Psychology
of
Motor Learning

Series in Health, Physical Education, Physical Therapy, and Recreation

Charles A. Bucher, Editor

SPORTS ACTIVITIES FOR GIRLS AND WOMEN
Mildred J. Barnes, Margaret G. Fox, Pauline A. Loeffler, and M. Gladys Scott

THE FOUNDATIONS OF HEALTH
Charles A. Bucher, Einar A. Olsen, and Carl E. Willgoose

A BEGINNER'S BOOK OF GYMNASTICS
Barry L. Johnson

INTRAMURAL AND RECREATION PROGRAMS FOR SCHOOLS AND COLLEGES
Viola K. Kleindienst and Arthur Weston

RECREATION TODAY: PROGRAM PLANNING AND LEADERSHIP
Richard Kraus

PSYCHOLOGY OF MOTOR LEARNING
Joseph B. Oxendine

TRACK AND FIELD FOR GIRLS AND WOMEN
Phebe M. Scott and Virginia R. Crafts

MOVEMENT EXPERIENCES FOR CHILDREN: CURRICULUM AND METHODS FOR ELEMENTARY SCHOOL PHYSICAL EDUCATION
Evelyn L. Schurr

THE MAKING OF AMERICAN PHYSICAL EDUCATION
Arthur Weston

Psychology
OF
MOTOR LEARNING

Joseph B. Oxendine
TEMPLE UNIVERSITY

Prentice-Hall, Inc., Englewood Cliffs, New Jersey

©1968
by PRENTICE-HALL, Inc.,
Englewood Cliffs, New Jersey

Printed in the United States of America

ISBN: 0-13-736595-0

Library of Congress Catalog Card Number: 68-12786

10 9 8

PRENTICE-HALL INTERNATIONAL, INC., London
PRENTICE-HALL OF AUSTRALIA, PTY. LTD., Sydney
PRENTICE-HALL OF CANADA, LTD., Toronto
PRENTICE-HALL OF INDIA PRIVATE LIMITED, New Delhi
PRENTICE-HALL OF JAPAN, INC., Tokyo

To
my wife,
ADRIENNE

Preface

The efficiency with which people learn motor skills is of increasing concern to physical educators. Their concern is stimulated by a growing realization of the importance of motor skills in daily life and by the crowded curriculum in today's schools. Serious efforts are being made, therefore, to insure that maximum learning occurs in the time available for skill instruction. Such efficiency can be reached only when a thorough knowledge of the learning process has been attained. During recent years research in learning theory has advanced at a rapid pace. Investigations have included gross motor skills as well as verbal and fine motor tasks. Therefore, a body of useful learning information is now becoming available for the field of physical education as well as for several related disciplines.

The purpose of this book is to present research findings and empirical evidence regarding motor learning and to synthesize these materials into useful concepts which will aid the teacher. Primary attention is devoted to presenting in the most useful manner what is known about learning. This book is similar to traditional psychology of learning texts in that research literature is reviewed and interpreted for basic truths about learning. However, this book differs in two important ways from most books which deal with the topic of learning. First, recent research and empirical evidence dealing with gross motor skills, in addition to skills involving verbal and fine motor tasks, are included. Second, generalizations and specific suggestions for teaching are made with special emphasis on regular physical education skills. Like most texts on learning, this book is not limited to an interpretation of the research but also includes the author's orientation toward learning and teaching.

A special text dealing with the learning of motor skills is needed not because physical educators have any deficiency in general learning theory (though some may have a limited background in the behavioral sciences), but because psychology of learning texts offer only limited guidance for particular teaching situations. Likewise, experimental psychology studies and resulting learning theories are usually not of great value in the teaching of gross motor tasks. It cannot be assumed that implications which are drawn for verbal concepts apply similarly to simple and complex physical activities. Consequently, applied research and rather specific interpretation must be combined with existing general learning theory.

This book delves into what appear to be the most basic issues relating to motor learning. It is organized into five parts. Part I outlines the nature and scope of motor learning and presents the major theories. This section provides a review of the historical developments in the study of learning and the contributions of the most prominent investigators. The classical theories are analyzed in terms of their implications for the learning of skills. Part II deals with the process of learning and is essentially an analysis of what is learned and how learning takes place. The role of reinforcement in learning, the matter of retention and forgetting, and transfer among motor skills are included.

Part III is devoted to an analysis of the state or condition of the individual which makes him receptive to, or "ready" for, a particular learning task. Readiness variables include both physical and psychological factors. The close relationships between physical development and ability to learn and perform skills, and between emotional excitement and performance are investigated. Part IV discusses the conditions which are most advantageous for the learning of motor skills. Primary emphasis is placed on types and conditions of practice and the structuring of units for instruction. Part V is devoted to individual differences which lead to important variations in motor learning and performance.

One problem encountered in the preparation of this book was deciding what to leave out. Numerous other topics dealing with method of instruction and with performance standards are somewhat related to the content of PSYCHOLOGY OF MOTOR LEARNING. However, since this is not designed as a methods book, specific techniques are offered only occasionally for illustrative purposes. In most cases, basic principles are presented, and it remains for the instructor to develop his own techniques for implementing them. There was some temptation to get into areas relating particularly to motor performance, such as physical fitness, kinesiology, or physiology of exercise. These topics, however, are more specifically handled in other texts.

The bibliographical references at the end of this book include the sources used in the preparation of the various chapters. In addition, each chapter is followed by a selected reading list to aid students in finding particularly relevant books and articles without having to search through the whole bibliography and without having to wade through only slightly related sources.

I wish to acknowledge the contributions of several persons who greatly aided me in the preparation of this book. I extend special thanks to Dr. Arne L. Olson of Temple University, who read the complete manuscript during the final stages; to Dr. Charles B. Corbin of the University of Toledo, who read the first seven chapters; and to Miss Ina Hawley and Miss Margaret Mackerras, graduate students at Temple University, who read the initial draft of the manuscript. Each of these persons made valuable suggestions which resulted in improvements. Appreciation is also expressed to the administration of Temple University which provided for the final typing of the manuscript.

Finally, I am indebted to the publishers and authors who have generously granted permission to use copyrighted materials which are acknowledged in the text.

J. B. O.

Contents

Part I

GENERAL LEARNING THEORY

Introduction

An investigation of the nature of motor learning must begin with an analysis of learning in general. Many of the principles established as general learning theory underlie the acquisition of all types of skills and knowledge. Learning theories were, in fact, established on the basis of research with a variety of tasks, including extensive use of motor skills. Nevertheless, it is becoming increasingly clear that special techniques and new applications must be sought if maximum efficiency is to be reached in the teaching of physical activities. It is with these techniques and innovations that the physical educator has recently concerned himself.

Typical of the concerns which have stimulated inquiry into the topic of skill learning are such matters as the general concept of learning, the different kinds of learning and the relationships among them, the prominent theories of learning and the current status of these theories, the points of general agreement among learning authorities today, the implications of learning theory for the teaching of fine and gross motor skills, the development of learning theory during the past century, and the establishment of proper research designs for the continued study of skill learning. It is toward the investigation of these matters that *general learning theory* is directed:

Chapter 1

The nature of motor learning

The topic of learning is of increasing concern to educators in general and to physical educators in particular. This concern is based on the realization that the effectiveness of teaching programs is dependent upon knowledge of the phenomenon of learning. Interest has also been stimulated by the "population explosion" which has resulted in more crowded schools, and the "explosion of knowledge" which has led to a more crowded curriculum. These developments have emphasized the need for *efficiency* in teaching and learning. For the physical educator, a thorough investigation of the learning process from a theoretical to an applied point of view, and from the learning of verbal skills to the acquisition of motor skills, is essential. It is for such an investigation that this book is intended.

The need for efficiency in teaching skills is apparent for a number of reasons. First, efficiency will save time and allow the teaching of more activities in the school program. Then, too, efficient methods will enable each individual to attain a higher degree of skill. In addition, with the best teaching techniques being employed, it is likely that the individual will develop a more positive attitude toward the particular activity. Certainly the individual who has attained early and rapid success in such activities as swimming, typing, or using a hand saw is likely to enjoy them more than the individual who has had a long and laborious learning experience and who tends to avoid participation as a result. Therefore, to promote enjoyment, fitness, and the other benefits of greater participation, efficiency in teaching skills is essential. Such efficiency will be attained only after the teacher has gained a thorough knowledge of the learning process as it relates to motor activities.

THE STUDY OF LEARNING

To the psychologist and the educator, learning is a very complex and perplexing problem. To the layman, however, learning has always been a rather simple matter. "We learn what we are taught," is often the attitude of the nonprofessional person. The concept of learning as a complex process is a relatively recent development. Long ago, parents taught children the skills necessary for livelihood. Artisans taught apprentices the skills for particular trades. Teachers taught in essentially the same manner in which they had been taught. There seemed little need for an elaborate or complex theory of learning.

As the nature of society changed, teaching gradually became the task of the school, and concepts of teaching and learning took on new and more formal meanings. Teachers found it impossible to familiarize students with all the activities and situations which they might encounter during their lives. For the sake of economy, therefore, teachers started emphasizing basic skills and generalized principles which could be applied to a variety of situations. As a result, the relevance of subject matter was not always clear to the students. Some children were not interested in these "foreign" concepts, and students often did not seem to learn well. Certain students caused trouble in the classroom, and some groups assumed that children would naturally dislike school.

Studies in learning have been conducted by the experimental psychologist and the educator. Both have maintained a keen interest in learning, and their efforts have contributed a great deal toward enhancing the effectiveness of the school. As a scientist, the psychologist seeks to know all about the phenomenon of learning because of its importance in determining human behavior. His quest for knowledge of behavior is ultimately aimed at predicting and controlling behavior. By use of pure research techniques, he seeks to gather objective, verifiable, and detailed evidence regarding learning and behavior. He then organizes this information into generalizations, principles, and laws which describe learning. In the late nineteenth century, experimental psychologists began to lead in the study of learning.

The educator also has an interest in learning. It is through the learning process that the goals of education are transmitted to individuals. The educator believes that the first step in becoming a good teacher is to understand how learning takes place. During the early twentieth century, educators welcomed educational psychology and aided its development as a science for disseminating knowledge, skills, and attitudes. Today, in a rather applied approach to the science of learning, the educator seeks knowledge which will help him to establish more effective educational programs.

Thus, general psychologists and educators have had a particular interest in the learning process. Both have made important contributions to the present knowledge of learning. But there has been a serious weakness in two separate approaches to the study of learning. The experimental psychologist, despite design and technique advantages, has been limited in his effectiveness by a lack of involvement with public school education. As a rule he has made little effort to solve the problems confronting school education. The psychologist's major effort, it must be remembered, has been the establishment of general laws of learning, not the development of their applications.

Educators, on the other hand, have been in contact with the school situation and have been especially interested in the application of research findings. However, their research in learning has often been loosely controlled. Perhaps this has resulted from too great emphasis on the "regular" school situation. The complexity of variables has been virtually impossible to control. It must also be pointed out that until recently educators have been somewhat negligent in relating appropriate findings of psychologists to their own applied research findings. The recent development of educational psychology as an important discipline is one of the most hopeful signs for the development, refinement, and application of sound learning principles to the process of school education.

The research and writings of educators and psychologists may be categorized into three major areas of concentration: (1) the learning process, (2) the learner, and (3) conditions for learning. Although these concepts are not distinct and mutually exclusive, they provide clues to how the topic of learning has been organized for investigation. These three areas also serve as the major focal points in the organization of this book.

Definitions of learning

The typical layman uses the term "learning" quite frequently and assumes that he has a clear understanding of its meaning. However, learning is extremely difficult to define adequately. Learning has been variously described as: (1) accumulation of knowledge, (2) improvement in an activity, (3) solving a problem, and (4) adjustment to changing situations. Although none of these definitions is completely adequate or inclusive, each one contributes to a broad understanding of the process because each is an example of learning in some particular situation.

For the purpose of this discussion, *learning* is defined as the process by which behavior is developed or altered through practice or experience. This definition is broad enough to encompass such diverse activities as memorizing a poem, acquiring the knowledge that fire can cause pain, realizing that being quiet in class will please the teacher, developing the ability to skate, or even improving one's skill in skating once the basic movements have been mastered. Learning undesirable behavior, such as antisocial conduct or the development of a faulty movement in a motor skill, is also covered by this definition. Therefore, new skills, changes in old responses, attitudes, rote memory, and highly complex concepts all represent learning. However, not all alterations in behavior are caused by practice or exposure to a learning situation. Such changes may result from fatigue, drugs, or maturation. In addition, reflexive behavior, such as the knee jerk, the eye blink, or pupillary response, does not result from learning, but is assumed to result from phylogenic development.

Motor learning, which is within the overall definition of learning, refers particularly to types of behavioral change which involve bodily movement. Usually motor learning is thought of as the acquisition of physical skills. The range of acquired movement responses varies widely. For example, the ability to kick a soccer ball accurately, proficiency in typing with speed and accuracy, and precision in controlling the vocal cords and the expiration of air in singing are all dependent upon practice or some exposure to the activity and the coordination of muscular responses. Obviously, some motor skills require different types of related mental activity than others.

The definition of learning as the process which alters or develops behavior through practice or experience is an attempt to describe learning by pointing to behavior which can be rather objectively observed. A different approach to the problem of definition has been taken by several authors who have attempted to *explain* the learning process by discussing the physiological changes which are assumed to take place in the nervous system. Kappers (1917) developed the growth theory of *neurobiotaxis* which explains learning as the growth of dendrites and axons in the nervous system. This theory indicates that as one practices by participating in or observing an activity, electrical impulses pass through the nervous system and cause the development of "connections" at the synapses. The greater the learning, the greater is the neural growth.

Kappers believed that in the first performance of any activity, impulses travel over new paths of sensory and motor neurons. The learning and performance of the new activity is assumed to be difficult because of the resistance of previously unused synapses to the transmission of impulses. The inability of these impulses to easily "jump the gap" results from a lack of neural development in the area of the synapse. As the individual repeats the activity, or as practice continues, the growth of dendrites and axons offers more connections, or "feelers," which help to transmit the impulse. This enables subsequent messages to travel over the nerve trunks more smoothly because of the greater growth of dendrites and axons in the area of the synapse. According to Kappers, therefore, learning is the development of neural connections which reduce resistance in the synapse.

Kappers' neurobiotaxis theory is not contradictory to the definition of learning suggested earlier. It is rather an early attempt to explain the dynamics of the learning process physiologically. Other psychologists, physiologists, and neurologists have expressed similar beliefs regarding structural changes in the nervous system as a result of learning. Some have agreed with Kappers essentially, while others have proposed different kinds of structuring or more elaborate theories.

Types of learning

Persons concerned with applying teaching principles to different situations wonder whether learning is a basic process which has similar characteristics regardless of the material or skills being learned. The topic of types, or forms, of learning has caused considerable discussion and study with only limited agreement among the authorities.

Some typical concerns have been questions such as the following: Is learning to ride a bicycle essentially different from learning to skate? Aside from the obvious differences in type of response and muscle groups used, is the learning process similar, or is it different? Is the intellectual functioning of a person who is learning dance steps the same as when he is learning to solve a complex mathematics problem? Can one assume that learning to type is similar to learning to catch a ball? Is there something essentially different about "verbal" and "motor" learning? Answers to these questions will have significance for teachers of all subjects.

Several authors have suggested different types or forms, of learning processes. Six theories have been summarized in Table 1, and it can be noted that there is only a limited amount of similarity or consensus among them. However, a few types, notably motor skill learning, problem solving, and the development of attitudes, do appear on more than one list. Some authors seem to describe learning according to type of material learned, while others emphasize the type of mental processes which are assumed to occur.

Deese (1958) has categorized all learning into two major types which he believes are basically different. Several other authors have agreed with this general notion. In the first type of learning, *classical conditioning*, the learner responds to a particular stimulus. The prime example of classical conditioning is the experiment of Pavlov in which a dog learned to respond with salivary secretion to a bell. In an experimental situation, the response is under the control of the investigator who decides when and how the subject is to respond and then trains him to respond that way. The stimulus which is used also serves as the reinforcer. This type of learning situation can be observed in and out of the schools.

Table 1

TYPES OF LEARNING AS SUGGESTED BY SEVERAL AUTHORS

Kingsley's forms of learning (1946)	*Harris and Schwahn's process of behavioral change (1961)*	*Tolman's types of connections or relations (1949)*
1. Development of motor skills and habituation of action	1. Skill learning—coordination of sensory and perceptual functioning in performance	1. Motor patterns—require simple conditioning
2. Problem solving	2. Reasoning—a rational approach to problem solving	2. Cathexes—acquired relationship between drive and goal
3. Development of attitudes and ideas	3. Attitudinal learning—involving the person's values	3. Equivalence beliefs—acquired relationship between drive and secondary or substitute goal
4. Development of understanding through observation, listening, reading, and generalizing	4. Conceptual learning—generalizations concerning situations and signs	4. Field expectancies—learned signs or cues facilitate problem solving
5. Memorizing ideas or verbal responses in fixed sequences	5. Group learning—interpersonal and social interaction are influential	5. Field-cognition modes (of a higher order than 4)—innate capacities contribute to readiness to learn in several ways
6. Development of perception and improvement of observation	6. Aesthetic creativity—application of original thought to aesthetic production	6. Drive discrimination—two modes of behavior are learned, depending upon the particular drive
7. Modification of emotional reaction		

Table 1 (continued)

TYPES OF LEARNING AS SUGGESTED BY SEVERAL AUTHORS

Kingsley and Garry's types of learning (1957)	Bloom's taxonomy of educational objectives (1956)	Gagné's types of learning (1965)
1. Perceptual motor learning	1. The psychomotor or motor domain	1. Signal learning— rather "involuntary" conditioned responses
2. Problem solving— learner must determine solution to a novel situation	2. The cognitive domain—development of intellectual abilities and skills	2. Stimulus-response learning—voluntary responses to a discriminated stimulus
3. Conditioning—both instrumental and classical	3. The affective domain—dealing with interests, attitudes, appreciations, and adjustments	3. Chaining—connecting a sequence of previously learned S-Rs
4. Trial and error learning—refers to inefficiency of earlier behavior		4. Verbal association— a type of chaining involving verbal materials
5. Discrimination learning—judgment between two or more stimuli is required		5. Multiple-discrimination learning— acquiring combinations of chains
6. Maze learning— learner must rely on memory of previous responses		6. Concept learning— internal or symbolic representation of environment
7. Verbal learning		7. Principle learning— acquisition of the relationship between concepts
		8. Problem solving— using two or more previously learned principles to develop new ones for specific purposes

In Deese's second type of learning, *instrument-operant conditioning*, initiative for the behavior is the subject's. Nothing is done by the investigator to elicit the response. After a correct response by the subject, however, the reward (reinforcement) is applied. Responsibility for the response rests with the subject. A particular response or behavior is required for the reward. The subject must do the trick before receiving the treat. Deese's two types of learning seem equally applicable to the learning of motor and verbal skills.

THE LEARNING OF MOTOR SKILLS

Motor learning refers to the acquisition of skills which require bodily movement. Discussions of motor versus verbal learning have occasionally led to the belief that little, if any, thinking was involved in the learning of motor skills. In Table 1, the separate listings of the two items "Skill learning" and "Reasoning" by Harris and Schwahn might seem to indicate that there is no reasoning associated with motor learning. Some authors seem to assume that all verbal learning is symbol-manipulative while motor learning involves only simple body stimulus-response associations. It is true that such a distinction seems apparent when one observes extreme examples of each type of learning such as the skill of mathematical computation and the skill of sharpening a pencil. However, a general dichotomy between verbal and motor learning is unreasonable since many tasks involve both processes. Learning to type, to play a musical instrument, to drive an automobile, or to perform a complex rhythmical maneuver involves both mental and physical coordinations.

Various motor skills require different levels and amounts of mental functioning. The learning of most skills is a thoughtful, active process. Blind trial-and-error efforts are not only frustrating but are largely ineffective. One child may observe another perform a cartwheel and then attempt to put his own body through this series of movements. He may attempt to determine the relationship between his actions and their results. He may receive advice from the instructor or his classmates and then try again, varying his response on the basis of external and kinesthetic feedback and his considered judgment of earlier trials. A learner may either attempt to duplicate an observed performance, or he may try to improve his own previous performance.

It is likely that certain motor activities are learned very slowly by some persons because these people are unable to understand the relationship between the response and the results. The teacher may aid the pupil by helping him to see this relationship. The pupil should gain not merely a verbal understanding, but a verbal understanding related to action. An individual may understand the physical principle of inertia but not readily apply it to his own actions with a tennis racket or in jumping. Action, feedback, evaluation, and repeated action are major factors in the successful performance of motor activities. Motor learning, therefore, is clearly a physical and a mental process.

The scope of motor learning

Careful observation of the student in school and the individual in adult life reveals that the activities which depend upon motor skills are extremely diverse. Rather than being restricted to recreational skills (which in itself is an important area), proficiency in physical activities is strategic to a wide variety of working skills, to locomotion, and even to communicative skills. Because of the diversity and universal importance of these skills, and because proficiency and enjoyment depend upon how they are learned, it is essential that motor learning be seriously investigated by all who have a part in the teaching of skills.

Motor skills may be divided into three broad categories according to the manner and purpose for which they are learned. First are the skills which are developed early in life and are primarily dependent upon maturation. These include activities such as crawling, walking, speaking, and general coordination of body movements. Although special teaching does not seem to speed the process, a favorable environment is essential for maximal development of these skills. Basically, the role of parents and teachers in regard to maturation is to provide the child with opportunities and encouragement for movement.

A second group of motor skills is those which are essential for the further development of educational objectives. This group includes communicative skills, such as handwriting, which are used as tools for more advanced learning. The primary grade teacher is particularly concerned with this type of motor learning, and teachers throughout the elementary school are interested in the development of the perceptual-motor skills necessary for effective reading. For example, as the individual learns to visually span two, three, or four words at a single glance, rather than one word, his reading efficiency will improve. In clerical courses, students develop typing and shorthand skills which may later aid in attaining other educational goals. The development of proficiency in these activities is dependent upon other mental components, but perceptual-motor factors are strategic.

A third category of skills is those which are taught for their own value, or for benefits which are directly related to learning them. Generally, vocational or recreational skills are in this group. Teachers in different areas of specialization and at different levels of the educational program are responsible for the teaching of these skills. The physical education teacher is naturally responsible for developing sports and certain other recreational skills as well as movement patterns and fitness levels essential for other specialized skill learning.

Other teachers in school are also interested in teaching fine and gross motor skills for their own sakes. For example, the industrial arts teacher aids the student in developing skill in the use of various manual and power instruments. These skills may later prove important for vocational or avocational pursuits. The science teacher demonstrates the proper techniques in using complex and fragile laboratory equipment. The home economics teacher promotes learning in the skills of sewing, cooking, and many other household tasks. The music teacher aids students in the development of voice control, projection, and enunciation. In music class, students may also develop skill in the use of a wide variety of instruments. These activities offer an opportunity for motor learning which may continue for many years. In the development of painting or drawing, it is clear that perceptual-motor factors come into use.

Even in advanced programs of study, the learning of motor skills is often important. Medical and dental students, as well as those in technical courses, often find the development of manual skill important in their programs. Anyone who has had a beginning dental student fill a tooth will likely be aware that motor skill is one of the prime needs in the training of dentists. Surgeons, engineers, and individuals in many other professions obviously need manual dexterity and skill in the use of instruments. Even this incomplete list is sufficient to show that motor learning is not restricted to the physical education class. Rather, teachers in a wide variety of subjects, from nursery school to the post baccalaureate levels, are often involved in the teaching of motor skills.

Types of motor skills

There are several ways in which motor skills may be categorized by type of response. There are *fine* and *gross* motor skills, depending upon the magnitude of the movement. Handwriting is a fine skill while a baseball swing is considered a gross motor skill. In addition, some activities are *discrete* while others are either *serial* or *continuous*. Discrete skills require a single exertion such as is used in tossing a dart. A serial skill involves a series of movements, each of which must follow in a particular sequence as in the bowling approach and delivery. Continuous movements require repetitive actions such as are evident in swimming, walking, or skating. Also, some tasks are referred to as *perceptual-motor* skills whereas others do not depend specifically upon vision. For example, a forehand stroke in tennis would be classified as a perceptual-motor skill, and swimming would not be described in the same manner. Therefore, the methods of typing motor skills are numerous and de-

pend upon the purpose for which the skills a
of comparisons to be made.

THE LEARNING PROCES.

A brief overview of the learning process, in g
as an important background for the study of the p.
istics of motor learning. This discussion of the essentia.
steps in the learning process will also be used to illust. ...mited
extent, the application of learning principles in relation t(,..ysical skills.

The necessary elements

At least four elements are necessary if learning is to take place:
(1) a living motivated organism, (2) an incentive which will lead to satisfaction of motives, (3) a barrier, or block, which prevents the organism
from immediately gaining the incentive, and (4) effort or activity on
the part of the organism to attain the incentive.

All *living organisms* can learn. It is true, of course, that some forms
of life reach greater and different kinds of learning than do others. In
laboratory situations, lower forms of animals have shown behavioral
changes which must be described as learning. These adjustments, or this
learning, also takes place in the organism's natural habitat. The different
capacities and different types of learning among various species have
long been of interest to the psychologist.

Incentives, which when attained will lead to the satisfaction of motives, are central to learning. Motivation, which is assumed to be an internal state of mind, arises from the organism's desire for certain incentives. Such incentives may take the form of food, a grade in school, or
success in the performance of a specific task. The intensity of drives,
wants, and needs determines the level of motivation. A comfortable or
satisfied individual is not as receptive to learning as one who has a
greater need for attaining a particular goal.

When the learner is *blocked* from immediately attaining the incentive which would satisfy his need, a learning situation exists. On the
other hand, if the incentive or goal is obtained without any serious effort on the part of the organism, this is an indication that the learning
has already occurred. An organism, if sufficiently stimulated, will make
repeated attempts to attain the incentive. Most learning theorists agree
that activity on the part of the individual is strategic for effective learning.

Initial *responses* may or may not prove successful. Goal-directed responses will often be inefficient and confused. Activity on the part of

...n may be overt, or it may involve mental functioning, pri-
...Occasionally, there may be chance successes. As the process con-
...ues, the more successful responses will be selected and more often
repeated, while the failures will be gradually eliminated. The attainment
of the incentive often involves the realization of a means-to-end connection on the part of the learner.

Regardless of the nature of the learning task, whether a child is
learning to walk, a student is learning a scientific concept, or an adult is
learning to drive a car, the essential elements are the same: a motivated
individual, incentives which will lead to a satisfaction of the motive, an
obstacle preventing the learner from easily attaining the incentive, and
activity on the part of the individual.

Steps in learning

An analysis of the steps or phases of the learning process is often
valuable in clarifying the overall topic of learning. One of the clearest
statements regarding the learning process was made by Woodruff (1948),
who described six sequential steps which he believed to be characteristic
of all types of learning. While placing strong emphasis on motivation,
his statement seems consistent with the majority of opinions on learning
theory today. Each learning step is presented as distinct and recogniz-
able by the keen observer. However, there seems to be no uniformity in
the speed or ease with which different individuals progress through the
different phases of the learning process. For example, an individual
might progress through one step quickly but get bogged down on
another one. The speed with which he learns the total task or progresses
through each of the steps may vary from a relatively sudden occurrence
to a very slow process.

According to Woodruff, the speed of learning depends upon (1) the
capacity of the individual, (2) the degree of motivation, and (3) the
nature of the task. First, more intelligent children, those with greater
capacity, generally learn tasks more quickly than children with lesser intelligence. Similarly, children who have greater motor ability will develop proficiency in physical skills more quickly than those who have less
coordination, strength, or general maturation. Second, when motivation is
high, learning occurs more quickly than when interest is slight or nonex-
istent. Third, a task which is simple or of short duration is generally
learned more quickly than one which is more complex. It is evident that
the speed of learning is dependent upon an interaction of these three
factors. Woodruff's six steps, discussed below, appear to be characteristic of all forms of learning.

1. "Motivation within the learner makes him receptive to stimula-

tion." Motivation refers to a condition of uneasiness within the individua which arouses or maintains activity. This is the most basic essential for learning and is a prerequisite for all the other steps. All purposive behavior results from motivation. Motivation is not injected into the child by the teacher but develops within the individual and is the result of his life experiences.

2. "A goal becomes related to motivation." When a general or undefinable state of motivation exists, the individual will seek some goal to satisfy his restlessness. As soon as the goal is selected, action toward that goal can begin. Depending upon the motivation, the goal selected might be of a physiological, social, or personal nature. In most school situations, the social or personal are more prevalent. A teenager's desire to be able to dance, bowl, or ride a surfboard is usually of social origin and acts as a strong force in getting him to practice these activities. The need for attaining a position on an athletic team in school can act as a powerful force for action. Aspirations to gain personal goals, such as the ability to read, swim, or to drive car are likewise strong incentives for action.

3. "Tension arises." When the goal is not immediately attainable because the individual cannot suddenly dance well, bowl, ride a surfboard, or drive a car, tensions arise. As in the case of all learning, a barrier exists. In these situations the barrier is the inability of the individual to suddenly exhibit proficiency in the tasks. If the individual strongly desires the goal, considerable tension is developed. This tension can aid learning by enabling one to make a vigorous and sustained attack on the task. For example, social and personal needs can cause one to practice football, swimming, or dancing long and hard despite physical discomfort, fear, and embarrassment. It has been shown, however, that tension or anxiety which is too great can interfere with the efficient solution of a difficult task.

4. "The learner seeks an appropriate line of action to reach his goal." In every learning situation there are usually several choices of action from which the individual may choose. The responses of the learner may vary from seemingly random or chance selections to those which are thought out and selected as logical or reasonable choices. For example, a novice bowler who is attempting to roll a hook might try different techniques such as variations in starting position, speed of the approach, height of the backswing, the release, and the follow-through. However, another novice bowler might try to reason out the action which will cause the ball to hook and therefore try different ways of releasing the ball. In the first example, there is little cause-and-effect consideration. In the second situation, much of the trial-and-error explanation is from mental rather than physical activity.

miliarity with a particular task increases, the degree of
activity decreases. For example, the novice golfer, after
lizes that something went wrong with his swing, but he
t it was. The more experienced golfer, however, will
down the problem to one or two alternatives. In either
..se, the golfer will try out the alternative which seems most appropriate. If that line of action is not correct, and the shot is not improved,
the learner starts over and tries other responses until success has been
attained.

5. "The learner fixes the appropriate line of action." Determination
of appropriate response usually comes from practice. Realization of the
correct action and its repetition tend to fix that response to the particular
goal. The first few successes might be rather accidental and, occasionally,
no relationship may be seen between the behavior and the outcome.
Sometimes the appropriate response is realized rather rapidly, after
the first or second trial. On other occasions, the correct action is suddenly realized after much practice, as when a performer after long effort
suddenly gets the feel of how to perform a skip or a somersault in gymnastics. But realization of the appropriate action may be a slow process
resulting from long practice. In most motor skills, learning takes place
gradually by small degrees. Handwriting skill, dance performance, or
swimming technique shows gradual improvement. The ultimate goal of
excellent performance is not fully realized each time progress is made.
Recognition of a small degree of success, however, results in some satisfaction, which leads to a reduction of tension. Tension is relieved in
proportion to the progress one has made toward the ultimate goal.

6. "Inappropriate behaviors are stopped." When the learner realizes
that certain activity is useless, he no longer uses it. In the early stages of
learning most motor skills, much of the activity is wasted. An example
is the running technique used by young children. Much of the action,
especially the lateral movement, is not only useless but is actually a
hindrance to running efficiency. However, when the junior high school
boy begins practicing with the track team, there is, hopefully, a reduction of movements which are not helpful in promoting speed. Efficiency
in running, as well as in other skills, is closely related to the elimination
of inappropriate behavior.

In physical education, some time is devoted to the teaching of new
skills whereas in other situations improvement in familiar skills is sought.
There is often some question whether the same process is followed in
both new learning and gradual improvement. In regard to both situations, Woodruff (1948) points out that:

They share in common these sequential steps: (1) motivation, (2) the setting-
up of a goal toward which action is directed, (3) the development of tension

and readiness to act, (4) discovering a way of acting which brings progress and (6) throwing aside or ignoring other ways which seem less promising. Whether the fifth sequential step (fixing the successful act) is present in behavior depends on whether one is trying to learn a line of behavior or is just trying to use one at the moment. . . . Nevertheless it is true that for both deliberate learning, and daily living and adjusting, the sequential steps are a sound basic formulation . . . (p. 59).[1]

Discovery and application of research findings

There are several approaches which the educator may take in conducting research and making use of the findings of experimental psychologists. He might rely entirely upon the psychologist to discover the basic laws of learning, and the teacher would then make direct application of these findings to his school setting. In support of this procedure, some authors have suggested that the classroom and the gymnasium are too complex for valid research.

However, the direct application of laboratory-established learning principles to the teaching of motor skills is not only questionable but quite difficult. For example, how does one apply the observed discrimination transfer in rats to the teaching of typewriting, sawing or basketball skills? Obviously, there is a question of *how* to apply much of the research, even if the teacher desires to make a direct application. Since research has shown that short practice sessions generally have advantages over longer practices, how short should these practices be for maximum efficiency? How many basketball free throws should a high school varsity player shoot a day? Should these throws be distributed in a certain way throughout the practice day? Is there a point of diminishing returns? Should practice schedules in tennis vary with different skill levels? Psychology does not offer specific answers to these problems, its contribution has been in the establishment of broad principles. In order for these principles to be most useful in a practical way, further research must be done with regular physical education skills.

Another approach to the problem of establishing and applying learning principles has been to encourage learning research in both the classroom and the laboratory. This procedure seems most promising for the discovery and implementation of useful laws of learning. Both teachers and psychologists may discover basic scientific truths in their own settings. The greatest advancement for the cause of learning research and the application of its findings is the coordination of the efforts of educators in the classroom and psychologists in the experimental laboratory. Combined efforts of these two groups will result in more rapid progress than will separate, isolated efforts.

[1] Used by permission of David McKay Co., Inc.

Selected readings

Bernard, H. W. *Psychology of learning and teaching.* (2nd ed.) New York: McGraw-Hill, 1965.

Bilodeau, E. A. (Ed.) *Acquisition of skill.* New York: Academic, 1966.

Bruner, J. S. *The process of education.* Cambridge, Mass.: Harvard, 1963.

Cratty, B. J. *Movement behavior and motor learning.* Philadelphia: Lea & Febiger, 1964.

Deese, J. *The psychology of learning.* (2nd ed.) New York: McGraw-Hill, 1958.

Gagné, R. M. *The conditions of learning.* New York: Holt, Rinehart and Winston, 1965.

Harris, T. L., & Schwahn, W. E. *Selected readings on the learning process.* New York: Oxford, 1961.

Kingsley, H. L., & Garry, R. *The nature and conditions of learning.* (2nd ed.) Englewood Cliffs, N. J.: Prentice-Hall, 1957.

National Association for Physical Education of College Women & National College Physical Education Association for Men. A symposium on motor learning. *Quest,* 1966, No. 6.

Chapter 2

Theories of learning

The purpose of this chapter is threefold: (1) to present the important contributions of some of the outstanding learning theorists and, in so doing, briefly review the recent historical development of the study of learning; (2) to suggest ways in which each theory might be used in the teaching of motor skills; and (3) to synthesize some points of general agreement among the several theories.

Learning theorists have traditionally sought to synthesize available knowledge about learning into principles, laws, and even broader interpretive systems. They have tried to discover relationships between variables and to evolve theoretical designs which would enable them to predict behavior under greatly differing conditions. Rather than being content to collect isolated information or to solve particular problems, theorists, past and present, have generally attempted to explain the learning process. As a result of this approach, not a great deal of attention has been devoted by these theorists to solving learning problems in special subject areas. This task has been left to educators who, in the development of their programs and teaching methods, have largely ignored the theorists.

There are several reasons why the teacher today should become acquainted with the major learning theories. An instructor cannot really judge the merits of different teaching methods without understanding the primary assumptions upon which they are founded. A thorough knowledge of learning theory will enable him to develop a systematic body of knowledge so that a central or developmental theme will be evident in his teaching. Where no such understanding exists, unrelated units or work assignments often prevail. The teacher does not have to develop a well-defined and explicit theory of learning, but study will enable him to avoid using a combination of contradictory techniques, a method which would not be advocated by any theoretical position. The teacher who is concerned with efficiency in his teaching, the teacher who is more than a technician, will look beyond the method or task at hand and seek an understanding of the basic truths upon which his program is founded.

Whether or not they realize or admit it, most teachers have theories about many aspects of learning. For example, the coach who stresses game situations in basketball practices shows how he thinks his players learn best. Some teachers introduce students to new skills early in the period and practice old skills later on the theory that the best time for learning is early in the practice period. Some years ago, the author knew a basketball coach who, at the end of each practice, required players to shoot free throws and then run laps around the gymnasium. The player who scored highest in shooting percentage was allowed to sit out the laps. This coach certainly had a theory about the role of motivation in learning and performance. Even the parent who says, "Children learn to walk just as fast if you don't encourage them," illustrates a theory of learning.

Human development theories are similarly prevalent among teachers and parents. Some examples of these beliefs are: Changing a child's handedness will lead to psychological problems; motor development promotes the mental development of school age children; spare the rod and spoil the child; all people are basically good (or evil); there are no bad boys, only bad parents. Individuals who hold these opinions may or may not be aware of evidence which may support their theories.

What is a learning theory?

Learning theories are attempts to explain what learning is and how it takes place. They summarize and synthesize the research findings (facts, principles, and laws) and opinions of the theorists into concise interpretations of learning. In this process, some specific details may be lost because the theories are developed for applicability to new learning problems rather than for use as specific rules. Each theory reflects the point of view of the author, including his terminology, research techniques, and the topics that he considered most important.

Most learning theories deal with the nature of the learning process, the role of the individual in learning, and the conditions for learning. These areas are important even to the nonscientific person in education. All learning theorists, however, do not investigate to find answers to the same set of questions. Because of particular interests, skills, and techniques of experimentation, the important pronouncements on learning vary in format and in emphasis. However, according to Hilgard (1956), a general theory of learning should deal with most of the following topics:

Capacity to learn. Living organisms differ in their capacity to learn. Man has greater learning potential than other living things; some animal species have greater capacity for learning than other species. Differences in learning ability are also apparent among individuals of the same species. Animal trainers, for example, quickly make judgments about the capacity of each animal they train. Theorists are principally interested in the capacities of man for learning. Whether the activity is learning to read, to swim, or to put together a jigsaw puzzle some individuals seem to get the idea more quickly than others. What kind and how much learning is possible? What effect do age and practice have on learning ability? Intelligence testing has long been an accepted procedure because it gives educators some basis for predicting probable learning and resulting behavior of the child.

Role of practice in learning. The old adage "Practice makes perfect" accurately emphasizes the need for practice in learning, but people do not necessarily learn more as they practice more. Psychologists today agree that there is no perfect correlation between the length of time spent in practice and the amount learned. Most learning theorists give considerable attention to the matters of desirable practice schedules, the organization and conduct of practices, and, in general, the role of practice in learning.

Motivation. Motivation indicates a condition in which the individual has needs, wants, drives, or interests. Very few people question the relationship of this condition to learning. Motivation in school is often centered on rewards and punishments which can be used to control learning and performance. Why rewards and punishments are important, and how they can be used most effectively in promoting learning, are matters of considerable importance to learning theorists.

Understanding and insight. The role of understanding in different learning situations has been of great interest to those who have studied the learning process. Some theorists have indicated that learning is a more or less automatic connection which one makes between a stimulus and a response. According to this view, little understanding of the total problem is essential. Others claim that the learner grasps the meaning of the task and solves problems without the customary trial-and-error procedure. The answers to some problems, therefore, seem to come suddenly while other solutions seem to be realized slowly and laboriously. Learning theorists differ greatly about the amount of understanding of a task which is required for learning.

Transfer of learning. Psychologists and educators have agreed that previously learned responses may be elicited in new situations. Also, new responses may be learned more easily because certain habits have been previously acquired. For example, advanced concepts in any area of learning may be mastered with more ease once the fundamentals have been learned. Authorities are not in agreement, however, about how much transfer is likely to take place and under what conditions. Neither is there a consensus concerning the elements which are actually transferred.

Retention and forgetting. People do not remember all they learn. Often they forget what they would like to remember and remember things they would like to forget. Sometimes after they have "forgotten" the answers to certain questions, they suddenly think of the answers for no apparent reason. Psychologists have been interested in determining whether forgetting occurs automatically with the passage of time or if there are other influential factors. They have also sought to find the conditions which are most favorable for retention.

All authorities on learning have considered several of these aspects, and theorists are often compared with each other by their positions on these topics. Not all theorists have done research or written on each of these questions. In fact, some of them spent most of their efforts on topics other than those mentioned. But capacity to learn, the role of practice, motivation, understanding and insight, transfer, and retention and forgetting are among the most common areas of interest. In addition to topic areas, learning theories also vary regarding the specificity of their predictions. Theories which include more precise predictions of behavior or learning are more usable in the school setting, but they are more vulnerable to attack.

Categories of learning theories

It is becoming increasingly difficult to break major learning theories into distinct categories. Some of the newer theories, and some interpretations of the older theories, do not fit into the traditional groupings. According to Deese (1958), taking of sides on the major theoretical positions is on the decline. Even the development of elaborate theories seems to be decreasing. However, Kingsley (1946) and Hilgard (1948) organized the major learning theories into *association* and *field* theories. Hilgard (1956) later categorized most of the theories as *stimulus-response* (approximating the association group) and *cognitive* (approximating the field group). Hill (1963) describes the two major theories as *connectionist* and *cognitive*, and Deese (1958) labels them as *association* and *gestalt*. Perhaps the most encompassing terminology is provided by Bigge and Hunt (1962) who label the two main categories as *stimulus-response associationism* and *gestalt-field*.

For this discussion, the theories of Thorndike, Guthrie, Hull, and Skinner will be classified as stimulus-response, while the concepts of Tolman, Lewin, and the gestaltists will be referred to as cognitive. Of course, the distinction between these two groups is not always clear since there are points at which theories in different groups agree. There are also issues of controversy among the individual theories in each major category. The differences within and between the major learning theories might be compared to the diversity in the Democratic and Republican parties in the United States. However, an effort will be made to show areas of distinction and identifying characteristics, or overriding concepts, of each of the two major groups.

STIMULUS-RESPONSE THEORIES

Stimulus-response and cognitive theories have developed into major influences on education during the current century, but each has roots in earlier centuries. In the United States the stimulus-response theories developed before the cognitive theories. Some impetus for the stimulus-response movement resulted from a desire among early American psychologists for theories more practical and objective than the relatively vague and subjective early German cognitive theories. The stimulus-response approach has been more "scientific." Stimulus-response proponents believe that behavior can be controlled by application of the *pleasure-pain principle*. Considerable attention is devoted to such matters as objective measurement, quantitative data, reflexes, and sequence of behavior.

The term *stimulus-response* (S-R) is used to indicate that a particular stimulus is connected or leads to a particular response. Stimuli which impinge upon the sense organs are found throughout our environment. Some of these stimuli cause automatic responses such as the reaction of the pupils to varying intensities of light. This behavior is unlearned. Other stimuli are connected to responses through learning, as when a typist sees the letter *t* and proceeds to hit the appropriate key, or a baseball batter notices the thrown ball curve and makes the necessary adjustment in his swing.

The association of a particular stimulus and response has long been recognized by psychologists. English psychologists of the eighteenth and nineteenth centuries established laws based on principles of association and used these laws to explain memory, perception, and reasoning. When mental processes occur close together or when the learner perceives several impressions at the same time, he tends to "link" them. In the eighteenth century, Hume determined the qualities essential for association to be resemblance and contiguity. Others gradually attached a cause-and-effect relationship to things which usually followed each other. Psychologists later decided that the association or connection was not an automatic link between ideas but the result of thought on the part of the learner. Stimulus-response psychology arose from this emphasis on the mental processes of the learner.

Stimulus-response theorists generally assume a direct cause-and-effect relationship with the learner seeing a connection between the stimulus and response. They also emphasize the importance of reinforcement of this connection, or *stimulus-response bond.*

To the stimulus-response theorists, learning is the process of building new bonds and organizing them into systems which develop into the knowledge, behavior, and personality of the individual. When stimuli are connected with responses which involve bodily movements, the connections are referred to as motor bonds. Simple motor skills might involve very few bonds, while complex skills might require many motor bonds.

The idea that learning consists of combining stimulus-response bonds, or "parts," into "wholes" is emphasized. The stimulus-response concept is therefore a molecular theory in which the individual learns through *particular* responses or habits. General understanding is not believed to take place to the extent assumed by the cognitive theorists. Rather, understanding is restricted to habits which are appropriate to the particular situation.

Determining how these connections are formed, and under what conditions, has led to the research upon which the stimulus-response theory is based. Following is a brief discussion of the works of some authorities who have been most influential in developing theories promoting the ideas of connectionism, conditioning, part learning, or trial-and-error learning.

Thorndike's connectionism

Edward L. Thorndike (1874–1949) probably contributed more to our present understanding of learning than any other individual. He established the basis for early scientific approaches to educational problems. His suggestions were especially effective because they were specific and could be investigated by scientific means. His influence on American education has been monumental. Most early learning theorists used Thorndike's views as a reference point and then conducted experiments to test his views as well as to establish their own. Tolman (1938), in reflecting on the influence of Thorndike, stated:

The psychology of animal learning—not to mention that of child learning—has been and still is primarily a matter of agreeing or disagreeing with Thorndike, or trying in minor ways to improve upon him. Gestalt psychologists, conditioned-reflex psychologists, sign-gestalt psychologists—all of us here in America seem to have taken Thorndike overtly or covertly, as a starting point (p. 11).[1]

Thorndike's learning theory is referred to as *connectionism* or sometimes as the *S-R bond theory* because of its emphasis upon the connection between the stimulus and response. He believed that learning requires the development of a bond between a stimulus and its appropriate

[1] By permission of the American Psychological Association.

response. Strongly influenced by the developing field of physiological psychology, Thorndike believed that the connections were products of biological changes in the nervous system. A major tenet in his theory is that learning takes place as a result of trial-and-error practice.

After conducting extensive research with cats in puzzle boxes, Thorndike established a number of principles for his trial-and-error learning. Among them are the following:

1. In the early phases of learning there is a great variety of activity and very little success.
2. The first successes are quite accidental and no connection is seen between response and desired result.
3. There is gradual elimination of wrong responses and useless activity.
4. The learner becomes aware of the connection between stimulus and response and gets the feel of the correct action.
5. Practice strengthens the correct response and the action becomes more efficient.

Thorndike's *laws of learning* have been used to a considerable extent as a guide for teaching technique for half a century. The most widely known are his laws of readiness, exercise, and effect. The *law of readiness* states that learning will take place most-effectively when the learner is prepared to respond. When an individual has reached a state of readiness, it is pleasurable for him to respond and unpleasant for him to be prevented from responding. Conversely, when an individual is not in a state of readiness, it annoys him to be forced to respond. Thorndike's readiness is a law of preparatory adjustment, primarily emphasizing psychological preparedness in interest and background knowledge. As an example of the need for background learning, one can imagine the difficulty which would be encountered by a person who takes an advanced course in statistics without having first taken the intermediate course. Today, the concept of readiness has been extended to include the interaction of maturation, prerequisite learning, and motivation. Thorndike, however, did not discuss maturation as a factor of readiness.

The *law of exercise* indicates that exercising or practicing a particular response under favorable conditions strengthens the connection between stimulus and response. Through repetition the bond is developed and strengthened; this is occasionally referred to as the *law of use*. Conversely, failure to exercise over a period weakens the connection, and this statement is sometimes called the *law of disuse*. Thorndike's early writings seemed to indicate that learning was almost automatic with practice, i.e., one learns in direct relation to the time spent in practice. Later Thorndike stressed the fact that conditions must be appropriate for learning to occur. One of the essentials for an efficient learning situation is described as a satisfactory effect, or reinforcement.

The *law of effect* Thorndike considered of great importance, and this law became one of his most controversial. It refers primarily to the strengthening of an S-R connection if the experience is pleasurable. For example, if a basketball player finds that a certain maneuver fakes his opponent out of the way so that he has an easy shot, this success is pleasurable and tends to strengthen the connection between the situation and the maneuver. Thorndike originally stated that when a response is accompanied by a painful or annoying experience, the bond is weakened. He later refuted this phase of the law by indicating that an unpleasant experience might indeed be well remembered.

Thorndike placed great emphasis on the use of motivational techniques to promote learning, and he encouraged the use of praise and rewards in support of his law of effect. He pointed out that rewards actually reinforce or strengthen the S-R bond. Although he emphasized motivation, he believed that above a certain critical minimum, additional motivation or greater rewards are not of value.

Thorndike believed that what is learned is a *specific* connection between the stimulus and response, and it is consistent with his view to assume that only such connections will be transferred. He stressed that only "identical elements" would be usable in a second situation. By identical elements he referred to substance (ability to handle spoken and written words, numbers, and symbols) and procedure (habits and attitudes regarding work). Thorndike's was a much narrower view of transfer than had existed prior to his time.

Implications for motor learning.   The following ideas related to the teaching of motor skills seem to reflect some of Thorndike's basic concepts about learning:

1. Practice must be under favorable conditions in order for effective learning to take place. Mere drill, or repetition of responses, does not insure desirable learning. Proper use of rewards and effective distribution of work periods are suggested.

2. The law of readiness is strategic to the learning of motor skills. This law has stimulated interest and research in maturational readiness, psychological readiness, and skill readiness (prerequisite, or fundamental, skills upon which more complex skills can be developed). Age level of the learners serves only as a rough guide in the selection of appropriate motor skills.

3. In organizing learning experiences for students, teachers should proceed from simple to more complex activities. Tasks should be subdivided and developed into sequences so that the parts are well learned. In sports activities, individual skills should be practiced and reasonably well developed before the total game is introduced.

4. Transfer of learning is by identical elements. Reactions are better in new situations which are similar to earlier situations. All physical con-

ditions of practice should, therefore, be as similar as possible to the game's conditions.

5. Rewards can be used to aid learning because they tend to strengthen the connection between stimulus and response. However, very expensive prizes or trophies are not essential.

Guthrie's contiguity theory

Edwin R. Guthrie (1886–1959) developed the contiguity theory which emphasizes the association between the stimulus and the response. He indicated that the mind tends to join things which come to it at approximately the same time. Guthrie believed that any response which is preceded or accompanied by a stimulus or a combination of stimuli will be repeated whenever the same stimulus or combination of stimuli is repeated.

Guthrie further believed that the connection between the stimulus and response is fully established in one trial. After this one-trial contiguous association, the strength of the association which has been established will not be altered by additional practice. This all-or-nothing theory (if a response to a stimulus is learned at all, it is learned to the maximum extent) is unique to Guthrie among the major learning theorists. According to this view, a specific response to a specific stimulus cannot be improved with practice.

One-trial learning would seem to eliminate the need for practice. However, Guthrie did advocate practice, and he emphasized drill. He believed that in every learning situation there are many connections made among the multiplicity of stimuli and responses. Skill learning results from repetition, therefore, because at each practice session additional associations can be made. Each learning situation presents a slightly different combination of stimuli. Correct responses (habits) need to be developed for each situation. Perfect performance results when the learner associates all appropriate responses with the right cues. According to Guthrie's theory, forgetting is not caused by disuse but by interference from subsequent learning. Drill helps the learner to make a greater number of correct responses, and more learned associations therefore result. Guthrie's explanation, though simple and plausible, is extremely hard to validate because of the difficulty in exactly duplicating a learning situation.

Guthrie was primarily concerned with things that could be seen or described. He was interested in the overt behavior which the individual exhibits in the learning process. He assumed a "black box" point of view regarding learning: we cannot really understand in a scientific way what takes place *in* the nervous system during the learning process. The role of the psychologist is, therefore, to match stimuli with their responses so that behavior can be predicted on this basis. Guthrie himself offered no clues regarding possible changes in the nervous system.

Guthrie disagreed with Thorndike's law of effect. He believed that motivation was not an important factor in the learning process, and he therefore did not emphasize praise or reward. Reward does not strengthen the stimulus-response connection directly, he stated. Rather, rewards are indirect aids effective in animal experiments because they remove the animal from the learning situation after a successful response. This removal prevents the animal from making incorrect responses which would interfere with learned habits.

Thorndike believed that the learner actually made a connection between the reward and response, whereas Guthrie discounted this suggestion of retroactive learning. He believed that rewards are important only as tools in promoting or discouraging learning *activity*. If it is desirable that a person continue practicing a skill in order to learn responses, then a reward may be effective in keeping him actively engaged in the learning process. Rewarding a person at the cessation of a practice period, however, would have no desirable learning effect, according to Guthrie. One learns a correct response because he *does* it, not because he is rewarded later.

Guthrie expected very little transfer of learning. He agreed generally with Thorndike about transfer of identical elements. His conditions for transfer were probably even more restrictive than those of Thorndike. Among the multiplicity of stimuli in a new learning situation, Guthrie believed that there would usually be enough differences to almost entirely negate the value of stimulus-response connections from old situations. To attain considerable skill in a new situation, therefore, a great deal of practice would have to take place.

Implications for motor learning. The following generalizations to motor skills seem consistent with Guthrie's theories:

1. Skill or proficiency in motor activities can be developed by drill in those activities. Motor activities involve a whole family of stimuli for which habits must be developed. By a great deal of practice, correct habits or responses will be developed for many sets of stimuli.

2. Rewards are of value only while they cause continued participation in a desired learning situation. As long as enthusiastic practice continues, prizes or other material or verbal rewards will not aid in learning. These motivational devices should be used only if the individual is reluctant to participate. Primary emphasis should be placed on overcoming the learner's negative reactions with activities which have inherent interest.

3. Newly learned responses interfere with older learning. Therefore, practicing failure (an incorrect response) will cause forgetting of the

correct habits. Teachers should emphasize practicing success. This might be accomplished by rigging the situation so that students usually attain success, even if it is slight. In addition, extraneous stimuli should be eliminated so that incorrect connections, or interference, will not be learned.

4. The amount of transfer of skills in Guthrie's theory is limited to the exact duplication of the stimuli. Therefore, the practice of skills for transfer purposes is not of great value. Conditions must be very similar in order for the old stimuli and responses to effectively overcome the new set of stimuli. Consequently, a basketball coach who is preparing his team for a game would do well to practice under conditions which are very similar to those which the opponents are likely to present in the game. Similarly, a player would always shoot free throws in exactly the same manner, i.e., bounce the ball the same number of times, stand at the same spot on the floor, and repeat every other detail.

Hull's reinforcement theory

Clark L. Hull (1884–1952) developed a theory which emphasized drive reduction as the prime essential in learning. According to Hull, an organism is usually in disequilibrium with its environment; the organism's *need* for something results in a *drive*. Needs are either primary (relating to physiological necessities) or secondary (relating to psychological wants). The drive causes energizing on the part of the learner. When the need is met the drive is reduced. The reduction of the drive is a reinforcement which causes the response to be learned. According to Hull's thesis, therefore, a stimulus causes a neural response which results in a drive. This drive evokes a response by the organism which ends in drive reduction. The drive reduction is the reinforcement which develops habits or learning.

Hull's theory of learning is an extremely well-developed system, although it does not have a highly integrated or centralized theme as is evident in the works of Thorndike or the Gestaltists. Hull's definitions are in great detail so that each aspect can be investigated scientifically. He established the technique for reducing theory to well-defined components, and he developed a system of postulates which were designed to *explain* learning when most theories were generally descriptive.

Hull's system established a clear rationale for educational programs designed to meet pupil needs. Since children learn only to the extent that a need is reduced, according to Hull, educational programs should be based on pupil needs. School authorities who had held a philosophy of meeting the child's needs were given psychological justification for their programs.

In regard to transfer, Hull proposed that stimuli need not be exactly the same in order to evoke the same response. If the organization of stimuli is approximately the same, the individual will respond as if the stimuli are identical. An old response may be evoked because of the new stimulus' similarity in intensity or quality to the old stimulus. In this belief, Hull differed from Guthrie, who believed that slight differences in the combination of stimuli would create new situations in which old learnings would be less valuable.

According to Hull, mere contiguous repetition only promotes inhibition. In his system, reactive inhibition is described as the tendency to avoid repeating a response which has just been performed. In addition, the greater the amount of effort in the performance or the more often the performance, the greater is the reluctance to repeat the act. This inhibition subsides with the passage of time. Learning, therefore, is not a function of a given amount of practice but depends instead upon reinforcement (drive reduction). To be effective, practice must be under conditions in which the learner has a physiological or psychological need. This concept is similar to Thorndike's law of effect but different from Guthrie's learn-what-you-do theory.

Implications for motor learning. The following general statements seem to be consistent with Hull's postulates on learning:

1. Learning which has been established in one situation will be transferred to a situation which is somewhat similar. The transfer possibilities are greater than those suggested by Guthrie. Teachers can increase transfer by establishing common elements in different activities.

2. Education is most effective when based on pupil needs. Teachers of motor skills who aid students in establishing psychological needs relating to activities will stimulate the students' more serious effort and increased learning. If students are impressed with the values of sports activity for personal or social reasons, they will be more receptive to the instructional program. Use of artificial rewards, in moderation, may also prove effective.

3. Careful attention must be given to the length of practice periods and the interest of these practices for the learner. Mere repetition in practice only promotes inhibition. Practice periods which are too long or void of reinforcement may actually be detrimental to learning.

4. The learning of skills should proceed from the simple to the more complex. However, emphasis should be placed on the relationship of skills to each other. In addition to being proficient in fundamental skills, the learner must practice in the game situation before thoroughly understanding the activity.

5. The teacher or coach should stress an *understanding* of the connection between the stimulus and response on the part of the learner. For example, the young pitcher must see the relationship between his

wrist snap and the resulting curve of the baseball. Similarly, the performer must understand the connection between follow-through and improved performance before he can learn to follow through properly.

Skinner's operant conditioning

B. F. Skinner (b. 1904) developed a theory which emphasizes the reinforcement of the response as the critical factor in learning. This theory is referred to as operant conditioning. An operant, according to Skinner, is a set of acts, or responses. *Operant conditioning* is the learning process which makes a response more probable or frequent by reinforcing the desired act. Reinforcement, therefore, is contingent upon the correct response. While Thorndike believed that reinforcement strengthens the bond between stimulus and response, Skinner emphasizes that the reinforcement merely strengthens the response.

Skinner believes that the learner will tend to repeat in the future what he was doing at the time of reinforcement. By rewarding certain acts, the experimenter can get the learner to repeat those acts or to behave in a certain way. A great deal of research was done with pigeons and other animals in the "Skinner box." A particular response was selected, and when the animal did it, a reward (food) was given. As a result the animal performed the rewarded response more often and, often exaggerated or improved upon the reinforced operant.

Skinner believes that people's learning in daily life is somewhat more complicated but has the same basic nature as operant conditioning. He found very similar properties in the learning processes observed in pigeons, rats, dogs, monkeys, human children, and psychotic subjects. The species seemed to make little difference in the essentials of the learning process.

Skinner has been very scientific and has indicated that psychology can become almost perfect science. He disagrees with the old axiom that "A horse can be led to water but cannot be made to drink." Rather, he insists that the science of conditioning can be perfected to assure that the horse will drink. If the environment of animals or humans is controlled, behavior can be accurately predicted, according to Skinner. Psychology should be able to determine what influences man and the extent of this influence. It naturally follows that the probability of man's responses can be predicted and his behavior controlled. Skinner's is a psychology of naturalistic determinism which is opposed to the philosophy of personal freedom. This determinism indicates that the behavior which results is the only behavior that could have occurred. Skinner has indicated that as the science of psychology develops, man will become more like a machine, in that his behavior will be predictable.

Skinner's psychology is concerned entirely with measurable behavior.

He believes that there is no place in scientific psychology for discussions about one's "inner self." Discussions about the subconscious are, to him, make-believe psychology and things of the past. Modern psychology has no need for mystical discussions about internal motives, Skinner feels, when a study of the environment could provide all the answers. Neither is the concept of "goal-oriented" behavior acceptable to him. Rather, behavior is the result of conditioning. People do not perform acts because they are seeking results similar to those of past responses. Skinner's theory differs from Thorndike's law of effect which requires a forward looking, incentive-seeking response. According to Skinner, it is not essential that the individual see a connection between the operant and the resulting reinforcement. Learning may take place, therefore, with or without the individual's awareness of the consequence of his response.

Skinner views the teacher as the architect of behavior. Having first determined the desired behavior, the teacher skillfully uses reinforcers to condition the learners in this behavior. A series of slight reinforcements is essential in effectively controlling the environment. Because not enough reinforcers are available in ordinary classrooms, the most effective control of learning requires mechanical or automatic aids. Skinner has concluded that teaching machines are essential for maximum reinforcement.

Skinner has suggested several reasons why teaching machines are especially effective in promoting learning. The individual is required to be active since he must actually manipulate the machine. The student must compose his own responses; he is not able to recognize and select the right answer. Very small progression steps are possible so that all learners can make some progress. Immediate reinforcement is available when the student makes the correct response. These mechanical aids are interesting enough to keep a child actively engaged for a long period. Each child in class is able to work at his own rate under the supervision of one teacher who can adjust the progression steps and the complexity of each student's program. In addition, teaching machines allow teachers to evaluate progress and apply supplementary reinforcement when needed.

Implications for motor learning.   The following ideas seem consistent with Skinner's theories of learning:

1. Since the teacher cannot fully reinforce all the essential behavior of even one child in a motor learning situation, mechanical aids, programmed instruction, or teaching machines should be sought. Mechanical aids have been used rather widely in remedial physical education programs, research laboratories, and in many individually prescribed programs of activity. Aids have taken the form of exercising apparatus which indicates status, or mechanical evaluative equipment. More varied

and extensive use of teaching machines should be made in all motor activities. Programmed instruction, which embodies most of the essential elements of teaching machines, offers great possibilities for future advancement in skills teaching.

2. Most individual-type motor activities encompass Skinner's idea of early reinforcement. In archery, shuffleboard, golf, and bowling one can quickly see results and often understand why a particular response results in success or failure. Teachers should encourage greater use of self-testing techniques for maximum operant conditioning.

COGNITIVE THEORIES

Cognitive theories of learning are based on the assumption that the learner organizes his stimuli or perceptions into a pattern or whole, as opposed to the stimulus-response concept which assumes the reception of particular stimuli, both singly and in groups. According to the cognitive theorists, stimuli from the environment are not discrete and independent from each other. All things derive their character from their relationship to other things. Stimuli are observed against a background, or *field*. A customer, for example, may or may not like a piece of wrapping paper or the general atmosphere in a store, and these background details would influence his opinion of the product. The cognitive theories include ideas which stress the learner's awareness of the total field or combination of stimuli. Psychological reality is what the individual makes of all stimuli that come to him. The individual, therefore, (1) relates stimuli to each other, (2) hypothesizes means-to-ends relationships, and (3) behaves in a goal-directed manner.

Another important characteristic of the cognitive theories of learning is their acceptance of the phenomenon of insight. It can often be observed in animals or humans that the learner suddenly "discovers" the solution to a problem. This "Ah, ha!" phenomenon is usually followed by rapid progress or much improved performance. It is generally assumed that insight results from conscious or subconscious consideration of the problem. Insight often appears to be much faster than the usually slow and awkward trial-and-error process. Very significant contributions to the study of insight were made by Köhler in his experiments with apes.

The cognitive concept has not been as scientifically exact as the stimulus-response theory because cognitive theorists recognize a greater number of intangibles which cannot be precisely measured by available evaluative tools. For example, cognitive theorists assume that behavior is a function of the total situation and a specific cause-and-effect relationship cannot always be shown. Motivation at any particular time cannot be attributed to a single stimulus but is the result of a combination of internal and external forces. Even success and failure are recognized as strong motivators, with success being accepted as a significant reward. The teacher adhering to cognitive concepts will work with students to help them see the need for learning and for establishing goals.

Cognitive theorists stress the importance of signs, symbols, total stimuli, and structuring. The learner is a moving and changing energy system. The environment is also dynamic. The individual's process of interacting, adapting, modifying, and changing results in learning.

Cognitive psychology developed more recently in the United States than the stimulus-response theory. The basic tenets of cognitive learning theory originated with the gestalt psychologists in Germany during the 1920's and 1930's and continued with the work of Tolman and Lewin in the 1930's and 1940's. According to Hilgard (1960), learning experiments in the tradition of cognitive theory have sharply declined in the last two decades. He believed that this decline resulted from the fact that (1) no major theorist came to champion this cause in the way that Hull developed the stimulus-response concept, and (2) the stimulus-response theory has been broadened to include many of the basic problems raised by early gestalt theorists.

The gestalt psychologists

The classical gestalt theory was more concerned with perceiving than with learning as such. However, since the learning process is so dependent upon how the learner discerns his environment, gestalt psychology has developed into one of the major learning theories.

During the first two decades of the twentieth century, three German psychologists, Max Wertheimer (1880–1943), Kurt Koffka (1886–1941), and Wolfgang Köhler (b. 1887), started conducting conditioning experiments which led to the development of gestalt psychology while stimulus-response and trial-and-error concepts were dominant in America. Wertheimer first presented the theory in Germany in 1912. A few years later, Köhler and Koffka were responsible for publicizing and establishing gestalt psychology in America.

To fully appreciate this theory and its application to learning, one must first understand the gestaltist concepts of *figure* and *ground*. The sensory field (visual, auditory, olfactory, etc.) is organized into a figure against a background. This can easily be observed when viewing a picture or any object against a background. One does not see the particular figure in isolation but observes the total visual field. Both the figure and the ground are important in presenting the total stimuli, or *gestalt*, to the learner. Wertheimer, generally regarded as the founding father of gestalt psychology, showed that when two optical stimuli are preceived by the human eye in quick succession, a simultaneous pattern is formed. This figure-ground concept applies to the other senses as well as to visual perception.

The emphasis upon *insight* has been a distinguishing characteristic of gestalt psychology. Köhler used this term to describe the sudden solution of a problem as the individual interacts with his environment. In his experiments with apes (described in *The Mentality of Apes*, 1925), he showed that the animals arrived at solutions without resorting to blind trial and error. In problem-solving situations, the apes were required to find an indirect way to obtain food. Such problems often involved placing boxes on each other or connecting poles to secure the food.

It became obvious that the apes were "figuring out" the answers, and Köhler therefore concluded that Thorndike's trial-and-error explanation of learning was inadequate. It is similarly clear in some classroom situations that the child reasons out answers to problems largely on the basis of related past experiences. The topic of insight had been largely ignored by American psychologists before Köhler's experiments.

Another important principle of gestalt psychology is that *the whole is greater than the sum of its parts*. The human mind not only connects the stimuli which come to it but transforms them into a pattern. According to the gestalt concept, the total pattern has properties of its own which are different from a mere accumulation of the individual stimuli. This idea differs from most stimulus-response theories (except Hull's), which assume that stimuli and responses are additive and that each stimulus or response is largely unitary and isolated.

Gestaltists believe that the organizing and reorganizing by an individual in interaction with his environment constitutes learning. They developed specific theories about the way in which the learner organizes his visual field.

Koffka (1933) was most instrumental in relating the gestalt theories to learning. He defined four laws of perception which seem to have implications for learning. His *law of proximity* indicates that the learner tends to group together things which are close in time or space. This appears similar to Guthrie's concept of association by contiguity. It seems logical to assume from this law that if the teacher organizes materials into groups, the children will perceive them in groups. If the learners see the material in proximity, it will be learned in proximity.

Koffka's *law of similarity* refers to the unintentional grouping of objects which are similar in shape, size, or color. This grouping of similar items applies also to the senses of hearing, touch, smell, and taste. Homogeneously grouped materials are more easily learned than materials grouped heterogeneously. More recent research has shown that material which falls into logical groups is learned more quickly and retained longer than isolated material.

Koffka's *law of closure* describes the tendency of the learner to complete any incomplete parts from the total field. The individual experiences a general uneasiness if a figure is incomplete or out of balance, and he is motivated to "complete" the pattern. Completion is satisfying to the individual and, according to Koffka, results in learning. For example, when three dots are shown to an individual he may view them as a triangle, even though the dots themselves do not make a triangle. The *law of good continuation,* which is similar to the law of closure, states that the individual tends to continue the impressions which make a more pleasant whole. Very often, an individual is stimulated to complete an interrupted musical piece or visual pattern. Koffka believed that this continuation is a pleasant experience and results in the learning of the response. Both the laws of closure and good continuation are somewhat similar to Thorndike's law of effect.

Implications for motor learning. Gestalt psychology would seem to have the following implications for the teaching of motor skills:

1. Since gestalt psychology emphasizes that an accumulation of the component parts is not equal to the whole, a sports activity must be perceived as more than the accumulation of separate skills. In teaching motor skills, therefore, the teacher must acquaint and keep the learner aware of the whole activity. Breaking an activity into parts or skills which the learner is unable to relate to the whole will prove detrimental to the learning of the total activity. Practice of the complete game or event, or meaningful subdivisions thereof, will not only lead to improvement in the separate skills, but will aid the individual in blending the parts into a workable unit. Previews and reviews can aid in the process of combination.

2. Patterns or relationships discovered in one situation may be recognized and used in another situation. According to the gestalt concept, transfer is not by piecemeal elements but by common patterns, configurations, or relationships. Teachers of motor skills should, therefore, schedule and teach activities in a manner to insure maximum carry-over among the activities.

3. Insight can take place if the problem is within the capacity of the individual. Sufficient background learning can make mental practice a valuable procedure in rapid motor learning. Problem solving in motor skills can take place if the individual has the tools or basic skills with which to execute the more complex movement patterns.

4. Understanding the relationship of the parts to the whole is essential for effective learning and performance. Relationships among different activities should exist not only within the area of physical education but among all phases of the school program. For example, mathematics, language arts, and citizenship may be interwoven with physical education for the mutual enrichment of each subject.

Tolman's sign-gestalt theory

Edward C. Tolman (1886–1959) was instrumental in combining many of the gestalt concepts and developing them into an acceptable learning theory. Previous to his work, educators had not widely applied the gestalt ideas of perception to education. Because of his sensitivity to opposing points of view, Tolman did not develop a tight or exclusive theory like Hull's systematic behavior theory.

While stimulus-response theorists indicated that a series of individual movements (responses) were learned, Tolman believed that the individual perceived the nature of the situation. Learners get the general idea or learn the solution to the problem as well as the specific responses. The learner is goal-directed and is following "signs" or cues to attain his end. He does not routinely follow a definite movement pattern but thoughtfully adjusts his behavior to his status in relation to his goal. According to Tolman, learning is the formation of cognitions, i.e., the recognition of signs and cues in relation to goals. His *sign-gestalt concept* refers to the organization or patterning of the stimuli which act as guides or signs to the learner.

Tolman's theory is one of behavior. Despite his assumption of thought by the learner, he believed that the exact nature of the related mental processes could not be determined with great accuracy. He believed, however, that a human being does not automatically and passively respond to stimuli. Rather, the intelligence of the individual plays a part in his behavior and learning. The learner *thinks* when he organizes stimuli, gives them meaning, and responds with a purpose.

Tolman's theory is molar (large and generalized) rather than molecular (small and specific). Stimulus-response theorists broke behavior into small, discrete parts. Tolman emphasized the fact that behavior cannot be fully understood unless patterns or masses of behavior are observed. According to him, the pattern or whole is lost if the molecular approach is taken. Tolman, therefore, used the gestaltist's "whole is more than the sum of its parts" concept to describe behavior.

Tolman worked extensively with insight. He believed that in learning there is considerable implicit trial-and-error practice. The learner mentally tries out different ways of solving a problem before suddenly arriving at a solution. Like Köhler, he reported that insightful behavior is not restricted to man. Animals also show evidence of figuring things out. Mental practice was therefore proposed as an important ingredient in all types of learning.

According to Tolman's theory, rewards and punishments are important because they can be effective in regulating behavior by providing the learner with motivations to try harder or to continue an activity after he would have stopped. Motivation is not connected to learning in other ways, according to Tolman. He did not believe in any retroactive effect of rewards as reinforcers of past learning. Thorndike's law of effect was therefore not acceptable to Tolman, whose position on the role of motivation in learning is very similar to that of Guthrie.

Implications for motor learning. From Tolman's sign-gestalt theory, one could conclude that:

1. Considerable transfer of skill or learning will take place if the relationship between the two situations is evident to the learner. General principles common to different activities should be pointed out for maximum transfer. Considerable time should be spent in developing basic skills or movement patterns which will be applicable to many activities.

2. Mentally trying out different alternatives aids in the learning and performance of skills. Encouraging mental practice seems desirable for learning an activity or for improving performance when rehearsal immediately precedes performance.

3. Rewards can be effective in motivating the learner to appropriate action. It can usually be assumed, therefore, that motivation which results in greater goal-directed activity will also result in greater learning.

4. Emphasis should be placed on organizing and presenting wholes which are within the understanding of the child. This may require breaking the total activity into several combinations or parts which relate to each other. Certain types of combination drills or lead-up games are examples of this concept.

Lewin's field theory

Kurt Lewin (1890–1947) developed a theory which emphasizes the complexity of stimuli acting on the learner. He was consistent with the gestalt theorists in his contention that the total pattern, or field, of events determines learning. He placed greater emphasis upon the role of motivation, however, than did the gestaltists. Lewin described the learner's "life space" as the external and the internal forces acting upon the individual. The internal stimuli are both physiological (resulting from hunger, thirst, heat, etc.) and psychological (including memories, dreams, and fears). External influences are received from other persons and from the multiplicity of stimuli that are encountered in the environment. Lewin compared this system of stimuli to a weather map which includes many high and low pressure areas resulting in cold and warm fronts, rain, wind, and other atmospheric conditions. His theory has often been referred to as *topological psychology*. The interplay of external and internal forces determines the behavior of the individual. The differences in organizational complexity of individuals results in a different interplay of forces for each, causing individual differences in learning and behavior.

Lewin described four types of learning, all of which deal with changes in cognitive structure. According to him, these changes might result from the cognitive field itself or from the motivations within the individual. Lewin believed that the change in cognitive structure (learning) might take place either suddenly or gradually as a result of repetition. Repetition might produce a change in the individual's knowledge of his environment or in his motivation. Not only might attractive goals occasionally become more attractive through repetition, but unattractive goals might also occasionally become attractive.

Lewin, more than anyone else, pointed to the distinction between incentives and goals and between reward and success. He emphasized that the individual's motivation or tension system involves more than reward. Motives are related to personal goals and not necessarily to a general incentive. Goals are established by the individual and are not the same as rewards which might be established by an external authority. A performer might, therefore, win first place or reach a recognized standard but not be very pleased because he had not reached his personal goal or level of aspiration. Conversely a student might finish last in an activity but still receive considerable satisfaction because he had attained the goal that he was seeking.

A related area of Lewin's work was that of social psychology, especially group dynamics. The major portion of his work in the rather new area of group dynamics came late in his life, and his basic tenets of group dynamics are consistent with the concepts of his field theory. Although group dynamics has not been firmly associated with Lewin's learning theory, both areas are based on similar assumptions.

Implications for motor learning. The following statement might aid the teacher in putting into practice some of the important elements of Lewin's statements on learning:

1. The teacher should aid the learner in establishing attainable goals and assist him in overcoming barriers which block achievement. Causing the child to set unreasonable goals by use of rewards often leads to frustration. Physical education teachers might use time standards, distances, or number of repetitions as attainable goals for the underachiever rather than winning the event.

2. Social development can take place only if the individual is allowed to participate in a social situation. Group interaction should be encouraged to a greater extent than has usually been the case. Leadership, cooperation, or competitive response will not be developed significantly in a lecture or any other teacher-dominated activity. Neither will the title of "captain" or "squad leader" be effective in promoting leader-

ship if the teacher proceeds to dominate the actions of the individual. Pressures in social settings, especially of the competitive sports type, can aid greatly in social growth.

3. Teachers should realize that the child's behavior is not a response to external stimuli alone, but to internal pressures also. An understanding of the complexity of forces acting on the child may aid the teacher in more effectively guiding his learning experiences.

SYNTHESIS OF THE LEARNING THEORIES

The differences in points of view expressed might well give the impression that the various theorists are in complete disagreement. In fact, some teachers feel that the philosophers and psychologists should theorize about the profound questions concerning learning and, "when they finally come up with solutions and agree among themselves, we'll put their recommendations to use in our programs." Neuman (1951) has suggested that for the teaching of practical athletic skills the psychologists' advice is worth about as much as a rabbit's foot. Although there is some logic to such lines of reasoning, the situation is not as chaotic as it may seem. An analysis of the theories reveals that there are a number of important principles which are characteristic of all of them.

Several attempts have been made to synthesize points of similarity among the major theories and to develop learning principles which are mutually acceptable to most scholars of learning. A number of difficulties are encountered when generalizing about the major theories. First, the theories were developed over a period of half a century and were largely independent of each other. Second, those who developed the theories used different experimental conditions for determining learning principles. These experimental conditions varied greatly in such matters as design, types of subjects, learning tasks, motivating techniques, and practice conditions. The learning periods ranged from a few minutes to many months, and evaluation of learning also differed. Third, the researchers themselves often had no chance to study opposing points of view. Nevertheless, several attempts have been made to establish basic points of agreement among the major theories.

Dashiell (1935) surveyed the major learning theories in the mid-1930's and attempted to develop a synthesis. On the basis of his study, he concluded that the following points were apparent in each of the theories: (1) the importance of motivation on the part of the subject, (2) the necessity of activity resulting from obstruction of motivated activity, (3) a multiplicity of responses to stimuli, (4) a gradual selection of appropriate responses and elimination of extraneous responses,

(5) reinforcement of the appropriate responses, and (6) variations in improvement from gradual to sudden solutions.

McConnell (1942) also considered points of agreement among the learning theories. His conclusions were similar to Dashiell's but were structured somewhat differently. McConnell reported that each of the theorists emphasized the following points: (1) Stimuli and responses must be seen in relation to each other; (2) motivation is essential in that it initiates and gives direction to behavior which is organized to attain a goal; (3) the individual must recognize the appropriateness of his response and modify future responses in light of this awareness; and (4) the success of the individual in learning is dependent upon his ability to discriminate between differences and generalize between similarities.

Perhaps the most extensive recent analysis of the major theories was conducted by Hilgard (1956) who, after reviewing the theories of learning established fourteen statements upon which he believed most current theorists would agree. These statements are practical ideas which Hilgard developed for the benefit of the teacher:

1. . . . Brighter people can learn things less bright ones cannot learn; in general, older children can learn more readily than younger ones; the decline of ability with age, in the adult years, depends upon what it is that is being learned.
2. A motivated learner acquires what he learns more readily than one who is not motivated. . . .
3. Motivation that is too intense (especially pain, fear, anxiety) may be accompanied by distracting emotional states, so that excessive motivation may be less effective than moderate motivation for learning some kinds of tasks, especially those involving difficult discriminations.
4. Learning under the control of reward is usually preferable to learning under the control of punishment. Correspondingly, learning motivated by success is preferable to learning motivated by failure. . . .
5. Learning under intrinsic motivation is preferable to learning under extrinsic motivation.
6. Tolerance for failure is best taught through providing a backlog of success that compensates for experienced failure.
7. Individuals need practice in setting realistic goals for themselves, goals neither so low as to elicit little effort nor so high as to foreordain to failure. . . .
8. The personal history of the individual, for example, his reaction to authority, may hamper or enhance his ability to learn from a given teacher.
9. Active participation by a learner is preferable to passive reception when learning, for example, from a lecture or a motion picture.
10. Meaningful materials and meaningful tasks are learned more readily than nonsense materials and more readily than tasks not understood by the learner.
11. There is no substitute for repetitive practice in the overlearning of skills

(for instance, the performance of a concert pianist), or in the memorization of unrelated facts that have to be automatized.

12. Information about the nature of a good performance, knowledge of his own mistakes, and knowledge of successful results, aid learning.

13. Transfer to new tasks will be better if, in learning, the learner can discover relationships for himself, and if he has experience during learning of applying the principles within a variety of tasks.

14. Spaced or distributed recalls are advantageous in fixing material that is to be long retained (pp. 486–487).[2]

Learning theory today

The trend today seems to be away from attempts to develop elaborate and all-encompassing theories of learning. A few years ago, those interested in learning tended to choose sides and debate the major issues from opposing points of view. Although such arguments continue to exist, their prevalence in literature seems to be on the decline. According to Deese (1958), there are several reasons for this change. For example, none of the current theories claim to explain all the questions about learning, so that there is no need to discuss the ultimate and exclusive correctness of one theory over another. In addition, there is a need for more detailed and specific answers to learning problems which would not be given by broad theoretical theses. Since no individual is able to answer all questions about learning, there is a need for a great many specialists, each of whom might contribute to the total field of knowledge.

The trend away from elaborate theoretical positions has led to the popularization of the *functional* approach to learning. Functionalism is not particularly concerned with establishing broad theoretical interpretations but emphasizes solving problems of interest to education. Functionalism assumes an eclectic position and has not been established as a major "theory" of learning. Actually, this approach to learning may be assumed by either the stimulus-response or cognitive theorists as well as by persons not in these groups.

Many educational psychologists would probably consider themselves functionalists. Their research has been conducted more frequently with human beings in a school setting than with rats or other animals in a laboratory. Functional theorists have been especially interested in investigating problems such as whole learning versus part learning, transfer of training, and reinforcement and practice distribution. As applied psychologists, they do not generalize far beyond the particular problem

[2] E. R. Hilgard, THEORIES OF LEARNING, Second Edition. Copyright ©
1948, 1956 by Appleton-Century-Crofts, Inc. Reprinted by permission of the publishers.

being investigated. In like manner, experimental psychology, which is directed toward the solution of specific problems, has become very popular within recent years. However, the problems investigated, and the results obtained, are not always clearly applicable to the classroom setting.

The functional approach has initiated research leading to the establishment of some principles of learning. Watson (1962) compiled a list of such established principles for the purpose of eliminating some of the confusion caused by the numerous learning theories. His list included fifty propositions "with which few knowledgeable psychologists of any school would disagree" (p. 4). These statements were established and organized into twelve areas important to education including learning process, maturation, individual differences, level of challenge, teaching method, discipline and learning. In regard to these principles, Watson indicated that, "The educator who bases his program on these propositions . . . is entitled to feel that he is on solid psychological ground and not on shifting sands" (p. 4).

SELECTED READINGS

Guthrie, E. R. *The psychology of learning.* (Rev. ed.) New York: Harper & Row, 1952.

Hebb, D. O. *The organization of behavior: a neuropsychological theory.* New York: Wiley, 1949.

Hilgard, E. R. *Theories of learning.* (2nd ed.) New York: Appleton-Century-Crofts, 1956.

Hilgard, E. R. Learning theory and its application. In W. Schramm (Ed.), *New teaching aids for the American classroom.* Stanford, Calif.: Stanford University Institute for Communicative Research, 1960.

Hilgard, E. R., & Bower, G. H. *Theories of learning.* (2nd ed.) New York: Appleton-Century-Crofts, 1966.

Hill, W. F. *Learning: a survey of psychological interpretations.* San Francisco: Chandler Publishing Co., 1963.

Hull, C. L. *Principles of behavior.* New York: Appleton-Century-Crofts, 1943.

Köhler, W. *Gestalt psychology.* New York: Liveright, 1947.

Lewin, K. *Principles of topological psychology.* Trans. F. Heider & G. M. Heider. New York: McGraw-Hill, 1936.

Skinner, B. F. *The behavior of organisms: an experimental analysis.* New York: Appleton-Century-Crofts, 1938.

Thorndike, E. L. *Educational psychology.* Vol. 2. *The psychology of learning.* New York: Teachers College, 1913.

Thorndike, E. L. *Selected writings from a connectionist's psychology.* New York: Appleton-Century-Crofts, 1949.

Tolman, E. C. Theories of learning. In F. A. Moss (Ed.), *Comparative Psychology.* Englewood Cliffs, N. J.: Prentice-Hall, 1934.

Watson, G. What psychology can we feel sure about? In W. C. Morse & G. M. Wingo (Eds.), *Readings in educational psychology.* Chicago: Scott, Foresman, 1962. Pp. 3–7.

Part II

THE LEARNING PROCESS

Introduction

The process of learning has, itself, been perhaps the most intriguing of all phenomena relating to education. A great deal of research, therefore, has been devoted to the problem of determining the nature of the learning process. Some typical questions related to this topic are: What precisely is learned? How much transfer can be assumed, and how is it best promoted? What is the nature of remembering? Is the learning process essentially the same for the different types of material and skills?

Each of these questions has been the focal point for considerable investigation and discussion. As a result, some specific principles or laws, as well as broad theories, have been established. This section on *the learning process* is devoted particularly to principles and their relevance to the teaching of skills:

Chapter 3. Reinforcement
Chapter 4. Transfer of skill
Chapter 5. Retention and forgetting

Reinforcement

One of the most important concepts relating to the management of learning is reinforcement. This phenomenon is the key to an understanding of the learning process, and as such, is of great importance to teachers in all subject areas. Teachers of perceptual-motor skills, however, can often make more direct and obvious application of reinforcement than can other teachers. This is because responses in motor skills can be more easily picked out and observed and, therefore, reinforced. Any lack of understanding of the concept of reinforcement, or lack of skill in its use, will seriously limit the effectiveness of those who seek to guide learning experiences. In this chapter, the strategic role of reinforcement in various types of learning experiences will be discussed. Special attention will be devoted to the use of reinforcement in motor learning.

The nature of reinforcement

Reinforcement refers to any condition which if it follows a response increases the probability that the same response will recur on subsequent occasions when similar stimuli are presented. In the laboratory, the animal that pushes a lever may be rewarded, or reinforced, by a pellet of food which appears. In athletics, the young baseball pitcher who makes the proper finger-wrist snap in his delivery has his response reinforced when he notices that the ball curves in the desired manner. As a result, this particular finger-wrist response will most likely be remembered and, therefore, repeated in subsequent situations when he desires to throw a curve ball.

Reinforcement is sometimes erroneously equated with the terms *reward* and *punishment*. Though rewards and punishments may on occasion be used as reinforcers, they are inadequate explanations of this concept. Whether they are of the extrinsic or intrinsic type, rewards do not always reinforce learning. An athlete, for example, might be rewarded at the end of a practice period by praise from the coach, promotion to the first team, or favorable comments by teammates. Though stimulating, this type of reward would probably not strengthen any particular response. In such situations, the performer does not know specifically which acts led to the reward. Therefore, no connection is made between motor response and reward. Rather, the player is likely to associate his reward to his overall effort for the day and be motivated to duplicate that performance on subsequent practice days. For a longer period of time, perhaps for a full playing season, the performer may win prizes, all-star selections, or other forms of recognition. Although these recognitions are generally rewarding, they are of little value in strengthening particular stimulus-response relationships.

Punishment may be equally vague and therefore ineffective as a means of reinforcing responses. A player might be punished by jeers from the spectators, criticism from the coach, or demotion to the second team. There is no assurance in these cases that the player forms a connection between the punishment and the specific response that led to failure. The lack of specificity in the usual administration of rewards and punishment makes them of little value in reinforcing learning. It is true, however, that some types of punishment or reward, if immediately and clearly connected to particular responses may well serve as reinforcement.

A second reason why reinforcement and reward cannot be equated is that reinforcement does not always result in reward or punishment in the ordinary sense. There is often a degree of satisfaction at the realization of success and dissatisfaction with failure. However, these impressions, often too subtle to be considered "rewards," do tend to reinforce actions which lead to success. An example of this might be seen when the novice soccer player learns to "give" with his body to more effectively trap the ball. Although there is some satisfaction in the successful performance of this act, the major result is not a reward in the traditional sense, but a reinforcement of the correct body action. In other situations, an act might lead to failure, which is a type of punishment. Nevertheless, the usual understanding of reward and punishment is not limited to the types of associations which reinforce learning.

Teachers use reinforcement techniques to change the response *probability* of a particular act. It may be desirable to increase the act's probability or, on occasion, to decrease the likelihood that the act will recur. All responses have a certain probability of occurring in a given set of circumstances. A particular eighth grader, for example, might be expected to serve a volleyball into the court area 50 per cent of the time, to make basketball free throws 30 per cent of the time, or to throw a baseball into the target area 40 per cent of the time. The teacher's aim is to increase the probability of success in each action to as near 100 per cent as possible. This he might do by reinforcing the desired responses or even the intermediate improvements that lead to the correct responses. The repetition of the desired responses with related reinforcement tends to form a strong habit. Athletic coaches and physical education teachers are interested in students acquiring the correct responses so well that they are done automatically without conscious thought. When the mechanics of a movement become habits, then the participant can devote more conscious effort to strategy, team play, or other mental aspects of the activity. Similarly, teachers of industrial arts or home economics and supervisors in numerous industrial jobs seek to teach motor skills in order to increase the probability of correct performance each time. Such a high level of probability is reached by repetition, or practice, which is supported by appropriate reinforcement.

On occasion, the teacher wants to reduce the probability that a particular response will occur. For example, an eighth grader might have a high probability of looking away from the volleyball before hitting it, or of jumping off the wrong foot when he shoots the basketball, or of looking at the ground just before throwing the baseball. A player might also have a high probability of arguing with the referee on all fouls called. The teacher's primary concern in such cases is to reduce the probability of these undesirable responses.

DEVELOPMENT OF THE REINFORCEMENT CONCEPT

The term *reinforcement* was first used in connection with learning at the beginning of the twentieth century. Reinforcement was closely associated with the idea of contiguity, i.e., any two ideas or concepts that were seen together in time or space would be connected. More recently, psychologists have concluded than contiguity alone does not insure a mental connection. Rather, the stimulus and the appropriate response must be related in some way to insure learning. Reinforcement is seen as the key to this connection.

Pavlov's stimulus substitution

Ivan P. Pavlov's (1927) well-known conditioning experiments with dogs led to the development of the earliest reinforcement theories which were based on the concept of temporal contiguity. In Pavlov's experiments, a dog was placed in a soundproof room. Attachments were made to the animals parotid salivary gland so the amount of salivation could be observed. It was noted that the sight, smell, and touch of food resulted in observable salivation. In the conditioning program, a tuning fork was sounded and food was then presented to the dog. Several sessions were held in which the sound of the tuning fork was always followed by the food. Later, the sound of the tuning fork alone resulted in salivation by the animal. The tuning fork had acquired the capacity for eliciting a salivary response because of its customary temporal contiguity to the food. Pavlov referred to the food as the unconditioned stimulus and the tuning fork as the conditioned stimulus.

Woodworth and Schlosberg (1963) interpreted Pavlov's first law as: "The occurrence of an unconditional reflex in temporal contiguity with a conditional reflex increases the strength of the latter" (p. 542). The second law is suggested as: "If a conditioned reflex is elicited without reinforcement by an unconditional reflex, the conditional reflex is weakened or inactivated" (p. 543). According to Pavlov's theory of reinforcement, conditioning is aided by reward (food) which tends to connect two stimuli. He assumed that without reinforcement, conditioning would not have taken place so effectively.

Thorndike's law of effect

A concept similar to that of Pavlov was developed in E. L. Thorndike's law of effect. His theory was based primarily on the belief that the effect of the response was strategic for reinforcement. In *The Psychology of Learning*, published in 1913, Thorndike states:

The Law of Effect is: When a modifiable connection between a situation and a response is made and is accompanied or followed by a satisfying state of affairs, that connection's strength is increased: when made and accompanied or followed by an annoying state of affairs, its strength is decreased. The strengthening effect of satisfyingness (or the weakening effect of annoyingness) upon a bond varies with the closeness of the connection between it and the bond. This closeness or intimacy of association of the satisfying (or annoying) state of affairs with the bond in question may be the result of nearness in time or of attentiveness to the situation, response and satisfying event in question (p. 4).[1]

His principle of reinforcement referred to any kind of reward or punishment which was instrumental in learning. This statement reflects the basic premise of reinforcement, although today the concept is not restricted to specific responses to isolated stimuli but is used more broadly.

Hull's drive reduction

C. L. Hull stated that any stimulus-response sequence which is followed by a lessening of the strength of the drive will be reinforced. This is consistent with his reinforcement theory of learning which indicated that learning takes place to the extent that a particular need is reduced. Such a need is connected to a particular drive which may be

[1] E. L. Thorndike, EDUCATIONAL PSYCHOLOGY, Vol. 2. THE PSYCHOLOGY OF LEARNING, New York: Teachers College, 1913. By permission.

either primary or secondary, biological or social. The value of the stimulus-response sequence as a reinforcer depends upon the strength of the relative drive. Hull emphasized that need-reducing reinforcement is advantageous to both learning and performance. In his later writing, he placed primary importance on reinforcement for improvement in performance. Thus, the attention-seeking child who disrupts the class and becomes its center of attention may be reducing his need for recognition. The reinforcement (need reduction) strengthens the tendency of the child to resort to similar behavior the next time this need occurs. An extension of this concept occurs on the athletic field when social needs may enable young athletes to practice long and play hard in games even in conditions of boredom and fatigue.

Skinner's operant reinforcement

B. F. Skinner founded his theory of operant conditioning upon the concept of reinforcement. His work has contributed a great deal toward a broader understanding of reinforcement. A discussion of operant conditioning seems important to illustrate how much reinforcement may be used in controlling learning.

Skinner identified two types of behavior, *respondent* and *emitted*. His explanation of respondent behavior is much the same as the earlier theorists', i.e., particular behavior is the result of a particular stimulus. An eye blink resulting from a sharp noise or a knee jerk are examples of Skinner's respondent behavior. Skinner differs from other theorists, however, in his discussion of emitted behavior. He describes emitted behaviors as those which are prompted by the individual himself and are not the responses to any identifiable stimuli. Skinner, who suggested that most human actions are emitted, referred to these unsolicited behaviors as *operants*. He has seriously questioned much that was previously assumed to be responsive behavior in a cause-and-effect way. There is no reason, for example, why a speech causes applause at its end. Nor does a lecture cause note taking by students. Certainly, a close play at second base does not cause the runner to slide. A zone defense in basketball does not cause the opposing team to use short, quick passes. According to Skinner, these behaviors are used because they have been rewarded in past situations.

Skinner stated that respondent behavior is not only very infrequent but is usually rather trivial. Since he feels that operant behavior is more frequent and more important, Skinner has devoted most of his attention to techniques for shaping emitted behavior by rewarding (reinforcing) desired operants and punishing undesired behavior. The learner makes a connection between the response and the reinforcement to develop most skills, knowledges, and attitudes, according to Skinner.

Skinner's ideas of operant reinforcement seem to be illustrated in athletics by both individual improvement and team strategy. For example, a basketball player might fail in three successive attempts to drive around the right side of an opponent to get to the basket. The fourth time, he might fake to the right and drive left for a successful lay-up. The reinforcement (an easy lay-up shot) for the maneuver would enable the individual to remember the maneuver the next time a similar occasion arises. A football captain might remember that in previous situations of second down and one yard to go, he had success in throwing long passes against unsuspecting opponents. It is clear that although such situations do not cause the particular responses, previously reinforced responses are strategic in this learning. A fifth grader might remember that once when he ran down the stairs he fell and was hurt. On another occasion, he carefully walked down and was complimented by the teacher who happened to be watching. Both consequences have a reinforcing effect and will aid the child in determining his descent of the stairs in the future. In these cases, according to Skinner's thesis, reinforcement is strategic in prompting the association of behavior with consequence.

There is considerable evidence to show that whatever the individual is doing at the time of drive reduction will be reinforced, even if that behavior is incidental. Head scratching by a chimpanzee has been reinforced when it happened to be the animal's activity at feeding time. Most superstitions probably have developed in this way. Farming practices, such as planting corn "by the moon," are apparently based on accidental successes which earlier farmers had when using that method. The connection between moon position and successful farming has generally been lost because it was not consistently reinforced. For more superstitious individuals, however, even occasional reinforcement is sufficient to "prove" a connection.

Athletes tend to remember odd happenings or conditions which were present at success or failure. These "signs" are often trivial such as the wearing of colored shoelaces, failure to shave, or having good luck charms. Nevertheless, reinforcement of these details leads to strong associations which stimulate great efforts to repeat "lucky" details and avoid "jinxed" ones.

Reinforcement in learning experiences

Feedback

Feedback and *knowledge of results* are popular terms for a type of reinforcement based on information which the individual is able to use to check or confirm his performance. Feedback is the most widely used type of reinforcement. An awareness of one's performance is important in learning not only because of its inherent reinforcement values, but because it tends to motivate one to continue work on the task. Performance in any task is more meaningful when the learner is aware of his progress.

The concept of feedback is closely related to the recent development of an "information theory" of learning which is described by Cratty (1964) and several other authors. The basis for this theory is reflected in the writings of Hebb (1949), K. U. Smith (1967), and Wiener (1961). The human learner is compared to an electric computer in that he receives (decodes) the stimuli and interprets (encodes) them for the most appropriate response. The information the learner receives may come from all the senses, but in complex movement activities the proprioceptors in the muscles, tendons, and points are especially important.

Authorities have long recognized that the learner improves more if he receives specific information about the relationship of his performance to his goal. Students often seek this information even if they are not aware of any learning advantages. For example, they are not always satisfied with a simple letter grade, pass or fail rating, or even "better" or "poorer." They will often ask, "How far did I miss?" "How was the performance weak?" "In what way was it better?" "Which questions did I get right and which did I get wrong?" Even though these inquiries are a source of annoyance to some teachers, they are often more than expressions of idle curiosity by the student. Answers to them can be instrumental in helping the student do better in his future attempts.

Thorndike (1931) conducted an early experiment to determine the effect of knowledge of results on subsequent performances. In his experiment, students made 3,000 attempts to draw a four-inch line while blindfolded. During their practice, they were not told how closely they approximated four inches. At the experiment's end, the students exhibited no greater skill in drawing a four-inch line than at the beginning. Kingsley (1946) conducted a similar experiment in which students attempted to draw four-inch lines 400 times and were not shown any of the results. No improvement was observed during this practice period. When same students drew four more lines and were informed of their margin and direction of error after each trial, a great deal of improvement in performance was shown in each attempt.

In Kingsley's experiment, the subjects were divided into two groups. One group was *told* the degree of error after each trial and, consequently, made considerable improvement with each successive trial. The second group looked at the results and *saw* how they had done. Their improvement was much greater than that of the first group. A greater understanding of performance and the making of necessary adjustments apparently resulted when subjects were able to personally observe the results. Second hand information (being told by someone else) regarding knowledge of results did not seem as effective.

Use of performance knowledge in teaching

Knowledge of results, or feedback, is automatic and easily observed in a great many motor skills. Archery, horseshoe pitching, typewriting, painting, bowling, and basketball shooting are some skills which provide early and definite feedback regarding success or failure. In other skills, however, *faults* which contribute to failure are not easily seen. Even when the end results can be observed the performer often does not know exactly why the performance failed. An experienced teacher can be especially helpful in showing the learner the particular movement which contributed to the results. The performer is often unaware of the contributing response and, therefore, must find the solution by trial and error. Even professional athletes of the first magnitude sometimes get into slumps and are unable to determine what they are doing wrong. They have to depend upon coaches to identify their faults. In such cases, the coach provides some strategic knowledge of results, i.e., the actions of the performer which are contributing to success or failure.

To be most effective, knowledge of results must be meaningful to the learner, specific in nature, and closely follow the performance. If the information provided the learner is not clearly understood, or if it is too general to be applied to a specific act, then it is of little value. This principle is important for both verbal and motor learning. In the classroom, it is not unusual for students to receive test papers or project reports from the teacher with no more than a letter or a numerical grade. Unfortunately, "correcting" papers today often means that the teacher applies a mark to the paper. With this limited knowledge of results the student can only guess at the strengths and weaknesses of his work. Even on objective examinations, the student may not find out which answers or solutions were correct or incorrect. If the teacher is to use tests as an educational as well as an evaluative device, he should provide specific performance information to the student. Ability to provide immediate, specific, and automatic feedback to the learner is the real strength of teaching machines and programmed instruction. Whether or not he uses these particular tools, the effective teacher will find some way to provide students with as much feedback as possible regarding their performances.

Perhaps teachers of motor skills have some advantage over teachers of verbal material in helping students to receive specific knowledge of results. After all, the batter in baseball either hits the ball or he does not. The direction and force of the batted ball can also be observed. Some feedback is therefore obvious. However, there is much additional information that the physical education teacher can provide. In addition to giving causal information regarding success or failure in activities where the performer can readily see the results of his performance, the teacher can provide valuable knowledge in activities in which the participant gets almost no feedback. For example, in the early stages of learning modern dance, diving, or intermediate swimming, the performer might have only a vague idea of the quality of his performance.

When students can readily observe the results of their efforts, the teacher may still increase the usefulness of this information as reinforcement in learning. Whereas the student may know the distance of his broad jump, his time in the 100-yard dash, or the number of push-ups performed, he often does not relate these details to previous performances in the same activity. Students do not often take a scientific or analytical aproach toward their abilities and their progress. The teacher can be effective in getting students to keep records of their daily and weekly performances. In this way, knowledge regarding progress can be emphasized. Greater emphasis on self-evaluation will result in greater concern for learning and greater effort to improve. Too often, students go to practice or perform without considering whether or not they are operating at maximum efficiency. Record keeping and competition against personal standards will probably result in greater motivation, more serious practice, and continued efforts to gain this type of detailed knowledge of results.

Rewarding approximations

In a discussion of stimulus-response reinforcement, it is often assumed that only a discrete and perfect success is rewarded. If this were the case, one might wonder about the role of reinforcement in *gradual improvement* or in very complex learning. After all, a student does not simply "make" a giant swing or a perfect one-and-one-half gainer. If the teacher waited until the perfect performance before reinforcing the learner, this would be clear evidence that learning could take place quite well without reinforcement. Use of reinforcement would then become a rather superficial extra, and would not be viewed as a necessary element in the learning process.

For effective reinforcement of more complex learning tasks, however, the teacher must reinforce *successive approximations* of the task. In other words, minor successes or progressions toward the major task should be reinforced so that they will be well learned. Such a technique is described by Skinner (1958) in an experiment in which he and two associates decided to teach a pigeon to bowl:

The pigeon was to send a wooden ball down a miniature alley toward a set of toy pins by swiping the ball with a sharp sideward movement of the beak. To condition the response, we put the ball on the floor of an experimental box and prepared to operate the food-magazine as soon as the first swipe occurred. But nothing happened. Though we had all the time in the world, we grew tired of waiting. We decided to reinforce any response which had the slightest resemblance to a swipe—perhaps, at first, merely the behavior of looking at the ball—and then to select responses which more closely approximated the final form. The result amazed us. In a few minutes, the ball was caroming off the walls of the box as if the pigeon had been a champion squash player (p. 94).

Teaching by progression levels. Since complex skills are learned by a gradual, sequential process, slight improvement must be reinforced in order to keep the person interested and to indicate progress. If the teacher withholds reinforcement until a perfect and complete performance is attained, he might lose the interest of most of his students. An effective technique for reinforcing approximations has been the practice of some physical education teachers to teach by progression levels. In this method, successive steps are made ends in themselves to be taught, rewarded, and later used as prerequisite skills for more advanced performances. This has been one of the most effective techniques in teaching complex body movement activities such as gymnastics, dance, and aquatics.

An example of the use of progression levels can be illustrated in the teaching of springboard diving. The child who has no experience and perhaps some fear of plunging into the water cannot be easily coaxed into taking a running approach dive off the board. Rather, he may start by sitting on the side of the pool with his feet in the water. From this position he is asked to put his arms and hands in front of his body, tilt his head forward and downward, and lean forward until he falls into the water. This act is rewarded verbally and practiced a number of times until the child feels comfortable entering the water that way. In the second progression step, the child kneels at the pool's edge and falls forward into the water. Again, this act is reinforced and practiced until the learner feels confident in this technique. Next, the child stoops, or crouches, and later stands at the side of the pool to make his entry. At this point he should not be afraid to enter the water from a standing position at the side of the pool.

He must now be taught to dive rather than merely fall into the water. Beginning work in diving can also be done from the side of the pool. The child is taught to dive, i.e., bend his knees and push off during his headfirst fall into the water. Later he is taught to increase the dive or push-off, while practically eliminating the forward fall of his body. After the child has learned to dive properly from the side of the pool, he is asked to walk onto the low diving board. While standing at the end, the child gets the feel of the board by bouncing slightly. He is then encouraged to dive off the end of the board in the same way he dived from the side of the pool. Much verbal reinforcement is needed to make the child feel comfortable and exhibit good form in the springboard dive. After some success has been accomplished in the standing springboard dive, attention can then be devoted to the approach. The student can be taught the four step approach on the deck rather than on the springboard. After the steps, hurdle, and two-foot take-off have been practiced until the student has them well learned, he can be taken back to the board to combine the approach and the forward dive. Then practice can continue for refinement of form on the standard forward dive and, later, for the different types of dives.

Similar progression-level teaching could be illustrated for many gymnastic routines, for dance, and for a variety of individual sports activities. This technique is effective only if each successive improvement is reinforced in some manner. The size of the progression steps will vary according to the ability of the learners because some learners will require less practice at each level and others may even be able to bypass some of the steps.

Instruction could be improved in most motor skills if teachers would establish specific sequential levels of learning. A thorough analysis of the different skills should reveal the movement patterns which are most fundamental and which act as prerequisites for the learning of more advanced movements. However, care must be taken to avoid the tendency to oversegmentize movement patterns which might be most effectively taught as a group. It is important to understand that rewarding approximations, which places emphasis on progressive and sequential advancement in the performance of a task, is distinctly different from teaching by the part method which may separate the activity into segments despite the relatedness of these parts to the whole.

Timing in reinforcement

Timing is the most important factor in determining the effectiveness of reinforcement. Immediate reinforcement has been found to be most valuable, with progressively longer delays resulting in a gradual reduction in effectiveness. After too long a delay, reinforcement is not effective at all because the learner does not make a connection between the response and the reinforcement. In some types of responses, if the learner has to wait even a few seconds, he may forget the exact kinesthetic sensation related to the movement. The length of the effective delay will vary according to the learner's capacity and the learning situation.

Shilling (1951) reported an experiment in which rats waited from 5 to 10 seconds after the response before a pellet of food was released. He observed that on the 5-second delay schedule the rats became conditioned, and after the appropriate response remained at the food cup and made anticipatory movements for the food. Rats that had to wait 10 seconds, however, generally moved away from the food cup and took part in unrelated activity. It appeared that the rats could remember up to 5 seconds and connect their response to the food. After a 10-second wait, however, they could not make the association. Spence (1956) observed that rats on a longer delayed reinforcement schedule might attain the same degree of learning, but that more trials would be needed. Most experimenters would agree that learning is slower when the reinforcement is delayed.

The delay of reinforcement in school learning varies widely. Some responses are rewarded or punished almost immediately, while in other situations minutes or even days precede reinforcement. For example, after a student answers certain questions on a written examination he may have to wait days before learning whether his answers were right or wrong. On the other hand, if he responds orally to a teacher's question in class, he receives almost immediate knowledge of whether his answer is correct or incorrect. In fact, the student often starts receiving feedback while he is still answering the question. Indeed, it is not unusual for a student to start answering in one way, and depending upon the kind of feedback, to alter or even completely reverse his answer. Some examples of feedback which are likely to cause him to change his answer are: the act of other students anxiously raising their hands when he is half through his answer; a surprised or amused expression on the face of the teacher at the beginning of the response; or a statement such as, "Are you *sure* about that?" at the conclusion of the answer. These nonsupportive responses cause the child to believe that he is on the wrong track. However, if the child receives an approving nod from the teacher, or if the hands of the students around him start to come *down*, the student is already receiving reinforcement for his answer. Much of the reinforcement from teacher to pupil and vice versa is extremely subtle.

Speeding reinforcement in motor performance.   In simple motor activities, delay of knowledge is usually short. Young children can immediately see results in handwriting, drawing, or cutting with scissors. When they are learning to whistle, they can almost immediately tell whether the lip formation and forced expiration are correct. The value of this feedback can be dramatically shown if the child is prevented from seeing his work. When his writing hand is covered, or he cannot see what he is drawing, his work becomes distorted. Without knowledge of his performance in these activities, improvement is much slower. The delay of automatic knowledge of results varies from one motor activity to another. In skeet shooting, the delay of reinforcement is particularly short. The baseball pitcher must wait approximately one-half second to tell whether the pitch will curve in the appropriate manner or if it will go into the strike zone. In horeshoe pitching, there is a delay of a second or two. In the track and field events of javelin and discus throwing, the delay between response and reinforcement is even greater.

It can be readily understood that a beginning bowler might forget the kinesthetic feel of a particular delivery by the time the ball strikes the pins. The thoughts, visual images, or distractions which enter his mind between the release of the ball and the time it strikes the pins all serve to minimize the effectiveness of the reinforcement. In discrete movement activities, it appears that even a slight delay can cause the person to lose an awareness of the intricacies of the movement. However, reinforcement may be aided by the early realization that the response will be successful. The basketball player who says, "I knew it was going in as soon as it left my hand," has a degree of reinforcement almost immediately. Teachers can often promote more immediate reinforcement by such techniques as spot bowling, which gives students feedback in about one-third the usual time. Although these interim reinforcements are not as definite as the final success, they do have special advantages because of the speed of the feedback. There are many activities which the teacher can select as checkpoints and encourage the students to use.

Another way in which the teacher may provide earlier reinforcement is by praising improvement or by pointing to errors in movement patterns *during* one's performance, regardless of whether the result of the response is successful. The coach may praise the young batter who swings without his customary hitch even if he misses the ball. Similarly, the tennis player who positions himself in the proper manner and makes a smooth, level stroke should be reinforced regardless of the consequence of his stroke. The young basketball player who is learning the jump shot might receive an immediate "That's the idea" as soon as the ball leaves his hand. These efforts to shorten the delay in reinforcement are extremely valuable and should be more widely used by all teachers.

The amount of intermediate reinforcement that the teacher can give to each student is limited. The learning process will be enhanced if students learn to analyze their own performances and predict probable results on the basis of cues which are received during performance. Kinesthetic awareness of proper performance should be stressed so that the learner is able to detect correct and incorrect responses. Just as the player knew the basketball was going into the goal as soon as it left his hand, other performers such as the place kicker in football, the golfer, the sprinter, the tennis server, or the horseshoe pitcher might also be able to predict results. A valuable drill to encourage one to analyze his performance is to have the performer predict his success by yelling *short, left, right,* or by guessing his time or distance as soon as possible. These exercises encourage performers to be sensitive to feedback during performance.

Long delay of reinforcement seems to diminish not only learning, but one's enthusiasm for the activity. A winning team is reinforced by the immediate knowledge of having won. This may be contrasted to a telegraphic or mailographic athletic contest in which each team performs at home and forwards the results to its opponent. The team must then wait hours or even days before finding out whether it won or lost. As a rule, the elation is not nearly so great as if the team had immediately been aware of winning.

Extinction

In physical education, as well as in other areas of the school curriculum, there is often a need for eliminating a particular response or some general behavior. This process, referred to as extinction, may be necessitated if the individual has developed a flaw in his response, if he has acquired the skill or knowledge incorrectly, or if he exhibits socially improper behavior. Extinction may result from various techniques of behavior. In the laboratory, many techniques for diminishing the strength of a response are used. This process is referred to as experimental extinction. For example, a rat which has learned to push a lever to get a pellet of food will respond in this manner each time it is hungry. If the experimenter wishes to eliminate the response, he does not give food when the lever is pushed. The rat will continue to depress the lever for a time, then it will gradually reduce and eventually eliminate this response. The connection between lever pushing and food getting will therefore be lost.

There is a tendency for the learner to continue responding for a while after the reinforcement has been discontinued. This resistance to extinction depends upon how well the response was learned originally. Behavior which has been effectively learned or thoroughly overlearned is most resistant to extinction. This has been demonstrated with animals in the laboratory and can easily be observed with children or adults in everyday life. Faults in motor performance which have been learned and practiced over a long period of time are the most difficult to eliminate. Physical education teachers and coaches have found, for example, that the baseball batter who is allowed to continue using a hitch in his swing or to step away from the plate has greater difficulty in learning the proper technique than does the person who is immediately corrected. Similarly, social behavior which is allowed to continue for a long period is most difficult to eliminate.

Eliminating improper social behavior.   Children in school forget a response or eliminate behavior when it is no longer rewarded. For example, a child may have developed a tendency to clown in school because he discovered that his antics got a laugh from his classmates. After using this technique for a while, however, he may find that the other children no longer applaud him. His behavior is, therefore, no longer reinforced. Eventually he loses the association between the clowning technique and a pleasant response from his classmates. Another child may be motivated to argue with teachers because of status satisfaction received from a group of classmates. In another class, however, he may find that arguing with the teacher is not popular with other class members. With no social reinforcement in this new situation, he would no longer be encouraged to argue. If baiting the umpire proves popular with teammates, a player is likely to develop this habit. On subsequent occasions, when baiting loses its popularity, he would reduce or eliminate the action. Attention-getting behavior, both acceptable and unacceptable, is used because of the pleasant response that it brings to the person.

Coaches are often confronted with the young athlete who has a tendency to be a show-off. His behavior often detracts from his concentration and that of his teammates in the game. Coaches, therefore, have attempted to eliminate such behavior by ignoring it, by punishing the show-off, or by rewarding alternative behavior. A universally effective method has not yet been determined. The effectiveness of any technique, however, will depend upon its capacity for eliminating the reinforcement of the show-off's behavior. In this process, coaches and teachers should exercise care to avoid undue damage to the self-image of the child.

Eliminating movement faults. In physical education and sports, both social learning and skill learning may be eliminated by nonreinforcement. Participants often develop errors of movement or faults in sports activities. A direct attack on this fault by the teacher (punishment of the child) might be one way of reducing the incidence of the habit or eliminating it. Another technique would be to reward what the performer does correctly while ignoring his faults. If alternatives to the fault are reinforced while the fault itself is not, the alternatives will be learned because of their association with success or approval. For example, a common fault among young baseball players is overstriding when preparing to swing at a pitch. The coach might aid a player in correcting this fault by first pointing out the weakness of this technique and then complimenting the batter each time the stride is shortened. This emphasis on the correct way of doing things is a simple matter of accentuating the positive.

The natural effect, or result, of a faulty response is often unpleasant in itself and will therefore prove instrumental in weakening the act. Such an unpleasant experience, or negative reinforcement, may be observed when the child who has been encouraged to tuck his head while doing a forward roll, forgets to do it. He will probably bump his head on the mat or floor with some degree of pain, and this natural punishment will tend to speed the association between the tucked head position and a more comfortable forward roll. In horseback riding, incorrect coordination of one's body movement with the trotting horse will result in some physical discomfort for the rider. Similarly, the diver who does not get his body in proper alignment will make a painful entry into the water. Improper body position while doing various stunts on the trampoline will become vividly apparent to the performer upon landing. The baseball player who hits the ball too near the handle of the bat will receive a somewhat painful sting. Occasions in motor activities in which improper performance is naturally punished with a painful or unpleasant experience tend to work to the advantage of the teacher who is attempting to promote a higher level of performance.

Inappropriate motor performance occasionally results in success. This is unfortunate for the teaching process since successful behavior becomes more resistant to extinction. For example, some beginning basketball players develop a tendency to take off on the wrong foot when attempting a lay-up shot. Naturally, the more this technique is practiced, the more right it seems. Each success (making the goal) reinforces this wrong foot takeoff. Efforts by the teacher to eliminate the fault are especially difficult because early attempts in the correct manner may not result in success. Similarly, right-handed players who always shoot and dribble with the right hand, despite floor position or circumstance, do so because of greater immediate success with this hand. The coach who is interested in developing left-handed proficiency for the long-range development of the individual's playing ability therefore encounters considerable difficulty because of the greater reinforcement which the learner receives from his particular manner.

Partial reinforcement

It would be unusual in everyday or school situations for reinforcement to be administered every time the correct response is given. Occasional or partial reinforcement is more often the rule. For example, the hound does not catch the rabbit in every chase. The cat only catches the mouse sometimes. Even the professional gambler does not win on every try. A fake maneuver in sports does not always fool the opposition. Nevertheless, partial or occasional reinforcement is still sufficient to keep the learner interested and working at the task. Humphreys (1936), for example, showed that reinforcement which was administered 50 per cent of the time was practically as effective as reinforcement 100 per cent of the time. Teachers should keep in mind, therefore, that reinforcement may be effective even if it is not given every time the response is emitted.

Retention is greatly affected by the regularity with which reinforcement has been administered during the learning period. Forgetting, or extinction, is much slower when the response has been only partially reinforced. Laboratory experiments show that animals which have followed a partial reinforcement schedule show greater perseverance in a particular response than animals which have been reinforced after every response. In fact, once a response has been learned, and the more infrequent the reinforcement was during learning, the more difficult is the response's extinction. The performer who anticipates only occasional success will persist much longer than one who is used to absolute success. The gambler, for example, will continue his pursuits with great expectations of success even after a series of responses has not been reinforced.

Habits which have been developed with partial reinforcement certainly seem more difficult to break than habits learned under full reinforcement conditions. The value of persistence, however, must be weighed against the value of speed of learning. Most authorities agree that learning takes place faster under conditions of very frequent reinforcement. For maximum learning *and* retention, the evidence seems to suggest a progressive decrease in the frequency of reinforcement, i.e., very frequent reinforcement in early stages of the learning process and less frequent reinforcement later.

Greater persistence resulting from partial reinforcement may apply to one's enthusiasm for an activity as well as learning. Perhaps this is why developing children who are star performers at the preteenage level appear more easily disillusioned when they get into more difficult competitions and occasionally experience failure. In comparison, children who are not in the habit of winning all the time seem less dependent upon the reward of winning.

Schedules of reinforcement. Travers (1963) has described three types of schedules for partial reinforcement. The first is the *fixed-ratio* schedule, in which the individual is reinforced for an established amount of work. Fixed ratios operate as merit rewards based on what the subject has done. For example, a rat would receive a pellet of food for depressing a bar five times, and a child might receive a reinforcement each time he swims one lap in the swimming pool. "Piece work" in industry, where the individual receives payment for so many units of work, is another example of the fixed-ratio of schedule. This schedule has been found valuable in keeping the individual interested in performing in a purposeful way. Because of its emphasis on maximum achievement, fixed ratios are widely applicable to the teaching of motor skills.

The second form of partial reinforcement is the *fixed-interval* technique in which the individual is reinforced according to a time schedule as long as he works. Such a schedule is used in the laboratory when the animal is rewarded at regular intervals. The same system might be used for reinforcing the child as long as he swims or the worker for the time that he works. Most industrial work uses the system of payment by the hour, week, or year. This technique is effective in keeping the individual active during the prescribed period, but it does not assure purposeful or enthusiastic participation. Because it does not emphasize maximum effort, the fixed-interval technique has not proven effective in sports activity or physical education.

Travers' third type of partial reinforcement is the *variable-interval* technique which rewards the individual at irregular and unpredictable intervals. This type of reinforcement is quite typical of many everyday situations. Variable-interval reinforcement has some weaknesses in promoting fast learning, but it has advantages in developing behavior which is very resistant to extinction. The individual is likely to continue his efforts because he realizes that reward could come at any time. Variable-interval reinforcement comes naturally in many sports activities. This irregular schedule is also the type most often used by teachers in the administration of verbal reinforcement.

Primary and secondary reinforcers

Travers (1963) described primary reinforcers as those which directly reduce a need of the individual. Food, water, pain reduction, and other biological needs fit into this category. Primary reinforcers are not restricted to biological needs, however. Emotional and social needs may also occupy a basic position in the individual's value system. For example, social recognition which results from victory in an athletic contest might serve as a primary reinforcer. Even the victory itself can be a primary emotional need for some persons.

The secondary reinforcer is one which is important as a result of its association with a primary reinforcer. This reinforcer has no quality in itself which reduces a need of the individual. An example of a secondary reinforcer is money. Very young children have no particular fascination for money. As years pass, however, they learn that money is associated with obtaining things which they want and need (primary reinforcers). Because of this association, money becomes a secondary reinforcer. Wolfe (1936) found that chimpanzees could be trained to insert chips into a machine to obtain grapes. After developing an association between chips and grapes, the chimpanzee would work for chips and even show some hoarding behavior. The chips, therefore, served as secondary reinforcers. However, the strength of chips and other secondary reinforcers for animals has not proven as strong or lasting as has money for human beings.

Secondary reinforcers in school.   Secondary reinforcers are more numerous than money, chips, or other items which relate to physical needs. Reinforcers relating to social needs are especially important in school situations. If victory in a low organization game is a primary reinforcer for a child, getting the best players on his side prior to the game could be a strong secondary reinforcement. Athletes in high school and college are very concerned about the conditions for the contest. Favorable conditions regarding wind direction, home field, equipment or facilities, and special rules may all serve as secondary reinforcers. Because of previous association with success or failure, each aids the individual in anticipating results. Realization of a special condition which is favorable to one's chances of success is in itself reinforcing.

For motivation in school, secondary reinforcers are most often used. Student behavior can be strongly influenced by skillful use of these forces. Teachers must keep in mind, however, that secondary reinforcers lose their effectiveness if used for a long period without being related to their primary reinforcers. It has been shown that the trained chimpanzee quickly loses his interest in chips if he finds that they are no longer effective in securing food. A performer would lose his concern for particular team members or conditions if he found that they were no longer related to victory. Even superstitions are lost if they are consistently unrelated to the primary force. Sports letters, trophies, or praise from the coach soon lose their attractiveness if they are given indiscriminately. In such cases they are no longer symbols of outstanding achievement.

There is little doubt that secondary reinforcement is related to the motivation of the learner. These reinforcers especially reduce the psychological and sociological needs of the individual. The amount and nature of various types of rewards have not been studied extensively with human subjects; however, it is probably justifiable to assume that above a certain maximum, larger rewards are not more effective. This assumption has been made concerning motivation in general. As a regular school reinforcement technique, very large rewards are certainly not practical.

In the use of reinforcement (praise or reproof), teachers should realize that different children, because of personal needs, react differently to the same stimulus. Teacher comments such as *good, correct, stupid,* or *disappointing* will evoke varying responses among children. If told, "You're the slowest runner in school," one child may try much harder the next time, while another child's subsequent performances may decline.

Coladarci (1955) suggested that teachers treat introverts and extroverts differently in regard to verbal reinforcement. The analysis of his data indicated that:

. . . (1) When introverts are grouped together, praise and blame are equally effective in motivating the work achievement of fifth-grade pupils. Either praise or blame is more effective in increasing the work output of pupils than no external incentives; (2) If repeated often enough, praise increases the work output of introverts until it is significantly higher than that of introverts who are blamed or extroverts who are praised; (3) If repeated often enough, blame increases the work output of extroverts until it is significantly higher than that of extroverts who are praised or introverts who are blamed. . . . Praise or blame should not be judged on an either-or basis but should be used to fit the case (p. 431).

In addition, factors such as age, sex, and peculiar circumstances should be considered in determining how, when, and where to administer reinforcement. Athletic coaches have often learned empirically that some athletes respond well to a tongue lashing while others perform best when kid gloves are used. Children in the classroom or gymnasium are no less complex.

SELECTED READINGS

Birney, R. C., & Teevan, R. C. (Eds.) *Reinforcement; an enduring problem in psychology.* Princeton, N. J.: Van Nostrand, 1961.

Deese, J. *The psychology of learning.* New York: McGraw-Hill, 1958.

Hull, C. L. *Principles of behavior.* New York: Appleton-Century-Crofts, 1943.

Keller, F. S. *Learning: reinforcement theory.* New York: Random House, 1954.

Pavlov, I. P. *Conditioned reflexes.* Trans. E. V. Anrep. New York: Oxford, 1927.

Skinner, B. F. *Science and human behavior.* New York: Macmillan, 1953.

Skinner, B. F. Reinforcement today. *Amer. Psychologist,* 1958, **13** (3), 94–99.

Travers, R. M. W. *Essentials of learning.* New York: Macmillan, 1963.

Chapter 4

Transfer of skill

A great deal of what is taught in schools today is based on the premise that children will transfer what is learned to out-of-school situations. All teachers agree that, to some extent, students generalize or apply the knowledges and principles learned in one situation to other situations. No other single topic in education has proven more popular during the past seventy-five years than the matter of *transfer of training*. Perhaps no topic is more important.

Teachers in all phases of the school curriculum assume that children will transfer the skills which are learned in each subject area. For example, children are taught to write themes in English class, not to help them write better themes in adult life, but because of the belief that this experience will improve their general effectiveness in communication. Teachers of motor skills also assume transfer. In teaching swimming, land drills are often used, not because of their value as a recreational or conditioning activity, but because of the assumption that movement skills learned on land will be used when the individual gets into the water. In teaching soccer, the technique of dribbling around obstacles is often used with beginning players. It is rare, of course, that the exact obstacle pattern used will be appropriate in a soccer game. General skill in dribbling, however, will be helpful. Parents often encourage their children to take dancing lessons more for the expected skills of poise and graceful movement than for improvement in dancing. When one considers the learning experiences used by the successful coach and the physical education teacher, it becomes clear that transfer of training is just as appropriate for gross motor skills as for verbal learning or fine motor skills.

Expectation of transfer is not limited to communication, swimming, soccer, or other skills. It is also assumed that acquired social attitudes and emotional responses will carry over to other areas of a person's life. For example, certain democratic procedures, such as allowing team members to elect their captain, are often used for citizenship-training values rather than to assure a wise selection. Kindergarten and first-grade teachers are interested in having young children develop positive attitudes toward initial school experiences in the hope that these attitudes will be transferred to other phases of the school program. In a particular subject, it is expected that attitudes developed in one phase will be reflected in other aspects of the course. An individual's negative attitude or anxiety concerning a particular teacher, coach, or opponent is expected to affect his behavior in a completely different activity with which the same teacher, coach, or opponent is associated.

According to McGeoch and Irion (1952), "Transfer of training occurs whenever the existence of a previously established habit has an influence upon the acquisition, performance, or relearning of a second habit" (p. 299). Transfer may, therefore, be positive or negative. The English teacher hopes that the writing of themes will have a favorable effect upon the student's written and oral communication. The swimming teacher also strives for positive transfer. However, it has been found that previously learned habits in swimming sometimes interfere with the learning of new habits, especially if faults had been developed during one's early training. Similarly, golf instructors have found that baseball players often transfer undesirable movement patterns from the baseball swing which may interfere with their ability to learn to play golf.

The question of transfer of skill is, therefore, a complex one. Since the beginning of the twentieth century a great deal of research has been devoted to questions such as: Does transfer occur at all? Are specific skills or general principles transferred? Can transfer be taught? How can transfer best be investigated?

Experimental designs in the study of transfer

Many studies have been conducted during the past several decades in an effort to determine the amount of transfer from one situation to another. The type of task (verbal and motor) and the nature of the learning situation have varied in these investigations. Two basic types of experimental designs have been used. One type has been arranged to investigate the amount of *proactive transfer*, i.e., the effect that the learning of a task has on the learning or performance of a second task which is practiced at a later time. For example, proactive transfer would be exhibited if students performed better in diving after engaging in a unit on rebound tumbling (positive transfer), or if students did worse in baseball batting after playing softball for a period of time (negative transfer).

To investigate proactive transfer, the following experimental design has been used:

Experimental group ....learn task *A* ....test on task *B*
Control group ....rest, or perform
                           some unrelated activity ....test on task *B*

If the two groups perform equally well on task *B*, it can be concluded that there is no transfer from task *A* to task *B* (assuming that the
two groups were equal on task *B* at the beginning). If the experimental
group performs better on task *B* than does the control group, it can be
said that there is positive transfer from task *A* to task *B*. Similarly, if the
control group performs better on task *B*, this is evidence that negative
transfer has taken place. In this general design, any number of experimental groups can be used. Different groups might vary the manner or
degree to which task *A* is learned. One experimental group might even
practice task *B* to determine how the transfer from *A* to *B* compares with
a procedure in which all practice sessions are devoted to the learning
of task *B*.

A second type of experimental design has been established to investigate *retroactive transfer*, i.e., the effect that practice on a particular
task has on the retention of a previously learned task. Retroactive transfer might be illustrated if students with an established level of skill in
tennis practice badminton for a series of lessons. If it is later determined
that their proficiency in tennis had deteriorated as a result of the badminton practice, this deterioration would be an example of negative retroactive transfer, also referred to as retroactive inhibition.

For investigating retroactive transfer, the following design is generally used:

Experimental
  group ....learn task *A* ....learn task *B* ....test on task *A*
Control group .....learn task *A* ....rest, or perform
                           some unrelated
                           activity ....test on task *A*

The important function of this design is to determine whether the learning of task *B* has any effect on the retention of task *A*. The critical comparison is made at the test on task *A*. Assuming that the two groups
originally learned task *A* to the same degree of proficiency, they should
perform equally well when this skill is tested, unless there has been
some retroactive transfer. If the control group performs better at the
test, this indicates that task *B* has a detrimental effect on the retention
of the skill in *A*. On the other hand, if the experimental group is more
proficient at the test for task *A*, it can be assumed that the learning of
task *B* has a favorable effect on the retention of task *A*.

HISTORICAL DEVELOPMENT OF STUDIES ON TRANSFER

Before the twentieth century, the traditional concept of *formal discipline* was prevalent in educational practice. This all-encompassing theory of transfer was dominant for several centuries in Europe and the United States. Basic to the concept of formal discipline was the theory of faculty psychology which postulated that the mind was composed of a set of faculties such as reason, will, attention, and judgment. Early educators believed that the study of certain subjects was especially valuable in developing the "faculties" for future use. The mind was assumed to be like a muscle which becomes stronger, quicker and more flexible with practice. Practice in reasoning, for example, would supposedly assist one in solving any kind of reasoning problem at some later date. Well-developed faculties were assumed to be helpful in all situations. Therefore, certain subjects were included in the school curriculum because of their "mental training" values.

In addition, the concept of formal discipline held that whatever was most difficult to learn was beneficial to the individual's development. In order to achieve maximum development, the *overload principle* was put to use. (In physical conditioning, the overload principle refers to the placing of unusual stress on the component to be developed.) The more difficult subjects in school were believed to be especially valuable in preparing one for subsequent hard work. The many failures in Latin and mathematics, for example, appeared to justify the belief that these subjects were hard and, therefore, most appropriate for training the mind.

The analogy between mental and muscular development seemed plausible and was, therefore, long accepted. It is true that effective use of a muscle can make it stronger, more flexible, and quicker in specific situations. However, studies have failed to produce any evidence that taxing the mind results in similar improvement. Consequently, modern educators and psychologists generally reject the doctrine of formal discipline.

Early experiments in transfer

Transfer was first objectively studied by William James and later by E. L. Thorndike. James (1890) tried to determine whether mental exercises were of any value in improving the mind. He and his students tested their memory abilities by learning Victor Hugo's poems. After an extensive training period of memorizing other authors' poems, they again tested their memory abilities on poems by Hugo. The difference in performance on the two tests was only slight. This led James to conclude that "one's native retentiveness is unchangeable. No amount of culture seems capable of modifying a man's *general* retentiveness" (pp. 663–664). He indicated that the best way to remember is to learn as much as possible about the material to be remembered. Many subsequent experiments were performed which indicated a lack of general transfer from one intellectual activity to another. Some later psychologists have concluded that James's views on transfer were too limited. However, his studies and writings opened a new era in the field of general faculty capacities and educational practice.

Early in the twentieth century, a number of teachers became interested in proving the theory of formal discipline. The subject areas of Latin and mathematics were most often selected because of the prominent claims that they were especially important in developing one's faculties. These early research studies often shared a characteristic structural fallacy. For example, at the end of a high school program, students who had taken Latin courses would be given a test of mental achievement. This group's test results would be compared with those of students who had not taken Latin in high school. It would usually be found that the Latin students had greater intellectual power, and it was assumed that study of Latin was primarily responsible for developing their greater reasoning ability. Weaknesses in this experimental design are obvious. A similarly structured study might be designed to compare the strength-building value of football and soccer. In such an experiment, the overall muscular strength of the football players (average weight, 170 pounds) would be compared to that of the soccer players (average weight, 145 pounds). Results would be easy to predict. Failure to select comparable groups at the beginning was a strategic weakness of the early transfer studies. Consequently, factors other than the experimental variables often played a major role in the results.

Later, when Latin was no longer advocated for mental discipline, a number of experiments were conducted to determine Latin's value in the development of English vocabulary or language knowledge in general. Hamblen (1925) reported that a Latin study group showed a gain in English vocabulary. The gain, however, was almost entirely in words which had a Latin origin. He suggested that perhaps a course in English would have been even more beneficial. Douglass and Kittleson (1935) and Pond (1938) reported no gains in English vocabulary following the study of Latin. Generally, it has been concluded from the Latin and mathematics studies that the difficulty of a school course, or other special intellectual activities, has no favorable effect on an unrelated subject or activity.

Thorndike's theory of identical elements

The work of E. L. Thorndike, along with that of James, effectively refuted the theory of formal discipline. In addition, Thorndike was the first person to develop a prominent theory of transfer. When challenged with the supposition that superior intellectual powers resulted from studying a particular subject, Thorndike (1924) said:

The chief reason why good thinkers seem superficially to have been made such by having taken certain school studies, is that good thinkers have taken such studies, becoming better by the inherent tendency of the good to gain more than the poor from any study. When the good thinkers studied Greek and Latin, these studies seemed to make good thinking. Now that the good thinkers study Physics and Trigonometry, these seem to make good thinkers. If the abler pupils should all study Physical Education and Dramatic Art, these subjects would seem to make good thinkers. These were, indeed, a large fraction of the program of studies for the best thinkers the world has produced, the Athenian Greeks (p. 98).[1]

Thorndike concluded from his work that the best way to develop knowledge or skill in any subject area was to study that subject. Humphreys (1951) drew the following conclusion from the work of Thorndike and his associates:

If you need accounting in your occupation, study accounting during your training and preferably the type of accounting you will need. If you want to read Cicero in Latin, by all means study Latin. If, however, you want to learn French, do not spend several years in the study of Latin, since you will be further ahead if you concentrate on French. If you want to learn to solve social problems, spend your time in the social sciences, not in the study of geometry (p. 213).[2]

Thorndike used newly developed intelligence tests to support his belief that there was no general transfer. Some of the tests involved novel problem-solving situations. He found that no high school subject was more effective than any other in aiding one to do better on intelligence tests. Generally, he advocated the direct teaching of any skill or knowledge which was to be learned.

Thorndike's famous theory of *identical elements* (1913) held that only specific skills, knowledges, or techniques are transferred. By identical elements, he meant "mental processes which have the same cell action in the brain as their physical correlate"; he explained, "It is of

[1] By permission of the American Psychological Association.
[2] Lloyd G. Humphreys, "Transfer of Training in General Education," *Journal of General Education*, V, 213. By permission.

course often not possible to tell just what features of two mental abilities are thus identical" (p. 359). He believed, however, that approximate decisions could be accurate enough for practical use.

He indicated both "substance" and "procedure" were transferable when they were identical in the second situation. Under substance he included abilities to handle spoken and written numbers, words, and symbols. By procedure he meant habits of observation and study, attitudes of neglect or pleasure, and feelings of dissatisfaction and failure. His definitions would seem to suggest a rather broad view of transfer. However, as a result of all his pronouncements on the subject, it has been assumed through the years that Thorndike held a rather limited view of the expected transfer of substance and procedure.

Thorndike's theory implied that transfer would occur to the extent that the same stimulus-response bonds were used in the second situation. Transfer would presumably take place if the stimuli were identical or if the responses to different stimuli were identical. Despite Thorndike's belief that approximate decisions regarding identical elements are of practical use, considerable difficulty and misunderstanding have resulted from the teacher's inability to know what is identical. In motor skills, for example, which movements or situations are similar enough to be considered identical? If the similarity were interpreted as strictly as Guthrie suggested, the possibility of any transfer would be remote.

In support of his transfer theory, Thorndike referred largely to studies of bilateral transfer conducted by himself and others. In these studies, it was found that similar movements or tasks *did* transfer to the opposite hand or foot. As a rule, Thorndike limited his predictions of transfer to the type which was measurable in these studies. It is difficult to relate his theory to transfer among different motor skills except to assume in a general way that transfer will take place to the extent that the skills are similar. For example, a person who had developed skill in tennis would have an advantage in squash only to the extent that the strokes are identical.

In view of Thorndike's explanation, one might expect enough identical elements to allow transference:

1. From rebound tumbling to diving, in which rotary and curvilinear motions as well as maximizing height could be used.
2. From the soccer kick to the soccer-type field goal kick in football.
3. From the overhand throw of a baseball to the overhead smash in tennis or in the tennis serve.
4. From the action of slinging a skipping stone across the water to the handball stroke.

Thorndike, with several other psychologists, effectively refuted the doctrine of formal discipline. He did not, however, offer a basis for an understanding of the full possibilities of transfer as now accepted.

Judd's theory of generalized principles

C. H. Judd differed sharply from Thorndike in regard to the nature and extent of transfer. Judd's theory of generalized principles emphasized that basic principles and laws, as well as specific skills, were transferred. He believed that the individual applied the general idea to a new situation.

Much of Judd's theory was supported by his classic study (1908) in which subjects threw darts at submerged targets. This motor skills study was designed to determine whether knowledge of a principle would aid an individual in a situation where the principle was applicable. In his experiment, two groups of fifth-grade and sixth-grade boys were required to throw darts at a small target which was placed under water. Prior to the testing program one group was given a good theoretical explanation of the principle of refraction. The other group was not given this information. In the first few trials (with the target 12 inches under water), there was no appreciable difference in the performance of the two groups. Judd observed that even with the theoretical knowledge, a certain amount of practice was essential before the principle would be put into practice. The submerged target was next raised to 4 inches beneath the surface of the water. At this point, there was a sharp difference in the performance of the two groups. The group with the theoretical knowledge performed better. Judd believed that the superior performance resulted from their understanding of why the angle required at the 12-inch depth would not apply when the target was placed at a 4-inch depth.

Hendrickson and Schroeder (1941) conducted an experiment similar to Judd's dart-throwing study. Eighth-grade boys practiced the skill of air rifle shooting at targets submerged under water. The authors reported that (1) knowledge of the principle involved was valuable in facilitating transference; (2) this knowledge was an aid in the original performances in the first situation (contrary to Judd's findings); (3) thoroughness of theoretical understanding has an effect upon the degree of initial learning and transfer; and (4) insight, or sudden learning, was apparent.

Other researchers have found that general attitudes and habits as well as theory and knowledge are transferable. Bagley (1905) found that when neatness habits were taught to children in a general way (as principles), these habits were more widely applied than when they were taught in relation to some specific school task. It would seem, therefore, that desirable habits should be taught in terms of their applicability to one's general experiences.

Judd's theory was therefore more liberal than that of Thorndike. Judd's generalized theory suggests the transfer of basic principles as well as peripheral knowledges and skills. In Judd's theory a great deal more transfer would be expected than would be assumed in Thorndike's identical elements theory.

In view of the general concepts of Judd's theory, one would expect the following types of transfer to apply to sports skills:

1. From tennis to squash not only would the forehand and backhand skills transfer but also the footwork, body positioning, and knowledge of rebounds and strategy.
2. Use of the concept of double teaming (2 on 1, 3 on 2, etc.) should be transferred among team sports such as basketball, soccer, field hockey, and lacrosse.
3. The follow-through technique should be transferred to throwing skills used in baseball, softball, football, and bowling, as well as to striking skills used in baseball, golf, tennis, or handball.

The theories of Thorndike and Judd have often been viewed as mutually exclusive, with one being correct and the other incorrect. Practice and research, however, have shown that transfer may take place either by identical elements or by general principles. As a result, recent educators have been concerned with establishing exact laws of transfer rather than proving one of the major theories right or wrong. This is consistent with the general trend in educational psychology to concentrate on functional principles rather than major theories.

CHARACTERISTICS OF SKILLS TRANSFER

Bilateral transfer of skills

The ability of an individual to more easily learn a particular skill with one hand after it has been learned with the opposite hand is referred to as bilateral or cross-transfer. In essence, bilaterality refers to the transference of any skill from one side of the body to the other side. However, this type of transfer may also be from the hand to the foot on either side of the body, and vice versa, or from one foot to the other. Studies back as far as the late nineteenth century have consistently shown examples of bilateral transfer. Reviews of research which has shown the consistency of this phenomenon have been prepared by Bray (1928), Weig (1932), and Ammons (1958).

Bryant (1892) found that tapping ability was transferable between hands for children. At the same time, he determined that cross-fatigue was independent of general fatigue. Woodworth (1899) showed that the ability to draw straight lines was transferable between limbs. In skills involving speed and accuracy, Scripture (1899) discovered transfer between limbs of the body. Swift (1903) conducted a study of gross motor skills in which subjects were required to juggle two balls with one hand. He found that they could learn this skill more readily after it had been learned first with the opposite hand. Cook (1934) and Baker (1950) demonstrated cross-transfer with fine motor skills. Studies substantiating the existence of bilateral transfer have involved such fine motor skills as mazes, mirror tracing, operating adding machines, and handwriting.

A vivid example of bilateral transfer is described by Munn (1932) in a 1932 experiment. In this study, one hundred college students practiced a novel task which involved flipping a ball into a cup, the ball being attached to the cup by means of a string. Both the experimental group and control group took 50 tries with the left hand. The experimental group then had 500 tries with the right hand, while the control group rested. Both groups were then given 50 additional practices with the left hand. From the first 50 trials to the second 50 trials, the experimental group improved 61 per cent, while the control group improved only 28 per cent. Munn concluded that the advantage for the experimental group resulted from their right-handed practice.

The existence of bilateral transfer indicates that learning when only one part of the body is overly involved is to some extent a general function. Certainly, this learning is not restricted to one particular limb or portion of the body. The reason for this transfer has not been entirely explained. However, neurological and muscular involvement may be comparable to the bilateral conditioning which apparently takes place in muscles. Hellebrant (1962) found that antagonistic muscle groups were developed with protagonist muscular development.

Ammons (1958) has suggested that bilateral transfer is facilitated by visual cues, knowledge of appropriate body position, techniques in eye movements, relaxing effects as a result of the previous learning, and a general feeling of confidence. Johnson (1960) also suggested that improved performance on the second task may be due to increased confidence, acquaintance with the problem, and improved techniques of learning. The conditions which Ammons and Johnson list are generally believed to facilitate transfer of all types, not just bilateral transfer. These conditions do not, however, suggest definite learning in the untrained body part.

The concept of bilateral transfer is one which is no longer seriously challenged. It must be kept in mind, however, that the most efficient and direct way to learn a skill with the left hand is to practice with the left hand, not the right one. The wise coach would not teach a right-footed boy to kick a football with his left foot for transfer value. Neither would the right-handed pitcher be taught to pitch left-handed. The most direct route in teaching these skills would be most effective.

In view of the advantages of direct teaching, of what value is bilateral transfer? While the punter in football and the pitcher in baseball would have little need to perform with their opposite limbs, numerous situations exist in sports and in everyday life in which bilateral skill is desirable. For example, the soccer player must develop kicking skill with both feet. Making effective use of transfer techniques may conserve practice time for the teacher. In addition, a more thorough analysis and understanding of the skill may result if the opposite side is used. Teachers who make use of the transfer concept will be able to promote more general or all-around skill development. By taking full advantage of bilateral training and transfer, teachers will avoid developing "one-handed" performers who can turn or break in only one direction.

The physical educator might make effective use of bilateral transfer in:

1. Teaching young basketball players to shoot and dribble well with either hand.
2. Teaching the wrestler to move effectively or to resist pressure from either side.
3. Teaching the dancer, the gymnast, or the diver to rotate the body to both the right and left.
4. Teaching the volleyball player to spike the ball with either hand.
5. Teaching the baseball player to switch hit.

General transfer among skills

Research and theories relating to motor learning have not been restricted to bilateral transfer. Rather, a greater amount of attention has been devoted to the transfer of movement skills from one task to others. The transfer theories of both Thorndike and Judd were based largely on research involving physical skills. Support for Thorndike's identical elements theory came mostly from studies on bilateral transfer of simple skills. Judd's classical study made use of a motor skill in which a knowledge of the basic principle of activity was strategic to learning. Stylus mazes, tracking devices, electronic apparatus, mirror tracing, mirror writing, and numerous other skills have been used. Ironically, findings from these studies have more generally been applied to verbal learning than to teaching of motor skills.

A limited amount of research has been devoted to the study of transfer among gross sports skills. Probably the most extensive investigation of the type was conducted by Nelson (1957a). He studied the transfer of learning in a number of gross motor skills which had some similar elements and patterns. Specifically tested was the amount of transfer from

(1) a badminton volley to a tennis volley (against a wall), (2) a volley-ball tap for accuracy to a basketball tip for accuracy, and (3) a track starting stance to a football starting position. In these experiments, six groups of unskilled college men were used. Nelson found that initial learning of the tennis volley favorably affected the learning of the bad-minton volley; initial learning of the basketball skill favorably affected the learning of the volleyball skill; and initial learning of the track starting stance favorably affected the learning of the football stance.

Nelson also found that (1) when skills are taught separately, teaching for transfer helps more than when skills are taught alternately, and (2) teaching for transfer did not aid in the track starting skills. Some negative transfer was apparent when similar skills were interspersed. He concluded that skills involving similar elements should not be learned concurrently.

In another experiment Nelson (1957b) investigated the effect of swimming on the learning of certain motor skills (volleyball tap for accuracy and running the high hurdles). In an investigation involving forty college men, he found that swimming had neither a favorable nor an unfavorable effect on the learning or performance of other skills. He reported that fatigue from swimming might have a detrimental effect on performance, but this was not a lasting interference. He detected no evidence of the negative transfer for swimming which has been assumed by many during the past few decades.

Lindeburg and Hewitt (1965) conducted an experiment to deter-mine whether practice with a basketball which was slightly larger and heavier than regulation size would aid or hinder one in performance with a regulation basketball. Experienced subjects were tested and re-tested with both the regulation and the experimental ball in the short shot, foul shooting, passing, and dribbling. The authors concluded that use of a basketball which was slightly larger and heavier than a regu-lation ball resulted in no differences in the shooting and dribbling tests. There was a slight negative effect on passing skills. In general, it can be assumed that use of a basketball which does not vary greatly from regulation size results in approximately the same development as would result if a regulation ball were being used. Teachers, therefore, who wish to use a larger than regulation size ball for young children need not be fearful of a great deal of interference.

Transfer of general principles

In recent years there has been a general tendency to emphasize principles in teaching rather than to attempt to cover all specific facts or knowledges. This practice was given a major boost by the work of Judd. As a result of this emphasis on principles, there are occasional criticisms that education is not practical enough. However, proponents of the principles approach in teaching point out that theory is the most practical technique. The rationale is that the individual who understands the theory or principle is able to use this knowledge in solving many problems. Consequently, greater useful knowledge can be gained from fewer concepts. On the other hand, the individual who understands specific facts without the underlying principles is limited to the application of only those facts. It is consistent with the principles approach to assume that the individual who has mastered basic movement or mechanical principles will be able to apply them to a wide variety of motor skills.

In accepting the generalized principles theory of transfer, there are dangers of assuming or expecting too much understanding and resulting application. First, it must be realized that teaching which is not understood by the learner can hardly be expected to transfer. Unless there is understanding, there will be no application. In motor skills, a basic or fundamental movement might be executed, perhaps accidentally, without any feel for the action or any appreciation for the general application of the movement. The wise teacher would, therefore, not assume that after one execution of a back somersault on the floor, a student would immediately be able to use this movement in a back dive off the springboard, a somersault on a trampoline, or at the end of a tumbling routine. The student must first get the kinesthetic feel of the movement and duplicate it *correctly* on the floor before he can transfer the correct movement to another environment.

In addition, it should be pointed out that even when the principle or theory is understood, it will not necessarily be applied to a second situation. Correct theory is not always applied to appropriate situations. Burack and Moss (1956) conducted a study to determine if an understanding of the principle of centrifugal force would aid students in the solution of a problem. They found that not all students who understood the principle applied it to a new task which required use of the principle. They concluded that (1) relevant past experience is not always drawn upon and applied to a present problem, and (2) knowing the general principles and even receiving examples do not necessarily enable subjects to apply the principle.

Aside from the studies of Judd and Hendrickson and Schroeder, which have been discussed previously in this chapter, there is little evidence regarding the application of basic movement principles or physical laws in the learning of new motor skills. One recent study, designed to investigate the influence of knowledge of mechanical principles, was conducted by Colville (1957). This study did not reveal any particular advantages resulting from an understanding of the appropriate principles. Colville had women of college age learn principles relating to rebound angles, momentum, and acceleration. The subjects then learned (1) a ball-rolling skill which involved a rebound, (2) a catching skill (using tennis and badminton rackets), and (3) archery shooting from 20 to 40 yards. Colville found that instruction regarding the mechanical principles did not aid in the acquisition of tasks which were seemingly related to the principles taught. Nevertheless, she states:

> However, since it appears that some part of the learning period may be devoted to instruction concerning general principles without detriment to the motor learning of the students, it would seem desirable to include such instruction in order to provide this additional opportunity for acquiring some related knowledge about principles of mechanics and the application of forces (p. 326).

Transfer and application of principles are, therefore, not automatic. Teachers have found that students often fail to generalize or make connections. On other occasions, learners try to make application where the principle does not apply. There is a need for closing the gap between understanding principles and applying them to new problems. The teacher should therefore point out similarities of general movement patterns among different activities.

Developing principles for transfer.   If an understanding of general principles or concepts is important in motor learning, a thorough knowledge of them is essential for maximum transfer. One should not equate the ability to state a principle with an understanding of its usefulness. Obviously, not all children understand the implications of poems they recite. The same holds true for verbal concepts, mathematical principles, or movement patterns. Of course, children with greater intelligence should understand principles and their applications more quickly than would less intelligent persons.

It is assumed that when students understand the principle of rebound, they will easily learn ball-playing skills in which this principle is important. Likewise, an understanding of the principles of inertia as reflected in follow-through is also expected to aid one in learning to perform certain sports skills. In order to promote rapid and thorough understanding of principles which are important for motor performance, it is often valuable to have students "prove" the concept in a practical way. For example, the principle of rebound angle and force can be effectively illustrated with a basketball rebound shot off the backboard or a bounce pass to a teammate. When shooting from the side of the basket, the beginning player has a tendency to bank the ball directly over the goal, thus causing it to miss the basket by coming down on the opposite side. In making a bounce pass he erroneously bounces the ball halfway between himself and his teammate, thus causing it to fall short of the target. In other situations, the principles of inertia and momentum may also be illustrated. The inexperienced third baseman who must throw on the run, and whose momentum is toward home plate, will usually throw to the homeplate side of the first baseman. The error in accuracy when one throws in a direction other than the one in which he is moving is reflected in numerous sports activities. A thorough understanding of the appropriate principles would make for more efficient performance.

Occasionally, the theory or principle underlying performance in a particular task may best be taught by an indirect method. Alternative activities can be effectively used. For instance, if the pupil is having difficulty in learning one movement skill, another skill to which the same principle applies could be taught. With his more thorough understanding of the basic principle, the student will more easily learn the desired skill. Teaching by transfer is often necessary when there is a lack of communication or if the student seems to have developed a psychological block to the first activity.

A valuable aid in making use of general principles in motor activities is mental rehearsal. This practice may be encouraged either by verbal description or by visual imagery of the task to be performed. There is considerable evidence that mental practice aids learning and performance. It seems reasonable, therefore, to assume that general concepts of movement may be gained by mental rehearsal and may then be transferred to the appropriate skill.

The value of general principles in motor skills is obvious. Such principles as follow-through, opposition of arms and legs, conservation of energy, momentum, and even general strategy techniques have wide application in sports activities. Much rehearsal is needed, however, to determine the manner in which basic principles may best be taught and transferred among a wide variety of skills.

According to a statement by the AAHPER (1965), "Development and learning proceed from the general to the specific, from the simple to the complex, and from the center toward the periphery" (p. 7). Although it seems contradictory to state that learning develops from the general *and* from the simple, an analysis reveals that each progression has implications for the transfer of skills.

Transfer from simple to complex tasks. Early participation in games and rhythmic skills requires very few rules and little group interaction. Organization and directions for the activities are slight. Later, the organization and functioning of these activities becomes more intricate, both in terms of skilled movement and in working with others in cooperation and competition. This progression from simple to more complex skills can be observed when one compares the types of activities recommended for first, third, and fifth graders.

Numerous situations exist in which simple skills may later be developed into more advanced movements or possibly be used as part of a more complex skill. For example, the childhood leaping activity of "crossing the brook" may aid in future activities such as the modern dance leap, or the takeoff for a lay-up shot in basketball. A rather simple skill is often combined with others to form a more complex task. In addition, the simple-to-complex concept may be illustrated when one transfers skill in such activities as rolls, headstands, handstands, leg scissors, and leg cuts from the mats to the parallel bars.

Transfer from general to specific skills.   At the same time that activities progress from the simple to the complex, they also evolve from the general to the more specific. Children must first get the notion of the task in a general way before becoming concerned with specific body movements or precise positioning. The general purpose of a low organization game must be understood before the child becomes interested in particulars. In performance, big body movements are dominant in the early stages of a child's development. As growth and learning take place, greater refinement of movement detail results.

Prerequisite learning

The development of skills and knowledges is a cumulative process. One viewpoint holds that all learning and performance in later childhood and adult life is the result to transfer from earlier learning. No doubt, there is a degree of validity in this theory. Teachers of motor skills, therefore, should start with more fundamental coordinations and progress toward more advanced activities. After the child develops basic skills, he will be able to perform finer, more integrated tasks.

A serious mistake often occurs in motor development as well as verbal learning, when fundamental learning is prematurely passed over for teaching of more refined skills. Not only does the learner have greater difficulty in learning the more advanced task, but certain movement fundamentals are omitted which limit other learning as well. It is possible to teach certain tasks to children before they have attained the optimum physiological or psychological level, but this practice results in an inefficient teacher-learning situation.

Learning and performance at each advanced level are best served if the instructor can assume certain prerequisite skills. The instructor in French II assumes that students have mastered certain concepts before beginning the course. The coach of a professional basketball team would assume that a candidate would have all of the basic moves. Similarly, a dancer applying for a role in a dance production is expected to have basic skills. It is essential, therefore, that teachers in the early grades concentrate on developing fundamental movement skills upon which a more sophisticated performance can be developed. The broader the base of early skills, the greater the possibility for developing proficiency in a wide variety of activities. Concentrating on the development of fundamental skills is often at variance with the sentiments of some overzealous athletic coaches who would have young performers specialize in a specific sport at a very early age. Although some success can be realized by specialization at a relatively early age, this practice will tend to limit one's ability to develop proficiency in other physical skills.

Considerable attention in recent years has been devoted to the use of basic, or fundamental, movement activities as prerequisites for the learning of more specific skills. At the elementary school level, greater effort is being devoted to the use of such movement skills as running, walking, hopping, balancing, lifting, kicking, skipping, rolling, and climbing. These activities are taught so that other skills which require these movements can be learned more readily. The nature of the transfer from basic to more specific skills has not yet been fully explored. One of the greatest needs in physical education today is the establishment of a sound system of progression from the most fundamental skills to the most intricate movements for all activities included in the program. This task would require concentration of study in an area which has been woefully lacking in research.

Developmental transfer among skills

The doctrine of formal discipline implied that certain basic capacities could be developed by engaging in developmental activities. The theory further stressed that the faculties which were developed would aid the individual in any reasoning situation in which they were needed. This concept is no longer generally accepted. In physical education, however, the idea of developmental activities appears to have merit. For example, no one would seriously question the idea that muscular strength can be developed through exercises. This added muscular strength, in turn, seems to aid the individual in the performance of a variety of activities.

The development of basic components of motor fitness has been encouraged as an aid in the learning and performance of specific activities which are dependent upon these components. A high degree of general muscular strength, endurance, speed, coordination, flexibility, and agility will undoubtedly aid one in the development of skill in certain activities. Individuals differ in their inherited capacities for developing each of the components of motor ability. Authorities do not agree on the extent to which each of these traits can be developed. There is little doubt, however, that the individual who has developed his general motor fitness capacities can more nearly reach his skill potential than can one who has not developed these components.

What are the components which can be developed and used in the learning and performance of skills? Balance? Speed? Coordination? Agility? Reaction time? While physical educators generally agree that muscular strength can be developed, the same consensus does not exist for several of the other physical components. Much research is needed before the answers can be provided to questions such as the following: What are the most important components for learning and performance in various types of motor skills? To what degree can each be developed or improved? In what manner can they best be developed? In what activities are they important?

Several research projects have been conducted in an effort to determine activities which might be valuable in developmental transfer. Bennett (1956) tested the value of modern dance, folk dance, basketball, and swimming activities in the development of general motor abilities among college women. Her subjects were freshmen who were enrolled in various physical education classes including classes in the particular activities being investigated. Comprehensive motor fitness tests were given at the end of 8 weeks and again at the end of 16 weeks of training. She reported that most of the activities were effective in developing agility, coordination, strength, and flexibility. The most effective activity for developing each of these components was swimming. Modern dance and basketball were equally effective. Folk dance, which was least effective, still developed measurable gains in strength, flexibility, speed, and balance. Improvements were greater at the end of 16 weeks than at the end of 8 weeks.

Calvin (1958) had a group of high school boys practice progressive resistance exercises over a four-month period. He found that this type of weight training was more effective in developing general motor coordination and improving anthropometric measurements than was a general program of physical education activities.

Speed exercises have occasionally been used by coaches and teachers because of the belief that they will aid the individual in quick movements when required in other activities. Lindeburg (1949) specifically studied the effect of "quickening exercises" on the speed of some simple and complex movements (reaction time and peg shifting). He had four two-month programs: (1) regular physical education, (2) table tennis, (3) physical education plus fast vertical and horizontal arm movements, and (4) no special activity. He found that none of the programs was effective in developing faster and more coordinated movements. He concluded that quickening exercises such as table tennis and fast arm exercises would not affect an individual's speed in a different activity.

Teaching for transfer

Most authors indicate that the amount of transfer can be increased if certain practices are followed by the teacher. The recommended teaching techniques for promoting transfer vary according to the particular author. After having summarized the literature relative to transfer, Nelson (1957a) recommended that the following steps be followed in order to facilitate maximum transfer:

1. Point out the possibility of transfer of learning.
2. Use real situations where possible.
3. Develop meaningful generalizations that are understood by the learner.
4. Provide practice in applying generalizations.
5. Direct learner activity through proper guidance. The more guidance a learner receives, the more efficient his discovery will be; the more efficient discovery is, the more learning and transfer will occur (p. 373).[3]

Davis and Lawther (1948) have suggested several ways of increasing the amount of transfer in physical education. Among their recommendations are the following:

1. When feasible, set up rules of procedure of general applicability.
   Examples:
      a. Habit of warming up before vigorous bodily exercise.
      b. Habit of keeping knees slightly bent for rapid start or change of direction.
      c. Knowledge of principle and methods of producing "English" on the ball in games.
      d. Acquaintance with methods best suited for arrangement and organization of material as an aid to retention.
      e. Familiarity with the principle of adding movement to movement in order to pyramid speed; for example, arm thrust and wrist snap to moving body.
      f. Awareness that irritability and tension are cues for needed recreational "antidotes."
2. Utilize patterns of response in a variety of situations.
   Examples:
      a. Practice desirable posture in sitting and standing, while moving and at rest, at home and at school.
      b. Practice use of natural activities and movement rhythms in a variety of sports and recreations.
3. Emphasize form and method.
   Examples:
      a. Learn graceful and efficient form in running or other natural activities.

[3] D. O. Nelson, "Studies of Transfer of Learning in Gross Motor Skills," *Research Quarterly*, 28, Washington, D.C.: AAHPER, 1957, p. 373. By permission.

b. Learn *methods* of caring for one's health as opposed to mere factual knowledge (p. 371).[4]

SPECIAL FEATURES OF TRANSFER

Learning how to learn

The phenomenon of learning how to learn, often referred to as *learning sets,* has been demonstrated on several occasions. This concept gives the appearance of transfer, or even formal discipline. On occasion there have been claims of a great deal of specific skill or knowledge tranfer when such was not the case. The learner often learns how to approach a task in terms of technique for solving the problem. He may then learn a second task more quickly than the first one, even if there is no similarity in specific material or theory. For example, some people seem to be able to solve puzzles or tricky problems easily. Their competence may come as a result of previous experience with problems which have a general similarity. It has been demonstrated that new lists of nonsense syllables can be learned better after lists of different nonsense syllables have been previously learned. Generally, if more lists have already been learned, the subject can more easily learn new lists. This technique of learning how to learn is often more important than any similarity of content.

Harlow (1949) showed that monkeys learn problem-solving techniques with practice. He later showed that children learn techniques which aid them in solving problems. As a result, he advocated that more attention be devoted to the development techniques, and he stressed that a great deal of time and attention should be spent on the early trials of any task. After a good base or understanding of the techniques has been established, less time is needed for later related problems. Therefore, teachers of motor skills might be wise to spend extra time and effort in teaching the beginning or basic movements of a new skill.

Woodrow (1927) showed that skills in learning can be taught. He instructed subjects in how to memorize poetry, prose, and other materials. His subjects showed greater improvement with practice than those who had not been instructed. Woodrow's techniques for improving memory were similar to many in education today, i.e., recitation, analysis of meaning, and association.

The existence of the learning-how-to-learn phenomenon no doubt helped to propagate the doctrine of formal discipline. The two concepts

[4] Elwood C. Davis & John D. Lawther, SUCCESSFUL TEACHING IN PHYSICAL EDUCATION, SECOND EDITION, © 1948. Reprinted by permission of Prentice-Hall, Inc., Englewood Cliffs, N. J.

however, are distinctly different since formal discipline emphasized the improvement of faculties which would have application to all circumstances, while learning how to learn is assumed to apply only to situations where the method of attack is similar.

It is assumed by psychologists and educators that the phenomenon of learning how to learn occurs with all types of tasks. In motor skills, this concept is most often exhibited in the performance of novel tasks. In stunts, especially those involving reasoning or problem-solving abilities, persons with previous experience in similar tasks often perform at a higher level.

Task difficulty and transfer

In attempting to refine techniques regarding transfer, several researchers have sought to determine whether the difficulty of the task is related to the amount of transfer. For example, will greater transfer take place from a difficult task to an easier one, or vice versa? How can the teacher best arrange the teaching of skills according to difficulty? If it is assumed that greater transfer takes place from simple to complex skills, then the early school curriculum should be composed primarily of relatively simple motor tasks which would be learned extremely well. Conversely, if the reverse principle is held, the physical education program should stress relatively complex and varied tasks. Clearly, the relationship of difficulty and amount of transfer is of great significance in the school curriculum.

Several conflicting and inconclusive reports have been made of task difficulty and transfer. Day (1956) summarized most of the published research relative to this topic. He reported that many different tasks and different methods have been used to vary difficulty. Pursuit rotors have probably been used more often than any other motor learning activity. Investigators using the pursuit rotor have varied the speed of the target as well as its revolving radius. Day suggested that it was impossible to synthesize the research on this topic. He did conclude, however, that the amount of transfer was dependent upon the difficulty of the problem. Lordahl and Archer (1958) used the pursuit rotor to examine this program. They reported that considerable negative transfer took place when the speeds were changed from fast to slow or from slow to fast.

Jones and Bilodeau (1952) reported an experiment in which greater transfer took place from a difficult to an easy task. The skills involved a two-handed target tracking situation. The two problems varied in the complexity of the path which the target followed. One group of subjects learned the task involving the more difficult pattern first and then the easier pattern. The other group followed the reverse plan. Positive transfer was shown in both situations. The investigators reported, however, that much more transfer took place from the difficult to the easy task than from the easy to the difficult task. In fact, it was reported that transfer from the difficult task to the easy task was equivalent to direct practice on the easy task. Jones and Bilodeau pointed out that the difficult task included all the features of the easy one, but the reverse condition did not hold true. In agreement with these authors, Baker, Wylie, and Gagné (1950) and Barch (1953) used motor skills to show that greater transfer occurred from a complex to a relatively easy task.

Although several studies have shown conflicting results, i.e., greater transfer from the simple to the complex or no difference, the majority of evidence seems to indicate that going from the complex to the simple problem is most effective for transfer. In order for this principle to hold true, however, it is important that the complex activity include all elements of the simpler one. Obviously, since the simple skill often does not include all aspects of the complex one, transfer to the second task will necessarily be limited.

Transfer from complex to simple tasks might be illustrated with a combination of sports activities. Let us assume that an individual has developed some proficiency in the games of basketball and soccer. The combination of these two activities, or the accumulation of skills involved, is more complex than the single sport of speedball. An analysis of the activities will reveal that practically all the special skills required in the game of speedball are also included in basketball and soccer. One could assume, therefore, that the individual who had learned the latter two sports would be able to quickly attain success in speedball. The player would simply have to learn to use old skills in a new situation. On the other hand, the person who had learned the game of speedball but had never practiced soccer or basketball would have a more difficult time learning those activities. The reason for this difference is that the activities of soccer and basketball involve practically all the skills needed for speedball. Therefore, practically no *new* skills would have to be learned. On the other hand, speedball includes only a few of the skills needed for participation in basketball and soccer, thus necessitating that the individual learn several new skills.

In situations where greater transfer has been shown from simple to more complex tasks, it appears that critical features of the second task were isolated and learned especially well in the first situation. Sometimes the important features can be separated and practiced in a concentrated way as when the athletic coach discontinues practice of the total game and devotes attention to certain critical phases of the activity. The complex-to-simple technique is desirable for transfer to the simple skills when this method allows for greater practice of the simple skills.

Degree of initial learning

A factor which has been important in determining the amount of transfer is the degree to which the initial task is learned. It has been demonstrated on numerous occasions that the transfer of verbal material is increased with additional practice of the first skill. Although this concept has not been fully investigated with motor skills, the same principle is assumed to exist. For example, an experienced driver can handle different types of automobiles with ease. However, a person who has not learned to drive his first car well will have great difficulty with different types of cars. Positive transfer can also be observed when an experienced musician learns a new instrument, or when a skilled typist learns to operate other office machines. Since much of what is taught in school is included for its transfer value, it is generally advocated that initial or basic tasks be overlearned for maximum transfer. The degree of desired mastery will often be more than the student thinks necessary.

Negative transfer

Transfer from one task to another may be positive and therefore beneficial, or it may be negative and a hindrance. Negative transfer occurs when one task interferes with or inhibits the learning or performance of a second task. While teachers are interested in promoting positive transfer, they are concerned with reducing or eliminating negative transfer. Experimental designs for determining negative transfer (proactive and retroactive) have been presented earlier in this chapter.

C. L. Hull (1943) used the term *inhibition* in reference to the detrimental effect which the learning of one task might have on a second activity. While inhibition and negative transfer are not synonymous, they are intimately related. Inhibition is a broader term referring to any reluctance on the part of the individual to perform the task immediately and correctly. One inhibiting factor is negative transfer. Hull describes the two types of inhibition as:

Proactive inhibition. This is interference that the learning of one task might have on the learning or performance of a similar task at a later time. That is, the second skill would be more difficult to learn because the individual had performed the first one

Retroactive inhibition. This refers to interference that the performance of a task might have on the retention of previous learning. Such inhibition results in the forgetting or weakening of performance of certain previously learned skills.

Numerous examples of negative transfer can be observed in motor skills. For example, the accomplished baseball player who takes up the game of golf often experiences considerable difficulty because of his tendency to swing the golf club like a baseball bat. This is an example of proactive inhibition. The well-learned tendency of the individual to swing across his body (outside-in) often retards the development of a proper golf swing (inside-out). Similarly, the interlocking or overlapping grip recommended for golf is often more difficult for the person who has grown used to the baseball grip. Other examples of negative transfer can be seen when a driver attempts to back a trailer into a driveway for the first time, or when a learner begins to practice mirror tracing.

Some retroactive inhibition may be experienced when the novice tennis player begins the game of badminton. It is likely that as he learns the fast wrist strokes of badminton, the individual will forget the proper (total arm swing) tennis stroke. In a retention test of the tennis stroke at a later time, the person probably would have a tendency to use the badminton stroke with the tennis racquet. His retention of the proper tennis stroke would likely be less than if he had never played badminton.

Switching from one-wall to four-wall handball might result in both positive and negative transfer. The person who is accomplished as a one-wall player will show positive transfer when the ball is played only off the front wall. However, when the ball bounces off the side or back walls the one-wall player will exhibit negative transfer. His initial movement response will be in the direction that the ball rebounds off the front wall. This response will tend to take him out of position for the second rebound off the side wall. The novice handball player will not be so likely to make this initial incorrect response.

Similarity and transfer

One of the most important factors in determining the amount of transfer is the degree of similarity between the tasks. This concept of similarity has been emphasized since the work of Thorndike which led to his identical elements theory. As has been pointed out earlier in this chapter, transfer can vary from highly positive (helpful) to neutral (no effect) to highly negative (interference). It is interesting to note that the relationship between degree of similarity and amount of positive transfer does not follow a straight line. Somewhat similar tasks may lead to interference, or negative transfer. Robinson (1927) illustrated this relationship (see Figure 1). The concept presented in this illustration is consistent with learning theory today.

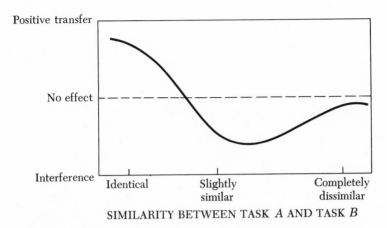

Positive transfer

No effect

Interference

Identical   Slightly   Completely
similar   dissimilar

SIMILARITY BETWEEN TASK *A* AND TASK *B*

Figure 1. EFFECTS OF TASK SIMILARITY ON TRANSFER. WHEN TASKS *A* AND *B* ARE VERY SIMILAR OR IDENTICAL, TRANSFER IS HIGH. WHEN TASKS *A* AND *B* ARE ONLY SLIGHTLY SIMILAR, INTERFERENCE IS GREAT. WHEN TASKS *A* AND *B* ARE VERY DISSIMILAR, INTERFERENCE IS SLIGHT. THIS IS REFERRED TO AS THE SKAGGS-ROBINSON HYPOTHESIS.

Source: The hypothesis was first proposed by E. S. Robinson, "The 'Similarity' Factor in Retroaction," *American Journal of Psychology*, 1927, 39, 297–312.

After surveying the research in the area of transfer, Kingsley and Garry (1957) developed a summary table to illustrate the amount of transfer which has been reported among several types of learning tasks (see Table 2). An analysis of their table reveals that tasks which are most similar can be expected to benefit from greatest transfer.

PRINCIPLES OF TRANSFER

On the basis of research evidence, opinions of learning theorists, and a consideration of the characteristics of motor learning, several transfer principles seem to emerge. Among those which are most widely accepted and which have implications for motor skills are the following:

1. The greater the similarity between two tasks, the greater will be the positive transfer. This principle has rarely been questioned, even by those with a very limited view of transfer, and it has been supported by research since the earliest studies on transfer. There is every reason to expect that this principle applies equally well to the learning of

Table 2

AMOUNT OF TRANSFER RESULTING FROM DIFFERENT TRAINING EXPERIENCES
IN EXPERIMENTS ON TRANSFER OF TRAINING

Amount of transfer reported	Training experience	Transferred to
Maximum transfer (over 50% gains)	Marking words	Other words
	Discrimination of shades of red	Discrimination of other colors
	Mazes	Other mazes
Considerable transfer (25%–50%)	Learning sets on object-equality discrimination	Similar problems
	Estimating areas of geometric figures	Similar mazes
	Memorizing techniques	Varied memory tasks
	Mental multiplication	Adding, dividing
	Biology, geometry	Biology and geometry tests
Moderate transfer (10%–25%)	Learning nonsense syllables	Learning prose, poetry
	Poetry	Prose
	Sound intensities	Brightness intensities
	Applying principles of refraction	Hitting underwater targets
Little to negative transfer (under 10%)	Poetry, prose	Dates, syllables
	Estimating line lengths	Similar task
	Cancellation of letters	Cancellation of nouns, verbs
	Card sorting	Reaction time typing
	Computation	Reasoning
	Latin	English vocabulary
	Latin	Spelling
	Biology and geometry	Other subjects

Source: Howard L. Kingsley & Ralph Garry, THE NATURE AND CONDITIONS OF
LEARNING, SECOND EDITION, © 1957. Reprinted by permission of Prentice-Hall, Inc.,
Englewood Cliffs, New Jersey.

motor skills. Numerous examples of sufficient similarity among motor
skills have been presented in this chapter. However, a great deal of
research is needed in order to clearly determine similarity characteristics of both substance and technique in regular physical education
skills.

2. Learning to make new responses to old stimuli results in negative transfer. This is evident when one attempts to break an old habit or to perform an established activity in a different way. The individual who learns to drive an automobile with a standard shift will experience some difficulty when attempting to drive one with an automatic shift. The stimuli are essentially the same, but different responses are required. The person will frequently stamp the floor with his left foot and reach for the gear shift with his right hand. Such behavior does not contribute to smooth driving performance. Similar difficulties result when the reverse learning procedure has been followed.

3. Learning to make old responses to new stimuli results in positive transfer. For example, a well-learned habit is easily applied to a new situation or a new activity. The experienced automobile driver, though exhibiting negative transfer when new responses are required, shows almost immediate proficiency when driving different vehicles requiring essentially the same response. Different model cars, trucks, tractors, or other machinery may be driven quite easily if, for example, they all have a clutch and a standard shift. Likewise, body control skills which have been developed in gymnastics are easily put to use in other activities such as dancing, diving, or other new stimuli situations where the old responses apply.

4. Transfer among similar tasks is not automatic. Several studies have shown that established skills and principles are not always used in new situations. Often the learner does not recognize the similarity between the situations or is not stimulated to make use of available skills. The teacher's strategic roles are pointing to situations where established skills may be used and motivating students to use these skills.

5. An understanding of principles or procedures underlying the initial task will result in greater transfer to a different activity. This statement is supported by convincing evidence from verbal and fine motor skills research. Although little research on this topic has involved gross motor skills, it is reasonable to assume that an understanding of the principles of momentum, rebound, and Newton's laws of motion would prove helpful in the performance of many sports skills. Techniques of learning and performing have also been shown to transfer. The instructor should show the learner the general applicability of principles and procedures.

6. The amount of transfer varies according to the difficulty of the learning material and the capacity of the learner. Persons more intelligent in the particular activity make greater transfer than do persons of lesser intelligence. Learners with greater ability are able to make broader application on the basis of fewer basic principles. The instructor, however, can promote transfer among learners of lesser ability by clarifying common elements among learning tasks.

Selected Readings

Bernard, H. W. *Psychology of learning and teaching.* (2nd ed.) New York: McGraw-Hill, 1965.

Cratty, B. J. *Movement behavior and motor learning.* Philadelphia: Lea & Febiger, 1964.

Deese, J. *The psychology of learning.* (2nd ed.) New York: McGraw-Hill, 1958.

Grose, R. F., & Birney, R. C., *Transfer of learning.* Princeton, N. J.: Van Nostrand, 1963.

Kingsley, H. L., & Garry, R., *The nature and condition of learning.* Englewood Cliffs, N. J.: Prentice-Hall, 1957.

McGeoch, J. A., & Irion, A. L. *The psychology of human learning.* (2nd ed.) New York: McKay, 1953.

Stephens, J. M. Transfer of learning. In *Encyclopedia of educational research.* (Rev. ed.) New York: Macmillan, 1960.

Travers, R. M. W. *Essentials of learning.* New York: Macmillan, 1963.

Woodworth, R. S., & Schlosberg, H. *Experimental psychology.* (Rev. ed.) New York: Holt, Rinehart and Winston, 1963.

Chapter **5**

Retention and forgetting

All learning experiences will be more valuable if the individual is able to remember them for a reasonably long time. Retention is essential if the person is to put to use what he has learned. If the information cannot be recalled on the appropriate occasion, the time spent in learning it has been largely wasted. In fact, there can be no improvement from trial to trial without some retention because the learning of advanced concepts or skills is contingent upon an understanding and retention of certain prerequisites.

It is axiomatic, therefore, that teachers should be concerned not only with learning, but with the retention of skills or materials which have been learned. Nevertheless, teachers in all subject fields have been traditionally concerned with immediate performance, often to the neglect of techniques which might improve long-term retention. There has existed a general assumption that if a high level of proficiency is exhibited in a particular task, this excellence will be retained. It has been shown, however, that the relationship between immediate proficiency and retention over a long period is not always high. A general concern for the fate of skills which are acquired had led to considerable investigation of retention and forgetting in recent years. Despite some success in establishing basic laws and general principles, much remains to be determined, especially in regard to the retention of gross motor skills.

Passage of time seems to result in two types of alterations in learned material: quantitative changes (the amount retained) and qualitative changes (variations in the organization or character of the learned material). *Retention* refers to the persistence of knowledges or skills which have been learned. Forgetting is the failure to retain that which has been learned. Retention and forgetting are essentially opposites of the same phenomenon. For example, 100 per cent retention is equal to zero forgetting and 20 per cent retention equals 80 per cent forgetting.

Theories regarding retention have long existed in the minds of teachers and laymen. Some of these beliefs are based on research evidence, or on empirical observation. Others are simply the result of traditional thinking. Teachers have long suspected that certain types of skills or knowledges are remembered longer than other types. It is also assumed that learning under certain conditions promotes retention. For example, it has been frequently stated that one never forgets how to swim or to ride a bicycle. On the other hand, the names of some state capitals, chemical formulae, or complex square dance maneuvers are seemingly more quickly forgotten. Practicing a task after it has been well learned seems to aid one in remembering. Relearning an old skill, which apparently has been forgotten, seems to be easier than learning the skill for the first time. Similarly, a poem learned during childhood is seemingly learned more quickly by the individual twenty years later. What is the nature of retention? How can it best be promoted among the different types of skills? These are only two of the important considerations which relate to the retention of school learning. This chapter is devoted to a discussion of the most important aspects of retention.

The retention curve

A retention curve illustrates the amount of skill which is retained at various points in time following the cessation of practice. The retention of an unpracticed skill or unreviewed verbal learning follows a decelerating curve. The shape of this curve is almost as well known as that of the learning curve.

The retention curve was first outlined by Ebbinghaus in 1885. His curve of retention, which was based on memory of nonsense syllables, was one of his most notable contributions (see Figure 2). The relatively straight line plotted against the logarithm of time indicates that most forgetting takes place soon after original learning. Studies since Ebbinghaus' have also shown that retention follows a decelerating curve. Several researchers have plotted retention curves against the logarithm of time (as shown in Figure 2) so that the long and short intervals can be gotten into the graph without unduly crowding the short periods. Also, this technique has been used to show that retention declines approximately in proportion to the log of time. A typical retention curve without the logarithmic adjustment is shown in Figure 3. Retention of both verbal and motor skills has been shown to generally decline with time. However, special conditions of practice or of the skill itself, may result in reminiscence, a temporary rise in the retention curve.

It appears that forgetting is never complete. Thus, the true retention curve never reaches the base line. This is consistently shown when a sensitive measure of retention is used. Motor skills or verbal materials which are experienced only once are often recalled under certain conditions.

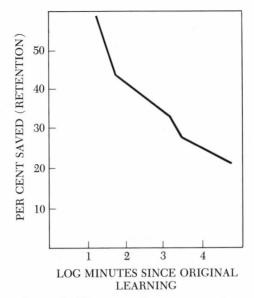

Figure 2. EBBINGHAUS' CURVE OF RE-
TENTION FOR LISTS OF NONSENSE SYL-
LABLES.

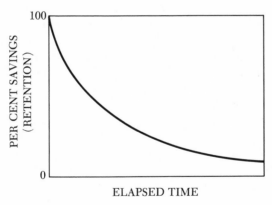

Figure 3. THE TYPICAL RETENTION CURVE.

Unusual or rare incidences of retention in everyday life seem to verify the belief that forgetting is never complete.

The descent of the retention curve is greatly affected by such factors as the type of material learned, its meaningfulness to the learner, the kind of practice schedule by which the material was learned, and the many experiences which come to the attention of the individual. Each of these factors will be discussed in some detail in this chapter.

Theories of forgetting

A number of theories have emerged which are attempts to explain the phenomenon of forgetting. Perhaps the oldest and most popular one has been the *fading* theory, which is based on the law of disuse. According to the fading theory, skills which are not used regularly will gradually wither away. Forgetting is therefore assumed to be directly related to the passage of time. This theory has surface validity and is supported by the observation that as time goes by, most verbal material seems to become less vivid and motor skills appear to deteriorate.

In recent years, some doubt has been cast on the accuracy of the fading theory. The fact that people remember certain things longer than others raises a question about the traditional belief that time is the critical ingredient in forgetting. Clinical literature lists numerous cases of *hypermnesia*, i.e., unexpected incidences of recall during certain psychological states. In addition, most individuals experience occasions when they are surprised at their remembrance of a number, a name, or other information which they have not thought about for a long period. Also, a relatively high level of proficiency in certain motor skills is sometimes exhibited after a long no-practice period.

Doubt has also been cast on the fading theory by several studies in which sleeping and waking subjects were compared. These studies generally showed that during sleep, individuals remember more of what has been recently learned than during an equivalent waking-period of normal activity. As a result, many current theorists believe that forgetting is not related to time, except that a longer period of time allows for more interruptive experiences. Therefore, the fading theory and the principle of disuse appear inadequate as a complete explanation of forgetting.

A more recent theory considers forgetting the result of *interference*. According to this view, time as such is not a critical factor in retention. Rather, the most important consideration is that of interpolated experiences. This concept holds that nothing is really forgotten, but previously learned habits or skills are altered or obliterated by new experiences. Therefore, the only reason that a person forgets how to tie a particular knot, or balance on a bongo board, or shoot billiards skillfully, is that other activities have been learned which interfere with the retention of these skills. This process of interference has been referred to as retroactive inhibition, and it has been strongly supported by studies on the retention of sleeping and waking persons. Because the research evidence is so convincing, the basic idea of the interference theory is widely accepted by educators today. General acceptance of this concept, however, does not necessarily mean that interference is the only cause of forgetting.

Another theory of forgetting was developed by Sigmund Freud and expanded by later psychoanalysts. This clinical view holds that forgetting is a result of *repression*: The individual subconsciously does not wish to remember an event or activity which threatens him. Forgetting is assumed to be a defense of the individual's personality. Usually the things most readily forgotten are unpleasant events or activities, especially those which evoke guilt feelings or shame. Forgetting is therefore viewed as an active process of expelling ideas or skills from one's self, but this process of elimination is at the subconscious level and is not an act of which the individual is aware. The theory of repression is used to explain the occasional development of "mental blocks" regarding people's names, places, or events. Most individuals can recall inexplicable and embarrassing lapses of memory, and repression seems to be verified by many instances among both children and adults. The theory of repression does not seem adequate, however, to account for all forgetting, especially the deterioration of skill.

One theory which has received limited attention explains forgetting as a *deterioration* of the neural connections which accompanied the learning in the first place. The deterioration theory is related to Kappers' theory of neural growth, which explains learning as the development of axons and dendrites around the synapse. The deterioration theory is similar to the disuse theory because as a previously learned activity or skill is not practiced or used, the neural connections gradually degenerate. The deterioration concept includes the assumption that lack of activity causes atrophy in the unused nerve areas, just as lack of activity results in atrophy in muscular tissue. Sports skills, therefore, deteriorate during long periods in which they are not used. However, most theorists have been primarily interested in the behavioral aspects of learning and retention and, therefore, have given little attention to the neurological explanation of forgetting.

The complex phenomenon of retention will be discussed in terms of the many variables which appear to influence it. Most of the factors which affect retention seem to fall into the following categories: (1) techniques of measurement, (2) the nature and degree of original learning, and (3) interpolated experiences.

TECHNIQUES OF MEASUREMENT

The retention of motor skills or verbal materials cannot be intelligently discussed without consideration of the conditions of measurement. Indications of the degree of retention will vary greatly according to the manner in which retention is evaluated. One method of measurement might register a zero for retention, while another technique would show a fairly high degree of remembrance. The most popular techniques for determining degree of retention have been recall, recognition, and re-learning. These methods vary greatly in sensitivity regardless of the type of learning being measured.·

The technique which is most frequently used in schools is *recall,* the least sensitive method. In recall, the individual is asked to draw from memory without any cues, the date of a particular event in history, the rules for a particular sports activity, or a poem which he has memorized. In short recall questions, the answers are usually entirely correct or entirely wrong, with no gradations. In other types of recall questions, such as reciting a poem, the individual can exhibit degrees of retention. As a rule, however, recall questions used in school do not measure the lower levels of retention, nor do they discriminate clearly between various degrees of competency.

The general technique of recall can be used quite successfully for determining retention in physical education skills. Such measures generally come in the form of retests. In movement skills, very low levels of retention are more accurately evaluated by the retest technique of recall than is possible with verbal material. The young basketball player who is asked to demonstrate the recently practiced skill of shooting the left-handed lay-up shot can exhibit widely varying responses. He may perform very clumsily and even jump off the wrong foot; he may exhibit a mechanically correct but awkward response; or he may give a well-executed performance. Unlike the right or wrong answer on certain memory tests, some estimation of basketball skill can be made even if a successful goal is not accomplished. In other activities, the student may be asked to demonstrate his retention in the cartwheel, archery, or rope skipping. In these activities, the performer rarely gets an absolute zero score for retention. In recall measures of verbal learning, however, the student often "draws a blank," or does not get the right answer, even if he has a vague idea.

In some types of physical education skills, however, the weakness of the recall method is just as apparent as with verbal knowledge. Consider square dancing as an example. The individual might "completely forget" the correct moves for a particular dance if he tries to walk through his assignment while depending entirely on memory without musical cues or other moving persons to guide him. On the other hand, if the person gets into a square in which the other people exhibit the right moves, their responses will very often evoke the correct moves on his part. The first situation, in which the individual attempts to recall his moves strictly from memory, is an example of the straight recall measure and is likely to result in either a correct or an incorrect response. The second situation, in which the dancer uses the cues of the other dancers and the music, is a recognition situation. Recognition is a finer measure and is likely to evoke a more accurate indication of the individual's retention.

Test-makers and teachers have long been aware that questions of the *recognition* type will elicit greater reproduction of the correct responses than will simple recall questions. For example, people are sometimes heard to say, "I'll recognize his name as soon as you mention it." They are expressing confidence in their retention if it is tested in a particular way. The recognition technique of using cues is a more sensitive measure of retention. As stated previously, the square dancer is likely to fall right in line, or quickly pick up his previously learned skills, if surrounded by skillful dancers. The movement of the others and the music tend to prompt him. He recognizes the moves as parts of a particular pattern. While the novice bowler may become completely confused when attempting to recall the sequence of arm and leg movement in the approach, he may immediately recognize the correct approach in others who are demonstrating various techniques. Similarly, as soon as he happens to get off on the correct foot and starts the sequence, he can immediately recognize the familiar kinesthetic sensations and continue in the proper manner.

Written questions of the recognition type are familiar to all teachers. Multiple-choice questions are perhaps the most popular type of recognition measure. Consider the following example: Which of the following persons is credited with having developed the game of basketball? (1) Abner Doubleday, (2) James Naismith, (3) George Mikan, (4) Tyrus Cobb, (5) Frederick Jahn. Many people who would not recall the name of the originator of basketball could look at the list and, through the process of elimination, arrive at the name "Naismith." A person who may not be able to illustrate or describe the correct movement of a square dance pattern may, when watching a group, realize whether the movement is done correctly or incorrectly. The individual who only vaguely remembers a particular movement response often is able to recognize whether or not his own movements are correct. This recognition appears to be based on cognitive and kinesthetic feedback as well as on the results of the movement. There is little question that the recognition retention measure is finer and more discriminating than the straight recall method. Although recognition is frequently observed in motor skills, it is not frequently used as a means of determining retention.

A measure of retention more sensitive than either recall or recognition is *relearning*. Occasionally, there is practically no evidence of retention when either the recall or recognition method is used. The student is sometimes not certain of any remembrance of the topic or skill. However, if he starts practicing the skill anew, he will probably find himself getting the feel of the activity quite rapidly. At the very least, he will find that the skill is learned in less time than it took him to learn it originally. This economy or "saving" in relearning is usually evidence of the individual's having retained some skill from previous experience. Saving may be detected in cases of very low retention such as when a person says, "I memorized that poem once, but now I don't even remember how it starts." It is also effective in cases of motor skills about which the person seems to remember nothing.

The sensitivity of the relearning technique was dramatically illustrated in an experiment by Burtt (1941) with his son who was less than two years of age. It was Burtt's practice to read traditional nursery rhymes to the child each day. For several weeks, however, he inserted three selections (twenty lines each) from Sophocles. These selections were read in the original Greek. Six years later, Burtt required the boy, who was then eight years of age, to memorize the same three passages of literature, and also three equivalent passages from the same volume. The boy required 435 readings to memorize the new passages but only 317 readings to learn those which had been read to him at the age of two. The earlier readings thus resulted in a 25 per cent saving. Burtt's experiment has been offered as evidence of the persistence of earlier exposure. It is clear that only the relearning technique would have shown any evidence of retention in this case.

Almost invariably when an individual starts practicing or reviewing a previously learned skill, it is found that proficiency returns rather rapidly. The difference in the learning time between the first and the second experience is an expression of the degree of saving. Most persons can recall taking part in some apparently forgotten activity and having it "come back" rather quickly. The relearning technique is clearly the most sensitive detector of retention for both verbal and motor learning.

Timing of retention measures

Measurement of retention is complicated not only by the type of measure used but also by the timing of the process. Retention curve charts can be interpreted clearly only when one realizes how the successive levels of retention have been established. Two common techniques have been used for determining the amount of retention at various periods after the original learning took place. The more traditional of these was the method of successive recalls in which a group would learn a task and would be given retention checks at various points in time. A retention curve would be plotted on the basis of the performance score at each test. The inherent weakness in successive recall was that some review was likely to take place at each test of retention. Performances on subsequent tests would, therefore, be somewhat enhanced.

The weakness of the successive recall technique may be eliminated by use of a second procedure which uses a single recall. In this system several groups learn the skill to a desired level of proficiency. A different group is then used to check the level of retention at each desired point in time. The retention curve can then be charted without fear that the performance scores have been contaminated by interim periods of testing (with related review). A third technique, which has been used on occasion, is to have one group learn some material and then give periodic retention tests on different but equivalent parts of the material. The difficulty in this procedure is in determining what materials or tasks are equivalent and likely accurately to reflect retention of the original material. If the retention material or tasks are similar enough to be adequate for comparison with the original task, they may, in essence, provide a review which will transfer positively to subsequent tests. This third technique does not seem appropriate as a means for establishing retention curves in motor learning.

Another factor which must be somewhat controlled if retention and retention curves are to be fully understood is the matter of mental review between original learning and the measurement of retention. Mental review will make a difference in both motor and verbal learning. Control of the interim mental process has been done effectively in the study of short-term retention. The most often used practice for eliminating or reducing mental review has been to assign an activity which demands the student's attention during the interim period. Practices such as counting backwards from 100 in intervals of three, working short arithmetic problems, or solving puzzles have often been used. The idea is to occupy the person's mind during the retention period so that the exhibited skill will be based on original learning rather than mental review which might follow.

THE NATURE AND CONDITIONS OF ORIGINAL LEARNING

An investigation of retention soon leads to the conclusion that the factors which influence learning will also have an effect upon the manner in which that learning is retained. The type of task, the degree of original learning, and the conditions under which learning took place all will make a difference when any sensitive test of retention is used.

Nature of the task

Several authors have suggested that not all learning tasks are remembered similarly. This assumption has been made especially when motor skills were compared with verbal material or when certain types of motor skills were compared with other types. However, statements about different degrees of retentiveness among different learning tasks are based more on empirical observation than on scientific investigation. The problem is especially difficult to solve by use of traditional research designs.

One problem which is encountered in attempting to compare the retentiveness of different tasks is the determination of equal levels of original learning. For example, if one learns to consistently shoot 70 per cent of his free throws in basketball, how does this compare with the ability to bowl a score of 130? Obviously, it is difficult to say whether the level of skill is equivalent for the two tasks. When one considers more commonly used experimental tasks, the same difficulties are encountered. Does the ability to recite twenty lines of a twenty-five line poem represent as high a level of learning as the ability to name forty of the fifty state capitals? How do these verbal skills compare with the ability to shoot fifteen out of twenty-four arrows into an archery target at forty yards?

Just as difficult as determining equivalent levels of original learning among different skills is the matter of establishing comparable degrees of retention. Suppose, for example, that at the retention test the student had dropped from 70 to 35 per cent in free-throw shooting. Is this comparable to a reduction in bowling score from 130 to 65? Similarly, if a learner is able to recite only ten of the originally learned twenty lines of poetry, is this equivalent to the retention of twenty of forty state capitals which were learned originally? Is *percentage* of retention an adequate means of comparing the retentiveness of different tasks? How can percentage of skating or swimming be measured? It is clear that these are not easy questions. Nevertheless, they are important in any attempt to determine and compare retentiveness among learning tasks.

Motor versus verbal learning

Despite a lack of scientific evidence, it has long been suspected that certain types of material or skills are remembered better than the other types. Differences in retentiveness seemingly exist between verbal and motor skills and between different skills within each of these categories. Carroll (1940) states, however, that the ability to retain verbal and motor learning is equal. Gagné and Fleishman (1959) believe that motor skills are retained longer than verbal material, but they indicate that much of the observed difference results from the fact that regular motor skills are often learned more thoroughly. Nevertheless, they believe that even when original learning is equalized, motor skills are still retained longer than other types of learning. Further, they conclude after reviewing several research studies that, " . . . it appears that the kind of human activities most resistant to forgetting are motor skills of the type which are continuous rather than discrete (p. 173)". Skating, swimming, and bicycle riding are suggested as continuous activities. It might be assumed that discrete activities would include skills such as a soccer kick, basketball jump shot, or fungo hitting in baseball.

After noting the apparent difference between the retention of certain school learning and the motor skills of bicycle riding and swimming, Trow (1950) pointed out that such comparisons were unrealistic. He stated that:

Bicycle-riding and swimming are relatively simple responses that have been many times repeated, while the items of knowledge are complex and numerous, and many of them have not been overlearned. A better comparison might be made between bicycle-riding or swimming and writing a capital letter A or giving the date for the discovery of America (pp. 605–606).[1]

According to Trow, therefore, the important factors in retention are the complexity of the material and the amount of overlearning, not whether the task is verbal or motor.

Leavitt and Schlosberg (1944) had subjects learn nonsense syllables and also develop skill in pursuit-rotor performance. An attempt was made to equate the amount of learning by having subjects practice each task for ten thirty-second trials with a thirty-second rest between trials. When they tested for retention of these skills they found a higher percentage of original learning was retained in the motor skill (see Figure 4). They suggested, however, that the greater retention of the motor skill could have resulted from better organization of that task. In a later study Van Dusen and Schlosberg (1949) made a particular effort to equate the organization of a verbal and a motor task. They reported no difference in retention at any point in time.

In one of the first studies on the retention of motor skills, Swift (1905) reported high levels of retention with juggling skills. He found considerable retention after periods of one and six years. He also reported a large saving in relearning the skill of typing after a two-year period. Swift's reports of high retention are not very helpful in comparing motor and verbal learning, however, because a comparable verbal skill was not learned and measured for retention. Also, practice in the interim was apparently not rigidly controlled.

Tsai (1924) reported a great degree of retention in the stylus maze habit. In this experiment, groups of subjects developed a high degree of proficiency in the skill. After periods of no practice from one to nine weeks, a very high level of skill was exhibited on retention tests. The skill retained varied from approximately 50 to 85 per cent after nine weeks. Bell (1950) reported a retention of 71 per cent in accuracy after a period of one year when the pursuit rotor was used. A very short period of practice was sufficient to bring the level of skill back to the orig-

---

[1] From EDUCATIONAL PSYCHOLOGY by W. C. Trow, used by permission of the publisher HOUGHTON MIFFLIN COMPANY.

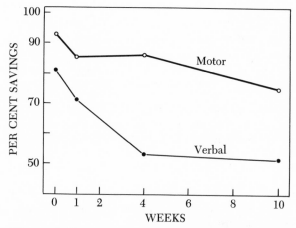

Figure 4. COMPARISON OF RETENTION OF A MOTOR
TASK AND A VERBAL SEQUENCE OF 15 NONSENSE
SYLLABLES. THE MEAN SAVINGS AT EACH INTERVAL
WAS OBTAINED BY COMPARING THE RETENTION
SCORE OF EACH INDIVIDUAL WITH THE SCORE ON
HIS LAST LEARNING TRIAL.

Source: After H. J. Leavitt and H. Schlosberg, "The Retention of Verbal and of Motor Skills," *Journal of Experimental
Psychology,* 1944, 34, 404–417. By permission.

inal point. The original learning involved twenty trials. After one year,
the original level of proficiency was reached after only eight trials. In
other studies involving the skill of typing, Towne (1922) and Rejall
(1913) reported high percentages of retention when subjects refrained
from practice for periods ranging from six months to four and one-half
years.

It is important to point out, however, that evidence of long-term retention is not restricted to motor skills. Depending on the type of verbal
material (especially its meaningfulness) and the manner in which retention is measured, great variation may be shown. Radosavijevich (1907)
and McGeoch and Whitely (1926) report studies in which high degrees
of savings were shown for both meaningful and nonsense syllables for
four-month periods. Periods of prolonged retention of verbal material
from five to forty-six years are reported by Worcester (1923), Ebbinghaus (1911), and Titchener (1923). Although experimental controls
were not rigidly enforced in these studies, they do give some indication
of the persistence of verbal learning.

Studies on the retention of school learning by young children indicate that school subjects are apparently retained in varying degrees, dur-

ing the summer vacation, and in some subjects achievement even shows a gain. Further investigation reveals that subjects with less likelihood of being practiced during the summer months show the greatest loss. Conversely, subjects which are likely to be practiced, directly or indirectly, show the least reduction (or greatest gain). General proficiency in physical education, reading, and possibly, social studies, remains highest during the summer months. While these observations have led some to conclude that physical education skills are retained longer, it is probable that the practice factor plays an important part in their retention.

Apparent differences. Claims for an inherent advantage in the retention of motor skills have probably overstated any actual existence of such a tendency. The appearance of greater retention is caused by a number of factors other than whether the activity happens to involve motor movement. The tendency to overlearn the skill is probably more prevalent among motor skills than among other types of learning. The likelihood of learning the motor skill very thoroughly is enhanced by the fact that the individual sometimes enjoys the activity and participates beyond the point of having learned how to perform the task. The tendency to overlearn is often not as strong with verbal skills. For example, in common motor skills, the individual is likely to participate in the activity as a recreational experience long after the original learning has occurred. The activities of swimming, bicycle riding, and skating may be performed quite regularly during an individual's early years. The individual is often surprised to find that twenty years later he can still show some skill in these tasks. He then compares his motor ability with his inability to recite a poem or perform another verbal skill which he learned at approximately the same time as the motor skill. The individual may not consider that the verbal material was not regularly performed as a recreational activity.

Another reason why motor skills appear to be retained longer than verbal material is the usual manner of measuring the degree of retention. Very often a recall technique is used for the verbal material while the relearning method is used to test the retention of motor skills. For example, the person may be asked to recite a particular poem, to name the capital of a state, or to provide a chemical formula. This recall technique will usually result in an all-or-nothing response. For the motor skill, however, the person may be asked to demonstrate skill in dribbling a basketball, swimming, or bowling. Theoretically, if 50 per cent retention existed for both the verbal and the motor tasks, this degree of proficiency would be exhibited in the motor skill, while a zero score might be obtained in the verbal material. After all, almost remembering a formula is of little value in a recall test.

Another point that is often ignored is that people do forget motor skills even when practice has been quite extensive. For example, the professional baseball batter who is apparently at the peak of his physical proficiency may go through a season with a batting average forty points lower than his average of the previous few years. Often this loss of skill or forgetting how to hit is not related to any physical disability but to the individual's inability to remember the fine points of his performance when he was at his peak. A clearer example of forgetting can be shown when the former high school baseball player goes out fifteen years later and attempts to hit fly balls for his son to catch. Former proficiency in hitting the ball accurately and consistently may be woefully lacking. Golfers, professional and amateur, slump from time to time without any reason except an apparent loss of skill because of forgetting. Performers in all sports activities forget how to perform for certain periods. This forgetting is reflected in a small or large drop-off in performance.

Meaningfulness of the task

Studies have consistently shown that *meaningful* material is remembered better than material which seems disorganized to the learner. The manner in which the material is structured, its relationship to the learner's previous experience, and the importance with which the individual views the material all help to determine the degree of retention. These details affect (1) the degree to which the material is learned in the first place, (2) the tendency of the person to think about it, or mentally practice, at a later time, and (3) the number of times that the person is reminded of the material in his everyday experiences. It also seems clear that the understanding or discovery of a principle which is basic to the material is an aid to retention. Materials which are learned by rote are not as well remembered.

Ebbinghaus' early experiments showed that meaningful material was retained better than nonsense syllables. Guilford (1952), similarly, found that poetry was remembered much better than nonsense syllables. Naylor and Briggs (1961) reported that the organization of material was important in its retention. They found that verbal and motor tasks which were arranged in an arbitrary sequence were not remembered as well as the same material organized in a more meaningful manner. It was concluded that the motor-verbal factors were not as important in retention as the organization and difficulty of the material. There is some evidence to indicate that materials or tasks which are learned by the whole method are remembered better than those learned by the part method, lending support to the belief that wholes are more meaningful than parts.

It has been reported on several occasions that the gist of a story is remembered longer than the minor or technical details. The basic ingredients are long retained, while names, dates, and numbers are quickly forgotten. Newman (1939) reported a study in which two groups of college women heard a story. In one group, the story was followed by eight hours of sleep. The other group followed the story by eight hours of normal daily activities. At the end of the period, both groups retained the general concepts of the story similarly. The working group, however, forgot a greater degree of the details of the story than did the sleeping group.

A similar study was designed to determine the verbal retention of elementary school children. In this project, one child was told a story and five minutes later was asked to tell the story to a second child. After five minutes, the second child was asked to tell the story to a third child. This procedure was followed until several children had listened, waited for five minutes, and told the story from memory. It was found that the basic ideas of the story were pretty well preserved while the details were obliterated. Names, places, and other specific information were forgotten and replaced by new information.

In like manner, the finer or more detailed points of a motor skill are forgotten more quickly than the basic features of movement. Fundamentals which are taught early and stressed as the most important elements of a skill are more likely to be retained over a long period. When skills begin to deteriorate, the fine points which lead to the highest level of performance are the first to be lost. Lawther (1966) reported that high levels of skill performance in piano playing, putting in golf, or other tasks where advanced performances may be exhibited, tend to drop down rapidly during periods of no practice.

Cook (1951) surveyed the research regarding retention and stated that learning involving problem-solving relationships and the operation of the highest mental processes are relatively permanent, and that unrelated facts and mere information are relatively temporal. Cook's contention seems to be supported by observation of high school or college students who appear to retain higher-level abilities and techniques longer than they recall formulae, names, dates and similar information.

Several authors have reported that materials which are pleasant or acceptable to the learner will be remembered better than unacceptable or neutral materials. Edwards (1942) indicated, however, that more important than the pleasantness of the material was the frame of reference of the learner. The concepts or information which are most consistent with the beliefs of the individual will be remembered most vividly. On the whole, the experiences which most closely agree with one's point of view are also the most pleasant. The movement skills which *seem* appropriate to the desired action will be acquired and retained more readily than actions which do not appear to be closely connected with the results. This tendency to remember experiences which are pleasant or which have greater meaning for the learner is just as applicable to motor skills as to other types or concepts.

Teachers of physical education may take advantage of the frame of reference by teaching certain rhythmical drills or dances while using familiar and popular pieces of music. The familiarity and pleasantness of the music may tend to evoke a positive reaction by the learner, and his greater interest will aid both learning and retention. Perhaps just as important is the fact that on future occasions when the particular piece of music is heard, it will evoke mental rehearsal on the part of the individual. No doubt, the matter of mental practice is a factor which contributes to the increased retention of meaningful material. Conversely, it is unlikely that materials which are not meaningful to the individual will be reviewed during his idle moments.

Speed of learning

Traditionally, it was generally believed that there was an inverse relationship between speed of learning and amount of retention. The general assumption was that the child who learned rapidly would also forget quickly. On the other hand, it was believed that the child who had to toil long and hard to gain a particular concept or skill would have this learning deeply implanted in his memory and would retain it longer.

Considerable psychological literature has been devoted to the task of eliminating this apparent misconception. The literature indicated a positive relationship between speed of learning and amount of retention. This conclusion was based on research which showed that students who learned fastest also retained most. However, Underwood (1954) conducted a study in rote learning which cast doubt on claims for a positive relationship. His study showed almost no correlation between time to learn and amount retained, but a positive correlation was shown between time to learn and time to relearn. When the relearning technique is used to measure retention, those who learned fastest originally would be expected to relearn faster.

Underwood believed that a basic weakness existed in most of the previous studies. The brighter children learned faster and, therefore, could learn *more* than the less able children. Those who learned most quickly had opportunities to overlearn or review when equal practice time was provided for all. Fast learners take greater advantage of equal *opportunity* for learning than do slower learners. However, when materials or skills are learned to a particular degree of proficiency, the speed with which they are learned seems to make little difference in retention. The technique for determining retention may give the appearance of correlation, i.e., when relearning is used, a slight, positive relationship is shown between speed of learning and retention.

Degree of original learning

A factor which is most strategic in the retention of any type of learning is the degree to which the material or skill is learned in the first place. The amount or degree of original learning is usually reported either in terms of (1) number of practice trials or amount of time spent in practice, or (2) the degree of exhibited proficiency. The level of proficiency is often measured in terms of the speed, accuracy, distance, or number of successful repetitions in motor skills, or the number of successful responses in verbal material.

The term *overlearning* refers to the continued practice or study of a task after it has been learned. Overlearning is used to describe the amount of original learning of a particular task. When the child can recite a poem once without making an error, it is assumed that he has learned the poem. Theoretically, overlearning is not practiced for the purpose of improving performance on a skill, but rather to "set," or reinforce, the learning so that it will be remembered longer. The child who recited the poem without error will not improve his performance with additional practice. The same is essentially true of the boy who continues to do headstands. Efforts to improve or refine a skill after success has been shown are not classified as overlearning. The diver who continues to practice a dive after it has been performed successfully is often attempting to polish or refine the execution of the task. Such efforts to make small changes and improvements are essentially new learning.

Overlearning is generally referred to in terms of the amount of extra practice that is taken. The amount of practice *after* the point of one perfect performance is compared with the amount of practice required to attain that level initially. A percentage of overlearning is computed from this comparison. For example, if the child required ten readings of the poem in order to recite it perfectly the first time, ten additional readings would represent 100 per cent overlearning. For a boy who required six tries before being able to do a back somersault on the trampoline, three additional executions of the skill would be 50 per cent overlearning. Most research studies report overlearning varying from 50 per cent to 200 per cent.

One of the early studies regarding the values of various degrees of overlearning was conducted by Krueger (1929). He had three groups of subjects learn one-syllable nouns, each group being given a different amount of practice. One group practiced only to the point of one successful repetition (thus no overlearning). Another group had 50 per cent overlearning, and the third group practiced to the point of 100 per cent overlearning. He found that 50 per cent overlearning was very valuable in promoting retention, and 100 per cent overlearning was only slightly more beneficial for retention (see Figure 5). The slight retention advan-

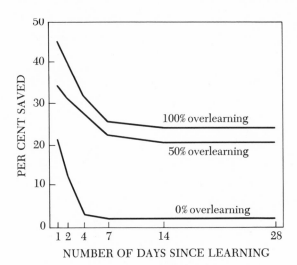

NUMBER OF DAYS SINCE LEARNING

Figure 5. RETENTION FOLLOWING DIFFERENT AMOUNTS OF ORIGINAL LEARNING.

Source: Based on data from W. C. F. Krueger, "The Effect of Overlearning on Retention," *Journal of Experimental Psychology,* 1929, **12**, 71–78. From Greogory A. Kimble and Norman Garmezy—PRINCIPLES OF GENERAL PSYCHOLOGY, Second Edition Copyright © 1963 The Ronald Press Company, New York. By permission.

tage of 100 per cent over 50 per cent overlearning did not seem to warrant the extra practice time. Krueger (1930) conducted a similar study with finger mazes and obtained approximately the same results. The tendency to get diminishing returns on retention for practice above 50 per cent overlearning is consistent with several other studies of this topic. In addition, the following generalizations may be drawn from recent research literature regarding overlearning:

1. The value of overlearning increases as the time for forgetting increases.
2. To be fully effective, overlearning must be practiced as seriously as the initial task and with as much attention.
3. Less interference or negative transfer will result from material which is overlearned.
4. Positive transfer increases if material has been overlearned.

Hammerton (1963) had two groups of subjects learn a difficult tracking task to an established level of proficiency. One group then continued to practice to a higher criterion. After six months, the retention of both groups was tested by having each relearn the task to the level of the first criterion. The results led Hamerton to conclude that if a task is sufficiently difficult, overlearning does not prevent forgetting, but it does reduce the decrement with the passage of time.

Garry (1963) stated that motor skills are overlearned more often than verbal skills and, therefore, give the appearance of having greater retention. With this in mind, one can refer to a poem learned during childhood or during the early years of school as a rough check. Many people who have not heard the poem in fifteen years would have no difficulty in completing the early portions of "Humpty Dumpty sat on the wall . . ." or "I think that I shall never see/A poem lovely as . . ." On the other hand, more recent (but less overlearned) knowledge might prove more difficult to retain. For example, if the typical adult were asked to give the formula for hydrochloric acid or copper, he would have great difficulty.

In motor learning, the practice of overlearning has long been advocated. Great stress has been placed on drills and practicing until one can perform blindfolded. Coaches have encouraged athletes to learn skills so well that they do not have to think about them. Conscious effort can therefore be devoted to higher-level activities. The good dribbler in basketball has learned this skill so well that he does not have to look at the ball and can concentrate on a teammate breaking for the basket. The advantages of overlearning in sports are obvious. The soccer player who has to think about how to kick the ball will find that he is usually too late in getting the ball to the player who was open. The athlete has to perform most of his skills by "instinct." This term (as used here) does not indicate that the player has inherited skills, but rather that he has learned them so well that he does not have to think about them.

Overlearning is usually a sound investment for teachers and students. Teachers must plan for overlearning. Too often there is a feeling that once you get the hang of it, you can stop practicing. The music teacher and the typing teacher use drills to enable the student to continue to practice skills which he has just learned, or at a level he has just reached. These drills tend to make the new (high) level of performance automatic. The individual will be less likely to regress to previous levels of performance at a later practice session.

The wise physical educator will try to insure that his students hold onto any new skills that they have learned during a particular session. He will have them go through their skills a few more times so that they will remember them the next day. The teacher or the coach, however, must be aware of the fatigue factor and not try to force new skills at the end of a long practice session. Too often, because of fatigue, players will lapse into earlier stages of performance or tend to learn and to practice faults.

Distribution of practice

Most material which has been learned over a long period of time (distributed practices) will be retained longer than that which is acquired over a shorter period (massed practices). Several studies have shown that distributed practices are advantageous not only for learning efficiency, but for retention as well. On the basis of his research evidence, Robinson (1920) reported that the advantages for distributed practice became more obvious with the passage of time. Hovland (1940) found that distributed practices aided retention when either the recall or re-learning technique was used for measurement. After conducting extensive research with rote learning, he concluded that distributed practices facilitate retention because of reduced reactive inhibition. Oxendine (1959) reported a greater amount of reminiscence in mirror tracing among groups using shorter practices.

A totally satisfactory reason for this phenomenon has not yet been offered. A possible reduction in inhibition has been suggested by several authors. The preservation theory (the tendency to continue practice at the subconscious level after overt practice has ceased) is also used frequently. McGeoch (1952) suggests that persons following a distributed practice schedule benefit from their numerous opportunities to begin the activity. They show initial proficiency in retention tests by more quickly orienting themselves to the task. Ammons (1956) likewise concludes that the warm-up time decreases as the number or resumptions increases. Whatever the explanation, most authorities concur that if two skills are equivalent, the one which has been learned over a longer period will, ultimately, be retained at a higher level. This principle holds true whether the task is motor or verbal.

INTERPOLATED EXPERIENCES

Very soon after practice ceases, a decrement in the skill or knowledge can be noted. Even with the occurrence of reminiscence (an increase in skill following the cessation of practice), a drop-off in learning begins in a relatively short period of time. The reason for this inevitable reduction in skill has been of interest to psychologists and educators for quite a long time.

Among the theories of forgetting discussed earlier in this chapter, it was pointed out that the interference theory seems to be most widely accepted among authorities today. This theory holds that nothing which is learned is ever really forgotten. Rather, certain skills or knowledges are interfered with as other learnings occur and alter or eliminate the original skills. Whether or not one accepts this concept completely, the cross-effects of learning are widely accepted and can be well documented. An understanding of the effect of interpolated activities on retention is important for all teachers.

C. L. Hull developed the concept of *retroactive inhibition* which refers to the interfering effects that certain experiences have on the retention of previously learned skills. This concept is essential to an understanding of retention. Teachers can most effectively manage school experiences only if they realize the role that certain interpolated activities have in the forgetting of previously learned skills.

In addition to cases of specific negative transfer, general interference is also evident in motor tasks. Not only may practice in football place kicking (with toe) interfere with the newly acquired soccer kick (with instep), but so may a variety of general movement activities. However, there is reason to believe that general and unrelated activities do not interfere as greatly as skills which are slightly related.

Several studies have been conducted in which it was shown that *general activity* tends to speed the forgetting of recently learned skills. Jenkins and Dallenbach (1924) compared the effects of sleep and regular, waking activity on the retention of nonsense syllables. The waking activity was unrelated to the tasks to be remembered. Two subjects took part in the study, and each was tested in the sleeping and waking conditions. Under both conditions, retention checks were made at one, two, four, and eight hours after original learning. The authors reported that a rapid drop-off in retention resulted under sleeping and waking conditions during the first two hours (though not as much for sleep). The sleeping subjects showed no further loss in retention from two to eight hours. However, the subjects continued to show a decrement when following the normal daily activities. A very high level of consistency is shown in the performance of the two subjects under each condition (see Figure 6). Van Ormer (1932) conducted similar studies and generally corroborated the conclusion that sleep tends to slow forgetting. The reason for the loss of remembrance during the first two hours of sleep and not afterward is not entirely clear. It has been suggested that this loss results because subjects do not go to sleep instantaneously after learning, and during the early stages do not sleep soundly. However, after the individual is fully asleep, there seems to be little interference until he awakens.

The relationship between amount of activity and retention has also been illustrated among animals. Minami and Dallenbach (1946) showed that the retention of inactive cockroaches was dramatically higher than that of cockroaches which were moderately active. The skill that was learned and remembered was a simple avoidance habit.

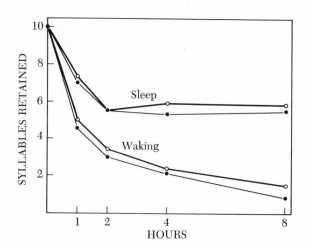

Figure 6. RETENTION OF SEQUENCES OF 10 NON-SENSE SYLLABLES BY TWO INDIVIDUALS AFTER VARYING AMOUNTS OF SLEEP IMMEDIATELY FOL-LOWING LEARNING.

Source: From J. G. Jenkins and K. M. Dallenbach, "Oblivescence during Sleep and Waking," *American Journal of Psychology,* 1924, **35,** 605–612. By permission.

Factors influencing retroactive inhibition

Retroactive inhibition occurs when the learning of a task or some material causes the forgetting of something previously learned. McGeoch and Irion (1952) suggested that the amount of retroactive inhibition resulting from interpolated activities is determined by many factors, of which the following were mentioned as the most important:

"Degree of similarity between original and interpolated activities. . ." Similarity between tasks may exist in meaning of the elements, methods by which they are performed, or serial position of the components. Research indicates that interpolated activities which are nearly identical in any of these aspects tends to aid retention of, or positive transfer to, the original activities. As the interpolated task becomes dissimilar, retention will be lower, to the point of interference. Totally dissimilar activities tend to have a neutral effect. Therefore, maximum retention results

when the interpolated and the original tasks are identical; least retention (highest interference) when the tasks are slightly similar; and a neutral effect when the tasks are not at all related.

"*Frequency of repetition of the original activity . . .*" Susceptibility to interference decreases as learning of the original activity increases. Therefore, both overlearning and review of the original task aid in retention.

"*Frequency of repetition of the interpolated activity . . .*" When the amount of original learning is held constant, an increase in the incidence of interpolated learning will result in reduced retention. Mandler and Kuhlman (1961) have shown that overlearning one motor skill increased the retroactive inhibition on a similar task. Of course, such factors as similarity and amount of original learning also play a part.

"*Amounts of original material . . .*" Several studies have suggested that longer lists or larger amounts of original learning are less susceptible to interference. Possibly this is an illustration of the principle that a greater degree of original learning tends to promote retention. When large amounts of material or long tasks are learned, certain parts of the activity are probably overlearned. The beginning phases of an activity are usually reviewed or performed anew as one continues to learn additional parts of a task. This well-learned material is, therefore, less susceptible to interference.

"*Amounts of interpolated material . . .*" Just as the amount of original material is related to the degree of learning (thus resulting in greater retention), so is the amount of interpolated material related to the retention of original material. Greater learning of interpolated materials will result in a reduction of retention of the original material. Twinning (1940) and Underwood (1954) showed that time which is spent in learning a variety of tasks or several aspects of one task is more damaging to the retention of original learning than when the same period is spent practicing a single task.

"*Sleep, inactivity, and other methods of filling the retention interval . . .*" Not only do particular related or unrelated tasks cause forgetting, but so do regular activities or daily routine. Sleep and relative inactivity result in less interference with learning than do active and varied experiences. Studies by Jenkins and Dallenbach (1924) and by Van Ormer (1932) support this principle.

"*Instruction, set, and isolation of materials . . .*" When an individual expects that certain material will have to be recalled at a later time, retention will be relatively high. Similarly, if he anticipates certain interpolated tasks, retention of original learning will be higher than if he is not expecting these occurrences. Apparently there is an attempt by the person to resist interference if he is aware of the need for retention and of the types of experiences to be encountered. The mind "set" of the subject, whether prompted by outside influences or originating within the individual, is important for the retention of learning.

"*The method of measuring retention . . .*" In the measurement of retention the techniques of recall, recognition, and relearning may be used. Recall shows the quickest measurable drop in retention, with recognition and relearning following in that order. A high degree of residual learning may not be revealed with a recall technique. However, the nature of retroactive inhibition is such that relearning, or improvement on additional recall trials, is especially rapid.

Theories of retroactive inhibition

The existence of retroactive inhibition is universally accepted today. There are differences of opinion, however, regarding the reasons for this occurrence. The explanations most often given have resulted in the development of two theories: the perseveration theory and the transfer, or competition, theory.

The perseveration theory.   This is a traditional concept of retroactive inhibition which was developed by Müller and Pilzecker (1900). According to this theory, there is a tendency for the learner to continue thinking about the task, or to perseverate, for a period after the cessation of overt practice. If a period of idleness follows practice, the individual engages in unconscious rehearsal which reinforces the learning that took place. However, if the individual takes part in other activity immediately after the work period, perseveration is interrupted and, as a result, the original activity is not learned as well. The exact nature or reason for the continuance of learning after practice has not been clearly established, although several physiological explanations have been offered.

The perseveration theory seems rather plausible, especially when one considers the tendency of certain visual images to linger in the mind. Also, most people have, on occasion, experienced difficulty in eliminating certain musical tunes or even unrelated ideas from their minds. The tendency to experience lingering ideas is especially apparent if an important event is followed by a period of idleness. The perseveration theory, however, assumes that the continuance of learning results from *subconscious* rather than conscious activity. There has been no definite evidence of continued neural growth because of perseveration, despite claims made by early physiologists in defense of the theory. In addition, if this theory were entirely adequate, the learned material should be rather free from interference once the perseveration is allowed to take place. But evidence indicates that a period of idleness following practice does not render one immune to interfering activities which may occur later. Consequently, the theory of perseveration is not widely accepted as a total explanation for retroactive inhibition.

The transfer or competition theory. This theory assumes that the loss of retention caused by intervening activity is the result of transfer from one activity to the other or of interaction between the two activities. Many studies have shown that the degree of retention of one task is influenced by its similarity to the intervening task. This concept differs significantly from the perseveration theory in which any activity following the original learning would interrupt the lingering mental activity and cause forgetting. According to the transfer theory, it appears that a person recalls the original and interpolated responses but is uncertain of which to use. The transfer theory is really one of *negative transfer* in which learning from one task intrudes upon the second task.

In consideration of the great variety and complexity of interpolated activity, one might wonder why we remember anything at all. Why is all learning not erased by more recent learning? There are several factors which seem to be crucial in preserving learning. Among these are the following: (1) Positive transfer is quite common among activities which are within the individual's experience; (2) many tasks are important and meaningful to the individual and, therefore, tend to be well remembered; and (3) much of what we learn is well learned or overlearned and, therefore, is likely to be long retained. The third factor is especially effective when the individual makes a conscious effort to retain the learned material or tasks.

Reminiscence

It is not an unusual occurrence in sports for an individual who returns to an activity after a few weeks or months to discover that he is a better performer than when he last participated. This discovery is contrary to what one would expect from the retention curves. William James, however, indicated that something occurs within the individual even if he does not practice. He postulated, for example, that people learn to skate in the summer and to swim in the winter. Do people really improve during periods of no practice? Under what conditions is the forgetting curve reversed?

The phenomenon of reminiscence is an interesting one which has long fascinated students of learning. Reminiscence refers to improvement during the period in which there is no practice. The term reminiscence was perhaps first specifically discussed by Ballard (1913). He found that children, after attempting to memorize a poem on a given day, could recite more of the poem on the following day than immediately after having studied it. This "improvement" during the period of no practice has been reported in various types of learning tasks and under widely differing circumstances. A typical experimental procedure is to allow practice on a particular skill, followed immediately by a test of proficiency; then a period of no practice, and a test of retention. As was indicated earlier, performance at the second test is occasionally at a higher level than at the test immediately following the practice period.

Various reasons have been offered to explain this phenomenon. The most common has been that some subconscious mental practice goes on in the individual even without his knowledge. This practice, or review, stands him in good stead at the time the retest is given. It has also been suggested that during rest periods the incorrect responses are more readily forgotten than the correct ones, possibly because the correct ones were reinforced.

Travers (1963) believes that reminiscence is not really a genuine phenomenon. He explains rather that the superior performance on the retention test results from the additional practice that the individual experienced during the earlier test period. A weakness in experimental design was therefore believed to be contributing to the erroneous assumptions. This idea was supported in a study by Ammons and Irion (1954) in which two groups were used. One group followed the traditional design of a test and a retest following the learning period. A second group omitted the initial test and, therefore, the practice which might occur from it. This second group did not exhibit the reminiscence phenomenon at the retention test. The authors concluded that the additional test was the source of additional learning, and that reminiscence did not, in fact, take place.

On a short-term basis in motor skills, it has often been shown that performance is higher after a period of no practice. This is possibly because of fatigue or inhibitions which may have developed during the period of intensive training. Much research is needed before definite conclusions can be drawn regarding the nature of reminiscence, or, indeed, whether reminiscence exists.

RETENTION OF MOTOR SKILLS

In comparison with verbal learning, many authors have reported a high degree of retention in motor skills. Several of these authors have been mentioned earlier in this chapter. Regardless of how the retention of motor skills compares with that of verbal learning, recent research seems to emphasize the fact that motor skills are retained at a higher level than is usually expected in verbal learning.

Purdy and Lockhart (1962) conducted a recent experiment to determine retention among five gross motors skills. College women learned novel skills including: (1) a nickel toss requiring timing and accuracy, (2) a ball toss involving hand-eye coordination, (3) a foot volley involving foot-eye coordination, (4) a lacrosse throw and catch requiring total body coordination and adjustments, and (5) balancing on a bongo board. Subjects were divided into three groups according to their ability to learn each of the skills. After a period of nine to fifteen months, thirty-six of the original seventy-five women were given a retention-relearning test on each of the skills. At this retention check, they practiced the skills for three days in the same manner as was followed from the original learning.

In analyzing the data Purdy and Lockhart found that:

1. A high degree of skill was retained after approximately one year of no practice. The total group retained 94 percent of its best performance on original learning. Eighty-nine percent of the subjects displayed reminiscence on one or more skills.
2. Relearning to previously attained skill levels was rapid after approximately one year of no practice. After three days of practice the total group regained the level of proficiency acquired in the ten days of original learning.
3. The skill groups retained their relative positions in learning, retention, and relearning of gross motor skills. The high skill group had significantly better scores than the average and low skill groups; the average skill group had significantly better scores than the low skill group.
4. When proportion of skill retained and relearned was considered, differences among the classified skill groups were small. The average skill group retained 98 percent of its best performance on original learning, the high skill group 93 percent, and the low skill group 83 percent. The average skill group relearned in proportion more than the other two groups, attaining 122 percent of its best original learning performance on the second day of the retention-learning experiment and 121 percent on the third day. The high skill group attained 112 percent on the second day and 110 percent on the third day, while the low skill group relearned 102 and 99 percent respectively on the second and third days (p. 270).[2]

After observing the high degree of retention in these skills, the authors suggested that teachers probably spend too much time reviewing previously learned skills. Intermediate and advanced performers should be able to go very quickly into more advanced skills. Long periods of review on more fundamental skills are generally a waste of time.

Ryan (1962) investigated the pattern of retention for two types of motor skills. He had eighty subjects develop skill in the pursuit rotor and the stabilimeter. The pursuit rotor involved rotary arm movement in

---

[2] B. J. Purdy and A. Lockhart, "Retention and Relearning of Gross Motor Skills After Long Periods of No Practice," *Research Quarterly*, 33, Washington, D.C.: AAHPER, 1962, p. 270. By permission.

which the subject attempted to keep a stylus in contact with a target which was revolving on a turntable. The stabilimeter was a total body balance task in which the subject attempted to maintain position with a minimum of movement while standing astride a bongo-board-type apparatus. After a standard amount of practice, subjects were divided into four groups to be retested after three, five, seven, or twenty-one days.

Ryan found that there was little loss in skill for periods up to twenty-one days. In fact, a gain in proficiency was shown on the pursuit rotor skill at all retention checkpoints. Retention on the stabilimeter usually showed a slight decrement. It should be noted that shorter practice periods were followed for the pursuit rotor (thirty seconds) than for the stabilimeter (one minute). Rest periods were a standard thirty seconds for both tasks. Since this constitutes a somewhat more distributed practice schedule for the pursuit rotor, Ryan suggested this as a possible reason for the greater retention. He concluded, however, that the two different skills are not retained similarly.

Fleishman and Parker (1962) investigated the long-term retention of a complex tracking skill. The task was one which simulated a pilot's actions in flying a radar intercept mission. The authors observed that retention of these skills over an extended period without practice is especially important. Seventeen practice sessions were held within a six-week period, each session including twenty-one 1-minute trials. Subgroups were then retained (as a test for retention) after periods ranging from one to twenty-four months. Some groups were retrained by use of a massed practice schedule (four continuous practice sessions), while other groups followed a distributed schedule (four practices scheduled one day apart). In analyzing the data, the authors found that (1) retention of this continuous perceptual-motor skill was very high, even for periods up to twenty-four months; (2) the small loss in retention was recovered in the first few minutes of practice; (3) no drop in the retention curve was shown between the first and fourteenth month; however, a decline was shown at twenty-four months; (4) the most important factor in retention seemed to be the level of original learning, not the conditions under which learning took place; and (5) retraining was more effective when practices were distributed rather than massed.

Ammons et al. (1956) conducted two experiments to determine the long-term retention of a complex type of compensatory pursuit skill and a second task involving sequential manipulation of controls. The task was learned by 538 male college subjects under twelve practice conditions, and they were given retention tests after periods ranging from one minute to two years. The authors found that loss in level of proficiency was not affected by degree of original learning. However, the groups with less original practice were poorer in proficiency at both the conclusion of practice and the retention test. Retraining to the earlier level of proficiency took longer for the groups having a longer no-practice period and for groups which had a higher original level of retention.

In two studies involving the skill of mirror tracing, Oxendine found practically no loss in skill for periods to four weeks. In one study (1959), junior high school boys practiced two days a week for five weeks. After a period of three weeks without practice, all groups showed reminiscence at a retention test. The subgroup which had followed the schedule of short practices showed the greatest reminiscence. In another study by Oxendine (1965), college students practiced mirror tracing daily for ten consecutive schools days. After a four-week period without practice, only a slight loss in retention was shown. In fact, all subgroups performed at a level which was equivalent to their ninth practice day.

Retention of continuous versus discrete motor skills

Earlier in the chapter it was pointed out that Gagné and Fleishman stated that continuous motor activities are remembered longer than those which are discrete. Naylor and Briggs (1961) and Fleishman and Parker (1962) support this statement. Continuous activities are those which require repetitive or sustained effort such as walking, swimming, skating, juggling or bicycle riding. Discrete skills require a singular exertion or short-term effort. Such activities as a dart throw, a billiard shot, a soccer kick, or a basketball foul shot are examples of discrete skills. However, the distinction between continuous and discrete activities has not yet been clearly delineated. Some tasks are serial, requiring a sequence of progressive movements which are not repetitive in nature. These tasks seem to fit into neither the continuous nor discrete category. Activities such as bowling, fancy dives, the high jump, and the basketball lay-up shot require a particular approach and execution of a rather complex task. Since the total sequence of their movements seems to fall between the continuous and discrete groups, perhaps the retentiveness of these skills should be moderate.

There is little clear evidence to support the Gagné and Fleishman theory regarding distinctions in remembering different types of motor skills. However, there is a traditional belief that people never forget how to swim or to ride a bicycle. On the other hand, people notice that after several years a great deal of proficiency may be lost in diving, a golf shot, the soccer kick, or in basketball shooting. There are two important reasons, however, why the continuous-type skills might seem to have greater retention even if no such advantage existed. First, the continuous activities usually involve a great deal of overlearning. Participation usually requires numerous repetitions of the same movement; for example, after a child first learns to walk, each step involves overlearning.

Each additional stroke in swimming promotes overlearning. The same holds true for skating, bicycle riding, or juggling. For most people, it is not likely that a springboard dive would be performed as many times as a running step, or that a hook slide in baseball would be performed as frequently as a pedal revolution in a bicycle ride. The factor of overlearning is, undoubtedly, strategic in aiding certain continuous activities to be remembered longer than many discrete skills.

Another factor which supports the appearance of greater retention of tasks such as swimming and skating is the fitness level of the performer. The man of fifty who has not been swimming for thirty years has the necessary fitness level to swim, at least for a short distance. He is physically fit for skating or riding a bicycle. At the same time, he might not have enough flexibility, leg power, and agility to perform very effectively a gymnastic stunt, fancy dive, jump shot, or hook slide. Although inability to *perform* certain tasks is not synonymous with *forgetting*, these two factors are often assumed to be the same.

A third reason why continuous activities may seem to be remembered longer is that a low level of skill is more evident in certain of these tasks. With 50 per cent loss in skill, the individual would still be able to exhibit basic maneuvers in skating, swimming, or bicycling. Perhaps the absence of more refined or advanced techniques is not immediately noticeable, especially when the individual expects a low level of performance. However, in certain discrete activities, a loss in accuracy, coordination, or speed is more obvious. For example, in billiards it is readily apparent that a shot is either successful or unsuccessful. The same is true in the basketball free throw, in horseshoe pitching, or in bowling. What is most apparent in discrete skills is not the overall body movement, as is the case with most continuous skills, but the *results* of the performance.

In summary

Retention of motor skills is quite similar to retention of verbal materials. Effective learning must take place before material will be well remembered. For motor and verbal tasks, meaningful or useful skills will be retained better than skills with no apparent purpose. Perhaps some physical skills are retained longer than verbal skills because such motor skills are more often overlearned. Skills which are overlearned will be retained better than those which are less well learned. Distributed practices are advantageous for retention as well as for original learning. Reviews should be most frequent soon after the learning has been accomplished. Practice with the intention of remembering and with an awareness of possible distractions will aid retention. Any activity following the learning period may interfere with material learned. However, interference is greater when the intervening activity is similar to the original learning. The more unique the learned activity, the less likely will be interference. Maximum retention can be promoted by overlearning skills and by regularly using them.

Good teaching involving appropriate motivating techniques, interesting learning tasks, and desirable practice conditions begets good learning. Good learning, in turn, begets good retention.

SELECTED READINGS

Deese, J. *The psychology of learning.* (2nd ed.) New York: McGraw-Hill, 1958.

Fleishman, E. A., & Parker J. "Factors in the retention and relearning of perceptual-motor skill." *J. exp. Psychol.*, 1962, 64, 215–226.

Gagné, R. M., & Fleishman, E. A. *Psychology and human performance.* New York: Holt, Rinehart and Winston, 1959.

Kingsley, H. L., & Garry, R., *The nature and conditions of learning.* (2nd ed.) Englewood Cliffs, N.J.: Prentice-Hall, 1957.

Krueger, W. C. F. The effect of overlearning on retention. *J. exp. Psychol.*, 1929, 12, 71–78.

Leavitt, H. J., & Schlosberg, H. The retention of verbal and of motor skill. *J. exp. Psychol.*, 1944, 34, 404–417.

McGeoch, J. A., & Irion, A. L. *The psychology of human learning.* New York: McKay, 1952.

Purdy, B. J., & Lockhart, A. Retention and relearning of gross motor skills after long periods of no practice. *Res. Quart.*, 1962, 33, 265–272.

Travers, R. M. W. *Essentials of learning.* New York: Macmillan, 1963.

Part **III**

THE STATE OF THE LEARNER

Introduction

Individuals vary a great deal in their readiness for learning at any given moment. Not only are differences shown among individuals, but also within the same person from time to time. No topic in education is more important than that of readiness to learn and perform. Determining readiness and promoting the proper state of preparedness are the basic aspects of this topic. This subject underlies the selection of appropriate tasks for the different age levels as well as the determination of proper techniques for teaching.

The physical educator has been concerned with the state of the learner in a different way than other teachers. He has been concerned with early physical growth and development as well as the mental maturity of young students. Not only must he select motor activities which the children are ready to perform, but he must also give consideration to which activities have the greatest potential for promoting readiness for more advanced skills to be encountered in the future.

Probably no type of human activity is more vividly affected by emotional arousal and general motivation than is the performance of motor skills. An investigation of the various states of arousal and their effects upon the learning and performance of different types of skills, is one of the major purposes of this section. Also of importance are techniques for promoting the desired motivational states for each type of performance. In this section, *the state of the learner* is considered in the following manner:

Chapter 6. Physical readiness
Chapter 7. Motivation

Chapter **6**

Physical readiness

At what age can a child be taught to tie his shoelaces, to do a cart-wheel? When can a boy learn to throw a curve ball, shoot a jump shot, or serve a tennis ball? When is a girl first able to handle a hockey stick effectively or thread a needle? Can special exercises lower the age at which these skills can be learned? These are all questions about *readiness*. They are extremely important for the educator who is interested in the grade placement of activities. Teachers are also interested in determining what skills and experiences are necessary prerequisites for the learning of these activities.

Parents, too, seek to know the age at which children will be able to perform certain tasks. For example, when should a child start walking? Will special practice enable one to be an early walker? How old must a child be before toilet training will be effective? What factors are involved in bringing about readiness for a boy to learn to tie a necktie or a girl to set her hair? During recent years, teachers in all subjects areas have developed a keen interest in the readiness of students to learn concepts and skills related to their particular subjects. The interest in readiness aims at matching instruction with pupil characteristics.

Individuals learn and perform best when they are ready. This state-ment, though true, is only of moderate benefit to the teacher who is interested in specific information for program planning. Teachers and parents need to know what "readiness" means for each activity. They need to know how readiness can be determined; how it can be hastened; and what type of readiness can be expected at various age levels.

Readiness to learn refers to a condition of the individual that makes a particular task an appropriate one for him to master. Readiness for motor learning is dependent upon a combination of physical and mental maturation, prerequisite learning, the individual's motivation for the task, and his feelings about the situation.

The scope of readiness

The topic of readiness is much more complex than was suspected a few years ago. Traditionally, it was assumed that motor learning depended solely on physical maturation, while verbal learning depended only on intellectual development. It has recently been pointed out, however, that the concept of readiness is not quite so simple. The interrelationship of physical, mental, and emotional factors in readiness has been emphasized by Cronbach (1954), Ausubel (1963), and Watson (1962). The following statement by Cronbach illustrates the complexity of the concept of readiness:

All aspects of development interact. A change in any facet of the child's readiness can alter his whole system of responses. When the normal sequence of development is interrupted in any way, effects are to be seen throughout the child's development.

Physiological maturing prepares one to profit from experience. Biological changes, especially in the nervous system, influence what one can learn. Pupils who differ in rate of maturing have different experiences and develop different personalities. . . .

Certain times in life are formative periods, which have a great effect on readiness for a particular activity. The period when a person first has a chance to engage in an activity is especially important. The formative period for physical skill is, roughly, from age 1 to 4. From the time he learns to creep through the "runabout age," the child is establishing a basic coordination pattern and developing confidence or timidity. The usual formative period for attitudes regarding one's intellectual abilities, reading, work with numbers, and school work in general is the first year or so of schooling. Success, failure, challenge, and conflict at that time precondition the reaction to all later schooling (pp. 89–90).

Ausubel (1963) states that the two principal factors in readiness are maturation (increments in capacity that take place in the absence of practice experience) and learning (specific practice on incidental experience). He indicates that a combination of the two is usually important, although for certain tasks only one might be strategic.

Numerous examples of the interrelationships of physiological and psychological phenomena can be pointed out. For example, a poor physical self-image can adversely influence all aspects of a young person's intellectual, social, and physical development. Physical exhaustion can greatly limit the extent of a student's intellectual pursuit. Similarly, a person who is limited in intellectual ability will have difficulty in learning a complex motor skill. In addition, he will have serious difficulty in adapting to intricate teamwork and strategy. It is therefore unwise to assume that mental and physical maturation are separate and contribute to only one phase of the individual's development.

It is readily apparent that different levels of physiological maturity are essential for the learning of different motor skills. Usually children are ready for large and simple movement skills earlier than for fine and complex movements. It is therefore largely a waste of time to offer specific instruction in a fine skill before children have reached an appropriate level of maturity. It is also clear that certain activities cannot be taught before an appropriate level of psychological maturity has been established. For example, children cannot learn to swim well while they are afraid of the water. Fifth-grade boys will have difficulty in learning to dance if they feel this activity is not appropriate for boys.

It is now generally accepted that interest is a strategic factor in affecting one's readiness to learn physical or verbal skills. Consider, for example, the reluctance of a group of eighth-grade boys to seriously practice dribbling a basketball properly. If this same group of boys had recently seen the high school star freeze the ball with his deft dribbling for the last sixty seconds in an important game they would be more ready to learn. Young children will be much more receptive to the learning of safety rules for descending stairs after a classmate has been injured on the stairs. The adolescent girl will be ready to learn to set her hair if her girl-friends are also learning the skill, or if she suspects a connection between hairdos and the interest of boys. These illustrations emphasize that readiness for the learning of a motor skill is not merely a matter of physical maturation.

Because of the interaction of physical, mental, and emotional factors in determining one's readiness for learning, it is often impossible to pinpoint the reason for a child's inability to learn a particular task. The difficulty may result either from physiological immaturity or simply from a lack of interest.

Despite the difficulty in discussing the various aspects of readiness separately, this chapter will be devoted primarily to the *physiological* factors of readiness for motor learning and performance. Chapter 7 will deal with factors related to psychological readiness.

Background of school readiness

The current interest in, and understanding of, readiness dates back to Thorndike's law of readiness (1913). This law referred primarily to emotional response to action or expected action. Today, the concept of readiness is broader than that proposed by Thorndike and is generally used in reference to learning or performance readiness. In the original law, the three circumstances for readiness are described as follows:

1. When a conduction unit is ready to conduct, conduction by it is satisfying, nothing being done to alter its action.
2. For a conduction unit ready to conduct not to conduct is annoying, and provokes whatever response nature provides in connection with that particular annoying lack.
3. When a conduction unit unready for conduction is forced to conduct, conduction by it is annoying (p. 128).

The rather vague term of "conduction unit" has been interpreted by Hilgard (1956) as "action tendency." In reference to this, he states that, "When an action tendency is aroused through preparatory adjustments, sets, attitudes, and the like, fulfillment of the tendency in action is satisfying, non-fulfillment is annoying. Readiness thus means a preparation for action (p. 18)". Hilgard indicates that Thorndike did not develop, or even foresee, readiness for learning in the broad sense that it is understood today. He says ". . . it would be historically inaccurate to construe his law of readiness as an anticipation of maturational readiness" (p. 19).

In recent years, the topic of readiness has developed into one of the major topics of interest at the elementary school level. Reading readiness has received perhaps the greatest amount of attention. Readiness for drawing, printing, and writing has also come in for considerable study. Relatively little attention, however, has been devoted to the necessary preparation for learning gross motor skills.

In regard to school learning, Bruner (1963) has stated that any subject can be taught effectively in some intellectually honest fashion to any child at any stage of development. Such a position would seem to deny the need for educators to give special attention to readiness for particular activities. At the same time, his *spiral curriculum* is designed to enlarge upon the more basic concepts as the child develops greater ability and supporting concepts. Bruner's theory is disputed by Piaget (1966) who believes that the biological character of development limits learning or the understanding of concepts to a particular level of difficulty. Havighurst (1966), by stating that many concepts are beyond the capacity of first graders to comprehend, also disagrees with Bruner.

Components of physiological readiness

For the purpose of this discussion physiological readiness for motor performances will include (1) maturation, (2) general motor development, and (3) prerequisite skills. These terms, with "growth and development," are often used almost interchangeably. Distinctions between them are not always clear because different authors indicate overlapping definitions. However, in this discussion, *maturation* is referred to as the early physiological development which increases the individual's motor capability or capacity to learn movement skills. Maturation is a phylogenetic development, only slightly affected by environmental conditions. This process occurs early in life, being most prominent in the first years but continuing into the teens or early twenties. Some authors even indicate that maturation continues throughout life.

General motor development refers to the improvement of one's motor abilities as a result of practice or experience. Such components as strength, coordination, speed, balance, and agility are fully developed only if certain exercise programs are available. The same is true for such basic movement tasks as running, skipping, climbing, throwing, and kicking. A deprived or seriously limited environment retards the development of each of these basic tasks. General motor development, as used in this discussion, most closely relates to growth and development as popularly used. Growth, however, simply refers to an increase in body size.

Prerequisite learning refers to the development of particular skills which are, in turn, used in the learning or performance of more advanced patterns of movement. Prerequisite skills are relatively basic movements upon which more sophisticated skills are built. For example, ability to do a simple two-step is a prerequisite to learning the polka. Progression in teaching a particular activity is usually a matter of developing the necessary prerequisites in logical order. The significance of each component of physiological readiness for physical education will be presented in the following sections.

MATURATION

Maturation is defined by Eichorn and Jones (1958) as the emergence of any characteristics whose form and timing are chiefly controlled genetically. The development of these hereditary characteristics is primarily dependent upon neurological functioning and occurs during the early life of the individual. Maturation is only slightly affected by variations in nutrition, exercise, and other environmental conditions; it occurs essentially without effort by the individual. Although it does not produce learning, maturation makes learning possible.

Motor skills are not developed until the child's neuromuscular system is sufficiently ready. When the required maturation level has been reached, the responses (grasping, walking, talking, etc.) will normally be made. However, the emergence of these skills does not occur suddenly and automatically with maturity. The child can be trained more easily and quickly if he has reached a full state of physiological readiness for the specific activity. Therefore, the role of the teacher and the parent in promoting motor skill learning is to determine the time at which children are ready to learn skills and then to arrange a learning situation which is most effective for the development of the skills.

Research in maturation has generally been designed to determine (1) at what age certain types of skills can be learned most effectively, and (2) if special training can speed the learning of certain skills. The studies have usually compared two groups of young children who take part in training at different chronological ages. This type of research has involved training in such diverse tasks as walking, talking, toilet training, climbing, throwing, and handling tools.

After studying different groups of children over two and seven year periods, Shirley (1933) and Bayley (1934) pointed out considerable consistency of behavior among them. Phylogenetic influences on early development seemed to be more influential than did environmental conditions. Children who had been compared by heredity seemed to develop the capacity to learn basic skills at about the same time. Several studies involving young twins have generally shown that the child who is untrained in the special task, with less practice at a later time is able to catch up to the trained child. Even though some early advantage might be shown for the practicing group, these advantages are usually slight and are generally lost when the nonpracticing group begins work on the task at a maturer physiological level. Both Shirley and Bayley observed that serious illness or restriction of activity can slow maturation somewhat, but the social status of the parents seemed to make no difference in the maturation process.

Most rapid changes in maturation take place during the early years. The rate of maturation follows a descending curve until its completion in the early twenties. Bayley (1936) found that gross motor coordinations mature more rapidly than mental functions during the first two years of life. After this age, motor progress is comparatively slower. She reported a moderate correlation between measured mental and motor development during the first fifteen months. The relationship was lower thereafter. She found that performance in motor tests was less consistent than in mental tests. Cratty (1964) describes maturation in a broader context. He indicates that maturation continues throughout the life of the individual and views aging as the terminal phase of the process.

Developmental stages

During recent years, various authors have identified several stages of early human development. A great deal of agreement can be noted among the different authorities. Piaget (1954) describes two stages of intellectual development: (1) Sensorimotor, which occurs during the first two years of life, and (2) conceptual, which occurs from two years until maturity. During the first two years, the coordination of simple actions seems dominant over the mental activity of the child. Piaget suggested that marked retardation in sensorimotor development at one year may be an indication of future conceptual retardation of the child. He differentiated the sensorimotor phase of development into six stages. The first month of life is referred to as the *reflexes* stage and is characterized by the prominence of simple reflexes. The second stage, which occurs during the second and third months, is referred to as *primary circular reactions*. During this period, the child engages in repetitive motor actions such as the opening and closing of fists or other simple movement of the hands. These actions are performed without any goal-directed purpose and without any result in which the child seems interested.

Piaget referred to the third stage of development as *secondary circular reactions*. The repetitive or rhythmical movements during this period (four to six months) seem to be performed because of the results which they produce. For example, the child may kick repeatedly because he enjoys the results of his actions. This kicking action may cause a suspended toy to swing vigorously over his crib or make his coach squeak or vibrate. Unlike the previous stage, the child seems to engage in these actions because he enjoys the change in environment that results. *Coordination of secondary reactions* occurs from the seventh to the tenth month. During this stage the child performs a learned response in order to obtain a desired goal. Simple problem solving, such as pushing a pillow out of the way in order to obtain a toy which is hidden under it, may begin during this period. Piaget refers to the fifth stage as *tertiary circular movements*. This developmental phase occurs from the eleventh to the eighteenth month and marks the beginning of trial-and-error experimentation. The child will use different responses to obtain the same goals. He learns that his actions can have considerable effect on the situation around him. The last of the six stages, *mental combinations*, takes place from the eighteenth month. During this period, the child learns to think through certain actions, considering possible consequences, before acting. This elementary foresight marks the beginning of conceptual thought. More advanced levels of conceptualization evolve during the remainder of childhood.

McGraw (1943) has identified four periods of neurological growth during the first two years of life which are similar to those described by Piaget. The first period covers roughly the first four months and is characterized by reflexes and rhythmical movements of the newborn child. The second period ranges from the fourth to the eighth or ninth month. There is a reduction of activity in the pelvic girdle and lower extremities with an increase in voluntary movement in the upper spinal region. The third period ranges from eight to fourteen months and is evidenced by increased control of lower spinal region. Months fifteen through twenty-four are included in the fourth period, which characterized by the rapid development of associational processes including communication.

Mussen, Conger, and Kagan (1963) suggest three major developmental trends during the child's early development. One of these is a *cephalocaudal* trend, which refers to the early development of the upper parts of the body. This tendency is evidenced by greater proficiency in head movements, visual skill, and eye-hand coordination during the early months, and the late development of walking and eye-foot coordination. Motor responses also develop in a *proximodistal* direction, from the central to the peripheral areas of the body. According to these authors, the shoulders, upper arms, and upper legs are controlled more quickly than are the forearms and hands, or the lower legs and feet.

The third trend described by Mussen et al. refers to a *mass-to-specific* muscular development, which indicates that children develop gross body movements and skills prior to the development of specific, or fine, skills. In addition, movements become more refined so that excess or wasted movements are gradually eliminated, and only necessary movements are used for more efficient performance.

Several studies have been conducted in recent years in an effort to determine the role of maturation in the learning of certain motor tasks, the age at which children can most effectively learn different skills, and whether special exercises or practice can speed maturation or physiological readiness.

Effect of special exercises

A number of maturational studies have involved identical twins. These co-twin control studies have advantages because the two subjects have identical hereditary characteristics. In these experiments, one child begins practice on a particular task such as walking, stair climbing, or on finer skills such as cutting with scissors. The second child does not begin practice at the same time, but usually begins a training program or is tested a few weeks or months later. The early practicing and late practicing twins are usually compared on (1) initial performance scores, (2) length of time required to reach a particular skill level, and (3) general proficiency at some later date.

Gesell and Thompson at the Yale University Child Development Center have conducted a number of studies with identical twins to determine the role of maturation in the learning of skills. In one study (1929), they had one child begin a daily program of stair-climbing sessions at the age of 46 weeks. After six weeks of this practice (at 52 weeks) the child was able to climb the staircase in 25.8 seconds. Practice was then discontinued for the first child, and one week later the other child began a similar training schedule. On the first practice day, the second twin climbed the stairs in 45 seconds. However, in just two weeks of training, this child was able to climb the stairs in 10.3 seconds. The two weeks of training at 53 to 55 weeks were therefore more effective for this task than were six weeks at the ages of 46 to 52 weeks. When practice was resumed for both groups at 56 weeks, the two children were practically identical in performance. McGraw (1943) reported similar results in a stair-climbing study.

Hilgard (1933) conducted an early study in which one twin (about five years of age) was given training in memory skills, tossing a ring over a peg, and walking a straight line on a narrow board. He found that the twin who was initially untrained caught up to the trained one in the performance of these skills and with fewer practices. He concluded that little was to be gained by early practice on complex skills. In another study, Hilgard (1932) trained children of two and three years in skills of climbing, buttoning, and cutting with scissors. In this study, the trained children showed superior skill immediately after the training session. After a very short practice period, however, the previously unpracticed group became as skillful as the trained children. He concluded that, when children are sufficiently mature for an activity, a short practice period is as effective as a much longer period before the children have reached the appropriate state of physiological readiness.

One of the most significant studies in maturation was reported by Dennis and Dennis (1940). They conducted a study with the Hopi Indians to determine the effect of freedom of movement on the speed with which walking would be learned. While most of the mothers bound their children to cradle boards, which limited the movement of most parts of their body, the researchers persuaded some women to free their children at an early age to allow greater movement of their legs. If walking were a skill which could be learned earlier as a result of greater activity, it seemed that the less restricted children should learn to walk earlier. In this study, however, it was reported that the bound and unbound children learned to walk at about the same time. The authors concluded that learning to walk was dependent upon maturation and would not be learned earlier because of greater freedom of movement.

Despite the inability of special exercises to appreciably speed maturation or the development of special skills, studies have shown some latent advantages for the exercising group. In one study, Gesell and Thompson (1929) reported that the twin who practiced stair climbing had greater agility, was more skillful, and less fearful than the control twin after both had learned to climb stairs. McGraw (1946) reported similar findings in a study of motor development. Whereas initial tests indicated that a program of regular practice was of little value in the early stages of learning, a four-year follow-up study showed that the trained subject was more skillful and confident in the skills which he had practiced. Mirenvo (1935) found that twins who were specifically trained in jumping, throwing for accuracy, and bowling showed greater improvement than siblings who were not specifically trained. Rarick and McKee (1949) showed that children who had better play facilities performed better on tests of running, jumping, balance, agility, catching, and throwing. Nevertheless, these authors have not generally advocated special exercise programs for children during the first two or three years of life.

Restricted activity and maturation

Although special exercises do not seem to be especially valuable for the early development of skills, lack of activity may prove a hindrance to physical growth and skill development. Individuals who have had an arm or leg in a cast for a period of a few weeks will agree that atrophy takes place in a rather short period. Situations in which lesser degrees of inactivity are imposed will result in a lesser amount of atrophy. A number of studies have been conducted in which the learner was deprived of normal activity. These deprivation studies have generally shown that unusual restriction of movement or experience will limit one's normal maturation.

Studies of controlled deprivation of children have not proven popular with parents. However, a number of studies have been conducted with animals to show that those which are seriously deprived of movement over a long period will not develop in a normal manner. Also, if other types of learning experiences are restricted, the animal will be limited in his development. In one significant study, Nissen (1951) reared a chimpanzee without restriction, except that it was unable to explore its environment with its hands and feet. These appendages were covered with cardboard tubes for two and one-half years. After the coverings were removed, the animal exhibited extremely retarded behavior and never developed normally thereafter.

Hebb (1958) reported an experiment in which a dog was reared in a situation where it did not have opportunities to learn normal self-protection techniques. When the animal was later released into a more typical situation, it showed an inability to avoid bumping its head on a low pipe. It took this dog far longer than the normal dog to learn routine measures of self-protection. On other occasions, when animals have been reared in darkness, they failed to show visual discrimination when brought into the light.

In light of these findings, it seems fortunate that children have the urge for activity and change. Exploratory movement, even random activity, is apparently essential for normal development. The capacity of children for getting bored, therefore, appears to be a desirable characteristic. Mednick (1964) reported a study in which university students were offered twenty dollars for every twenty-four-hour period they would spend in an especially unstimulating environment. The subjects were to lie on foam rubber beds with cardboard cuffs around their arms and with translucent goggles over their eyes. In addition they were to stay in a soundproof room. They could earn one hundred dollars for five days of this nonactivity. Few of the students, however, were able to continue this regimen for more than two or three days. The subjects reported that they experienced hallucinations and sometimes became panicky. In addition, they had difficulty sleeping or even thinking clearly. They performed poorly on intelligence tests which were given while they were in the room. Upon emerging from this restricted environment, many were confused, nauseated, disoriented, and fatigued for periods up to twenty-four hours.

Monkeys, rats, and other animals also show a need for activity and stimulus change. Researchers have shown that animals learn in some situations when the only reward is a change in scenery. Monkeys can be trained to push a particular panel which allows them to observe other monkeys, or even people, in a different room. On subsequent occasions, they open the panel to watch what is happening on the outside.

The need for change, both in movement and in what one observes, is strong enough to cause both men and animals to bring about changes. Normal activities and stimulations appear to be strategic for normal maturation. Special restrictions in activity seem to result in restricted development.

Hicks (1931) reported that young children benefited very little from practicing the complex task of hitting a moving target. He concluded that, for young children, the important need is for general environmental activity rather than specific skill practice. A study of Williams and Scott (1953) on motor development during infancy supports the need for activity during this period. Two groups of Negro infants from sharply contrasting socioeconomic backgrounds were compared. The low economic group showed significantly greater development in motor skills than did the higher economic group. The authors belived that this difference was attributable to a permissive atmosphere and absence of cribs, play pens, high chairs and similar restrictive equipment in the low socioeconomic homes.

Lawther (1959) indicated that the great developmental need of children is practice or opportunity for development at a time when they can benefit from it. He especially encouraged the use of developmental facilities and equipment at home and school. Further, he reported that basic skills, such as eating and drinking, are best established if children are allowed practice without pressure or punishment. Lawther pointed out, however, that special practice or parental encouragement prior to the child's maturational readiness is largely futile.

GENERAL MOTOR DEVELOPMENT

In addition to maturation, which usually takes place as a normal function of growing older, physical educators must also concern themselves with the development of motor capacities and the physical growth of the students. Physical fitness and general motor capacities are to a large extent dependent upon exercise or practice. These capacities are, in turn, important in establishing one's readiness to learn and perform more advanced skills.

The student cannot learn a routine on the parallel bars without first developing a degree of arm and shoulder strength. Agility and skill in footwork are essential for successful participation in handball. General body coordination and balance are needed for the learning of precise movements in a dance activity. Components such as strength, endurance, flexibility, and eye-hand coordination are strategic for participation in many motor activities. Different tasks are dependent upon, or emphasize, different capacities. Of course, various levels of performance require greater or lesser degrees of these capacities. A very important function of the teacher is to determine the most essential components and the levels necessary for each type of activity and to guide the students into these activities when they are ready. Another critical function, of course, is to promote readiness by developing the basic motor capacities.

The activity of an individual through his elementary school years will, to a great extent, determine his readiness for a wide variety of activities or a few specific sports at the junior high school level. Activity tends to promote readiness for further activity. The best way of promoting readiness for learning and performance in motor activities is by encouraging general physical activity. This broad base of activity can be instrumental in the development of basic components essential for participation in a wide variety of activities.

Numerous studies have shown that children of various ages who take part more regularly in physical activities score higher in motor capacity tests than do those who are less active. Rarick and McKee (1949) showed that superior performers in the third grade had a history of greater activity participation than did children with inferior performance. McCraw (1956) reported that junior high school boys who took part in varsity athletics scored higher than nonparticipants in tasks of running speed, the standing broad jump, and the softball throw. There are dangers, however, in generalizing from these studies about the value of these activities in motor development. It is not clearly established whether superior motor capacities were the cause or the result of greater participation in these activities. Most likely there is substance to both of these possibilities. There can be no doubt, however, that under well-controlled conditions, an increase in physical activity can result in improvement in most motor capacities. This improvement often represents an increase in readiness for various activities.

It is universally agreed today that muscular size and strength can be developed by physical activity. Numerous research reports describe the role of exercise in this process. Studies generally show that athletes exhibit greater development in all basic components of motor capacity than do nonathletes. McCraw (1956) reported that during a school semester athletes grew more in height and weight than did nonathletes. Kusinitz and Keeney (1958) found that favorable anthropometric changes took place in adolescent boys as a result of weight training. In these boys, waist girth declined while other measurements increased. Jokl (1964) compared men who were gymnasts with their twin brothers who did not take part regularly in any sports activity. The gymnasts had broader shoulders and were stronger and heavier than their brothers. The effect of exercise on muscular size and strength can usually be seen when one compares the most-used and least-used arms of professional baseball pitchers, bowlers, tennis players, or even carpenters.

Developing basic motor capacities and movement skills is a prime responsibility of physical educators, especially at the elementary school level. At the same time, it is difficult to develop basic skills among children who come to class with great variation in ability, without making the class especially repetitious and uninteresting for the advanced students. Unnecessary repetition has often been a valid criticism of many physical education programs. It seems possible, however, that practice on a particular trait might occur without repetition of the same activity. The needed skill can be incorporated into a new activity. For example, the skill of skipping may be used as part of a basic rhythm unit in the first grade. Perhaps not all of the students will develop a high level of proficiency at this time. In a later grade, a different activity such as "Skip to My Lou" might be used. This activity, which involves practice in skipping, may be new to the children. As a greater proportion of students learn to skip well, less time should be devoted to this activity. Other basic skills, such as throwing, catching, and kicking, can be brought into several activities in the same manner. The technique of changing the activity to improve the same skill will prove more valuable for students who develop early proficiency than will continuing practice of the same activity.

Motor development during childhood

Children today are maturing earlier and are taller and heavier than their parents were a generation ago. Much of this earlier development is assumed to result from improved dietary practices. The increase in physical size is apparently greater than any difference in general motor ability or capacity. Despite outstanding athletic performances by a few teenagers, today's young people in general do not appear to be stronger, faster, or more flexible than the children of forty years ago. For tests in which comparable scores can be obtained, such as in strength and motor educability, today's children do not have the same superiority they do in physical size.

General statements about the readiness of an individual or group are of limited value. Readiness is always relative to the particular subject, topic, level of difficulty, and method used. Any age group in school represents different stages of development. Even a single individual may, for a time, waver back and forth in his readiness for a particular task. However, norm tables regarding age-level characteristics provide some information regarding average or typical development.

During the preschool years, there is a gradual improvement in the child's ability to run smoothly, to turn corners sharply, and to start and stop. These locomotor skills continue to develop into the primary grades. Gutteridge (1939) compared the motor development of children from three to seven years of age. Very rapid development was seen between ages four and seven in hopping, skipping, throwing, and galloping. At age seven, nearly all children were rated as proficient in each of the activities. Gross motor movement and coordination develop especially fast during this period.

Seils (1951) investigated the motor development of children in grades one, two, and three. Boys and girls were compared on a variety of motor ability tests according to grade level and age (broken into three-month groups). The children were tested in running, balance, agility, jumping, throwing, and striking. Generally, Seils found a gradual or consistent improvement in each of the components from grades one, two, and three. A few exceptions were found among girls, who often did not exhibit a significant improvement between grades one and two. However, grade three scores were always higher than those for grade two. When students were further grouped according to three-month age differentials, they generally showed a consistent improvement with each succeeding advancement in age. In addition to better performance at each level, it was found that students were taller and heavier. The increase in size was reasonably steady. While a moderate correlation was shown between performance and skeletal maturity, the relationship of physical size and age to performance was considerably lower.

It has been shown in research, and observed in general practice, that children who are strong or who have outstanding motor skills, retain essentially the same relative position in the group as they grow older. It is rare that these skills or capacities develop suddenly or are lost rapidly. Slight changes, however, may be made. Children who are low in motor capacities are often raised to the normal range. It appears more difficult to develop the average performer into an outstanding one.

Children become stronger as they grow older. Furthermore, the increase in strength is greater than the increase in body size. There appears to be a qualitative as well as quantitive change in muscle tissue. Rarick (1965) indicates that the muscle tissue actually becomes stronger or has the ability to mobilize more units. In addition, Asmussen and Heebell-Nielsen (1955) report that the effective use of strength becomes greater as the nervous system matures. This is exhibited in such activities as running and jumping.

Sex differences in motor development

Bontz (1948) found that elementary school girls were superior to boys in fine movement activities. Boys proved to be superior to girls in gross motor activities. Bayley (1934), however, found little difference between boys and girls in motor ability. Garry (1963) reported that the motor ability of boys and girls is similar until adolescence. Table 3 contains some average physical performance scores for boys and girls from ages five to seventeen. It can be noted that, among young children, boys perform better than girls in practically all items included. Boys seem to have a distinct advantage in throwing and in strength items. The only measure in which girls perform as well as the boys is in the Brace Test of Motor Educability. It must be pointed out, however, that the types of items included here are those which culture emphasizes more for boys than for girls. Perhaps if skipping, balancing, or coordination activities had been included, girls would have performed as well or better. Differences in performance, therefore, apparently result from cultural as well as biological factors.

Rarick and Thompson (1956) showed that from an early age, the male possesses more muscle tissue per unit of body weight, and that he is stronger per unit of muscle mass than is the female. Sex hormones play a prominent role in motor performance. In males, hormones favor strength development more than in females. Bayley (1951), however, showed that girls who ranked high in the masculinity physique were stronger per unit of body weight than were boys who had a feminine-type physique.

Sex and heredity play a major role in determining body type and composition. Research has shown that, as early as age two, girls have greater fat composition than do boys. Boys have heavier bones and greater muscular tissue. As children grow older, the differences in body composition become greater, reaching a peak during adolescence. Sheldon (1954) and several other authors indicate that body types are determined primarily by heredity and do not change a great deal from childhood.

Table 3

SOME MOTOR CAPACITIES OF CHILDREN FROM AGES FIVE TO SEVENTEEN

Age (years)	Yards run (per second)	Standing broad jump (inches)	Jump and reach (inches)	Brace motor educability (score)	Distance throw (feet)	Hand grip strength (pounds) right	Hand grip strength (pounds) left	AAHPER sit-ups (number completed)	600-yard run walk[a] (minutes and seconds)
BOYS									
5	3.8	33.7	2.5	–	23.6	–	–	–	–
6	4.2	37.4	4.0	5.5	32.8	–	–	–	–
7	4.6	41.6	6.1	7.5	42.3	28	28	–	–
8	5.1	46.7	8.3	9.0	57.4	31	31	–	–
9	–	50.4	8.5	10.0	66.6	38	38	–	–
10	5.9	54.7	11.0	11.0	83.0	44	43	41	2:33
11	6.1	61.0	11.5	11.1	95.0	51	50	46	2:27
12	6.3	64.9	12.2	12.7	104.0	62	59	50	2:21
13	6.5	69.3	12.5	13.1	114.0	74	67	60	2:10
14	6.7	73.2	13.3	14.5	123.0	89	81	70	2:01
15	6.8	79.5	14.8	15.2	135.0	101	92	80	1:54
16	7.1	88.0	16.3	16.2	144.0	–	–	76	1:51
17	7.2	88.4	16.9	15.9	153.0	–	–	70	1:50

150

Age (years)	Yards run (per second)	Standing broad jump (inches)	Jump and reach (inches)	Brace motor educability (score)	Distance throw (feet)	Hand grip strength (pounds) right	left	AAHPER sit-ups (number completed)	600-yard run walk[a] (minutes and seconds)
GIRLS									
5	3.6	31.6	2.2	—	14.5	—	—	—	—
6	4.1	36.2	3.5	5.5	17.8	—	—	—	—
7	4.4	40.0	5.7	7.5	25.4	23	22	—	—
8	4.6	45.9	7.7	9.0	30.0	28	27	—	—
9	—	51.3	8.7	10.0	38.7	31	31	—	—
10	5.8	—	10.5	10.5	47.0	37	36	31	2:48
11	6.0	52.0	11.0	11.1	54.0	42	42	30	2:49
12	6.1	—	11.2	11.8	61.0	53	51	32	2:49
13	6.3	62.1	11.0	11.8	70.0	60	56	31	2:52
14	6.2	62.7	11.8	11.9	74.5	66	61	30	2:46
15	6.1	63.2	12.2*	11.5	75.7	64	59	26	2:46
16	6.0	63.0	12.0	11.8	74.0	—	—	26	2:49
17	5.9	—	—	—	—	—	—	27	2:51

[a] Low numbers represent better scores.

Source: Data from the Figure "Relative strength indices for boys and girls" by Anna Espenschade from SCIENCE AND MEDICINE OF EXERCISE AND SPORTS edited by H. M. Barrow and R. McGee in A Practical Approach to Measurement in Physical Education, Philadelphia: Lea & Febiger, 1964, and the American Association for Health, Physical Education, and Recreation, AAHPER Youth Fitness Test Manual. Washington, D.C.: the Association, 1965. By permission.

Table 4 includes average height and weight records for boys and girls from ages five to eighteen. It can be observed that boys are slightly taller and heavier than girls up to age ten. For the next three years, girls take the lead over boys in both of these measures. The size differential in favor of girls reaches a peak at about age thirteen. After this, the growth spurt of the boys carries them past the girls in physical size.

Table 4

HEIGHT AND WEIGHT RECORDS FOR BOYS AND GIRLS

Age (years)	AVERAGE BOY		AVERAGE GIRL	
	Height (inches)	Weight (pounds)	Height (inches)	Weight (pounds)
5	43.8	42.8	43.2	41.4
6	46.3	48.3	45.6	46.5
7	49.6	54.1	48.1	52.2
8	52.0	60.1	50.4	58.1
9	53.3	66.0	52.3	63.8
10	55.2	71.9	54.6	70.3
11	56.8	77.6	57.0	78.8
12	58.9	84.4	59.6	87.6
13	61.0	93.0	61.8	99.1
14	64.0	107.6	62.8	108.4
15	66.1	120.1	63.4	113.5
16	67.6	129.7	63.9	117.0
17	68.4	136.2	64.0	119.1
18	68.7	139.0	64.0	119.9

Source: Adapted from HEALTH OBSERVATION OF SCHOOL CHILDREN by George M. Wheatley and Grace T. Hallock. Copyright 1951 McGraw-Hill Book Company. Used by permission of McGraw-Hill Book Company.

Motor development during the preteenage and adolescent years

Individual differences in body size and in motor ability become greatest during the adolescent years. This is especially apparent when one observes early maturers and late maturers. Boys and girls who mature early literally take off and leave the others. Early maturers, however, stop growing sooner and the late maturers close the gap to some extent but never completely.

Girls reach the maximum growth spurt approximately two years earlier than do boys. As a result, girls are taller and heavier at ages twelve and thirteen (see Table 4). Differences in time of maturation can cause considerable apprehension, especially for early maturing girls (who will appear unusually tall) and late maturing boys (who will be especially short).

Early sexual maturation influences strength development and motor performance in preteenage and adolescent children. Gain in strength is greatest as boys and girls approach puberty, but this increase slows down afterward. Late maturers may follow early maturers in this change by as much as three years. The increase in strength during the pubescent period is greater for boys than for girls. During this period, and thereafter, boys are superior in strength, jumping ability, speed, and power; while girls often excel in balance, hopping flexibility, and coordinated movements.

In general motor performance, girls usually show only slight improvement after the age of thirteen or fourteen. In fact, Table 3 shows that there is a decline for girls in some activities after this period. It is probable that this decline results more from cultural than from biological influences. There seems little doubt that girls *can* continue to improve motor performance for a time after age thirteen or fourteen. This has been shown by championship performances in many sports activities.

Readiness for fine muscular skills

The readiness of adolescent children to perform motor activities depends upon the particular activity to be performed. An example of the relationship between physical maturity and readiness to perform certain motor tasks can be cited from an experiment conducted by Fuzak (1961) with junior high school boys. He observed that:

After several years of teaching experience in industrial arts, it was observed that many junior high school pupils did not achieve reasonable success in a number of manipulative processes which they were expected to perform. It seemed not to matter how hard they tried, how much the teacher varied his teaching techniques, nor how intelligent they were; the pupils still did not achieve satisfactory results. At the same time, it was observed that older beginning pupils achieved satisfactorily on the same manipulative processes, with much less expended effort by the teacher and pupils. It was noted that the troublesome processes usually involved finger, wrist, elbow, and shoulder coordinations. The question, therefore, was raised as to the relationship of physical maturity to the readiness of pupils to learn to perform complex coordinative processes in industrial arts classes (p. 366).

In his experiment involving 322 junior high school students, Fuzak developed four tests to measure manipulative processes commonly carried on in industrial arts classes such as marking, scribing, rotating, tracing, and paring. The students' skills in each of these activities was then compared with a measure of maturity. The prime criterion for maturity was strength of grip, as measured by a simple hand dynomometer. The data showed a high positive relationship between hand strength and skill in the manipulative tests as indicated by test scores and judgments of raters.

Fuzak urged industrial arts teachers to screen their learning experiences and plan their programs so that larger muscle activities would be presented at the earlier grade levels and the more complex finger coordinations later. He concluded that:

Implications of a similar sort affect many portions of the junior high school program, where complex finger coordinative activities are carried on. Attention should be given by these teachers to the physical readiness of their pupils to satisfactorily engage in the learning experiences provided. Many pupils are driven away from learning activities involving complex finger coordinations (p. 379).

Fuzak's summary reflects a concern which is also felt by many physical educators regarding the appropriateness of certain complex motor activities in the elementary and junior high schools. General statements and hypotheses can be made regarding types of activities which are appropriate for children at different grade levels. However, specific information cannot be obtained without detailed investigation of maturation and motor capacities in relation to each activity.

Children in endurance activities

It has traditionally been assumed that vigorous or endurance activities are inappropriate for children and preteenage youth. Medical authorities and educators have generally believed that such activities were injurious to the health of children, and further, that children were incapable of these activities. Several persons in recent years have questioned both of these assumptions. Cureton (1964) and Astrand (1952) have recently reported research dealing with cardiovascular and respiratory functioning among children who are engaged in activity programs. In a study of the aerobic capacity of young children, Astrand reported that boys seven to eleven years of age and girls seven to nine years old reach practically the same oxygen intake as adults. In studies to determine endurance capacities of children, Cureton has used such measurements as oxygen intake, rate of oxygen debt, blood pressure, and electrocardiograms to determine physiological responses to exercise. He has concluded that there is no evidence that a graduated progressive training program is injurious to the health of children.

Incidents are frequently reported in which young children perform outstanding feats of athletic strength or endurance. It was reported recently that an eight-year-old boy in New Jersey regularly competes in races of five to ten miles. Enough similar cases are observed to indicate that many children can perform activities of greater endurance than are usually recommended for regular school programs. Some physical educators who are convinced that children *can* engage in greater endurance events question the advisability of such activities. Cureton suggests, however, that programs which are limited in vigorous endurance activities (as are most school programs today) do not effect important changes in motor development. Rather, he recommends more endurance activities such as running, swimming, rowing, and cycling.

Nevertheless, medical authorities encourage caution in the selection of vigorous activities for health reasons. In view of the possibility that greater development may result from endurance programs, more research is needed on this topic. Continued acceptance of traditional beliefs (even of medicine) without evidence is unwise. Not to be ignored, of course, are the possible psychological implications of programs of strenuous activities. Longitudinal studies are necessary to determine the physiological and psychological implications.

Readiness among adults

Despite the adage that "Old dogs can't learn new tricks," adults and adolescents often have a greater readiness for learning than younger children. Ausubel (1963) states that older persons can learn any new material easier than younger children when neither have any background in the particular discipline. He surmises that this is because older persons can draw on transferable elements of their overall ability and make applications. Apparently, older people understand methods of investigating problems better than younger children. These methods aid one in learning new material. This readiness on the part of adults for learning motor skills is, of course, dependent upon their having the physical capability for *performing* the specific task.

There are occasional situations where children are more ready to learn certain materials or skills than adults. This is true in the case of negative transfer on the part of adults. If an adult has learned a skill the wrong way, he must unlearn the incorrect response before learning the right way. This would give the person with no previous experience an advantage. Occasionally older persons have less enthusiasm than young children for taking part in a certain activity. This motivation, of course, would affect readiness to learn material. Nevertheless, the adult or older child is generally more ready to learn than the younger child.

In today's world of greater leisure, early retirement, and longer life, there is greater interest in the capability of adults. When does one reach his physiological peak? How does this period vary for different activities? Is there a rapid decline in performance potential? These are some questions which have gained importance in recent years.

A newspaper recently carried a report of an eighty-year-old man who made a bicycle trip from New York to California. A man in North Carolina recently ran fifty-nine miles in one day to celebrate his fifty-ninth birthday. A thirteen-year-old boy was the top United States figure skater in the 1964 Olympics. A number of girls at the ages of thirteen and fourteen years have made the Olympic swimming and gymnastic teams. These statements are not particularly startling, since such occurrences have become rather commonplace in today's world. Age differences among Olympic participants usually span more than fifty years. These facts show that traditional ideas about a short period of peak performance potential, assumed to be in the early twenties, with a sharp decline thereafter can no longer be accepted. Age does not appear to be the restrictive factor that it was considered a few years ago.

At almost any adult age, individuals seem to be able to participate with success in a wide variety of activities. Skills requiring accuracy, speed, steadiness, great energy output, and endurance are characteristic of the activities of all ages. One of the most complete studies of age and athletic performance was reported by Jokl (1964) with members of the 1952 Olympics in Helsinki. He found that, although there were differences in mean ages and ranges of age for participants in the different sports, a great deal of overlapping existed among the participants' ages.

Average ages, and age ranges for participants of different events did reveal some general patterns in Jokl's study. The mean age for all men swimmers was less than twenty-two years. This may be compared with an average age of thirty-seven for those in shooting competition. The youngest competitors were engaged in cycling, boxing, running short distances, and jumping. The oldest participants (average age over thirty) were found in fencing, marathon running, walking, equestrian, and shooting events.

It has often been asserted that the violent or anaerobic events were associated with younger performers, while older persons excelled in the longer endurance events. This was generally supported by Jokl's study, but there are notable exceptions. For example, the grueling five-hour cycling event (190.4 kilometer road race) included participants with an average age of only twenty-two years. The swimming endurance race also involved young men whose average age was twenty-one years. Of course, in these activities, whether the distance was short or long, young men tended to enter more often than older men.

In reference to a longer participation life, Jokl states:

On the basis of favourable endowment and good environment, physical training may render an adolescent boy or girl maximally efficient physically and enable him to maintain a high level of bodily fitness until near the end of his life . . . Participation in athletic activities of one kind or another is now possible almost throughout the whole length of life. This conclusion is supported by the description of several hundred gymnasts, male and female who competed in the Marburg Alter-Turn-Fest, with many of the men over seventy-five, and many of the women over fifty-five years old . . .

Individual cases of middle age and old men or women with outstanding physical performance capacity have been known for a long time. What is new is that nowadays such cases become common, as the age distribution in the various Olympic events illustrates; and that even top level performances in athletics are now within the reach of men and women above 40 and 50 and 60 (pp. 92–93).[1]

Physiological readiness for learning and performing motor skills lasts for a long period. Maximum readiness appears to be reached during the midteenage years. There is, however, no rapid drop-off in ability to learn new skills. If an adequate level of motor fitness is maintained, many individuals' abilities to learn and participate in skills will not be appreciably reduced.

PREREQUISITE SKILLS

In addition to maturation and the general physical development of the individual, specific prerequisite learning is often essential in preparing one for particular physical tasks. The mere fact that a person is physically mature does not mean that he can, at a given time, learn certain types of activities. The more fundamental skills or movements must be learned prior to the more advanced ones. Children who have taken part in particular types of activities are often more ready for certain subsequent skills than are children who have not been exposed to the first activities. A mature individual cannot learn a jump shot before he has learned to shoot the ball and to jump. Neither can he learn the more advanced gymnastic stunts before he has learned the fundamental skills. This is as obvious as saying that a person could not do well in advanced calculus before he had the first course in algebra.

The concept of prerequisite learning is basic for progression in any subject area. Bruner (1963) seems to deny and support this idea. Although his statement, ". . . any subject can be taught . . . at any stage of development" seems to refute the need for progressive learning, his spiral curriculum emphasizes basic concepts which are enlarged upon from year to year. The ability to enlarge upon or refine these basic concepts seems to be dependent upon the child's having gained greater understanding and supportive concepts.

Prerequisite skills may be divided into two general types. First are

[1] From Jokl, Ernest, MEDICAL SOCIOLOGY AND CULTURAL ANTHROPOLOGY OF SPORT AND PHYSICAL EDUCATION, 1964. Courtesy of Charles C Thomas, Publisher, Springfield, Illinois. By permission.

the basic skills which are used as such in the performance of more complex activities. For example, fundamental movement skills, such as leaping, balancing, throwing, side-stepping, pushing, and bending, are used in many sports activities. One must first learn these movements in order to learn and participate in activities making use of them. The second type of prerequisite skills are the simple movements upon which more complex or refined tasks are dependent. Intricate or advanced movements in skating, diving, or gymnastics cannot be mastered without first learning an elementary version of that type of movement.

Prerequisite skills as component parts

Some basic movement skills are used in many sports activities. Therefore, it seems desirable that they be well learned at an early age. A boy cannot play basketball very effectively without having first learned to sidestep without crossing his feet. This very important movement should be taught at the primary grade level (not just for its use in basketball, but because of its usefulness in a wide variety of activities). Several activities can be used to teach side-stepping. For example, in the early school years, it may be developed by carefully selecting and teaching folk dances, singing games, and other simple activities which require side-stepping. During the intermediate grades, the student can be put in a game in which he must move sideways in order to prevent a soccer ball from crossing a line. In addition, dodging games, trapping drills, and advanced folk dances may be used. Then the learner can be put into sports situations such as basketball, football, wrestling, and soccer, where the technique of lateral movement will be practiced and developed. Other movement fundamentals such as skipping, rolling, twisting and striking could be developed in the same manner.

Accurate judgments regarding weight, space, and time are important for effective learning and performance in many motor skills. An understanding of these factors and an appreciation of each in the performance of motor activities can apparently be developed by certain exercises. For example, an understanding of weight may be developed by having children push, strike, lift, catch, and throw objects of different volume and intensity. Balls, bats, rackets, bean-bags, and other pieces of equipment and supplies can be used for this development. The concept of space may become clearer if objects of varying sizes are handled at various distances from the child. These objects may be slowly rolled, bounced, thrown, or pushed through distances. Similarly, the child may move between points by various means of locomotion. Such activities are likely to develop a greater understanding of space perceptions.

An appreciation of time may be gained if the child moves between two points by first running, then walking, side-stepping, skipping, crawling, and pushing or pulling a heavy object. The child might also compare running for a given distance to walking through water at waist depth, or to swimming the same distance. Running through an open area can be compared to running through an obstacle course. Catching or chasing balls which are bouncing at various speeds can also help to develop an awareness of time which will be useful in many motor activities.

Activities which are particularly designed to develop an understanding of such concepts as weight, space, time, and movement should aid the student in using these ideas when he is confronted with a new physical activity. These concepts are especially valuable in sports involving the throwing, hitting, or catching of a ball. Specific attention, as opposed to a trial-and-error process, can speed the learning of weight, space, time, and movement concepts and thus prepare the child to develop a high level of proficiency in a skill at an earlier date.

Prerequisite skills as a foundation for refined skills

While some skills are important prerequisites because they serve as basic ingredients of a more complex activity to be learned later, others are important as developmental stepping-stones to more refined movement. The latter skills are especially prevalent in the early school years. Catching, throwing, striking, kicking, and jumping do not start out as refined or efficient movements. Rather, these processes occur in cruder stages and must be practiced for most efficient development.

Children in the first grade may be unable to catch a tennis ball when it is thrown from a long distance. However, they will be able to learn to catch a large playground ball when it comes from a short distance. Therefore, the teacher at this level can more effectively teach catching by starting with large balls and gradually introducing smaller ones as the skill level progresses. Several researchers have reported that, given a choice, more advanced children will select a small ball for play, while less mature children will select a larger ball. In like manner, it has been found that young children experience great difficulty when trying to hit a baseball or a small rubber ball with a bat. For developing early skill in coordinating one's swing, timing the swing in relation to the speed of the ball, and actually batting the ball effectively, the teacher might be wise to start with a larger ball, perhaps a softball or even a playground ball.

To develop proficiency in body movement skills, basic or easy stunts should be used in the beginning. For example, in developing skill and confidence in balancing, a wide and low balance beam might be used. General competence in swimming seems desirable before refined techniques for particular strokes will be very valuable. Basic dives in various positions (pike, tuck, straight) are prerequisites for more sophisticated dives. The need for progressing from the simple to the more complex can be pointed to in all areas of skill development.

Many situations can be cited in which developmental steps seem essential in the learning of skills. For example, the forward roll and the backward roll are desirable prerequisites for learning a somersault in a forward or backward direction. To develop an effective jump shot in basketball, one must first learn to stop short, make a two-foot take-off, and shoot an overhead push shoot. Although the game of Newcomb is not an essential prerequisite for volleyball, it does aid in the rapid development of the concepts and some of the skills needed for volleyball play.

Even the prerequisite skills mentioned are dependent upon more fundamental learning. For example, to effectively learn the backward roll (which may prove valuable in learning the backward somersault) certain progressive steps must be taken. First the children should learn the proper tucked position and rock back and forth in this position. Further, they should be able to show how to place their hands properly and should experience the feeling of being in an inverted position, as well as the momentum involved in the backward roll.

Certain tasks or games are composed for a hierarchy of skills which must be learned in sequential order. The essentials for advanced learning may involve the understanding of concepts or movement skills or both. An understanding of space and movement concepts, as well as movement skills, is involved in some folk dances. Before children can learn a circle dance effectively, it is desirable that they understand such concepts or skills as: (1) how a group can form a circle by clasping hands; (2) how a circle can be made smaller or larger by having the group step toward the center of the circle or way from the center; (3) clockwise and counter-clockwise direction; (4) the effect of movement in one part of the circle or movement in another part of the circle; and (5) speed and fluidity in the skills related to individual and group movement. If the pupils have mastered certain basic elements, they can add one or two new movements, such as a two-step or schottische, which may be used in a new dance. On the other hand, children who have not been exposed to rope skipping, balancing, and rhythmical activities would not be as ready for the particular dance.

For certain activities, taking part effectively is more dependent upon prerequisite skills than upon maturity level. In a class of normal junior high school children, the range in maturation or developmental age may be as much as four to six years. One way in which readiness for the learning of particular skills may be more or less equated is by emphasizing prerequisite skills. In this way, the students may be prepared to take part in the same activity without its being too advanced for some and too simple for others. To an extent, emphasis on prerequisite skills can tend to offset the disadvantage of differences in developmental level.

DEVELOPMENTAL ACTIVITIES

In order to fully prepare children for the types of activities they will encounter in the school program, certain developmental experiences are necessary. A systematic program of such experiences will tend to raise the minimum level of readiness for all pupils. Such a program will also insure that physical competencies are attained as soon as the child is mature enough to gain them.

As stated earlier, readiness for motor activities is dependent upon maturation, general physical development, and specific prerequisite learning. Little, if anything, can be done to speed maturation. With adequate nutrition and freedom from unusual restrictions of activity, maturation is relatively unaffected by parents and teachers. Special developmental activities are therefore not of importance for maturation. Prerequisite learning is related to proficiency in a particular activity. This concept has been discussed earlier in this chapter. In respect to the other essentials for readiness, several authors have recently suggested that *general* readiness for motor activities can be affected by the parent and the teacher.

Developmental or readiness training of very young children is primarily the responsibility of parents. Children who seriously lack basic readiness skills when they come to school may be regarded as retarded. However, the school will be able to speed the development of these skills if attention is devoted to them in the kindergarten or first grade. It would be even more helpful to establish a program of such developmental activities in prekindergarten programs such as Headstart and Get Set. When a child is retarded in the development of basic skills, his condition can be somewhat overcome by establishing a program of basic skills which is geared to his actual readiness level. Several motor development programs have been established especially for handicapped or retarded children. Among the most popular are those developed by Radler and Kephart (1960), Frostig (1964), and Getman and Kane (1964). An analysis of these programs, however, seems to indicate that many normal children would benefit from the activities during the early years.

Early developmental training should be aimed at establishing basic levels of proficiency in a wide variety of activities rather than excellence in a few. Exposure to a great many experiences is therefore essential. In regard to this, Radler and Kephart state:

From a developmental point of view, the optimum condition is *not* high degrees of skill. *It is minimum ability in a wide number of motor activities. . . .* In any motor performance there is a minimum degree of ability which permits the child to perform the activity. This is the degree of ability which is important for his future development . . . The law of diminishing returns sets in after the child has learned to perform the task adequately. *From the point of view of development, the acquisition of spectacular degrees of skill is not worth the effort required* (pp. 119–120).[2]

Developmental activities need not be uniform for all pupils. Individual differences demand that some flexibility and variety be built into the program. In any group, some children need to start at a more elementary level than do others. Equipment or apparatus of different size, shape, or complexity might be used. For example, some children can play with and control a relatively small playground ball, while others need a large one. Some children can bypass certain steps in the learning of stunts. Some can work with faster-moving pieces of equipment, navigate greater distances or heights, or combine several stunts into one operation. Opportunities should be provided for children to develop basic motor abilities at their own rates.

Radler and Kephart indicate that motor skills are valuable in developing all-around school preparedness, not just readiness for physical education activities. They indicate that the kindergarten curriculum demands a level of readiness in the following areas of behavior: motor, symbolic, social, and numerical. Competencies in three of these areas may be enhanced by physical skills. These competencies assume a mastery of major and minor muscle movements, eye movements, eye-hand coordination, and a sense of laterality. In regard to motor behavior, the authors believe that the kindergarten child should be able to hop on one foot, skip, broad jump, high jump and throw a ball accurately. In addition, he should be able to build with blocks and to draw simple forms as squares, circles, and crosses. Symbolic readiness may be exhibited by such physical tasks as drawing an object or a scene, or by reproducing forms or images with one's body. Social skills of a physical nature are developed when the child learns to dress himself, tie his shoelaces, or perform many of the social graces which require movement. Havighurst (1966) outlines the developmental tasks needed by young children as motor coordinations, learning to play in a group, oral language, moral consciousness, and concepts of the physical world. He outlines the need for more complex skills as the child grows older.

During the early school years, many school functions are dependent upon motor development. For example, penmanship is a complex sensorimotor skill which may be aided by specific motor development. By the

[2] D. Radler and N. C. Kephart, SUCCESS THROUGH PLAY, New York: Harper & Row, 1960. By permission.

time the child is five years old, he is able to begin associating visual and kinesthetic sensations so that he can coordinate the muscular movements necessary for writing. During the early learning stages, handwriting should be large and free. Penmanship will improve as perception, memory for details, hand and finger dexterity, and strength are developed. These capacities can be developed through special physical exercise. Even the capacities of perception and memory of letter forms in penmanship, which are more removed from physical skills, can be developed by special activities. Two programs which have been designed to develop readiness for school through motor activities will be discussed in some detail.

Radler and Kephart's program for developing perceptual skills

Radler and Kephart (1960) base their book, *Success Through Play*, on the assumption that skills which are essential in establishing readiness for school can be learned. Their program emphasizes visual skills as a means for understanding one's self and one's environment. According to these authors, 40 per cent of entering school children have poor visual skills which prevent their being entirely successful in regular school work. These skills can be improved by special exercises designed to enable the children to *see* well. In this context the ability to see is not restricted to the 20-20 concept of vision. Rather, such components as kinesthetic awareness, balance, and general coordination are all considered parts of perception. The authors state that a child's ability to copy circles, squares, triangles, and other figures is more closely related to school achievement than is the standard intelligence test score. In fact, measurable increases in general IQ scores (up to fifteen points) were shown after children who had visual problems took part in the training program. Radler and Kephart's program is composed of the following six exercises which are designed to improve and also to reflect motor ability:

Angels in the snow. In the traditional game, the child lies in the snow, moves his arms and legs into different positions, and then gets up to observe the pattern which has been created. The authors suggest a modification of this game for indoor use to help the child develop an awareness of his body, to develop a sense of laterality, and to practice muscular control. In this activity the child lies on the floor and goes through various exercises, such as moving the feet apart, clicking heels together, clapping hands over head and moving the arms and legs in combination and to a time pattern. The teacher may *touch* a body part to help the child become aware of its position and movement. Later, he may *point* to the body part, then *name* it and ask for certain responses. The authors believe that such experiences develop laterality, space perception, and timing, and that these capacities underlie such activities as reading, writing, and drawing.

Walking board. This activity involves simple stunts on a homemade balance beam which is placed very close to the floor. The child participates in balancing activities which become progressively more difficult. These activities are designed to develop muscular control in balance, postural responses, and lateral movement.

Balance board. This activity is somewhat similar to the walking-board except that the child does not move about but rather balances on a rocking board at one position. After some proficiency and confidence has been developed in standing on the balance board, the child begins to perform simple stunts such as bouncing a ball on the floor, throwing objects at targets, and other hand and foot exercises. The purpose of the activity is to develop dynamic body balance.

Drawing games. This is one of the most important activities in Radler and Kephart's program. The purpose of these games is to enable the child to see the relationship between visual perception and kinesthetic awareness. All activities are performed at a blackboard. The following are typical tasks: The instructor makes two dots on the board some distance apart. The child then attempts to connect these with a straight line. Several other dots are drawn and the child is encouraged to connect all of them. Emphasis is placed on drawing straight lines and making neat curves when approaching and leaving a particular dot. Some children tend to have difficulty starting and stopping, but this exercise appears to help in the development of directionality. The child is then taught to draw vertical lines, horizontal lines, curving lines, and forms. The ability to copy a square appears to be an index of developmental level. For this reason, it is used on several intelligence tests. These drawing exercises seem to be important for subsequent skills in drawing and writing. Awareness of the relationship between feeling a particular bodily movement and the resulting illustrated lines is seen as strategic for the development of school readiness.

Pegboard games. Acoustical tiles and golf tees (with smoothed points) are used in this exercise. The child inserts a sequence of tees into the board to "draw" particular figures. Because it is a slower process performed piece-by-piece, pegboard drawing is more difficult than chalk drawing. Pegboard games are assumed to be valuable in developing reading readiness because of their emphasis on short, small steps in form perception.

Ball games. For these games, a ball is attached to the end of a string and suspended in air. The ball is swung back and forth like a pendulum while the child watches by rolling his eyes, touches with his finger or strikes. These activities are designed to develop eye control, eye-hand coordination, and timing. Coordination between the visual and motor systems is required. A great deal of progression can be used with this type of activity. The child may start by making contact with a stationary ball or by lying on his back and rolling his eyes to follow the ball. Level of difficulty may be increased so that the child is required to use a smaller ball which is swinging faster. With this ball he may bunt or bat the ball with a stick. This technique is sometimes used by baseball coaches to help the batters watch the ball and time their swings. A further progression is to have the players hit a bouncing or jerking ball on the end of a string. The latter activity is somewhat comparable to batting a curving baseball.

Getman and Kane's program of perceptual exercises

Getman and Kane (1964) have outlined a program of developmental exercise which is similar to that of Radler and Kephart. Getman and Kane's program is a series of visual activities which are designed to promote readiness on the part of young children. According to the authors, the activities are similar to those which the child might normally experience if he had a chance to be outdoors and to come in contact with nature. However, in our particular culture, he is often deprived of these rather natural activities. Getman and Kane's prime emphasis is placed on perceptual readiness which underlies performance in all areas of school achievement. The authors believe that readiness for school learning *can be developed* by the following types of activities:

Practice in general coordination. This practice involves general exercises to develop greater awareness and control of body parts. Head lifts, head rolls, bilateral arm movements, bilateral leg movements, and combinations of head, arm and leg movements are used. Exercises such as jumping, skipping, and rolling are used to familiarize the child with gravity.

A typical coordination exercise is one involving head and alternate arm movements. For illustrative purposes, the following instructions (for the children) are presented.

1. Until now we have moved both arms and both legs in the same way. Now we are going to move one arm up and one down at the same time. Do it slowly at first with each arm moving at the same speed so that when you reach the top with one hand you will slap your side with the other hand. Keep your arms relaxed but your elbows straight. Slide your arms across the floor at a smooth even speed.
2. Starting position.
3. Look at ceiling. Ready: Now raise your RIGHT hand to the overhead position and hold it there until we start. Pretend you are holding a long

pole between your hands. As your left arm reaches the overhead position, the right hand should slap your side. Ready: 1–2, Right—DOWN, left—UP, left—down, right—up, etc.

4. This time we'll add head movements to the arm and leg movements. Begin in the starting position with your right hand up. Now turn your head AWAY from the up arm (to the left). As your right arm comes down, roll your head to the RIGHT slowly. When your right arm reaches your side, you should be looking to the RIGHT. Lead with your eyes as in the HEAD ROLL exercise.

5. Return to starting position. Right hand up—head turned to the left. Ready: Right down—head turn RIGHT, left down—head turn LEFT, right—left, right—left, 1–2, 1–2, etc.

6. Look at the ceiling (p. 23).

Practice in balance. The purpose of this type of activity is to have the children gain an understanding of the laterality of their bodies and the types of movements necessary for balance, as well as to enable them to direct their movements for better balance. The apparatus as well as the types of tasks (walking forward and backward, turning, viewing peripheral targets, etc.) are similar to the walking-board exercises of Radler and Kephart.

Practice in eye-hand coordination. The child draws lines, circles, and other forms on the blackboard, sometimes with both hands simultaneously. These activities integrate visual and tactile experiences and fluidity in spanning material are both stressed.

Practice in eye movement. Several exercises are designed to develop ocular skills which are prerequisite to learning. Detailed inspection of one item and fluidity in spanning material are both stressed.

Practice in form recognition. A template (form board) is used to help the child develop precision in the drawing of geometric forms. It has been found that young children have an especially difficult time in stopping chalk at the right spot or in turning corners accurately. Exercise in drawing forms tends to develop the child's awareness of correct muscular movement, hand bilaterality, and visual discrimination of basic forms.

Practice in visual memory. A tachistoscope is used to project images on a screen momentarily. The child is required to reproduce the flashed form on a chalkboard, or a work sheet, by tracing it in the air, or by naming it. As some skill is developed, additional forms are flashed on the screen, and the speed of the flashed form may go from half a second to one twenty-fifth of a second.

These ideas are recommended by Getman and Kane to prepare the child for regular school learning. They are especially needed if the child has been restricted from a wide variety of adventurous childhood activities, or if he has been rushed into school before he was ready. Once a general state of readiness has been developed for school activities, a more traditional approach can be used.

Additional developmental activities

The two programs just described offer some excellent ideas for developing general school readiness. The programs are based on movement and observation and are designed primarily to develop kinesthetic control and precision in movement. This design makes the programs especially valuable in the development of physical readiness. However, a complete program of developmental activities for physical education requires expansion upon these, plus additional activities. Radler and Kephart's program, as well as that of Getman and Kane, emphasizes the components of balance, hand-eye coordination, foot-eye coordination, and general precision in body movement. Additional physical components such as muscular strength, speed, agility, and flexibility need to be developed to their full potential. These require a program of rather vigorous activities.

Through a program of movement exploration in the early school years, most of the components needed for physical performance can be developed. Some concepts which are popular in movement programs were suggested by Radler and Kephart (angels in the snow) and Getman and Kane (tracing forms in the air). Movement skills involving vigorous motion are needed in the early years. The concept of movement education has almost unlimited possibilities for the development of all motor capacities needed for future, more advanced learning and participation.

In addition to the movement exploration concept, more formal programs such as circuit training, stunts and tumbling, and rhythms also provide opportunities for the development of physical capacities. Such traits as strength, speed, and flexibility can be sometimes more directly emphasized by formally organized activities.

One danger of formal programs, however, is that they may not be especially helpful to children at the top or the bottom of the performance scale. Serious attention must be devoted to individual differences if maximum development is to take place. Many authors suggest homogeneous grouping as a means for solving this problem. Havighurst (1966) indicates that students should be grouped according to proficiency in each particular school activity. Despite the merits of such a system it could prove rather cumbersome, and still would only partially solve the problem of meeting individual differences. Another valuable method is to encourage individual activities in which one child is not dependent upon another's level of readiness, and each child has opportunities for unlimited development. Track activities, circuit training, gymnastics, or even the ball games suggested by Radler and Kephart seem to meet these criteria.

One developmental concept which has not received sufficient attention from physical educators or from the authors of the programs discussed is the matter of rhythm in general motor performance. Emphasis upon rhythm in the performance of motor skills results in smoother coordination and sometimes increases speed. The effect of rhythm has been illustrated in typewriting and in learning cursive writing. The work songs of manual laborers further illustrate this principle. Occasionally rhymes have been used with the bouncing of balls or rope skipping. Music from records, the clapping of hands, or the metronome seems to have value in promoting more rhythmical movement.

Aside from formal programs, children will develop and use a wide range of motor abilities if given the opportunity to engage in normal play activities. Perhaps particular traits will not be developed as fast in informal play, but the variety of responses is great and the movements are the types needed for future participation in regular work or play activities. Sapora and Mitchell (1961) classify the fundamental movements used in play into two categories: (1) locomotion, or movements in which the player moves his own body, and (2) handling objects, or actions which result in the movement of other bodies. Locomotion is accomplished mainly by use of the lower limbs with the arms and the trunk being used only incidentally. Conversely, handling objects is performed mainly by the hands and arms, with incidental use being made of the trunk and legs.

According to Sapora and Mitchell, physical play involves the following types of locomotion: creeping, walking, running, dancing, jumping, climbing, swimming, and diving. Use of each of these is dependent upon the developmental level of the individual and the nature of the play activity. These activities vary in their potential for contributing to the overall development of the individual. Some bodily movements involved in handling objects are: throwing, catching, striking, swinging, pushing, pulling, carrying, and lifting. The variety of movements involved, as well as the range of difficulty levels which may be used, tends to insure that general or all-around skills will be developed if children are given the opportunity and are encouraged to engage in these types of play activities.

MEASURING DEVELOPMENTAL READINESS

Determining the child's readiness for regular motor activities is essential before establishing an appropriate program for him. Arbitrarily setting up a physical education program without seriously considering the developmental level of the children will certainly prevent the program from reaching its full potential. Activities are likely to be too advanced for the children, thus resulting in constant failure and frustration; or too elementary, resulting in boredom and a lack of challenge.

Traditional beliefs about readiness cannot be continually accepted at face value. Relatively little scientific investigation has been devoted to the purpose of determining the proper grade placement of motor skills. Most often, activity selection has been based upon what had previously been taught at the same grade level. Examples of inaccuracies in such a process have been frequent. Most often, it has been found that children could learn skills previously considered too difficult for them. For example, Mead (1958) reported that Manus children in New Guinea are expected to swim at three years of age, and to climb trees even earlier. Further, she indicated that a child of five years who could not swim would be comparable to an American child of five who could not walk. Occasionally, skills have been moved back to a later maturational level when it was found that they could best be learned at that level.

Several problems are faced when one attempts to determine readiness for physical education activities. One of these is that readiness seems to vary with different activities, i.e., it is specific for each task. For example, one child may be more advanced than another in rhythmic activities, but less advanced in swimming or basketball.

One way of determining readiness is to expose the child to the task. If he learns the activity, he was ready to learn it. If he does not learn, readiness is only one of the factors which may have been missing. However, such a slow and methodical process is similar to a high-jumping contest which starts with a minimal level of competence and progresses to the maximum level of anyone in the group. A class which is presented with a new activity would start at the lowest level that all students could surely perform. Then the class would advance to progressively more difficult levels until all class members had reached a challenging point. This trial-and-error procedure appears to present a rather unstimulating program for more advanced students.

General developmental level can be roughly determined by chronological age and physical size. Simon, Shaw, and Gilchrist (1954) investigated the relationship between physical and mental maturity in a study of fifty failing and fifty outstanding Caucasian first-grade students. The failing students tended to be more immature than did the successful students on a battery of anthropometric indices. Differences were found in age, intelligence, head circumference with leg length, and waist circumference with leg length. Simon indicated that these measurements were the most sensitive indicators of school readiness.

The most obvious and practical means for determining readiness for activity or maturity is physical size. Investigators are unanimous in reporting that within a given age range the larger children are more mature. Olson (1961) found a correlation of .54 between standing height and skeletal age. Larger children are therefore readier for higher-skilled activities than are smaller, less mature children. Hale (1959) showed that champion Little League baseball players were up to two years advanced in maturation. The fact that physical abilities generally increase with size supports the assumption that size is a reasonably valid, though crude, indication of physical maturity. With exceptions, size seems to an important criterion for determining readiness for physical activities.

The Wetzel Grid (1940) provides an easy means for determining the child's *developmental level*. This scale, which includes age, height, and weight, compares the child's physical size with that of other children his age. In this manner, one is able to determine if the child is as advanced as most other children of his age. Wetzel states that, "The grid is a record of the child's growth as reflected by height and weight, as well as visual demonstration of whether or not his growth is progressing satisfactorily and the extent to which this is so. The grid provides a means of determining the direction of growth and the rate at which growth occurs from infancy to maturity" (p. 3).

Perhaps the most popular means of estimating general performance level was developed by McCloy (1934). He showed that age, height, and weight were important in grouping boys for athletic activities. He developed a *classification index* for grouping children for physical activity. His scale included a combination of age, height, and weight, each of which was weighted according to its importance at a given grade level. He found that height was not a strategic criterion of motor ability for elementary school children. At the college level, age did not seem to be important in motor performance. All three characteristics, however, were found to be important at the high school level. Neilson and Cozens (1934) developed a classification formula which closely resembled McCloy's and involved the same components. Although these scales are easily usable in a practical situation for grouping students in an activity, they are not especially valuable as indices of sexual maturation.

Recently, interest has focused on skeletal maturity as a means of determining the child's developmental level. Generally bone growth techniques have been found to provide a reliable index for maturity. Recent ossification studies indicate that skeletal growth probably offers the greatest possibility for accurate maturity determinations. Through such studies the following growth periods have been identified: (1) from birth to about age five secondary centers of ossification make their appearance; (2) from age five to age twelve in girls or age fourteen in boys ossification spreads from these centers; (3) from age twelve or fourteen until full maturity in the early twenties the epiphyses fuse with the diaphyses, leading to a cessation of growth in length.

Secondary sex characteristics have also been used as a means of determining maturity when children are approaching adolescence. Crampton (1944) classified boys as prepubescent, pubescent and post-pubescent on the basis of pubic hair changes. Tanner (1955), after pointing out the close relationship between biological age and the maturity of the reproductive system, recommended that pubic hair and genital development be used as an index of the maturity of the reproductive system. Greulich and Pyle (1959) also showed a close relationship between the maturation of the reproductive system and skeletal development. They pointed out that this relationship was so close that onset of menarche could be predicted by assessments of X-rays of the hand and wrist during the prepubertal period. In the regular school setting, however, secondary sex characteristics can be used only as a rough guide in determining maturational level.

SELECTED READINGS

Cratty, B. J. *Movement behavior and motor learning.* Philadelphia: Lea & Febiger, 1964.

Cureton, T. K. Improving the physical fitness of youth. *Monogr. Soc. for Res. in Child Develpm.* 1964, **29**, No. 4 (Serial No. 95).

Frostig, M., & Horne, D. *The Frostig program for the development of visual perception.* Chicago: Follett, 1964.

Getman, G. N., & Kane, E. R. *The physiology of readiness.* Minneapolis: PASS, Inc., 1964.

McGraw, M. B. *Neuromuscular maturation of the human infant.* New York: Columbia, 1943.

Mussen, P., Conger, J., & Kagan, J. *Child development and personality.* (2nd ed.) New York: Harper & Row, 1963.

Piaget, J., *The origins of intelligence in children.* New York: International Universities Press, Inc., 1952.

Radler, D., & Kephart, N. C. *Success through play.* New York: Harper & Row, 1960.

Rarick, L. Growth and development theory and practice: implications for physical education. *Mich. Osteopathic J.,* 1965, **30**, 20–24.

Chapter 7

Motivation

One of the most universally accepted concepts regarding learning is that the individual must be interested in a particular task before effective learning can occur. It is, therefore, best if the child in school is somewhat aroused or excited about a specific task or learning situation. This principle of motivation has been generally agreed upon through the years from the early learning theorists to today's classroom teachers. A "motivated" condition is essential not only for *learning*, but also for effective *performance* in motor skills. For this reason, educators in general, and physical educators and coaches in particular, devote considerable effort towards motivating students.

Motivation as used in this discussion refers to the process whereby needs are created within the individual which force him to seek particular goals to satisfy those needs. Motivation refers to an *internal* state of the individual which may be initiated from within the person, as in the case of a biological need, or from the outside, as in the case of a social need. If the need is a basic or urgent one, a state of intense emotional arousal may develop. Generally the motivated person is more active than one who is not motivated. This activity is directed toward particular goals, which, when attained, satisfy the individual and lead to diminished activity. In the school setting, the goals most often sought are achievement, recognition, belonging, or other personal and social motives. It is by making effective use of these desires that the teacher is able to motivate students to outstanding accomplishments.

An aroused or highly motivated state most obviously affects the individual in three ways. First, such a condition results in *physiological changes* which takes place within the person. These changes usually involve an increase in heart rate and blood pressure, a flushed face, and other processes which are more difficult to observe, except by scientific measurement. Second, within the individual there are *conscious sensations* which accompany excitement. These sensations are attributable to physiological changes and are not usually noticed by other persons. Third, an aroused emotional state is usually reflected in *more activated behavior* on the part of the individual, who will often exhibit gross and strong movements and may become awkward and clumsy. This activated behavior can be easily observed and measured. Physical educators have been particularly interested in physiological changes and in resulting motor behavior.

People in everyday life and in the sports world are often impressed with the physical performance of persons who are highly motivated or emotionally aroused. The following case was described in a newspaper a few years ago. A man, after having jacked up his station wagon to change a tire in his driveway, was called into his house. Moments later, one of his children, who had been observing the proceedings, ran into the house to tell his father and mother that the car had fallen off the jack and on another child. Both parents ran outside, and the quick-thinking father immediately began resetting the jack in order to lift the car off the child. The mother, seeking more immediate results, took hold of the car and manually lifted it so that the child could crawl out from under! So great was the strain that, in the process, a bone was broken in her back. Certainly this feat was outside the expected performance possibilities for the woman, who was described as average in size. Other incidents of unusual physical acts under emotional stimulation are within the experience of most individuals.

Physical responses resulting from stimulation are strange and varied. Motivation or stress may result in *positive* effects, such as increases in (1) speed of movement: the running speed of a frightened child or sprinter under pressure of intense competition; (2) strength: the angry man is stronger than the contented one; the woman who was able to lift a car because she was emotionally aroused; and (3) endurance: the athlete will endure or persevere longer without showing fatigue if the competition is especially exciting.

At other times, *detrimental* effects may result from a high state of emotional excitement. Quite often there is a reduction of bodily coordination. For example, an excited young pitcher might lose his control in a close game; a basketball player might miss more than his share of easy shots; or a child who has recently learned to tie his shoelaces might be all thumbs when pressured by the teacher to hurry. Mental performances also are sometimes adversely affected by emotional excitement. Consider the case of the child (or adult) who forgets his well-learned speech when he stands up before a group. Some adults indicate that their minds occasionally go blank under pressure.

FOUNDATIONS OF MOTIVATION

The basis for motivation has traditionally been explained with reference to the concept of *homeostasis*. Homeostasis refers to the tendency of the body to take compensatory action for the purpose of maintaining a physiological balance at all times. Adjustments are regularly required. For example, the human body contains mechanisms for maintaining its temperature at approximately 98.6° F. Men occasionally work for short periods of time in temperatures ranging from below 0° F. to above 170° F. Even under such extreme conditions a variation in body temperature by as much as six degrees would not be expected. The ability of the body to maintain an even temperature balance is one of the clearest examples of homeostasis.

Homeostasis is also revealed in the tendency of the body to maintain a reasonably constant supply of blood sugar, despite wide variations in intake of sugar. Similarly, the acidity-alkalinity balance in the blood is held reasonably constant regardless of variations in intake. To maintain healthy conditions for life, similar internal adjustments must be made regarding the water content of the blood and lymph, the oxygen content of the blood, and the numerous minerals in the body. In the event of a failure in homeostasis, the individual is forced to seek a body balance by other means. The seeking of substances to meet bodily needs, therefore, becomes the basis for motivated activity.

Richter (1942) conducted extensive research with animals to illustrate how a disturbed homeostatic state results in overt behavior on the part of the organism. In his studies, various ductless glands were removed from rats in order to upset the normal homeostatic ability of the body. The rats responded by taking compensatory action such as selecting unusual but appropriate food to obtain certain minerals, or building larger and warmer nests to make up for unusual heat loss. He concluded that ". . . in human beings and animals the effort to maintain a constant internal environment or homeostasis constitutes one of the most universal and powerful of all behavior or drives" (p. 64).

There can be little doubt that there is merit to the homeostatic theory of basic drives. However, this concept, when restricted to biological conditions, does not appear to be broad enough to include the total range of human motivation. Man is not merely a biological being. Personal and social conditions play a major role in influencing his behavior. In fact, even lower animals give evidence of reacting to social influences. It has become very clear that psychological or sociological needs may act as stimulants for action, just as do physiological deficiencies.

Needs and drives

Needs and drives form the basis for human motivation. Both are often related to the concept of homeostasis. A need generally refers to a deprived state or a lack of an essential element. This deprivation may exist in the physical, psychological, or social necessities. A physical need therefore is not suitable for stage use, as the most skillful operator can handle but two at the same time and it is doubtful if even then he can bring them smoothly and correctly to exact readings. The more useful kind is somewhat akin to the rotary-resistance dimmer in that it can be mounted with others in a bank and has a protruding handle that makes manipulation simple, and this handle can be interlocked with those of its neighbors.

SWITCHBOARDS FOR RESISTANCE AND AUTOTRANSFORMER DIMMER CONTROL

Because the smallest stage should have provision to control individually no fewer than twenty different stage circuits—and for any quality of production far more are needed—it is pointless to think of dimmers except in relation to complete controlboards. In general design there is little difference between a switchboard utilizing resistance dimmers and one with autotransformers.

Any such board should logically be arranged so that banks of dimmer handles can be manipulated with ease by a minimum number of operators. All elements that pertain to any one circuit—dimmer handles, switches, pilot lights, fuses or circuit breakers, and if possible the stage-load plugs—should be placed in a logical association with one another. Mastering handles, master switches, and the like should be in one central location. All elements should be clearly identified. Running lights (lights by which the operators can see to manipulate the board) must be provided. Ideally, these should have a choice of brightnesses: high for usual operating conditions and a dim glow for use during stage blackouts. Clips to hold cue sheets, scripts, and notes in plain and easy view are a necessity often overlooked. And, most important, the board should be placed so that a clear, unobstructed view of the stage is provided at all times. Obviously, it should have all proper safety devices and precautions, physical as well as electrical.

STAGE CIRCUITS. One aspect that is frequently overlooked in controlboard consideration is just how many stage circuits are to be connected through it. The days when each dimmer was inflexibly wired to a certain instrument are happily gone. Present thinking demands that about the stage there be located at appropriate spots and in appropriate numbers outlets to any one of which any instrument in stock may be connected. Much as the wall outlet in a kitchen may serve at different times the percolator, the toaster, the electric iron, the fan, and even the hair curler, so an outlet in the stage floor may at different times be used for a backing flood, a fireplace effect, a special side-lighting spotlight, or one color circuit in a striplight.

CROSS CONNECTING. Now in order to make possible the connection of any stage outlet to any dimmer or indeed to place several stage loads under the control of a single dimmer of suitable capacity, flexible systems, variously referred to as interconnecting, crossconnecting, or patching, have been devised. These operate in any number of ways: by rotary switches, by plugs that can be pushed into jacks as on a telephone switchboard, push-button tables, crossing grids of busses with contacts provided by movable clips. Each one has its own advantages and many refinements, and which should be employed in any particular case must be a matter of a study of the specific situation, the number of dimmer circuits and of load circuits, the probable amount of use, and particularly the experience and *competence* of the probable users.

MECHANICAL MASTERING.   Because intensity control is frequently required over several if not all stage circuits simultaneously, various provisions may be incorporated into a properly designed controlboard to make this possible. The simplest and most obvious of these is interlocking. The handles of a number of dimmers mounted side by side may have their handles connected to a shaft that runs the length of the bank. By means of a long master handle the shaft is turned and all the dimmers locked to it will simultaneously move to the same readings.

The drawback is obvious. If we want one dimmer to stop at a reading different from the others, it will take some fast and dexterous work on the part of the operator to disengage the proper handle at the proper place. If several dimmers must be dropped off at different readings during a fairly rapid dim, the whole process becomes impossible. Further, those that are dropped off correctly will have reached their desired readings while the other lights are only part way to theirs.

Of course, the same thing happens in reverse when dimmers are set at different readings and the attempt is made to use the interlocking mechanism to take them to "out" simultaneously. Those dimmers that are set at the higher readings will start down first, and their lights will be part way out before dimmers set at lower readings are picked up by the revolving shaft. Interlocking, therefore, while better than no master control whatever, is an awkward, inartistic makeshift.

ELECTRICAL MASTERING.   In order to get truly proportional dimming, a master dimmer of large capacity may be employed to control a number of smaller ones and their respective loads. Obviously such a master must have a capacity equal to the total capacities of the lesser dimmers combined—a limiting factor indeed. And of course, if these are resistance dimmers, all including the master must be loaded to full capacities for proper performance.

Obviously, the large-capacity dimmer is tied up to the single task of being a master, even at times when it would be more useful as an independent dimmer with its own stage load. To meet this situation various systems of wiring and switching have been devised to permit the large dimmer to serve either as a master or otherwise as the particular situation warrants.

In many small theatres a transfer switch is associated with a large-capacity dimmer, such as a master, to enable it to be used to control the houselights. With the switch thrown one way, the dimmer can take out the house. Then the switch is thrown the other way, and the same dimmer brings up some of the stage lights. At the end of the act the process is reversed.

PACKAGE BOARDS

A recent innovation in the field of stage lighting control is the so-called "package board"—an attempt to provide all things for all people, with the to-be-expected results.

Invariably using the autotransformer dimmer, the typical package board offers several control circuits, often with provisions for mastering and interlocking. Switches, fuses or circuit breakers, and some type of flexible plugging are incorporated. The whole is advertised as being readily movable, but it takes four husky lads to handle the larger sizes.

For extremely small stages, where very little artistic effect is needed, one of these devices is hardly adequate. Two might be considered a minimum. But when more than two are employed, one might better invest his money in a conventional and permanent board.

One situation in which the package board does have merit is that found in many schools where plays are performed in a number of different locations. And in some places the drama group is requested, and expected, to provide lights for a dozen extraneous occasions: the dance in the gymnasium, the swimming extravaganza, the concert under the stars. Here a package board may be very useful, and when not on its social travels, it can earn its keep as a small auxiliary to the regular stage control system.

ELECTRONIC CONTROL

But the ultimate in intensity control will not be found in such devices, ingenious as some of them may be. Far more advanced apparatus is on the market today and installed in many places, here and abroad. These various forms of control fall under the general heading of electronic, but there are several ways in which the problem has been attacked. Still newer methods coming over the horizon may presently render obsolete our current systems.

TYPES OF ELECTRONIC CONTROL. Of the various types of electronic control, a few may be mentioned briefly. The first truly successful system was put into operation at Yale University by George Izenour in 1947 and consists of two thyratron tubes—one for each direction of a-c flow—that modify the typical sine-wave form of the current into a succession of pulses of greater or lesser length. A second system and one that has been used in Europe successfully and has been installed in a few places in this country consists of three thyratrons, one for each phase in a four-wire service. A third method, growing out of the old reactor principle, is today known as the magnetic amplifier—a choke coil control over a transformer wound on an 8-shaped coil. Each of these has its advocates and its disadvantages.

Of extreme importance in the present state of development are the so-called solid-state devices, or semiconductors, of which the silicon-controlled rectifier has the greatest application in the field of stage lighting. A number of leading manufacturers are producing dimming units based on this form of apparatus, improvements are noted almost daily, and it seems that the future holds still greater promises.

THE AIMS OF ELECTRONIC CONTROL. The object of all these devices is not mere gadgetry, and certainly not complexity for the glorification of the technician. Rather the purpose is to free the artist from the tyranny of the crude mechanisms with which he has formerly worked. Under old methods a simple shift of emphasis in the stage lights required that the designer must instruct several operators (who probably could not even see the results) in what he expected them to do, and then coach them carefully and repeatedly in the timing he wanted them to follow. Then, if he saw exactly what he desired executed correctly once out of five times, he considered himself fortunate.

With modern control systems the artist may, with flicks of his fingers, set each light to the exact level he desires, then set them again to the levels to which he wishes them to change, and the operator who will execute his wishes can see and comprehend at all times just what is being attempted.

If sometimes the lighting of a show under the modern methods proves a rather long-drawn affair, it is not because the designer is taking longer to accomplish that which was formerly done in a shorter period of time, but rather that his dreams, released from the older bondage, are now soaring with dozens of ideas that he could never even attempt before. The penny-whistle band has been superseded by the pipe organ.

LOCATION FOR CONTROL PANELS

All electronic systems have one important aspect in common—namely that a low-voltage, low-amperage current is all that is required to control the actual dimming device, be it a tube, a transformer, or a semiconductor. And this low-amperage current permits the controlling operator and the apparatus he directly handles to be placed at any distance from the stage and in any location that seems appropriate. The projection booth at the rear of the balcony has been utilized in some houses, and while this is not a bad location from which to run the show, it is a very poor place for the designer to light it because of the bad angle, the impossibility of seeing the backgrounds, and the distraction of light patterns on the stage floor. An orchestra pit is better, though a little too close for the designer to view the stage picture as a whole. Of the practical places, the rear of the main floor of the auditorium is unquestionably the best. In any event, it is inexcusable to place the control panels backstage, though the cross-connecting system may be there and the actual dimming apparatus—be it tubes, magnetic amplifiers, or other—can be tucked away in the basement or other convenient location. The very newest devices promise to eliminate such concentrations entirely by placing tiny dimmers at the instruments themselves.

ELECTRONIC MASTERING. More important than remote control, however, is the ease with which the various control circuits may be brought under the mastery of comparatively small devices. This permits all instruments on the stage to be dimmed simultaneously by means of a small handle, knob, or other convenient device. It also allows the practice known as "presetting," in which the intensity of each light in each successive portion of a scene is recorded in advance and set up in an appropriate memory apparatus. Then, on cue, the single operator may change from one complete set of readings to another at whatever speed is indicated by the action of the play.

PRESETTING. Now this does not mean simply fading the lights from dark to their desired intensities and back to dark again. It means that each instrument may start at any desired reading and change to any reading—some becoming more bright, some less so, some going out, some coming on, and some remaining as they were—all simultaneously and in perfect unison.

Some form of "infinite presetting" is the demand today by light designers who have worked extensively with existing electronic systems. And equipment manufacturers have responded by placing on the market several systems that make this flexibility and artistic freedom possible.

THE FUTURE

Because new systems of electronic control are being devised and the older ones are undergoing constant refinement, it would be misleading to recommend any one type over the others. The prices also are in process of change, for the most part downward, it is pleasant to report. Certain systems may be obtained in forms that compare in cost very favorably with obsolete methods of control, while offering vastly more for the same investment. No one planning a theatre that claims to be approaching adequacy in artistic possibilities can afford to overlook electronic control.

19

LIGHTING EQUIPMENT
FOR THE
NONCOMMERCIAL STAGE

THE THEATRE

Recommendations for equipment to complete a satisfactory inventory must depend on a number of factors which differ sharply among all noncommercial theatres. The first and most obvious is, of course, the size of the theatre plant itself. A huge auditorium that calls for a throw for the front lights of forty feet or more is necessarily going to need more powerful spotlights than the modest little hall where downstage areas can be lighted from a location barely a dozen feet away, and wide-beam instruments are essential.

Furthermore the choice of instruments should be governed by the possibilities of improvements in the existing plant. Often new locations for hanging instruments may be provided without great trouble or expense and such instruments that are added should be purchased with such future plans clearly in mind.

ARRANGEMENT OF THE STAGE.   Size and distances are not the whole story in the theatre. How well the stage itself is arranged and equipped is of prime importance in selecting lighting instruments. Can those hung overhead be flown up and down—indeed, can they be mounted above the stage at all? What about the cyclorama or other ultimate backing? Will there be a vast expanse, necessitating an elaborate set of lights for its proper illumination? Or will only a few feet be available for dramatic backgrounds? What provisions are there for the intensity control of the lights? If very limited, can this control be expanded to take care of the new instruments?

PRODUCING HABITS.   Of grave concern are the producing habits of the resident group. Do they confine themselves to single-set interiors of a rather realistic nature? In such an event they can get along nicely with a comparatively modest layout of instruments as to both type and number. But if they wish to expand into more imaginative forms of dramatic presentation, with full-stage pictures and action flowing down to the apron or even beyond, then a far larger and more complex inventory becomes essential. Nor must changing tastes be overlooked—what has been done in the past may not be wanted in the future.

In fact, this last thought ties in with the practical matter of planning a step-by-step accumulation of a very complete inventory. It would be quite foolish, of course, to buy in the first year all the spotlights one hopes ever to own, to the neglect of the other types of instruments. Often it is wise to plan the purchase of new equipment and expansion of inventory in very tight coordination with the expected production plans of the years to come, with a careful analysis of the plays that will be produced, their probable mode of production, and even preliminary sketches of the scenic aspects involved.

PERSONNEL.   One very important consideration that merits the deepest and most honest thought is the factor of personnel. Will the organization have artists capable of making imaginative use of new equipment and technicians able to care for it properly? It is with the keenest disappointment that one views, all too often, beautifully appointed lighting apparatus used merely to flood the stage in a manner that could as readily have been done with rows of gas jets. Or to see fine and expensive instruments ruined through misuse and neglect.

BUDGET.   And the last, of course, brings us, where it must ultimately in all practical matters, to the actual money involved. Stage lighting instruments are not cheap, yet even a large inventory of them will amount to considerably less than many expenses that go into building a theatre or maintaining a producing group. And because more and more today our designers and directors are depending on light to give them the environment and emotional background they need for their plays, a well-planned selection of lighting instruments and their adjuncts may be a great saving over the older, more costly forms of production and scenic display.

With these things in mind, let us consider the stage instruments themselves and what would be needed of the various kinds to give a theatre a well-rounded inventory.

SPOTLIGHTS

FOR THE DOWNSTAGE AREAS.   Spotlights should be the first considered, for these instruments are the most effective for lighting the various acting areas as described in Chapter 11. In order to make use of the highly important 45-degree angle—indeed, to put light on the face of the actor at all—it is necessary to place the spotlights for the downstage areas somewhere overhead in the auditorium itself.

In some smaller, informal theatres, this may be a pipe or cross beam, with the instruments in plain view of the audience; in the commercial theatre the balcony front (though really too low) has become almost a convention for want of a better place. But in many a theatre currently designed there are openings provided in the ceiling, often disguised by a false beam, from which the desired angles are easily attained. Whatever the location the ellipsoidal-reflector spotlight because of the qualities described in Chapter 15 is the only instrument that we can consider seriously for this purpose.

If the throw to the stage is very long, the 8-inch types, burning the 750-watt lamps, seem the best to use; for a shorter throw, the 6-inch variety with 500-watt lamps; and if the distance from mounting position to acting area is extremely short, the still smaller types give enough light and the additional breadth of spread needed for this throw.

Because we conventionally divide the stage into six subareas, and three of these are in the downstage band, and two instruments are required for each, it is obvious that six ellipsoidal spotlights is the minimum requirement for the most modest scale of production. An additional three would permit more flexibility in allowing two sets of color on one side of the stage, these to work with a single set on the other side. Of course, two instruments on each area from each side, making a total of twelve ellipsoidal spotlights, come close to the ideal.

If the stage is exceptionally broad, it may be necessary to divide the downstage section into four acting areas, and the number of front spotlights must be increased accordingly. And, of course, there may be any number of sound reasons for using some different number of subareas. The six-area system is not sacred, by any means. It is simply a system that seems to work in a great many cases, and we use it here as a basis for discussion.

THE UPSTAGE AREAS.   Similarly the upstage band of acting areas will be covered by spotlights, and here the 6-inch Fresnel-type instrument is usually the answer. These areas may be reached effectively from what is often called the first-pipe location: the first mounting position behind the proscenium, the housecurtain, and any masking piece hung overhead. Sometimes a "light bridge" (a catwalk with mounting pipes attached) is located here, a very great convenience in the proper placing and focusing of stage lights, operating follow spots, and such pursuits. Whatever the actual provisions may be, in this position some device must be found for the upstage-area instruments and others. It is a most critical location.

Just as the minimum number of ellipsoidal-reflector spots for the downstage areas is six, so the upstage areas demand at least six Fresnels. And if additional instruments are to be used on the downstage band, then more should be provided for the upstage areas, so that the possibilities for variation may be consistent on all portions of the stage.

EXTRA SPOTLIGHTS.   While the acting areas must be the prime consideration in choosing spotlights, there are many additional uses for these instruments. Accenting special areas, throwing light into odd corners of an irregularly shaped setting, punching a strong light in through a window or door all call for spotlights of one sort or another. Even the most modest inventory should allow a couple of 6-inch Fresnels and as many 6-inch ellipsoidal-reflector spotlights for these various purposes. While a more elaborate setup would probably find good use for a half dozen 6-inch Fresnels, a pair of the 8-inch type, and at least twelve ellipsoidal-reflector spotlights about equally divided among the three sizes.

FLOODLIGHTS

Floodlights are the next consideration. For the small stage a few adjustable sockets with R-type lamps might be perfectly satisfactory; these can be useful adjuncts in quite large layouts as well.

More conventionally, the ellipsoidal floodlight is the proper instrument to use, and a half dozen of the smaller type are extremely valuable for door and other small backings. For larger backing areas, particularly curving cycloramas, the larger floodlight is necessary. There should be no fewer than one such instrument for each ten feet of background to be lighted in each color. So, for a 3-color setup on a cyclorama measuring fifty feet along its top edge, fifteen floodlights would be a minimum requirement. And more would be desirable if a great deal of light is required on the cyclorama.

However, as will presently be discussed, the use of striplights rather than floodlights for lighting a backdrop or cyclorama is recommended.

BEAM PROJECTORS

The beam projector, with its narrow and extremely powerful beam of light, has scarcely any use on the very small stage, if a few extra spotlights are available for sunlight effects through windows and the like. But on a larger stage this instrument is invaluable, and a minimum of four of the 10-inch size must be recommended. For the really big stage on which musicals and other nonrealistic dramas are frequently presented, the number of beam projectors that can be found useful is almost limitless.

STRIPLIGHTS

Striplights should be chosen with a view of their use in a variety of places on the stage, depending on the requirements of the particular production. As was suggested in Chapter 16, strips without reflectors but burning the R- and PAR-type lamps are the most valuable today. They should be wired in 3-color circuits, and the 6-foot lengths made standard with a few exceptions noted below. Such instruments can then be successfully employed for any of the usual striplighting purposes with the simple changing of lamps for the various requirements of intensity and beam form.

FOOTLIGHTS AND X-RAYS.   Footlights, if used, and they are often invaluable, should extend not more than about two-thirds the width of the proscenium opening, otherwise they will throw unnecessary and distracting light on the tormentors and walls of the setting. For any stage opening up to thirty feet, three 6-foot strips should suffice. A larger stage can use four such lengths.

In like manner first border strips sometimes called "X-rays" hung from the same pipe as the upstage area spotlights (or one immediately adjacent) should not extend over half the stage width, so two 6-foot lengths, spaced two or three feet apart at the center, are sufficient. Both these sets of strips may well use the colored R-lamps to good advantage, though clear 150-watt floods with gelatin may be substituted.

THE BACKDROP.   If the backdrop is straight, rather than in curved cyclorama form, striplights overhead are preferred to large floodlights. Total footage of these would be little less than the actual length of the backdrop, so if this should measure forty feet at least six 6-foot lengths would be required. For this overhead position, the power of 150-watt PAR spots or even 300-watt R-spots would be needed. Gelatin color media would be used. In some places, striplights are used even with a curved cyclorama, with several short

4½-foot lengths making the curve possible. Regardless of what are used overhead, the striplights at the foot of the background are a necessity. Again, the total length of these would be approximately that of the surface to be lighted. Because these instruments must be fairly close to the backing, widespread distribution, as from R or PAR floods is essential. Because these are focused upward, the accumulation of heat on the color media is terrific. Gelatin and plastics will quickly burn out, so colored-glass roundels become necessary.

Cycloramas.   When cycloramas expose a very great height, say thirty feet or more, to the view of the audience, it may be necessary to use duplicate sets of instruments at top or bottom. One very effective method is to put a second set of striplights at the base of the cyc with PAR-150 spots which are focused on approximately the middle of the backing, thus giving three zones of lighting, which, of course, are carefully overlapped and blended. Even if identical colors are used—and this is not at all necessary—by varying the different circuit dimmers, limitless color effects can be achieved.

On the other hand, on a very small stage, or with a setting that exposes to the audience's eyes only a small amount of backing, it may be possible to light this from one direction—top or bottom—only. Obviously fewer color changes can be worked in such a situation. And some stages are so arranged that it is impossible to use lights from overhead on the cyclorama. Then double instrumentation at the bottom is essential.

A great convenience in the effective lighting of a backdrop or cyclorama from the bottom is a "cyc pit" or trough, let into the stage floor at the foot of the drop or cyc, and carefully following its curve, if any. The cloth piece should descend into this trough, which should be at least three feet wide and deep enough to hide the bottom of the cyc from the spectator seated at the rear of the uppermost balcony. The striplights are placed in this pit, conveniently hidden from the audience. Naturally, such a trough should be planned with the new stage. Rarely can it be incorporated easily into an already existing plant.

BORDERLIGHTS

The custom of using several rows of borderlights across the stage at various intervals from the front to the rear has practically been abandoned in this country except for ballet, revue, and such musicals as still employ wing-and-border-type settings. At best it provides a stylized form of lighting that modern taste does not entirely approve. And it is quite impossible of course with a ceilinged interior. But if it is essential for one of the types of productions stated above, then three or four 6-foot lengths may be hung from battens, behind appropriate masking, across the various zones of stage action, usually three, including the front zone covered by the first border strips. With a low trim, colored lamps might be suitable for these, but the use of gelatin might be preferred with PAR-floods for a short throw, or R-spots for a longer one.

As can be seen, it is not possible to state exactly how many lengths of striplights are necessary unless the dimensions of the stage, and its background provision, as well as the general production scheme, are known. Possibly for a modest stage layout three lengths for footlights, two for first borders, and five for cyclorama foots—a total of ten 6-foot lengths—might be recommended, it being understood that these same instruments may be used for other purposes as occasion demands. For larger installations this number might well be doubled, but two or four of the shorter 4½-foot lengths substituted for the same number of longer ones.

BACKING STRIPS

A small, so-called "backing strip" is a very handy instrument. In its commercial form, this is a very short metal trough holding three or four small-wattage lamps. It can be used instead of a floodlight for small backings, placed behind narrow headers over doors, and employed in any number of tight places to throw a general illumination of low intensity. Half a dozen of these can be useful on any stage, but for the budget-minded group much less expensive, and practically as useful, devices can be put together merely by mounting sockets on boards, or on the scenery itself by means of spring clips, and using bare lamps. The 40-watt side-silvered T-shaped lamp is especially useful for this purpose.

R'S AND PAR'S

While the use of R's and PAR's has been enthusiastically advocated for striplights, and suggested as a substitute for more conventional floodlights, it must be pointed out that these lamps are totally unfitted for employment as spotlights except in the most rudimentary layouts. They lack the punch for a really long throw, but, more important, their beams are so impossible to control, to shape, to mask, that the side spill is distracting and annoying even to a not very discriminating audience. Even with the use of the hoods that are available, they cannot substitute for the smallest conventional spotlight. One exception to this statement must be noted. A 1000-watt, low-voltage PAR lamp has recently been incorporated into a new type of follow spot—a very effective instrument and one easy to operate.

SPECIAL INSTRUMENTS

EFFECT MACHINES. Because of the increasing employment of projected effects on the modern stage, and the good use that these can be put to if sensibly employed—and with artistic taste—it would be well for even a modest producing organization to provide itself with one or more lens projectors. They need not be elaborate. If some old plano-convex spotlights are available, as they usually are, it is only necessary to buy the apparatus that goes to make up the effect heads. In fact, it is not recommended that any producing group, except under the most special circumstances, utilize any other manner of projecting images from slides.

As was pointed out, the commercial equipment houses sell holders for the second condensing lenses (or Dutchmen), the slide holders, and the holders for the objective-lens systems. A small inventory of objective lenses of various focal lengths should be obtained. In this way, a completely satisfactory lens-projecting machine can be made up for whatever purpose is desired. Probably a pair of such projectors are advisable for almost any stage. Additional parts are readily obtainable for the more elaborate production that would require such equipment.

LINNEBACH PROJECTORS. A Linnebach projector, or a pair of them, to enable cross-fading from one scene to another, are extremely handy things to have around. They can be easily mocked-up from sheet metal by anyone handy with tin snips and rivets; or other sheet material might be used, local fire laws permitting. Linnebach effects, on a small scale, can even be achieved by use of a large plano-convex hood with the lens removed.

FOLLOW SPOTS. It seems that follow-spotting is undergoing a revival in the American theatre, even for productions of quite realistic character. Inasmuch as the nature of a follow spot requires that its beam be seen above all the other lighting on the stage picture, extremely powerful instruments must be used. For the very largest installations, the carbon arc has not yet been surpassed, but for anything smaller, the new incandescent follow spots, including the recently developed type that uses a low-voltage PAR lamp, should suffice. But unless the auditorium provides a location for the instrument and its operator out of view of the audience, yet offering a clear view of the entire stage, no follow spot can be used at all. Whatever instrument is selected must be chosen on the basis of the location and length of throw from such a position.

RÉSUMÉ OF INSTRUMENTS

In résumé, then, for the smallest and most modest stage, the very minimum of equipment that can be recommended would be as follows:

Ellipsoidal-reflector spotlights for the downstage areas		6
Fresnel spotlights for the upstage areas		6
Miscellaneous spotlights for various purposes		4
Small floodlights for backings, and the like		4
Striplights in 6-foot lengths,		
for footlights	3	
for first borders	2	
for backdrop	3	
total striplights		8

A group starting out in a new plant and with no other equipment available would find this list barely adequate to accomplish anything particularly artistic or imaginative. But these instruments would serve as a firm base on which to build.

CONNECTIONS

STAGE CONNECTIONS.   But merely to own a good supply of instruments, including their adjuncts such as lamps, color media, mounting devices, and the like—is not enough. One must have suitable wiring about the stage and auditorium to permit the electric service to be brought to each instrument wherever it may be mounted.

In the commercial theatre this is accomplished awkwardly and inefficiently by stringing cable directly from the control board to the various spotlights, floodlights, and so forth. And this may also be necessary for such groups as play only occasionally and in places that are ordinarily devoted to other pursuits than the dramatic. But any real theatre should have permanent wiring laid in conduit, and the planning for this should be done with care.

FRONT-OF-HOUSE CONNECTIONS.   If we are considering the smallest possible theatre in which we expect to use no more than six spotlights from the auditorium location—be it false beam, balcony front, or wherever—we shall need six outlets at this position. Eight would be a more realistic number, for surely a special instrument or two will be used here on occasion. And if we expect our inventory of instruments to increase, additional circuits should be laid in at the very start to care for everything that we logically can expect to acquire.

Of course, each outlet should be furnished with an appropriate connector, so that instruments may be readily changed, and each outlet should be serviced by its own wiring, laid in conduit, back to the control board or cross-connect panel, so each instrument will be on its own dimmer control independent of each other instrument. This wiring should be standardized, not only here but throughout the stage, for 20-ampere-current flow. This is a logical capacity, great enough to take care of the largest lamps this theatre will use.

STAGE-FLOOR CONNECTIONS.   Outlets must be provided in the stage apron where footlights will be placed. At least three circuits will be needed here, one for each color circuit of the foots. With a larger stage, the footlights may be used in sections, thus requiring more outlets, and occasionally small spots are located here, so provision should be made for them.

Around the stage floor there should be an abundance of connections to accommodate a great miscellany of instruments. Again, each such outlet should have its own wiring back to the control. The system of serving opposite sides of the stage with the same circuitry is antiquated. On the smallest stage at least six connections should be provided along each side, and many more are preferable.

OVERHEAD CONNECTIONS.   Along the first pipe position is where the greatest accumulation of stage outlets is required. The upstage areas are lighted from here, many accenting specials are mounted here, and here is where the X-ray strips are hung. Twelve is the very minimum number of connections for the most modest layout.

Depending on the size of the stage, additional outlets should be furnished over its central areas. These may be used for occasional second-border strips, for back- and top-lighting instruments, and for chandeliers and other overhead specials. Again, the needs of a minimum stage suggest three, with more desirable.

CYCLORAMA OUTLETS.   And special attention must be given to hooking up the instruments that are to light the cyclorama or backdrop, both from above and at stage level. If our stage has no more than twenty-five feet of backdrop exposed to the view of the audience, it will require four 6-foot strips to wash it evenly. This means a total of forty-eight lamps, or sixteen lamps per color circuit. And if we use 150-watt lamps, we have 2400 watts or 24 amperes per circuit which is too much for our general wiring.

So either we must split the strips between two sets of outlets, or else provide heavy-duty wiring that will take this high current flow. In like manner, the overhead lights must be planned for.

On a very modest stage, it is probably better to settle for one capacity all the way round and provide extra outlets to cyc-foot and overhead locations. This would have the added advantage of permitting different color effects on the opposite sides of the stage, a not infrequent desire. So we should furnish twelve outlets all together for the backdrop area. Of course, if the stage is so low that not over fifteen vertical feet of the backdrop is seen by the audience, we can eliminate either the overhead or the stage-level outlets, but not both.

TOTAL OUTLETS.   Fifty connections is not a bit too many for even a small stage—say twenty-five feet wide at the proscenium by twenty deep. We would much prefer to have seventy-five. For larger stages, with more equipment and where more elaborate productions are planned, the number will easily jump to a hundred and fifty.

Of course, not all these outlets will be used at the same time, but the convenience and safety involved in not needing to string cables for long distances—not to mention the increased artistic possibilities—should more than compensate for the comparatively modest first investment, if, indeed, permanent wiring costs as much as equally long runs of good stage cable.

CROSS-CONNECTIONS.   Obviously we are not recommending that a dimmer be permanently assigned to each of these circuits, nor is this ever done today in other than the crudest layouts. Some form of cross-connecting device, of which several types were mentioned in the previous chapter, must be provided, so that any instrument may be hooked up to any dimmer of whichever form of control board is used, subject, of course, to a proper regard for circuit and dimmer capacities.

A cross-connecting panel also should allow several stage circuits to be hooked up to the same dimmer. Although we like to have completely independent control over each instrument, sometimes this is not really necessary, or the lack of a sufficient number of dimmers may make it impossible. Again, it may be highly desirable to have certain instruments operating under one control. A properly designed cross-connecting panel is the ideal place to handle such "ganging."

CONTROL BOARDS

Various types of these were discussed in Chapter 18, but how many circuits should be included in a new installation—and of what capacity—is a subject for considerable consideration, no matter what kind of control is used.

In the electronic systems the smallest dimmer is usually about 2000-watts. Being multicapacity, this is satisfactory for all loads up to its rating. For the smallest stage, with the most modest pretenses, twenty-four such dimmers would be an absolute minimum based on separate control for each of the six acting areas (two instruments apiece), thus leaving a mere twelve circuits to be distributed among footlights, X-rays, and cyc lights (three apiece), not to mention door-backings, sunshine and moonlight specials, chandeliers, wall sconces, and table lamps, fire effects, special accenting lights, and others beyond count.

On a stage with a large expanse of backdrop, the demands jump very rapidly. With a 40-foot cyclorama, for example, lighted by 300-watt R-40 lamps, each color circuit would draw 60 amperes, necessitating dimmers of 6,000-watt capacity, otherwise several smaller dimmers would be forced to do the job. Incidentally, on such a stage it would be advisable to lay in heavier capacity wiring to such outlets as would usually be used for these lights, both at stage level and at the head of the backdrop.

For any stage larger than the one discussed above, the number of dimmer circuits must be increased, in line with the elaborateness of the productions to be done on it, especially if artistic distinction is hoped for and planned. Fifty control circuits, have proved scarcely sufficient for a large—but not immense—stage, even with some pretty dextrous replugging on the cross-connection panel.

20

LIGHTING DESIGNS
FOR TYPICAL
PRODUCTIONS

So far we have investigated the various tools of the light-designer's trade: instruments, color media, and control methods. Now let us see how these are employed in actually designing the lighting for a play. Because there are many forms of production these days, we will consider four typical but quite different sorts of presentation: a realistic interior, a realistic exterior, a wing-and-border setting, and a "space stage." Each of these has its own special problems.

First, we must decide in what manner of theatre these will be produced. So let us assume that it is of medium size. The stage will have a thirty-foot proscenium opening. There will be ample provisions for hanging scenery and instruments above the stage. About twenty feet from an actor

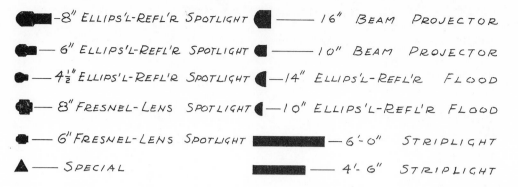

Figure 20–1. CONVENTIONAL SYMBOLS FOR INSTRUMENTS AS USED IN LIGHTING LAYOUTS

playing at the proscenium line will be a "beam" for mounting front spot-lights.

DESIGNING ON PAPER

The importance of planning on paper the lighting design for any production cannot be exaggerated. It unifies the designer's ideas, enables him to foresee and eliminate many problems of both artistic and physical nature, and, when all the details are put down on paper, others are able to execute his wishes with assurance and precision.

A good layout shows the scenery in place on the stage and all the instruments in their proper locations—all drawn to scale to eliminate self-deception. Figure 20–1 shows the conventional symbols for instruments as used in most layouts. Instruments are numbered in a logical manner, and on an accompanying schedule they should be identified as to type, position, and purpose. Other details, such as lamp, color, and the like should also be specified. For some involved settings, it may be advisable to show a cross section of the stage as well as the plan. Corrections and additions should be marked on the layout and schedule as the work progresses.

THE REALISTIC INTERIOR

A realistic interior usually calls for some variation of the conventional box setting with a ceiling cloth overhead. The primary interest is within the walls of this set, while the backgrounds seen through windows and doors are of less importance. The lighting is sometimes completely motivated by apparent sources; in practically all cases it is realistically plausible.

In Figure 20–2 is shown such a setting. On the stage-left wall is a door, leading to some other room or passage. In the up-left corner a flight of stairs comes down into the room from off left. In the center of the upstage wall is an archway opening into a corridor with an entrance at the stage-left end.

The stage-right wall contains a window and a fireplace. Through the window is seen a backing with painted sky and a scene of distant hills.

Two scenes are involved. In Act I bright sunlight streams in through the window. In Act II it is dark night outside and a fire is burning on the hearth.

DOWNSTAGE AREAS.   In dividing the stage into acting areas, we find that though the conventional three will be needed across the front section, only two will be required for the upstage band. To cover areas 1, 2, 3, the downstage group, we mount 6-inch ellipsoidal-reflector spotlights in our front position. We select the ellipsoidal-reflector type over the plano-convex spotlight because of its far greater efficiency and punch of light, and over the Fresnel spot because the latter, though quite powerful, has such side spill that we would have light all over the proscenium wall to the great distraction of the audience. For a longer throw than the one we have assumed for this theatre, we would naturally use the 8-inch ellipsoidal-reflector spot with its narrow, more powerful beam. For a much shorter throw we could use the smaller, wider-beamed type.

In choosing the mounting positions for these instruments we attempt to achieve the ideal 45-degree angle, but note that we must mount the Area 1L instrument somewhat in from the end of the beam in order to reach the extreme downstage-left corner of the stage without being cut off by the proscenium. In like manner, Area 3R must come somewhat nearer the center.

Therefore, we have sacrificed to some extent the ideal angle in these cases, but this is a necessary compromise. The remaining four instruments can be placed just about where we prefer them. All six instruments are carefully framed so as not to spill distracting light on the face of the stage apron, on the overhead teaser, and, in the case of numbers 2 and 5, on the proscenium.

UPSTAGE AREAS.   To cover the upstage areas, numbers 4 and 5, we will select 6-inch Fresnel spotlights and mount them on the first pipe. Fresnels are picked for this location because the soft edge of their beams makes blending between the areas much easier, and no sharp, distracting beam patterns will appear on the walls of the set. Numbers 7, 8, and 12 can be focused at close to the 45-degree angle for their respective areas, but number 11, focused on Area 5R, must move in a little in order to keep spill light off the stage-right wall.

All five areas must be consistent in regard to colors. Because in both acts warm light (sunbeams and fireglow) seems to come from the right of the stage, we can use a warm gelatin in instruments 4, 5, 6, 11, 12. The opposite side of the room would need a cool color for comparison in instruments 1, 2, 3, 7, and 8. Brigham Gelatin No. 62 (light scarlet) and No. 26 (light sky blue) make an excellent combination for such a situation without appearing too strong in either shade.

THE STAIRWAY.   Of course, the stairway must not be overlooked. But rather than consider it another area, it is preferable to handle it as a special problem, due to its different levels. To catch it properly, yet to avoid spilling light where it is neither needed nor desired, we can use an ellipsoidal-reflector spotlight from the first pipe, framing its beam to the stairs themselves, and only high enough to cover the actor moving up and down. This would be instrument No. 9, and because its beam is substantially at the same angle as the other stage-right instruments, its color should agree with these: a No. 62. To light the stairway from the other side, and particularly to catch the face of an ascending actor (always a fine effect) another ellipsoidal-spotlight (No. 13) can be mounted on a high stand (or from an overhead line) at the head of the stairs, about eight feet offstage. The beam from

Figure 20–2.   A REALISTIC INTERIOR SETTING.   *Below:* Instrument schedule. *Opposite page. Above:* Sketch of setting. *Below:* Layout of lighting instruments.

No.	INSTRUMENT	LOCATION	PURPOSE	LAMP	COLOR	REMARKS
1	6″ ELLIPS'L-REF'R SPOTLIGHT	BEAM – L	AREA 2 L	500 T 12	26	
2	″ ″ ″ ″	″ ″	″ 1 L	″	26	FRAME OFF RETURN
3	″ ″ ″ ″	″ ″	″ 3 L	″	26	
4	″ ″ ″ ″	BEAM – R	″ 1 R	″	62	
5	″ ″ ″ ″	″ ″	″ 3 R	″	62	FRAME OFF RETURN
6	″ ″ ″ ″	″ ″	″ 2 R	″	62	
7	6″ FRESNEL-LENS SPOTLIGHT	1ST PIPE – L	AREA 4 L	500 T 20	26	MAT TOP
8	″ ″ ″ ″	″ – C	″ 5 L	″	26	″ ″
9	6″ ELLIPS'L-REF'R SPOTLIGHT	1ST PIPE – C	STAIR SPECIAL	500 T 12	62	FRAME TO STAIR
10	″ ″ ″ ″	″ ″	ARCH SPECIAL	″	62	FRAME TO ARCH
11	6″ FRESNEL-LENS SPOTLIGHT	1ST PIPE – R	AREA 5 R	500 T 20	62	MAT TOP
12	″ ″ ″ ″	″ ″	″ 4 R	″	62	″ ″
13	6″ ELLIPS'L-REF'R SPOTLIGHT	STAND – L	STAIR BACKLIGHT	500 T 12	57	
14	10″ FLOOD LIGHT	SCENERY – L	DOOR BACKING	250 G 30	57	HIGH ON SCENERY
15	″ ″ ″	FIRE PLACE	FIRE GLOW	100 A 21	61	GANG WITH #24
16	16″ BEAM PROJECTOR	R- STAGE WALL	SUNLIGHT	1000 G 40	–	HIGH AS POSSIBLE
17	6″ × 6′-0″ STRIPLIGHTS				RED	3-COLOR CIRCUIT
18	″ ″	APRON	FOOTLIGHTS	75 R 30 FL.	BLUE	ROUNDELS
19	″ ″				GREEN	FEED THROUGH
20	″ ″	1ST PIPE	X – RAYS	150 R 40	RED	
21	″ ″			COLORED	BL. WHITE AMBER	
22	6″ × 4′-6″ ″	FLOOR – R	SKY BACKING	″	RED, BLUE, AMBER	
23	6″ × 6′-0″ ″	BEHIND ARCH	HALL	″	RED, BLUE WHITE, AMBER	
24	SPECIAL	FIREPLACE	FIRE EFFECT	2- 60A21	VARIED	GANG WITH #15
25	DESK LAMP	UL CORNER	LAMP	150 A 23	–	SHIELD TOP & SIDE
26	WALL SCONCE	L OF ARCH	WALL FIXTURE	15 FC/V		GANG - CANDELABR.
27	″ ″	R OF ARCH	″ ″	″	–	SOCKET ADAPTERS

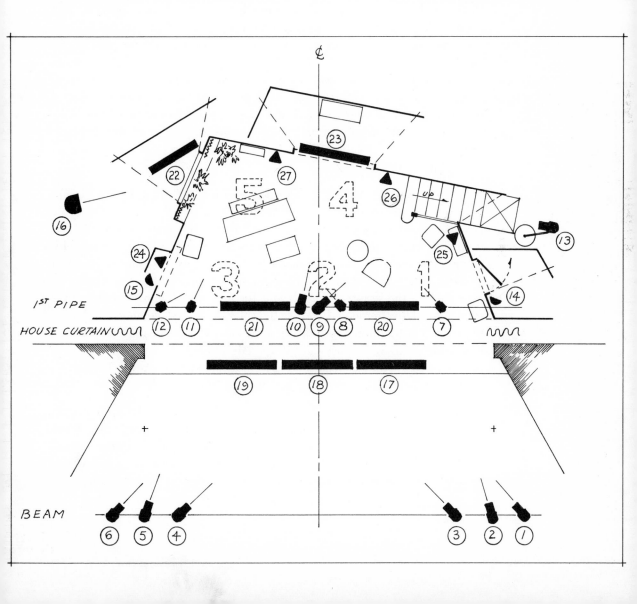

this instrument may be presumed to come from a hall light at the head of the stairs, and a No. 57 (light amber) gelatin could be used here for realism.

THE ARCHWAY.   An acting area of utmost importance is that immediately beyond the archway. Here the most vital entrances are made, and the actor must be well lighted as he prepares to come into the room. In fact, the director may even play brief, but important scenes in just this location. To cover this instrument 10 may be mounted in the center of the first pipe and framed carefully to the opening of the archway. As no particular angle is involved here, any plausible color may be chosen, such as the warm and flattering No. 62.

FLOODLIGHTS.   Having listed the spotlights, we should next see what flood-lights are desired. Two of the small, 10-inch variety are useful. No. 14 is placed behind the downstage-left door to throw illumination on the backing so this will not appear as a dark hole whenever the door is opened. This flood is placed at least ten feet high on the scenery to throw its light down-ward as from a ceiling or wall bracket. A 250-watt G-30 lamp will give ample illumination, and a No. 57 gelatin will provide a color that resembles the warm light usually associated with such household fixtures.

No. 15 has a very different use: it is placed in the fireplace to throw a warm glow over all who approach it. It need not be—in fact should not be—too brilliant (and hence distracting) so a 100-watt A-21 is all that is neces-sary, with a No. 61 gelatin (orange), a more realistic color for fireglow than the traditional red.

SUNBEAMS.   A large spotlight might be used for the strong beams of sun-light entering the window, but a beam projector is better still, because of the powerful punch of its parallel rays. No. 16 should be mounted well offstage, if possible even farther than our layout indicates. A producing group with ample equipment might even use two or more such instruments for this purpose. The height above the floor would depend on the hour of day as expressed by the script; a great height for near mid-day, a low, flat, angle for dawn or late afternoon. Likewise the color to be used would depend upon the time. It is traditional to think of sunlight as having a strong amber hue, but actually this is the case only in the late afternoon. For such a scene a No. 58 (medium amber) could be used. But noonday sun is much closer to white, and for such an effect it is best to use no color medium at all.

FOOTLIGHTS.   To give a unifying tone of color to the setting, footlights have been installed: three 6-foot lengths, each burning twelve lamps, wired in 3-color circuits. No strong burst of light is desired for this purpose, so that the 75-watt R-30 floods will be ample behind red-, blue-, and green-glass roundels. Of course, care is taken to place the glass so that the colors run alternately through all three lengths, and to connect the strips so that each circuit contains a single color only.

The best method for designating striplights connected in this manner is to give each length its own instrument number, and use the name of the color to designate each circuit for the run of the strips. Thus these footlights have been shown in our layout and schedule as instrument numbers 17, 18, and 19, and the circuits as red, blue, and green.

X-rays. Borderlights have also been hung: two 6-foot strips on the first pipe, spaced slightly apart to allow certain spotlights to be mounted between them. A little more punch is needed for these "X-rays," so we have used 150-watt R-40 colored lamps in instruments 20 and 21, with the circuits being designated as red, blue-white, and amber. Of course, the regular 150-watt R lamps with appropriate gelatins would be perfectly satisfactory. Considering that these lights are to blend and tone an interior, we need not bother with any greens, nor very strong blues, while the cheerful warmth of the amber will be useful in both our sunlit and firelit scenes.

Backing Strips. Instrument 22 is a 4½-foot striplight placed on the floor before the sky backing and focused on it. Considerable variation in color is desired here, so the 150-watt R-40 lamps would be in red, blue, and amber. The amber and blue mix to make a light blue daylight sky, while a rich night sky can be obtained by adding a little red to a blue on low reading. It should be noted that if people in the rear of the auditorium can see this striplight through the low window, or if there are balcony spectators who would surely see it, the better technique is to hang the instrument overhead and focus it down on the backing.

A 6-foot strip, No. 23, is hung behind the header over the archway to light the passage and its back wall. Again the 150-watt R's can be used, but these may well be amber, blue-white, and red lamps as a more useful combination for this interior corridor.

Note that different length strips are employed for these two backings, because the area that can be seen by the audience varies: about 9 feet in one case, and 15 in the other. Such an analysis is always essential and is plotted carefully on the layout from the "worst seat" on each side of the auditorium through the extreme limits of the openings to the backgrounds.

Specials. With the regular instruments cared for, we can turn to the specials. No. 24 is a fire effect: two 60-watt lamps hidden behind two or three logs. Their light will be seen through pieces of colored glass, or crumpled gelatins, to give the effect of glowing coals. Though this will be seen by only a small segment of the audience, it is a worthwhile device to give the fireplace a touch of realism and warmth.

In the corner between the wall and the stairs is another special, No. 25, a conventional desk lamp with cord running offstage to connect with the regular stage cable. Because its shade has been made more dense by use of a brown-paper lining, a 150-watt lamp may be used to throw a strong downward light.

Finally on the upstage wall are two sconces or wall brackets, No. 26 and No. 27, one on either side of the arch. These have unshaded lamps; therefore ones of small wattage must be used to prevent glare uncomfortable to an audience. The 15FC/V lamp, a flame-shaped decorative style, is employed. Because these have candelabra-sized bases, adapters must be placed in the regular sockets of the sconces, unless these are already of the proper, small size.

CONTROL.   Modest as this layout is, it would still require no fewer than thirty dimmers to control the lights properly. There are twenty-seven listed instruments, but the two sconces can be ganged, as can the fire glow and fire effect. On the other hand, the striplights each have three color circuits, each demanding its own control. The largest load would be 1200-watts (10 amperes) for each circuit of the borderlights. The beam projector would pull almost 9 amperes, and each circuit of the footlights 8. For the rest, 500-watt dimmers would suffice.

If the control board could not furnish the necessary circuits, some ganging would have to be done. Great ingenuity is often displayed in doing this, but a truly artistic use of lights and color values could not be maintained with much less than thirty dimmers.

REALISTIC EXTERIORS

The realistic exterior setting is one of the most difficult to light effectively, due to the many maskings needed to prevent the audience from seeing into the wings or up into the hanging space. These maskings—flat surfaces painted to resemble natural objects—are never very convincing and tend to catch stray, unwanted beams of light.

An exterior setting almost always includes a large sky area or a painted scene in the background that needs special attention. Apparent motivation is necessary for all the lighting.

AN EXTERIOR SETTING.   Figure 20–3 shows a typical exterior setting including many of the features frequently encountered. On stage left three sets of woodwings, painted as tree clusters, serve to mask the wings on that side of the stage. On the right there is a cottage which masks that side. In connection with the downstage woodwings, leaf borders cross the stage to mask overhead. Across the back of the playing areas is a ground row, three feet high in its lowest portion and representing hills in the middle distance.

The backdrop consists of a translucency, the lower portion of which is painted with opaque media to represent rolling hills and woods; above this the translucency is painted with dye colors to permit the light to pass through from the rear for greater luminosity and depth.

There are two scenes involved. In Scene 1 brilliant sunshine pours in from stage left. In Scene 2 moonlight floods the set from the same direction.

AREA SPOTS.   The front lights are placed substantially as they were for the realistic interior, but because the sunlight and moonlight make two different effects necessary, the stage-left instruments are double-hung; that is, there are two instruments focused on each area from this side. One set works in the first scene, the other set in the second. Or they might be used together at different intensities.

The three upstage areas are handled the same way, but because the first leaf border will hang so low, the usual first pipe location cannot be used. Instead this pipe is moved behind the leaf border. Great care must still be taken to prevent stray beams from touching corners of the second cloth border. In fact, the most careful planning cannot predict this with exactness, and much remounting and refocusing will probably be needed on the actual set.

DOUBLE-HUNG SPOTLIGHTS.   The stage-left instruments that will work when the sun is shining are called the Left-warms and they have No. 57 (light amber) gelatins to give the effect of warmth on that side of the stage. Opposite them, in the stage-right spotlights, we use No. 17 (special lavender), a medium gelatin that will appear quite cool opposite the warm No. 57. But in Scene Two, when the moon is apparently lighting the left side, the Left-cools contain No. 29 (special steel-blue) which is so very cool that the special lavender actually seems warm in contrast. This use of a medium or "neutral" gelatin on one side of the stage to work alternately against a warm and a cool on the other is a device that is often of extreme value when instruments or control circuits are not too abundant.

Because the space just beyond the fence would be frequently used, especially for entrances, we are considering it a seventh area, with instruments (numbers 19, 20, and 21) mounted behind the second border. To make sure that an actor leaving or entering at stage right is completely covered, we place an additional spotlight (No. 22) off right. The sunlight and moonlight coming in from stage left (as explained below) will take care of that side of the stage.

SUNLIGHT AND MOONLIGHT.   For a completely realistic effect, a great many powerful instruments would probably be needed for the sun and moon light. But to keep our example within proper bounds, we will use only four for each. Because the moonlight need not be as bright, we have used 8-inch

Figure 20–3.   A REALISTIC EXTERIOR SETTING.   Below: Instrument schedule. Opposite page. Above: Sketch of setting. Below: Layout of lighting instruments.

No.	INSTRUMENT	LOCATION	PURPOSE	LAMP	COLOR	REMARKS
1	6" Ellips'l-Ref'r Spotlight	Beam –L	Area 2L–Warm	500T12	57	Soft Edge
2	" " " "	" "	" 2L–Cool	"	29	" "
3	" " " "	" "	" 1L–Warm	"	57	Frame Off Torm.
4	" " " "	" "	" 1L–Cool	"	29	" " "
5	" " " "	" "	" 3L–Warm	"	57	
6	" " " "	" "	" 3L–Cool	"	29	
7	" " " "	Beam–R	" 1R·	"	17	
8	" " " "	" "	" 3R	"	17	Frame Off Torm.
9	" " " "	" "	" 2R	"	17	Soft Edge
10	6" Fresnel-Lens Spotlight	1st Pipe–L	" 4L Warm	500T20	57	
11	" " " "	" "	" 4L Cool	"	29	
12	" " " "	" "	" 5L Warm	"	57	
13	" " " "	" "	" 5L Cool	"	29	
14	" " " "	" "	" 6L Warm	"	57	
15	" " " "	" "	" 6L Cool	"	29	
16	" " " "	1st Pipe–R	" 4R	"	17	
17	" " " "	" "	" 5R	"	17	
18	" " " "	" "	" 6R	"	17	
19	" " " "	2nd Pipe–L	" 7L Warm	"	57	
20	" " " "	" " "	" 7L Cool	"	29	
21	" " " "	2nd Pipe–R	" 7R	"	17	
22	" " " "	3rd Pipe–R	" 7 Special	"	17	Mat Off Drop
23	8" Fresnel-Lens Spotlight	1st Pipe–L	Moonlight	1000G40	26	Focus on Area 2,3
24	" " " "	" " "	"	"	26	" " " 1,2
25	" " " "	2nd Pipe–L	"	"	26	" " " 5
26	" " " "	3rd Pipe–L	"	"	26	" " " 7
27	10" Flood	Scenery–R	Door Backing	250G30	58	Mount High on Scener
28	16" Beam Projector	1st Pipe–L	Sun Light	1500G40	54	Focus on Area 2,3
29	" " "	" "	"	"	54	" " " 1,2
30	" " "	2nd Pipe–L	"	"	54	" " " 5
31	" " "	3rd Pipe–L	"	"	54	" " " 7
32	6"×6'-0" Striplights					Focus on Painte
33	" "				Amber	Portion
34	" "	On Floor Behind	Translucency	300R40	Blue	Roundels
35	" "	Ground Row	Front Light	Flood	Bl-Green	
36	" "					
37	6"×4'-6" Striplights	4th Pipe	Translucency	150 Par 38	36	
38	6"×6'-0" "	Behind	Backlight	Spot	67	3-Color Circuit
39	" "	Translucency			40	Feed Through
40	" "	Very High				Focus on
41	" "					Translucent
42	6"×4'-6" Striplights					Portion

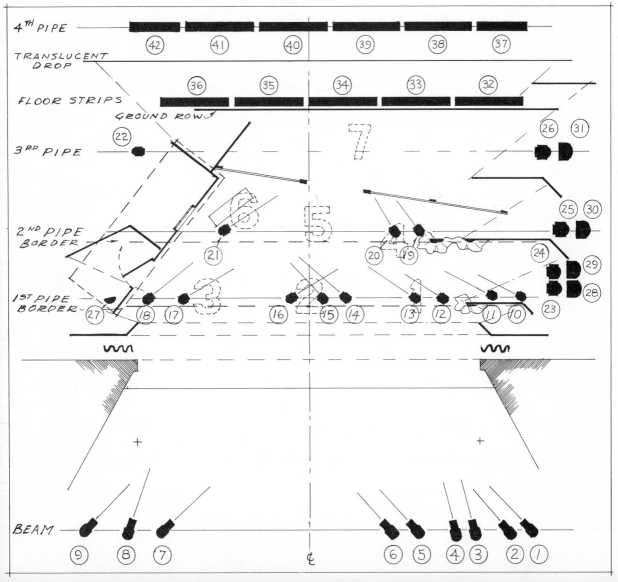

4ᵀᴴ PIPE

㊷ 42 ㊶ 41 ㊵ 40 ㊴ 39 ㊳ 38 ㊲ 37

TRANSLUCENT DROP

FLOOR STRIPS

㊱ 36 ㉟ 35 ㉞ 34 ㉝ 33 ㉜ 32

GROUND ROW

3ᴿᴰ PIPE

㉒ 22 ㉖ 26 ㉛ 31

2ᴺᴰ PIPE BORDER

㉑ 21 ⑳ 20 ⑲ 19 ㉕ 25 ㉚ 30 ㉔ 24 ㉙ 29 ㉘ 28

1ˢᵀ PIPE BORDER

㉗ 27 ⑱ 18 ⑰ 17 ⑯ 16 ⑮ 15 ⑭ 14 ⑬ 13 ⑫ 12 ⑪ 11 ⑩ 10 ㉓ 23

BEAM

⑨ 9 ⑧ 8 ⑦ 7 ⑥ 6 ⑤ 5 ④ 4 ③ 3 ② 2 ① 1

₵

Fresnels, which give a much smoother and broader beam. Nos. 23 and 24 would be placed behind the first woodwing with their focuses overlapping across the stage. The remaining Fresnels, Nos. 25 and 26, would be mounted one each behind the other two wings. No. 26 gelatin (light sky-blue) would give quite a realistic appearance as moonbeams.

The powerful beam projectors with 1500-watt lamps will be necessary for sunlight, to cut through the general light on the stage. These have been mounted in the same manner as the Fresnels ("moons") and a No. 54 (straw) gelatin used with them to give them a bit more warmth than the natural light from these instruments. This light will still appear whiter than the stage-left area lights with their No. 57.

It is not unusual on the stage with limited equipment to employ the same instrument for suns and moons, changing the color media between scenes, of course.

TRANSLUCENT BACKDROP.   And finally we come to the background with a distant view painted opaquely at the bottom. This portion of course, must be lighted from the front and therefore five 6-foot lengths of striplights are placed on the floor, not too close, so that their various beams may have room to blend smoothly over the surface. They should be as close to the ground row as possible, so as to be hidden from the audience (this is especially important if there is a balcony). As the light to be thrown on this portion is limited to the realistic daylight and night-time colors, we may use amber, blue-green, and blue roundels over the 300-watt R-floods. Glass is essential here, for gelatin would quickly burn out over these powerful lamps.

The upper portion of the backdrop is a true translucency, and therefore its light should come from behind. Four 6-foot lengths and two shorter lengths of strips with 150-watt PAR-spots are flown well above the highest visible part of the translucency and are focused down it to give it a sheet of light. A plain, white cloth might also be hung behind these, to reflect additional light through the drop. This is a particularly effective device to furnish extra punch. As these strips are focused downwards, gelatin may be used safely. Quite a variation of color is needed for this sky, so the three circuits may well have No. 36 (nonfade-blue), No. 67 (fire red), and No. 40 (light blue-green). By mixing the first and last, a daylight sky can be achieved; the 67 and 40 can give a sunset amber, while a touch of 67 added to the strong blue will provide a rich night sky. Many variations of these are possible.

It will be noticed that neither footlights nor X-ray strips are employed with this setting. Footlights would throw unwanted shadows—of the cottage, the trees, the fence, the ground row—on the background, unless they were

kept at such a low reading that they would serve no useful purpose. Likewise, strips in the usual X-ray (or first border) position would light up the
overhead cloth borders, representing leaves and branches, but actually designed solely for the utilitarian task of masking the overhead stage machinery. Such maskings are best left unlighted—and the audience, therefore,
undistracted.

CONTROL.   In a setting of this nature it is amazing how rapidly the dimmer
requirements mount up. Certainly the twenty-two area spotlights each
deserve individual control. The four moons could be ganged but would then
require a dimmer of 4000-watts capacity. Similarly the suns could be controlled together, but would need a 6000-watt dimmer—or two of 3000-watts
each.

The translucency front strips make up as three 20-lamp color circuits of
6000 watts apiece. There are 22 lamps per color circuit in the rear strips,
at 3300 watts each.

If the largest dimmers are 2000-watts (many places don't approach this)
then the moons will require two, the suns four, translucency fronts nine,
and rear six—a total of twenty-one dimmers!

On many boards this would necessitate ganging area spotlights, always a
great pity, with the resulting loss of artistic control. Of course it may be
necessary to fall back on awkward replugging between scenes, using the
same dimmers for the moons in the second scene as were used for the suns
in the first—and the left area cools in place of the warms on the same group
of controls.

WING-AND-BORDER SETTINGS

The wing-and-border setting presents problems very different from the
realistic exterior and interior types. Here realism and plausibility are usually
of little concern. Rather, the large expanses of flat scenery demand flat
lighting, and against these brilliant backgrounds the actors must be picked
out by powerful lighting directed on them. The use of follow spots for
this purpose is universal.

SETTING FOR A MUSICAL.   Figure 20–4 shows a wing-and-border set for a
typical musical. Because a traveler show curtain with appropriate design
is hung immediately behind the house curtain, the house tormentors and
teaser have been removed and their functions assumed by a show portal hung
just upstage of the show curtain. The zone across the stage just above the
portal is usually referred to as "In One." Its upstage boundary is marked
by a second traveler, a second portal, and a drop beyond. In turn, some
feet upstage of this group is yet another consisting of a second drop, a third

Figure 20–4.   A WING-AND-BORDER SETTING.   *Page 342.*
Instrument schedule. Page 343. *Above:* Sketch of setting. *Below:*
Layout of lighting instruments.

No.	INSTRUMENT	LOCATION	PURPOSE	LAMP	COLOR	REMARKS
1	6" Ellips'l-Ref'r Spotlight	Beam - L	Area 2L warm	500 T12	3	
2	" " " "	" "	" 2L cool	"	26	
3	" " " "	" "	" 1L warm	"	3	Frame to portal
4	" " " "	" "	" 1L cool	"	26	" " "
5	" " " "	" "	" 3L warm	"	3	
6	" " " "	" "	" 3L cool	"	26	
7	8 Ellips'l-Ref'r Spotlight	Beam - C	Follwspot	750 T12	Clear	
8	"			"	"	
9	6" Ellip's'l-Ref'r Spotlight	Beam - R	Area 1R warm	500 T12	62	
10	" " " "	" "	" 1R cool	"	17	
11	" " " "	" "	" 3R warm	"	62	Frame off portal
12	" " " "	" "	" 3R cool	"	17	" " "
13	" " " "	" "	" 2R warm	"	62	
14	" " " "	" "	" 2R cool	"	17	
15	" " " "	1st Stand - L	Crosslight	750 T12	29	Focus on Area 2, 3
16	" " " "	" "	" "	500 T12	29	" " " 1, 2
17	6" Fresnel-Lens Spotlight	1st Pipe - L	Area 5L warm	500 T20	3	
18	" " " "	" "	5L cool	"	26	
19	" " " "	" "	4L warm	"	3	
20	" " " "	" "	4L cool	"	26	
21	" " " "	" "	6L warm	"	3	
22	" " " "	" "	6L cool	"	26	
23	" " " "	1st Pipe - R	4R warm	"	62	
24	" " " "	" "	4R cool	"	17	
25	" " " "	" "	6R warm	"	62	
26	" " " "	" "	6R cool	"	17	
27	" " " "	" "	5R warm	"	62	
28	" " " "	" "	5R cool	"	17	
29	6" Ellips'l-Ref'r Spotlight	1st Stand - R	Crosslight	750 T12	57	Focus on Area 1, 2
30	" " " "	" R	"	500 T12	57	" " " 2, 3
31	" " " "	2nd Stand - L	"	750 T12	29	" " " 5, 6
32	" " " "	" - L	"	500 T12	29	" " " 4, 5
33	" " " "	" - R	"	750 T12	57	" " " 4, 5
34	" " " "	" - R	"	500 T12	57	" " " 5, 6
35	" " " "	3rd Stand - L	"	750 T12	29	Focus Far
36	" " " "	" - L	"	500 T12	29	" Near
37	" " " "	" - R	"	750 T12	57	" Far
38	" " " "	" - R	"	500 T12	57	" Near
39	16" Beam Projector	2nd Pipe - L	Downlight	1000 G40	2 & 62	Focus Downstage
40	" " "	" - L	"	"	2 & 62	" "
41	" " "	" - R	"	"	2 & 62	" "
42	" " "	" - R	"	"	2 & 62	" "
43	6"x6'-0" Striplights				R	
44	" "	Apron	Footlights	150 R40	G (Roundel)	3-Color Circuit
45	" "		Flood	B		Feed Through
46	" "			"		
47	" "	1st Pipe	1st Border	150 R40	58	
48	" "		Spot	40		
49	" "			"		
50	" "	3rd Pipe	2nd Border	150 R40	58	
51	" "		Spot	40		
52	" "			"		
53	" "	4th Pipe	Back Drop	300 R40	"	
54	" "		Spot	32		
55	" "			57		

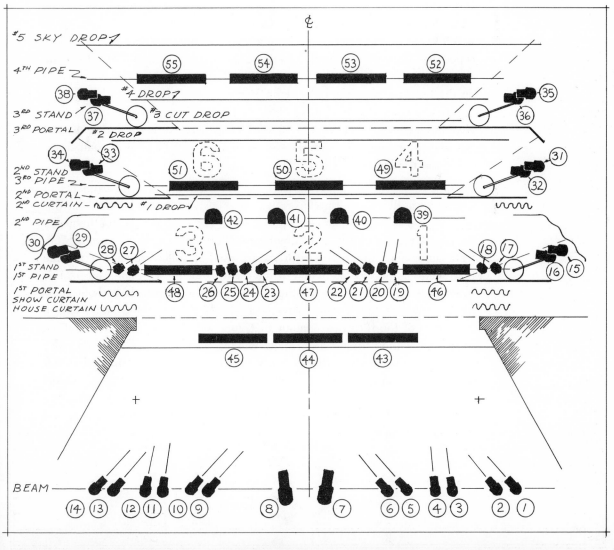

¢

#5 SKY DROP

4TH PIPE

55 54 53 52

38

#4 DROP

3RD STAND

37

#3 CUT DROP

35

36

3RD PORTAL

#2 DROP

34 33

2ND STAND
3RD PIPE

51 50 49

31

32

2ND PORTAL
2ND CURTAIN

#1 DROP

2ND PIPE

30 29

42 41 40 39

28 27

1ST STAND
1ST PIPE

18 17

16 15

1ST PORTAL
SHOW CURTAIN
HOUSE CURTAIN

48 26 25 24 23 47 22 21 20 19 46

45 44 43

+ +

BEAM

14 13 12 11 10 9 8 7 6 5 4 3 2 1

portal, and then two more drops. Finally, beyond all is a sky-blue backing.

The several drops will not all be solid cloth; some will be in part cut out so that the audience sees through to other scenic elements beyond. The various drops will work with the curtains and portals in different combinations as the show progresses, while set-pieces, furniture items, and the like will be moved on and off stage for different scenes. Often special lighting is needed for such pieces.

In the sketch are shown the three portals, drop No. 2, representing a cut-out of trees, and drop No. 4, a distant view.

LIGHTING THE IN-ONE ZONE.   In order to provide the punch of light on the actors required by this type of presentation, we have double-hung all the area lighting spotlights. This means that in the beams there are twelve 6-inch ellipsoidal spotlights, two to a side on each of the three "In One" areas. Care must be taken to focus these spots far enough downstage on the apron to cover the probable movement of the players. In this style of production it is not uncommon for the actors to be brought clear down to the very edge of the stage, and they must be covered there just as much as when they are confined by the imaginary "fourth wall."

With four instruments on each area, considerable variation in the colors is possible. Rather than simply use the same tints on the opposite side of the stage, we prefer to put the flattering No. 3 (flesh pink) as the warm color on the left and No. 62 on the right. For most productions of this type, a generally romantic feeling is desired, so the cools should not be extreme. No. 26 is a deep enough blue to be used on the left, while the rather neutral No. 17 (special lavender) on the right will appear quite cool in comparison to the warm colors used with it.

FOLLOW SPOTS.   Frequently, it is desirable to have special instruments in the beams to illuminate the decorative show curtain. But to keep this layout on the modest side, we have foregone these and will let the footlights do the job. But a pair of 8-inch narrow-beam ellipsoidal spotlights, burning 750-watt lamps and equipped with irises are used as follow spots. We assume that operators may be stationed in the theatre's beam. In plants where this is not possible, some other location must be found. Musicals without spotlights to accent the leading players on the brightly lighted stage lack a great deal of the theatrical glamor that goes with this sort of presentation. Most of the time these follow spots will be most effective with no color medium at all. If any is used, a No. 2 (light flesh-pink) is appropriate. Of course, for occasional and particular purposes other and stronger colors may be used, including a very dense blue filter especially made for ultra-violet effects. With an operator in constant attendance, color changes are easily accomplished.

THE IN-TWO ZONE.   Moving to the "In-Two" zone, that between the second and third portals, we light the three upstage areas by means of twelve 6-inch Fresnel spots hanging from the first pipe. Their colors match the downstage area spotlights, as usual. These instruments must be carefully focused to pass under the second portal without touching the edges with a distracting glare. Many times a third set of spotlights is employed for the "In-Three" zone, but because ours is not deep and we are trying to be economical with instruments, we shall hope that the extra light is not needed this far upstage.

SIDE LIGHTING.   Side-lighting—lighting from the wings—has become a convention with the wing-and-border setting. It has three important aspects. Its low angle from the side adds to the plasticity of the actors' appearance. It can add extra color effects. And it helps to tie together the zones across which it is focused. In each of our six side entrances we have provided two 6-inch ellipsoidal spotlights, mounted on stands. The upper instrument is focused across the stage to catch both the center and the far acting areas, and, because of this long throw, it burns a 750-watt lamp. The lower one, mounted at least ten feet above stage level, ties in the near and the center areas and uses the 500-watt lamp. Because we are not using strong colors for our regular area spotlights, in these sidelighting instruments we choose No. 29 (special steel-blue) from the left and No. 57 (light amber) from the right.

DOWN LIGHTS.   Another feature that is becoming almost a "must" for musicals are the downlights which we have placed over the "In-One" zone. These are hung quite high and just downstage of the traveler curtain and the second portal so that they tend to back-light the actors standing at the front of the zone. A combination of No. 2 and No. 62 gelatins in these 16-inch Beam Projectors with their 1000-watt G-lamps will throw a flattering high light on the head and shoulders of the actors and set them out from the scenery. A second set of down lights over the "In-Two" zone might not be amiss, but our list of instruments is already startlingly long.

FOOTLIGHTS.   Striplights have been used extensively to tie in the various portions of the stage, to give tonal washes over scenery and actors, and generally, to provide quite a bit of the illumination. The footlights consist of the regular three 6-foot lengths, in this case burning 150-watt R-40 lamps behind glass roundels in the primary colors. The unusually high wattage here is to provide a strong wash of light for the show curtain. In general, musicals and revues demand rather strong footlights to supplement the regular front lighting especially for chorus-line sequences, to throw illumination under large hats, to wash the company with special colors, and the like.

BORDER LIGHTS.   For the first and second borders, three 6-foot lengths each are used. Those of the first pipe must be placed well apart to leave room for area spotlights to be mounted between the lengths; on the third pipe less space is needed. But in both cases somewhat wider extension into the wings is necessary in order to wash properly the scenery hanging upstage of each set of strips. 150-watt R-40 floods are used with colors approaching the secondaries: No. 11 (medium magneta), No. 58 (medium amber), and No. 40 (light blue-green) a combination that should allow almost any tint desired to flood the stage.

THE BACKDROP.   And for the background, the cloth or other surface painted to represent the sky, there have been hung four lengths of strips, as far downstage from the surface as other flown elements permit, so that as smooth a wash as possible can be achieved. Here it is necessary to go to the 300-watt R-40 spots, as a good punch will be needed. A good dark night sky can be achieved by use of a No. 38 (dark Navy-blue) and if this is a bit too deep it can be lightened a little by mixing in No. 27 (light blue). For a bright daylight sky we add No. 57 (light amber).

CONTROL.   There are twenty-four area spotlights, all of which will be working at the same time in several scenes, so no replugging is possible in this

Figure 20–5.   A SPACE-STAGE SETTING.   *Below:* Instrument schedule. *Opposite page.* *Above:* Sketch of setting. *Below:* Layout of lighting instruments.

No.	INSTRUMENT	LOCATION	PURPOSE	LAMP	COLOR	REMARKS
1	6" ELLIPS'L-REF'R SPOTLIGHT	BEAM - L	DR SPECIAL	500 T 12	29	
2	8" " " "	" "	FOLLOW SPOT	750 T 12	54	
3	6" " " "	" "	R-CENTER SP.	500 T 12	NONE	
4	" " " "	BEAM - R	DL SP. #1	"	57	
5	" " " "	" "	" " #2	"	26	
6	6" FRESNEL-LENS SPOTLIGHT	1ST PIPE-L	L- STEPS	500 T 20	3/62	KEEP OFF CYC.
7	6" ELLIPS'L-REF'R SPOTLIGHT	" " "	UC SPECIAL	500 T 12	NONE	
8	" " " "	" " "	"HORROR SP."	"	41	FRAME TO TRAP
9	" " " "	1ST PIPE-C	ARCH SP. #1	"	58	
10	6" FRESNEL-LENS SPOTLIGHT	" " "	R - STEPS	500 T 20	17	
11	6" ELLIPS'L-REF'R SPOTLIGHT	1ST PIPE-R	ARCH SP. #2	500 T 12	30	FRAME TO ARCH
12	" " " "	PLATFORM-DR	FOLLOW SPOT	"	26/29	
13	6" FRESNEL-LENS SPOTLIGHT	2ND PIPE-R	UR STEPS	500 T 20	18	
14	6" ELLIPS'L-REF'R SPOTLIGHT	" " "	DS STEPS #1	500 T 12	26	
15	" " " "	" " "	" " #2	"	57	
16	16" BEAM PROJECTOR	3RD PIPE UL	ARCH BACKLIGHT	1000 G 40	54	FOCUS THRU ARCH
17	LINNEBACH PROJECTOR	BEHIND PLATFORM-L	PROJECTION ON CYC	1500 G 40	SLIDE	HIDDEN OPERATOR- ADDITIONAL SLIDES
18	14" ELLIPS'L-REF'R FLOOD	BEHIND PLATFORM-R	FIRE GLOW ON CYC	500 PS	60	
19	" " " "	"	"	"	67	GANG TOGETHER
20	" " " "	"	"	"	63	
21	6" x 4'-6" STRIPLIGHTS	1ST PIPE - L	X - RAYS	150 PS OR R40-FL.	29 58 41	3-COLOR CIRCUIT FEED THROUGH
22	" "	" " -R	"			
23	SLIDE PROJECTOR	2ND PIPE - L	PROJECTION ON CYC	1000 G 40	SLIDE	8" PLANO-CONVEX SPOT WITH EFFECT HEAD

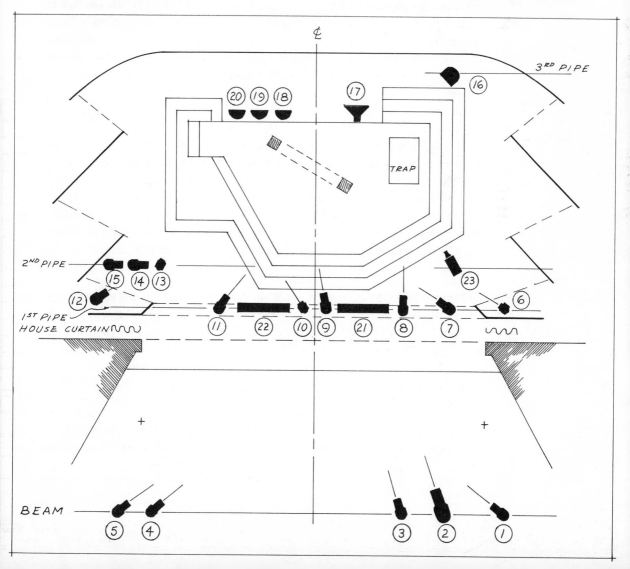

production. While it would be pleasant to have an individual dimmer assigned to each cross-lighting instrument, we can get along by ganging the pair at each location, holding the dimmer requirements to six. Likewise the down lights may well be ganged, if a 4000-watt dimmer is available—or on two 2000-watt dimmers.

The footlights and first and second border will each require three 1800-watt circuits—nine all together. But the backdrop calls for three circuits of 4800 watts apiece. On boards with only small capacity controls, these loads must be split up in some manner, depending on what is available.

Obviously individual control over the two follow spots is absolutely essential. The total and minimum demands for this layout, therefore, would be forty-three dimmers that can handle up to 2000-watts each, and three of far greater capacity. And this is a very modest plot for a musical play.

SPACE STAGES

Increasingly popular today is the type of presentation that is often referred to as "space staging." In this form of production realism is completely lacking in the scenery, which is generally a dark background, an arrangement of platforms, and a form or two of suggestive but not very accurate shape. No specific locales are intended, or the locales may change as the play progresses. For example, a presentation of *Macbeth* might be given with the same scenery serving at various times for "The Heath," "Macbeth's Castle," "Dunsinane," and so forth.

The lighting is usually done in limited areas at a time—a single actor pinpointed by a spotlight, or a compact group covered by a slightly larger pool of light. Entrances are made from the dark. Often groups of actors stand in half darkness. Every instrument becomes, in effect, a "special." A grave problem is to keep the spill light off the background, to hold the beams to tight focuses, to eliminate insofar as may be done, reflections from the floor. To this end the instruments are usually mounted quite high and as nearly vertical as possible, and focused with care and precision.

A TYPICAL SPACE SETTING.   Figure 20–5 shows a typical space-stage arrangement. Surrounding the stage is a cyclorama and wings of a soft, black material to absorb as much light as possible. Center stage is an irregular platform with steps from three sides—all painted a flat black. An arch that might be accepted as a number of things from a church window to a bower, and painted a dark shade of brown, stands on the platform. There is a trap to the left of it in the floor.

LIGHTING THE SPACE STAGE.   In the beams four 6-inch ellipsoidal spotlights are used for the stage-level areas at quite sharp angles to avoid as far as possible letting their beams strike the cyclorama. One 8-inch spotlight to be used as a follow spot is also mounted there, while a 6-inch spot is placed high on a special platform in the right wing. Other 6-inch instruments, including a few Fresnels with hoods to control side spill are used from the first pipe to light the platform and step areas. Two cover the arch opening, a very important acting position, another is carefully focused on the trap. A large beam projector is also employed as back-lighting through the arch from the upstage side.

Despite the blackness of the cyclorama, it can be used for special projections to good advantage. A Linnebach will throw general pictures as backings to the archway, while sharper images can come from the effect machine hung from the second pipe. A general glow is produced by three floodlights placed behind the up-right corner of the platform. Two spotlights are hung from the second pipe to wash the downstage portion of the steps. And two striplights are intended to give a very general low-intensity tone to the whole stage for scenes involving large groups.

CONTROL.   This is a very modest layout—no doubt an actual script would suggest many more instruments than those to which we have optimistically limited ourselves. Frequently in such a production the demands for color changes force the hanging of identical instruments, side by side, and covering the same portions of the stage.

But those instruments we have used must—beyond question—have individual control. This should not be too difficult, as only twenty-two dimmers are required, and none need have a capacity greater than 1500 watts.

In plays of this nature the effects are largely achieved through the most delicate dimming and cross fading. The biggest problem of control, therefore, is the timing on the control panel. If this is located, as is sadly the usual case, somewhere in the wings, the operators must be driven and drilled until they can accomplish their blindfold task adequately. But if the controlboard is properly located where the stage may be easily viewed, then the operator can perform his work with taste and understanding and become, in effect, an additional and very important "actor."

21

DESIGNING THE LIGHTING
FOR NONPROSCENIUM
PRODUCTIONS

ARENA PRODUCTION

So far we have discussed only the types of production presented on a conventional stage with practically all action separated from the audience by
"the fourth wall." But there are other forms rapidly gaining in popularity in
which the division between audience area and acting area is less clearly
marked. These vary from a regular stage with action coming out into the
auditorium on side stages, ramps, and steps to the complete arena form in
which the audience surrounds the playing area on all four sides. Obviously
the techniques that are useful for lighting in-the-round stages must differ
from those used for the more conventional types.

The designer need not be bothered with lighting the scenery in a truly in-the-round production for little scenery exists and what there is is adequately lighted by the same beams that strike nearby actors. But this same lack of scenery deprives the designer of valuable mounting positions for his instruments, and, more important, denies him a background. He must light the actors from all sides, just as they must play to all sides.

Accuracy of Focus. With the spectators crowded closely—often too closely—about the playing areas, instruments that have hard-to-control beams are of little value. Floodlights are impossible. Striplights may be used discreetly and with side maskings to give an over-all tonality of rather low intensity. Fresnel spots must be focused with particular accuracy and in addition a funnel must be added to control the beam spill.

Functions of Arena Lighting. Visibility remains, of course, the primary function in arena-production lighting, and this means that the actors must be effectively lighted for all members of the surrounding audience. Composition takes the form of holding the spectators' attention to the acting areas and thus demands that the lighting must have definition and form of great precision. Some plays suggest that certain sections of the stage be always related to certain locations, which adds another duty to composition—that of holding these areas to closely prescribed limits. Mood must be accomplished by means of general intensity and in color toning, but both within very limited ranges.

Mounting Positions. Because there is such great variation among the different arena stages and the buildings surrounding them, it is difficult to suggest a typical lighting arrangement. An arena stage in the center of a large gymnasium floor, for example, would probably offer all sorts of lofty and convenient mounting places for overhead lighting instruments, while a formal hall with a plastered ceiling of no great height presents the utmost difficulty, ranging close to the impossible. However, let us assume a reasonable amount of overhead flexibility in our discussion of this form of presentation.

Arena Lighting Areas. It is convenient to divide the arena stage into a number of acting areas, each of which can be effectively covered by the beam of a spotlight mounted along the 45-degree angle. Just what type of spotlight this would be would depend on the mounting locations and their distances. If a good, long throw is possible, the narrow-beam ellipsoidal spotlight with a 500-watt lamp would be fine; for much shorter throws, say of 15 to 20 feet, the 6-inch plano-convex spotlight, using 500-watt or 1000-watt lamps can be very useful, or the wide-beam ellipsoidal.

On the proscenium stage it was basic that each area be covered by two spotlights, ideally each 45 degrees on the actor, but in an arena with the actor seen from all sides, more instruments are a necessity. There are two popular approaches to the solution. One is that three instruments per area be used, evenly spaced about the area and thus at 120 degrees from one another. The second approach is to use four spots on each area, putting them 90 degrees from each other.

COLOR IN THE ARENA.   With either, the system of one warm and one cool color on each area is no longer applicable. With the three-spotlight plan the third instrument is assigned a "neutral" color, such as No. 17 (special lavender) which, we have seen, appears "cool" opposite a warm gelatin and "warm" opposite a cool one. No. 3 (light flesh-pink) is also a possibility for scenes that are basically warm and romantic. Or no color at all can be quite effective, and would permit lower-wattage lamps in such instruments as have no gelatin to cut down the output.

With the four-instrument system two variations suggest themselves. In the first, a warm and a cool are used on opposite sides, while the two intermediate instruments have a "neutral" medium. The alternate system is to use two warms, opposite each other, and two cools, also opposite each other. Probably the latter is the more satisfactory.

A word of warning about the choice of colors in arena productions is advisable: because the directionality of the spotlights on each side of each area is so definite, colors show up much stronger on the actors than in a proscenium production where there is far more mixing of different beams. Or perhaps the very closeness of the audience makes this seem true. At any event, the stronger gelatin colors are rarely advisable.

BLENDING.   The use of blending strips to give a tonality to the scene, much as first border strips are used on a proscenium stage, may be quite effective if properly handled. Two or three of the 6-foot lengths might be hung down the center line of the arena, or two strips may be placed along opposite sides and focused across the stage. In a permanent arena setup, it might be easier yet to mount sockets on an overhead rig surrounding the stage and focused toward it, wire these in three circuits, and use the colored R-lamps. Striplights, so used, must be provided with "blinders" (side maskings) that will prevent their beams from falling on the audience, particularly that portion of it seated on the opposite side of the stage.

UNMASKED INSTRUMENTS.   It is useless in a temporary arena setup to attempt to hide the instruments from the audience. They can, of course, be hung and maintained in a neat manner, with wiring carefully tied off and the like. But a frank acceptance of the fact that the instruments are there for all to view is better than a lot of makeshift, dust-catching, and fire-prone draperies.

However, if a stage house is designed especially for arena production, a false ceiling should be provided with openings through which the beams of light may be focused from instruments hung well above and out of sight. Catwalks must be installed, so the electrician can reach all instruments with ease: for maintenance, for focusing, and for color changes. Provision should also be made for closing off any unused openings.

BLINDING THE SPECTATORS. But the most difficult problem in any form of arena production is the matter of keeping the beams of the area spotlights out of the eyes of the spectators seated on the opposite side of the stage. As long as light persists in traveling in a straight line, and as long as directors wish to play their actors at the very edge of the arena stage, just so long will a compromise be necessary between a well-lighted actor and a half-blinded spectator. If the first row of the audience can be raised higher than the stage level, or be set back from it, or both, the problem is greatly eased. But in any event, this is one of the greatest problems confronting the light designer in arena production.

DESIGNING THE LIGHTING FOR AN ARENA PRODUCTION. On page 354 is a sketch of one variation of arena staging with properties in place on the stage floor. There are two "boxes" in which lighting instruments may be hung overhead. Figure 21–1 presents a layout and an instrument schedule for a suitable lighting design.

The designer has divided the stage into five subsidiary areas, which have been numbered clockwise from one through four, with area five in the center. Dotted lines on the layout mark the approximate limits of these areas, though it is, of course, understood that actually they will overlap one another and their lights will blend smoothly. The instruments have been systematically numbered, from the top, clockwise around the stage, in the outer box first and then the inner.

From each corner of the outer box a pair of 6-inch ellipsoidal-reflector spotlights are focused on the two closest areas, giving each of these two beams of light at approximately right angles to one another. From the inner box two plano-convex spotlights are focused on each of the same areas. The plano-convex type of instrument is used here because the upper portion of its beam can be effectively matted to prevent light from glaring into the eyes of spectators seated on the opposite side of the stage.

Area 5, in the center, is hit from the four corners of the inner box by 6-inch Fresnel spotlights. Here the danger of spill light annoying the audience is less marked than with the outer areas, but funnels are used on the instruments just the same. The typical soft-edged Fresnel-beam pattern is useful to blend this center light with the illumination on the adjacent areas.

The color system used is that of opposite warms and opposite cools. The

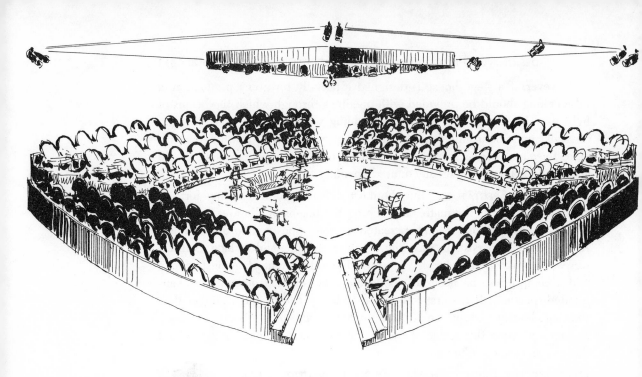

Figure 21–1. AN ARENA-PRODUCTION SETTING. *Above:* Sketch of setting. *Opposite page. Above:* Layout of lighting instruments. *Below:* Instrument schedule.

warm light, working diagonally out of the upper-right corner of the lay-out is from a No. 62 (special scarlet) gelatin. The identical color might have been employed also from the lower left, but the designer preferred to use a slightly different tint, No. 54 (light straw). In like manner, the cools are not identical: from the lower right is a No. 26, or light sky-blue, while opposite it is a No. 17 (special lavender). No. 17 is not an especially cool color, but it has been chosen here because we are assuming that this is a warm, pleasant type of play. Had it been a cold, stark drama, we might have selected such combinations as No. 29 and No. 26 for the cools, while the versatile No. 17 might have been one of the warms, with, perhaps, no color at all in the opposite instruments.

A few specials have been provided. On the right side there is an 8-inch Fresnel with a double No. 29 gelatin to give the effect of moonbeams for a brief scene. Instrument No. 6, an ellipsoidal with large-wattage lamp, is focused carefully on the divan with a romantic medium-pink gelatin for a tender moment. Toward the upper-left corner is another divan special with No. 70 (chocolate) for a different scene. Also on the left a wide-beamed ellipsoidal-reflector spotlight without color serves as an accent on the central area for some special action there. And the two table lamps at either end of the divan are practical fixtures, ganged on the same dimmer, but capable of being turned on and off at their individual switches.

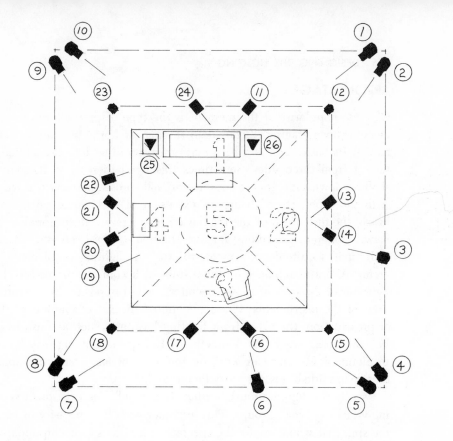

No.	INSTRUMENT	PURPOSE	LAMP	COLOR	REMARKS
1	6" Ellips'l-Ref'l Spotlight	Area 1	500T12	62	
2	" " "	" 2	"	62	
3	8" Fresnel Spotlight	Moonlight Special	1000G40	29/29	Focus Center
4	6" Ellips'l-Ref'l Spotlight	Area 2	500T12	26	
5	" " "	" 3	"	26	
6	" " "	Divan Special	750T12	4	Frame to Divan
7	" " "	Area 3	500T12	54	
8	" " "	" 4	"	54	
9	" " "	" 4	"	17	
10	" " "	" 1	"	17	
11	6" Plano-convex Spotlight	" 4	1000G40	62	Mat Top
12	6" Fresnel Spotlight	" 5	500T20	62	Funnel
13	6" Plano-convex Spotlight	" 3	1000G40	62	Mat Top
14	" " "	" 1	"	26	" "
15	6" Fresnel Spotlight	" 5	500T20	26	Funnel
16	6" Plano-convex Spotlight	" 4	1000G40	26	Mat Top
17	" " "	" 2	"	54	" "
18	6" Fresnel Spotlight	" 5	500T20	54	Funnel
19	4½" Ellips'l-Ref'l Spotlight	Center Accent	500T12	Clear	Focus Center
20	6" Plano-convex Spotlight	Area 1	1000G40	54	Mat Top
21	" " "	" 3	"	17	" "
22	" " "	Divan Special #2	"	70	Mat to Divan
23	6" Fresnel Spotlight	Area 5	500T20	17	Funnel
24	6" Plano-convex Spotlight	" 2	1000G40	17	Mat Top
25	Fixture	Table Lamp #1	40A	-	Gang with #26
26	"	" " #2	40A	-	" " #25

APRON STAGES

Of great popularity at the moment is the type of presentation known variously as open staging, Elizabethan staging, or apron staging, among other names. Its basic form is a bare platform protruding into the audience, who face it from three sides. Sometimes this is all there is to it, sometimes a shallow downstage zone of a conventional, proscenium-style stage is used with the "open stage" being an extension of this. Some open stages are nearly the full width of the regular stage—merely a deep apron; others are narrow tongues, protruding far into the house. The open stage itself, especially if it is quite deep, presents most of the lighting problems of the full arena. With the audience on three sides, it becomes a problem to keep the light out of the eyes of those spectators seated opposite the mounting positions of the instruments. If a conventional theatre is adapted to this style of presentation, the usual front lighting locations, such as false beams and balcony front, may be used effectively. But special rigging may be required to mount lights that can work on the sides of an extensive apron. If the theatre has side boxes, they may be put to this use.

Usually the lighting must be sharply defined. There is much spotting of individuals or small groups. This, together with the necessity of controlling the spill that would annoy the spectators, indicates that ellipsoidal-reflector and plano-convex spotlights must be used almost exclusively. Floodlights and striplights have no place in the picture at all. Of course, if a portion of the conventional stage itself is also used, it could be lighted by the more conventional means, depending on its depth. Usually these areas serve primarily as backgrounds, with overhead striplights employed to wash broad drops or large scenic pieces. But on the extended apron only highly controllable spotlights should be used.

OUTDOOR PRODUCTIONS

Theatrical Lighting Practice by Rubin and Watson gives an excellent description of lighting practices for outdoor productions on the grand scale, auditoriums seating 3000 spectators or more. But we are concerned here with more modest presentations. Many schools, for example, give annual productions in a courtyard with a school building as background, others have a more-or-less permanent outdoors auditorium with planted hedges to create a proscenium wall, side wings, and a backdrop. Often there is no permanent area but an outdoor stage is improvised almost any place about the grounds.

Open-air theatrical productions would appear to have one advantage over those held indoors in that a truly all-enveloping darkness would seem to be an actuality. But even assuming that the outdoor stage is not located close to lighted areas and the performances do not start before night has fully closed in, there is rarely such a thing as complete blackness, even in rural sections. Moonlight, even starlight, must be reckoned with. Blackouts are not long effective. And as conditions will vary from night to night, it is impossible to set definite dimmer levels.

ELECTRIC SERVICE.   There are a number of problems facing the producers of open-air theatres, two of which deal with the supply of electric current. A permanently established outdoor layout will have made adequate arrangements to secure the proper service to the theatre, just as one would for a new theatre of any sort. But all too often a temporary outdoor presentation is attempted, and it is found at the last moment that adequate service is not available, without considerable expense, for running long cables or the hiring of a portable—and noisy—generator.

PERILS OF WEATHER.   Secondly is the matter of weather. Cable and instrument connections, switches, dimmers, and other current carrying parts that are perfectly satisfactory indoors are a hazard when exposed to rain, or even a heavy dew. Special equipment is needed for some parts, special housing for others. Equipment that has been rain-soaked and apparently dried out successfully may later reveal hidden and permanent damage. This is no field for the amateur electrician to risk his life and that of his fellows.

Artistically the weather may effect the best planned outdoor lighting by ruining gelatin color media. Gelatin when exposed to dampness, loses its form completely and is entirely beyond control. This can occur as the result of condensation even under a roof in a very moist location. Outdoors it is an impossible situation. Color media of glass or of plastic become essential.

FRONT LIGHTING.   Front lighting is often a problem in an outdoor theatre. In order to attain anything close to the desired angles, it is usually necessary to erect poles beyond the seating area so as not to obstruct sight lines. Frequently this makes the throw to the stage an extremely long one, and the largest ellipsoidal-reflector spots, or even beam projectors, must be used.

These front lights may have to serve the entire stage, unless one is so fortunate as to have properly masked positions on the sides. Occasionally shrubs or trees are so located. Some permanent outdoor theatres have dense hedges that serve as proscenium wall and woodwings and these are admirable to hide side-lighting spotlights. If natural features are lacking, it may be necessary to build towers near the stage with masking for the spotlights thereon.

Naturally no overhead lighting can be provided, so all thought of first and second pipes, border strips, and so on, may be discarded. Footlights, particularly if hidden by a low hedge, or similar natural device, can be effective in giving a general, low toning to the actors, and any realistic scenery. Rarely in outdoor productions is there a large expanse of background corresponding to a backdrop or cyclorama. In fact, in many such presentations the background consists of trees or a hedge. In such cases no special lighting is desirable, and is even less so when the stage is backed by a view over a lake or of distant hills.

TV AND MOVIES

One tremendous advantage possessed by the television and movie lighting designers is that it is not necessary to mask instruments. Because the camera sees only what it wishes to, and its shots are carefully planned ahead of time, the lighting man need merely to keep his instruments and their associated equipment out of the picture. True, this is not always the easiest matter, but it is distinctly a help, particularly in the case of "tight" shots or close-ups when spotlights may be brought to within a foot or two of the actors.

BASIC TECHNIQUES. With this nicety of positioning possible, a great deal of precision can be brought to lighting a small scene, say a single commentator at his desk. Techniques vary, but a common one is to throw a general "fill light" on the actor from the front and then to set him apart from his background by means of low-hung spotlights coming in from behind to highlight his head and shoulders. To replace the plasticity lost by the flat-fill lighting and to suggest a motivating source, a spotlight is used from one side at high intensity. For tight close-ups a second spot may be used from a different angle.

A refinement of this uses spotlights entirely. The fill light is from one spot, set to one side and of lower intensity than another spot on the other side of the actor. Top lighting remains the same, but the background light is very tightly controlled by means of still a fourth spotlight.

GROUP PROBLEMS. While these procedures are excellent for the lone actor, they need modification where there are two or three performers in a group. One head may throw a shadow on a neighboring face unless the instruments are placed with extreme care and foresight. An effect that flatters one of the actors may be uncomplimentary to his fellow who is facing in a different direction.

INSTRUMENTS. The spotlight most frequently employed in the television field is the Fresnel type, from the smallest 3-inch size burning the 150-watt lamp up to the 10-inch models with 1000-watt lamps. Almost universal is the employment of "barn doors," shutters designed to cut the shape of the beam from round to a flatter pattern. This is necessary to eliminate the shadow of the microphones hung low above the actors' heads, while at the same time getting the full horizontal spread of the beam. A recent development has been an oval Fresnel lens that accomplishes the same purpose. Ellipsoidal-reflector spotlights are not used to any great extent, their principal occupation being the throwing of patterns on a rear drop or background by means of "gobos" at the gate position. Follow spots—either the largest ellipsoidal-reflector type or arcs—are used in most large studios.

While striplights are occasionally employed, floodlights are more common. R lamps in clip-on holders, the ellipsoidal flood called a "scoop" with lamps up to 2000 watts, a boxlike flood with 750-watt lamp referred to as a "broad," and "pans" containing several fluorescent tubes are the common varieties. It is a rare studio that does not possess several of each type.

To keep the floor areas as clear as possible, most instruments are hung from overhead, though a few floods are kept on handy, castered floor stands, while the clip-ons, as the name suggests, are completely flexible.

FULL-STAGE SCENES. When a scene becomes larger than a tight group of two or three actors, the lighting more nearly approaches the kind used in a conventional proscenium theatre. And when a full-stage picture, such as a dance sequence, is shown the similarity is quite marked. Although a discreet camera view allows greater liberties in placing of instruments, there are problems created by the medium that are not encountered on the legitimate stage, such as the danger of cameras, microphones, and personnel throwing shadows into view.

TV makes great use of projected scenery on translucent screens. But because directors frequently move their actors close to these, very delicate focusing problems can arise.

INTENSITY CONTROL. Control over intensity levels is of far less importance in television than on the regular stage. Intensities are adjusted more by the size and location of instruments, or the use of noncolor filters. Scenes do not run long enough to need fades to suggest the passage of time, so the switching of circuits off or on suffices. And the camera itself, and its associated controls, can quite effectively handle many adjustments that on the stage require the most precise dimmer readings and changes.

SUMMARY

Regardless of the technical differences that lie between proscenium-stage lighting and lighting for arenas, outdoor stages, and the eye of the camera, the same basic principles still hold true. The designer still uses the four tools of light: intensity, color, form, and movement. He still applies these, in varying degrees, to arrive at the desirable visibility, plausibility, composition, and mood for the play or the scene. And these, in turn, still contribute to the ultimate concern of the designer: to assist the actor interpret his part in a suitable environment.

ADDITIONAL READING
ON SCENE DESIGN

The following books are recommended as additional reading to increase the reader's understanding of the philosophy and historical background of scene design as part of the art of theatre.

THE DESIGN CONCEPT

Appia, Adolphe, *Adolphe Appia—A Gospel for Modern Stages. Theatre Arts Monthly*, August, 1932.
Entire issue devoted to Appia's influence on present-day scene and lighting design.

Brown, John Mason, *The Modern Theatre in Revolt*. New York: W. W. Norton & Co., Inc., 1929.

Cheney, Selden, *Stage Decoration*. New York: The John Day Company, Inc., 1928.

Craig, Edward Gordon, *On the Art of the Theatre*. New York: Theatre Arts Books, 1956.

Fuerst, Walter R., and Hume, Samuel J., *Twentieth Century Stage Decoration*. New York: Alfred A. Knopf, Inc., 1928. Vol. 1, text; Vol. 2, ill.

Gassner, John, *Form and Idea in the Modern Theatre*. New York: Holt, Rinehart & Winston, Inc., 1956.

Gorelik, Mordecai, *New Theatres for Old*. New York: Samuel French, 1940.

Jones, Robert E., *The Dramatic Imagination*. New York: Duell, Sloan & Pearce, Inc., 1941.

Kernodle, George R., *From Art to Theatre*. Chicago: University of Chicago Press, 1943.

Laver, James, *Drama, Its Costume and Decor*. New York: The Viking Press, Inc., 1951.

Nicoll, Allardyce, *The Development of the Theatre*. New York: rev. ed. Harcourt, Brace & World, Inc., 1947.

Oenslager, Donald M., *Scenery, Then and Now*. New York: W. W. Norton & Co., Inc., 1936.

Pierson, William H. J. F., and Davidson, Martha (editors). *Arts of the United States* (Stage Design section). New York: McGraw-Hill Book Company, Inc., 1960.

A collection of color slides assembled by the University of Georgia under a grant by the Carnegie Corp. of New York. Contains an excellent essay by Donald Oenslager on the U.S. scene designed. Slides by SANDAK INC. New York.

Simonson, Lee, *The Art of Scenic Design*. New York: Harper & Brothers, 1950.

Simonson, Lee, *The Stage Is Set*. New York: Harcourt, Brace & World, Inc., 1932.

DESIGN APPLICATION

The following are recommended to broaden knowledge of the practicable application of design principles to modern theatre practices and related theatrical forms.

Albright, Halstead and Mitchell, *The Principles of Theatre Art*. New York: Houghton Mifflin Company, 1955.

Boyle, Welden F., *Central and Flexible Staging*. Berkeley: University of California Press, 1956.

Bretz, Rudy, *Techniques of Television Production*. New York: McGraw-Hill Book Company, Inc., 1958.

Carrick, Edward, *Designing for Moving Pictures*. London and New York: The Studio Publication, 1941.

Dean, Alexander, *Fundamentals of Play Directing*. New York: Holt, Rinehart & Winston, Inc., 1941.

Koenig, John, *Scenery for Cinema*. Record of Exhibition, Baltimore Museum of Art. Baltimore, 1942.

Lambourne, Norah, *Staging the Play*. New York: The Viking Press, Inc., 1956.

Levin, Richard, *Television by Design*. London: The Bodley Head Ltd., 1961.

Selden, Samuel, and Sellman, Hunton, *Modern Theatre Practice*. New York: Appleton-Century-Crofts, Inc., 1935.

Southern, Richard, *Proscenium and Sightlines*. New York: American Photographic Book Publishing Co., Inc., 1939.

Traube, Shepard, *So You Want to Go Into the Theatre*. Boston: Little, Brown & Company, 1936.

Wade, Robert J., *Designing for TV*. New York: Farrar, Straus and Cudahy, Inc., 1952.

DRAWING AND PAINTING

The following books are recommended to the student scene designer to help develop his skill as a visual artist and draftsman.

Clark, Arthur Bridgman, *Perspective*. Stanford, Calif.: Stanford University Press, 1944.

Container Corporation, *Color Harmony Manual, Ostwald Theory of Color*. Chicago: Container Corporation of America, 1948.

Evans, Ralph M., *An Introduction to Color*. New York: John Wiley & Sons, Inc., 1948.

Field, Wooster Bard, *Architectural Drawing*. New York: McGraw-Hill Book Company, Inc., 1922.

French, Thomas E., *A Manual of Engineering Drawing*. New York: McGraw-Hill Book Company, 1941.

Graves, Maitland, *The Art of Color and Design*. York, Pa.: The Maple Press Company, 1941.

Guptill, Arthur L., *Drawing in Pen and Ink*. New York: Pencil Points, 1928.

Guptill, Arthur L., *Sketching and Rendering*. New York: Pencil Points, 1929.

International Printing Ink Corp., *Three Monographs on Color*. New York: International Printing Ink Corp., 1935.

Jacobson, Egbert, *Basic Color, An Interpretation of the Ostwald Color System*. Chicago: Paul Theobald, 1948.

Luekiesh, M., *Color and Its Application*. Princeton, N. J.: D. Van Nostrand Co., 1921.

Munsell, A. H., *A Color Notation*. Baltimore, Md.: Munsell Color Co., Inc., 1941.

Munsell Color Co., *Munsell Book of Color*. Baltimore, Md.: Munsel Color Co., 1942.

Ostwald, Wilhelm, *Colour Science*. Winsor and Wenton Limited, 38 Rathbone Place, London W. 1, England.

Parker, Oren, *Scenographic Techniques*. New Haven: Oren Parker, 1957.

Patten, Lawton, and Rogness, Milton, *Architectural Drawing*, Rev. Ed. Dubuque, Iowa: William C. Brown Co., 1961.

Pope, Arthur, *The Language of Drawing and Painting*. Cambridge, Mass.: Harvard University Press, 1949.

Scott, Robert, *Design Fundamentals*. New York: McGraw-Hill Book Company, Inc., 1951.

FURNITURE AND DECORATIONS

The following are recommended as general reference material for designing furniture and decorating interiors.

Aronson, Joseph, *The Encyclopedia of Furniture*. New York: Crown Publishers, 1938.

Gottshall, Franklin H., *How to Design Period Furniture*. Milwaukee, Wis.: Bruce Publishing Co., 1951.

Hardy, Kay, *Beauty Treatments for the Home*. New York: Funk & Wagnalls Co., 1945.

Hunter, George Leland, *Decorative Furniture*. Grand Rapids, Mich.: Dean Hicks Co., *Good Furniture Magazine*, 1923.

Jones, Bernard E., *Furniture Making*. Philadelphia: David McKay, Publisher.

Jones, Owen, *The Grammar of Ornament*. London: Bernard Quaritch, 1910.

Potter, Margaret and Alexander, *Houses*. London: John Murray, 1948.

Potter, Margaret and Alexander, *Interiors*. London: John Murray, 1957.

Speltz, Alexander, *Styles of Ornament*. New York: Grosset & Dunlap, Inc., 1936.

Strange, T. Arthur, *A Guide to Collectors: English Furniture and Decoration*. London: McCorquodale & Co., 1903.

Strange, T. Arthur, *Historical Guide to French Interiors*. London: McCorquodale & Co., 1903.

ADDITIONAL READING
ON TECHNICAL PRODUCTION

The following books are recommended as additional reading to give the reader a greater insight into scenery construction techniques and general shop practices.

SCENERY CONSTRUCTION

Burris-Meyer, Harold, and Cole, Edward C., *Scenery for the Theatre*. Boston: Little, Brown & Company, 1938.

The Complete Woodworker. New York: David McKay Co., Inc., N. Y., n. d.

Cornberg, Sol, and Gebauer, Emanuel L., *A Stage Crew Handbook*. New York: Harper & Brothers, 1941.

Dykes Lumber Company, *Moulding Catalog*, No. 49, Dykes Lumber Co., 137 West 24th Street, New York 11, N. Y.

Fitzkee, Dariel, *Professional Scenery Construction*. San Francisco: Banner, 1931.

Haines, Ray E., *Carpentry and Woodworking*, Princeton, N. J.: D. Van Nostrand Co., Inc., 1945.

Lacey, John L., *Handy Man's Carpentry Guide*. New York: Arco Publishing Co., Inc., 1955.

Parker, H., and Kidder, F. E., *Architect's and Builder's Handbook*. New York: John Wiley & Sons, Inc., 1932.

Popular Science Monthly, *Power Tools, Do It Yourself With*. New York: Popular Science Publishing Co., Inc., 1955.

Ramsey, Charles G., and Sleeper, Harold R., *Architectural Graphic Standards*, 3rd Ed. New York: John Wiley & Sons, Inc., 1941.

U.S. Forest Products Laboratory, *Wood Handbook*. Washington, D.C.: Government Printing Office.

THE HANDLING OF SCENERY

The following provide a more specialized knowledge of the various methods of moving scenery, backstage organization, and rigging techniques.

Barber, Philip W., *The Stage Technician's Handbook*. New Haven, Conn.: Whitlock's Book Store, Inc., 1928.

Burris-Meyer, Harold, and Mallory, Vincent, *Sound in the Theatre*. Mineola, New York: Radio Magazine, Inc., 1959.

Gassner, John, *Producing the Play*, with *New Scene Technicians' Handbook* by Philip Barber. New York: Holt, Rinehart & Winston, Inc., 1953.

Gillete, A. S., *Stage Scenery*. New York: Harper & Brothers, 1959.

Halstead, William P., *Stage Management for the Amateur Theatre*. New York: Appleton-Century-Crofts, Inc., 1937.

How to Put Rope to Work, Plymouth Cordage Company, North Plymouth, Mass.

Irving, J., *Knots, Ties and Splices*. New York: E. P. Dutton & Co., Inc., 1934.

Kranich, Friedrich, *Buhnintechinik der Gegenwart*, Vol. I. Berlin: Verlag Von R. Oldenbourg, 1929.

Rose, A., *Stage Effects* (George Routledge and Sons, Ltd.). New York: E. P. Dutton & Co., Inc., 1920.

Southern, Richard, *Changeable Scenery*. London: Faber & Faber, Ltd., 1952.

Southern, Richard, *Stage Setting*. London: Faber & Faber, Ltd., 1937.

SCENE PAINTING

The following are recommended to expand skill in scene-painting techniques.

Appleton Publishing Co., *Theatrical Scene Painting*. Omaha, Nebr.: Appleton Publishing Co., 1916.

Ashworth, Bradford, *Notes on Scene Painting* edited by Donald Oenslager. New Haven, Conn.: Whitlock's, 1952.

Atkinson, Frank H., *Scene Painting and Bulletin Art*. Chicago: Frederick J. Drake and Co., 1916.

Brown, Van Dyke, *Secrets of Scene Painting and Stage Effects*. New York: E. P. Dutton Co., Inc., 1913.

Polunin, Vladimir, *The Continental Method of Scene Painting*. London: C. W. Beaumont, 1927.

GENERAL

The following books are recommended as supplementary reading in the generalized area of scene design, technical production, and stage lighting.

Adix, Vern, *Theatre Scenecraft*. Cloverlot, Anchorage, Ky.: Children's Theatre Press, 1956.

Friederich, Williard J., and Fraser, John H., *Scenery Design for the Amateur Stage.* New York: The Macmillan Company, 1950.

Helvenston, Harold, *Scenery, a Manual of Scene Design.* Stanford, Calif.: Stanford University Press, 1931.

Selden, Samuel, and Sellman, Hunton D., *Stage Scenery and Lighting*, rev. New York: Appleton-Century-Crofts, Inc., 1959.

Smith, André, *The Scenewright.* New York: The Macmillan Company, 1926.

ADDITIONAL READING
ON STAGE LIGHTING

The following books are recommended as supplementary reading, either to broaden the reader's view of the field or to assist him in understanding knotty problems. They would form an invaluable nucleus for the private library of anyone genuinely interested in the field.

The "General" list contains books of broad approach to the whole stage-lighting picture, and offers material of value in several facets of theatre lighting. The titles under the heading "Supplementary" contain matter related to specific aspects.

GENERAL

Bentham, Frederick, *Stage Lighting*. London: Pitman & Sons, Ltd., 1950. Covers the field well, but the American reader is warned that British terminology is sometimes confusing.

Fuchs, Theodore, *Stage Lighting*. Boston: Little Brown & Co., 1929. Certain portions are somewhat outdated today, but there is much pure gold still to be found in it.

Gassner, John, *Producing the Play*, rev. New York: Holt, Rinehart & Winston, Inc., 1953. Contains a capsule survey of the field by one of Broadway's most successful lighting practitioners.

McCandless, Stanley, *A Method of Lighting the Stage*. 4th Ed. New York: Theatre Arts Books, 1958. Though not going into the more technical aspects, this is probably the most influential book ever published on the subject.

McCandless, Stanley, *A Syllabus of Stage Lighting*. 10th Ed. New Haven, Conn.: Published by himself, 1958. A reference book and dictionary of all stage-lighting terms.

Selden, Samuel, and Sellman, Hunton D., *Stage Scenery and Lighting*, 3rd Ed. New York: Appleton-Century-Crofts, Inc., 1959. A complete and useful text.

Williams, Rollo G., *The Technique of Stage Lighting*. London: Pitman & Sons, Ltd., 1952. Especially good on color. British terminology may confuse.

SUPPLEMENTARY

Bowman, Wayne, *Modern Theatre Lighting*. New York: Harper & Brothers, 1957. Some good comments on practical electricity.

Century Lighting Company, New York. Their equipment catalogues are a mine of information regarding instruments.

General Electric Company, Cleveland, *Fundamentals of Light and Lighting*, 1956. Excellent material on color, sources, and the behavior of light.

General Electric Company, Cleveland, *Large Lamp Bulletin*. Almost a textbook on sources. Excellent illustrations.

General Electric Company, Cleveland, *Lamp Bulletin*, 1956. Another fine and complete publication on lamps.

Illuminating Engineering Society, New York, *IES Lighting Handbook*, 3rd Ed., 1959. Pertinent information on color, instruments, equipment, and usage.

Kliegl Bros., New York. Equipment catalogues of all stage instruments.

Navy Training Courses, *Basic Electricity* (NavPers 10086-A). Government Printing Office, Washington 25, 1960. Clear and simple presentation of the fundamentals of electricity. The best available text.

Rubin, Joel E., and Watson, Leland H., *Theatrical Lighting Practice*. New York: Theatre Arts Books, 1954. A survey of the usual lighting practices of all types and levels of dramatic production.

GLOSSARY

ARC LIGHT: A spotlight that has for its source an electric current arcing between two carbon rods. The term is often misapplied to mean any brilliant light.

BACKSTAGE: Much the same as OFFSTAGE but generally in reference to stage workers and stage machinery rather than to actors.

BAG LINE: Pick up or bull line on a sand bag to lift the weight of the bag while trimming or clewing a line-set.

BOOK: To set a two-fold of scenery in an open-book position.

BOOM or BOOMERANG: A vertical pipe for mounting spotlights.

BREAK: To fold or unfold scenery.

BREAKAWAY: Scenery or properties rigged to break on cue.

BREAST LINE: Fixed line to wall or gridiron that drags or breasts a piece of hanging scenery into an excentric position. Also called a DRAG LINE.

BRIDLE: Means of dividing the load of each liftline by spreading the pick-up points along the batten.

BULL LINE: Heavy, four-stranded hemp rope used on a winch to lift uncounter-weighted scenery.

BUMPER: Low platform downstage of portal against which castered wagons bump.

CLEWING: Several lines are held together by knots or clew so as to handle as a single line.

CUE: A visual or audible signal from the stage manager to execute a predetermined movement of lights or scenery.

CYC KNUCKLE: Hardware for attaching side arms of a cyc batten to a regular pipe batten.

DECK: Stage floor.

DIM: To change the intensity of a light, either brighter or less bright.

DIMMER: Apparatus to alter the flow of electric current, so as to cause a light to be more or less bright.

DISAPPEARANCE TRAP: Special counterweighted elevator trap used as a quick exit or disappearance by an actor.

DOLLY: A type of wagon.

DONKEY: Electric winch.

369

DOWNSTAGE: The area nearest the footlights and curtain.

DRAW LINE: Operating line of a traveler curtain rigging.

FEEL-UP: To take slack out of lift lines prior to setting the trim.

FLAG: Small piece of cloth inserted into the lay of the purchase line as a trim mark.

FLAT: In the commercial theatre FLAT refers to the stiffening of two or more hinged wings into a flat plane or wall.

FLIPPER: Jog hinged to a single wing.

FLOODLIGHT: A lighting instrument that produces a broad spread of light. Often misapplied to other lighting apparatus.

FRESNEL: (Correctly pronounced Fr'nel). A lens recognized by its concentric rings. The spotlight designed to use this lens.

FRONT LIGHTING: Illumination on the stage from instruments placed in the auditorium.

GOBO: A metal cut-out used with a spotlight to obtain a patterned beam.

GRIP: Stage hand.

GRIPPING: Running scenery on the floor by stage hands or grips.

HEAD BLOCK: Multigrooved pulley or multipulley sheave in a line-set.

JACK: Framed brace to hold scenery upright.

JACK KNIFE: Pivoting wagon movement like the action of blades in a jack knife.

JOG: Narrow width wing.

JUICE: Commercial jargon for electricity.

KLIEGLIGHT: A type of spotlight sold by Kliegl Bros. KLIEG is often used as a synonym for any bright light.

KNIFE: Steel guide for a tracked wagon.

LAMP: In the commercial theatre the term for any lighting instrument, particularly a spotlight.

LEFT STAGE: To the actor's left as he faces the audience.

LEKOLITE: A type of spotlight sold by Century Lighting, Inc. LEKO is often used as a generic term for any ellipsoidal reflector spotlight.

LINE SET: A group of from three to five lines using the same head block to lift a pipe batten or unit of scenery.

LIP: A beveled three-ply strip attached so as to overhang the edge of a framed unit of scenery and thereby conceal the open crack of a joint with an adjacent unit.

LOFT BLOCK: Individual pulley on the gridiron of a line-set.

MAKE-UP: To put together a setting.

MASK: To conceal from the audience, usually by scenic pieces or neutral hangings, any portion of the backstage area or equipment.

MULING BLOCK: Pulley to change the horizontal direction of a moving line.

OFFSTAGE: Out of sight of the audience. Away from the center of the stage.

ON AND OFF: Referring to scenery sitting parallel to the footlights.

ONSTAGE: In sight of the audience. Toward the center of the stage.

PEEK: To expose the backstage or see past masking.

PICTURE: The general composition of the setting as seen from the average and not extreme sightlines seat.

PRACTICAL: Can be used by the actor, as a window sash that can actually be raised, or a light that can be switched on and off by him.

PROP: Short for "property." Also refers to anything not real or practical.

PURCHASE LINE: Flyman's operating line in a counterweight system.

RAKED: Referring to scenery angled to the footlights.

RETURN: Element of scenery that returns the downstage edge of the setting off stage to the right or left.

RIGHT STAGE: To the actor's right as he faces the audience.

SANDBAG: Counterweight for pin-and-rail flying system.

SNATCH BLOCK: Pulley block with removable side to permit its insertion into rigging or tackle system without having to rethread all the line.

SNATCHING: To hook and unhook a flown piece of scenery during the shift.

SPIKE: Mark on the floor to locate the working position of scenery or properties.

SPOT LINE: A fixed line spotted on the gridiron directly over its working position.

SPOTLIGHT: A lighting instrument with a lens that throws an intense light on a defined area. The term is often misapplied to other lighting instruments.

SPOT SHEAVE: The special placement of a loft sheave on the gridiron for an additional or single running line.

STAB: Low trim or tie-off on the bottom rail of the pin-and-rail flying system.

STAGE LEFT and STAGE RIGHT: *see* LEFT STAGE and RIGHT STAGE.

STAGE PEG and PLUG: Bolt-threaded peg which fits into an inside threaded plug.

STAGE SCREW: Screw-threaded peg.

STRIKE: To take down a setting. To remove properties or lights.

SUNDAY: Knot used to clew or hold several lines together.

SURROUND or SHROUD: Carry-off platforms that surround a turntable.

SWITCHBOARD: Fixed or movable panel with switches, dimmers, etc., to control the stage lights.

TAILS: Lines dropped from a batten to hang scenery several feet below the batten.

TEASER: Top or horizontal member of the adjustable frame downstage of the setting.

TORMENTOR: Side or vertical members of the adjustable frame downstage of the setting.

TRAPS: System of openings through the stage floor.

TRICK LINE: Small line used to trigger a breakaway or trick device.

TRIM: Mark designating the height of a line-set. HIGH TRIM: Height of a flown piece when in *out* position. LOW TRIM: Height of flown piece when in an *in* (or working) position.

TRIPPING: To raise a piece of soft scenery from the bottom as well as from the top.

UP AND DOWN: Referring to scenery sitting perpendicular to the footlights.

UPSTAGE: On the stage but away from the audience.

WAGON: Low platform on casters.

WILD: Hinged portion of a setting that is free to move.

WING: In the commercial theatre the term *single wing* refers to the basic unit of framed scenery, commonly called a *flat* in the non-commercial theatre.

WINGS: Area offstage right and left, stemming from the era of wings and backdrops.

X-RAYS: Old expression designating the first row of border lights.

INDEX

would be illustrated by a body depleted of its food supply. The physiological need for food eventually results in an awareness of this need and a desire to overcome the deprivation. The desire to obtain food is referred to as a drive. The physiological need, therefore, results in a psychological drive.

Needs are sometimes categorized as primary and secondary. This classification, however, can be misleading since the so-called secondary drives are, on occasion, stronger than the primary drives. Cole and Bruce (1959) classify the needs and drives into *physiological* and *psychological*. This classification is more descriptive, but even it can lead to confusion because of the difficulty in always clearly distinguishing between the physical and the psychological or sociological influences.

Physiological needs and drives

Cole and Bruce suggest the following as the most important of the physiological needs which may result in drives:

Food and Drink. The body survives on chemical ingredients supplied by food and water. Obviously, food and drink are important, and their unavailability will result in powerful drives.

Rest. The fatigued tissues of the body are repaired during rest periods. When man is sufficiently tired, he will rest in spite of external efforts to stimulate him to action.

Sexual gratification. When a state of excitement exists, sexual gratification becomes one of the strongest human drives.

Self-protection. All human beings have a need for protection from physical harm or destruction. Safety and a feeling of security are among the strongest needs.

Elimination. Regular elimination of waste products from the body is a strong physiological need for all persons.

Several other authors list essentially the same physical needs. In addition, Leuba (1961) and Bortner (1962) include the drive for *activity,* or the urge for action, as being a strong characteristic of all persons except the very old or ill.

Psychological needs and drives

Maslow (1943) presents the following as representing the most important needs in the psychological and sociological areas:

Belongingness and love. All normal human beings need affection, warmth, acceptance, and a place in a group. After the physiological needs have been satisfied, love needs emerge as perhaps the strongest drive.

Self-esteem. Individuals have a strong need for self-respect, self-confidence, and a feeling of adequacy. This need is satisfied to a great extent when one receives the recognition, attention, and appreciation of others.

Self-actualization. Individuals in our society need oportunities to realize their full potential. When this has been achieved, the individual experiences a fulfillment which is conducive to a healthy adjustment.

Bortner (1962) presented a rather similar list of social drives which he considered the most common and most demanding. They included the following:

1. The drive for security
2. The drive for mastery
3. The drive for recognition
4. The drive for belonging

Bortner pointed out that it is essential that these drives be satisfied in order for the child to develop a healthy, integrated personality. These needs and drives provide the teacher with a sound basis for motivating students.

Thomas (1923), Symonds (1934), Carroll (1940), and Leuba (1961) discuss psychological needs and drives which are similar to those mentioned by Maslow and Bortner. Primary differences are in terminology and length of the lists. The longer lists contain greater specificity and refinement of the general concepts mentioned by Maslow and Bortner.

How needs become drives

A drive is a tendency to behave in a manner to fulfill a need. Needs give rise to drives, and drives give rise to behavior. Physiological needs result in psychological drives. For illustrative purposes, Cole and Bruce (1959) describe the following sequential stages in the hunger cycle to show how drives, or motivated activity, may result:

Physical deficit. The stomach is empty and the blood's supply of food is depleted.

Body tensions. The physical deficit of food may be accompanied by contractions of the stomach, tensions in the muscles, and general irritability.

Psychological awareness of these changes. With the conscious awareness of hunger, there is a craving for food.

Seeking food and eating. Motivated action eventually results in the individual's securing food.

Full stomach. The need is eliminated, and there is a relaxation of physical tensions.

With the conscious awareness of hunger, the need for food becomes a motive for action. Obviously, this motive can be very strong, driving human beings to determined actions. Other physiological needs can be broken down and analyzed as the source of emotional arousal in much the same way. The psychological and sociological needs, though more complex to break down, might also be logically analyzed in this manner.

The relative strength of different drives

As suggested by Maslow, not all needs and drives are equally strong. Some seem to underlie or act as prerequisites for others. For example, certain needs do not manifest themselves until hunger and thirst have been satisfied. Persons who have been deprived of food and water for long periods, report that intellectual, sexual, or social matters fade in importance during these periods. This effect of starvation is illustrated in a study reported by Cole and Bruce (1959) of a World War II experiment in which conscientious objectors volunteered for fasting studies designed to gain information helpful in the rehabilitation of starving people. Despite the initial enthusiasm of the volunteers, as time passed, their thoughts centered more and more on food. As their preoccupation with food reached an obsessive height, some subjects secretly secured food for consumption and other experienced severe psychological repercussions from their conflicting drives. Travers (1963) pointed out that Buddha is pictured with a fat belly because of the belief that the mind can be fully devoted to serious matters only when physical needs have been met.

A number of personal and environmental factors affect the strength of the various drives. This adds to the difficulty of organizing needs by strength or importance. However, Maslow (1943) listed the following broad categories of needs in rank order, from strongest to weakest:

1. Physiological needs
2. Safety needs
3. Love and belonging needs
4. Esteem needs, including achievement and recognition
5. Self actualization needs
6. Desires to know and understand

Although Maslow's ranking may meet with general approval, certain of the personal and social needs at the end of the list occasionally become stronger than the physiological and safety needs. Extreme examples of domination of personal and social needs are seen in the individual who becomes a martyr, goes on a hunger strike, or commits suicide, and by the parent who sacrifices himself for his child. Therefore, classification of needs into primary and secondary groups, or into lists on strengths and weaknesses, must be viewed with certain reservations.

Needs and drives in the school

Along with the process of maturing, and with education, comes the ability to control drives or to delay gratification. For the infant, this capacity does not exist at all. However, the individual is gradually able to be reasonably satisfied with a promise of "Not now, but later." The capacity to delay gratification satisfactorily may never be fully attained; thus adults vary in their ability to discipline their desires for satisfaction. Psychopaths are especially weak in the ability to delay the satisfaction of a drive. One major concern of educators is to develop appropriate drive control and restraint in children.

Teachers should organize and conduct their programs so that each child has an opportunity to meet needs. Whether the need is basic or derived, teachers will be more effective if they work in accordance with, rather than contrary to, needs. In today's typical school setting, the children's physiological needs have been cared for quite well. On occasion, slight difficulties may arise regarding uncomfortable classroom temperature, furniture, lighting, or the like. In physical education, however, the total range of physiological, psychological, and sociological needs can be encountered in a manner that is unique in the school situation.

Quite a wide range of physiological needs and drives becomes evident in physical education classes and in varsity athletes. The individual is often encouraged to withstand some degree of pain, fatigue, and fear of impending danger. A strong tendency to surrender to these needs may be countered by other needs, such as achievement, recognition, and belonging. For example, the undersized high school football player may experience mixed feelings when faced with the necessity of hurling his body into the path of a hard-charging fullback. The need for self-preservation encourages him to avoid contact while the need for accomplishment demands that he stop his opponent at all costs. The personal need to excel in front of one's peers may on other occasions cause the young person to practice long and hard for perfection or to continue an all-out effort in a wrestling match long after fatigue has appeared. The physical educator and the coach are, therefore, in a unique position to manipulate personal and social needs for developmental purposes.

Physiological responses during emotional excitement

During periods of excitement certain physiological changes occur which are measurable with modern scientific equipment. The particular responses will depend upon the nature and the extent of the emotional arousal. W. B. Cannon (1929), probably the most influential pioneer in the study of emotional reactions, has described bodily changes during pain, hunger, fear, and rage. Other authors have discussed these and additional emotional states, including joy, sorrow, stress, anxiety, and jealousy. Although different conditions may evoke somewhat different responses from the nervous system, these differences are not always clearly distinguishable. There is considerable overlapping in physiological responses among several of the emotional states.

Cannon worked extensively with both men and animals to identify physiological responses to various types of situations. He pointed out that strong emotions prepare the organism for vigorous activity during emergencies. To illustrate the types of physiological changes which take place during periods of stress, he cited the following situation:

If a cat is quietly eating and digesting its meal and is suddenly confronted by a barking dog, the following changes take place within the cat:

1. Digestive movements of the stomach stop.
2. Blood pressure rises.
3. Heart rate speeds up.
4. Adrenalin is secreted into the blood system.
5. The cat arches its back and is ready to fight.

Cannon pointed out that adrenalin when secreted into the blood system (a) increases the blood pressure, (b) builds up the supply of sugar in the blood, (c) causes the blood to clot more easily, and (d) makes the cat less sensitive to pain. Most of the responses which were observed in the cat can also be measured in man.

Physiological changes in response to emotional excitement are controlled by the *autonomic nervous system,* which regulates the secretions of the endocrine glands and controls the smooth muscles of the body. The autonomic nervous system is made up of the sympathetic and parasympathetic systems, each of which influences the same bodily organs but generally with opposite effects. The sympathetic system acts as an emergency system, being most active during excited states, and serves to mobilize the body for violent action. The parasympathetic system functions primarily during normal or quiescent states and takes care of regular metabolic functions. For example, the sympathetic system stimulates the adrenal gland and thus increases the heart rate. The parasympathetic system is instrumental in slowing down both of these processes.

The physiological responses which are initiated by the autonomic nervous system during excitement are many and varied. The full range of reactions is not yet known. However, some of the bodily responses which have been described by various authors are as follows:

Galvanic skin response. During periods of excitement there is a detectable increase in the electrical impulses which take place on the skin. This response, which is intimately related to sweat secretion, is one of the most widely used indices of one's level of activation. The galvanic skin response (GSR), also referred to as skin conductance and skin resistance, may be measured in microamperes by use of an ammeter or galvanometer. One important advantage in using the galvanic skin response as a measure of excitement is the immediacy of the measure. Whereas certain other types of physiological analysis (gas, blood, urine) usually require a relatively long time, skin responses to sudden stimulation can be detected in a few seconds. These measures may be taken by attaching electrodes to the palms or, in some cases, by placing the fingers on the poles of an ammeter. Harmon and Johnson (1952) and Fort (1959) have used the GSR in studies of athletic performances.

Heart rate. During periods of excitement the heart rate speeds up and becomes more intense. The rapid, pounding heart is one of the most obvious signs of excitement. Even routine mental activity stimulates the heart to a faster rate than exists during sleep or other quiet periods. Testers who have sought to use the pulse rate as an indication of physical fitness have found that one's emotional state at any given time is often more important in determining his heart rate than in his physical condition.

Blood pressure and volume. Blood pressure is almost always higher during periods of excitement. Startling occurrences cause dramatic increases in blood pressure and circulation. In certain emotional states (extreme depression or shock), the blood pressure may be lowered. Also, there is sometimes a displacement or movement of the blood supply, for example, into the tissue near the skin of the face when blushing or of the neck when angry, away from the surface of the face when one is frightened.

Blood composition. During periods of emotional excitement, the endocrine glands secrete certain harmones into the blood to aid the body in its responses. Perhaps the most important of these hormones is adrenalin, which aids the body in performing many physical feats. Variations in hormone secretions can best be measured by a blood test or urinalysis. In addition to hormones, extra red blood cells may also be released into the blood to aid the body in obtaining more oxygen. The extent of this hormonal secretion may be determined by a blood test.

Muscle tension and tremor. This is one of the most obvious and common reactions to a stressful situation. The individual is unable to relax because of conflicting internal desires. This tension leads to an inability to control fine muscular movements as efficiently as when one is relaxed. Considerable evidence (Duffy, 1957; Malmo, 1959; Woodworth and Schlosberg, 1963) has been collected to show that the tension level of various muscles reflects the motivation level and, generally, the level of activity or arousal.

Eason and White (1960) have shown that tension level of the head, neck, shoulder, and arm muscles reflects the amount of effort exerted during performance of physical tasks. Evidence shows that muscular tension, measured electromyographically, will reveal how well an individual performs a task in relation to the amount of effort he exerts, i.e., how *efficient* the performance is. This technique has possibilities for showing whether fluctuations in performance are due to motivation or a change in skill.

Respiration. During certain types of excitement, respiration may become faster and shallower, so that there is sometimes a gasping effect. Deep breathing is difficult during excitement. On the other hand, when the individual's level of excitement is less than normal or he is bored, he may show signs of lack of air, such as yawning or sighing.

Pupillary response. During emotional excitement, the iris contracts and, as a result, the pupils of the eye dilate. This seems to happen especially during pain, anger, or extreme tension. During quiet states there is a tendency for the opposite reaction to occur.

Pilomotor response. During certain types of emotional situations, goose pimples may appear on the skin. This may happen when an individual hears a screeching sound, or even when he is affected by a profound emotional experience. The same circumstance will often cause the hair to stand on end and give a person a creepy feeling.

Salivary secretion. Research indicates that there is a reduction of salivary secretion during most periods of emotional excitement. Many athletes experience dry mouths before important contests.

Encephalography. During stressful situations, there are changes in the nature of brain waves. The development of accurate and simplified techniques for measuring the brain waves may hold the key to the determination of emotional states in the future.

Among the other physiological changes within the body during excitement are a slight rise in oral or skin temperature, a change in gastrointestinal activity, and an increase in the frequency of blinking. However, information regarding the exact nature of these changes is not refined enough to be of special importance to most physical educators.

Conscious awareness

People often become aware of certain changes in internal functioning when excited. Emotional arousal is therefore a physiological and a conscious experience. *The James-Lange theory* of emotional reaction, which resulted in considerable debate soon after it was introduced, was based on the concept of the individual's awareness of physiological responses. Their theory was the reverse of traditional ideas about the sequence of emotional response. It had generally been assumed that (1) man observes an impending dangerous situation, (2) interprets the hazards and becomes frightened, and (3) reacts in a manner to reduce the danger to himself and possibly others.

During the 1890's William James, of Harvard University, and George Lange, in Denmark, independently disputed traditional beliefs about the sequence of emotional responses. According to their theory, man reacts rather instinctively to dangerous situations, and conscious awareness of danger comes *later*. This theory holds that we become afraid after we run from danger, and we become sad after starting to cry. The physiological response which accompanies one's general reaction was seen as a strategic factor in promoting emotional arousal. The theory is based on the concept that man has the capacity for acting appropriately in hazardous situations without foresight. Nature then takes care of the necessary bodily functions to prepare man for fight or flight. After one has acted appropriately, he then becomes aware of bodily changes. Despite the interest and debate caused by this theory soon after it was introduced, it has never gained general acceptance among psychologists. It does, however, emphasize the awareness of physiological phenomena associated with emotional excitement.

What physiological changes are people aware of during excitement?

Table 5

SIGNS OF FEAR DURING AERIAL COMBAT

"During combat missions did you feel":	*"Often"*	Per cent reporting *"Often"* or *"sometimes"*
A pounding heart and rapid pulse	30	86
Feeling that your muscles are very tense	30	83
Being easily irritated, angry or "sore"	22	80
Dryness of the throat or mouth	30	80
"Nervous perspiration" or "cold sweat"	26	79
"Butterflies" in the stomach	23	76
Feeling of unreality, that this couldn't be happening to you	20	69
Having to urinate (pass water) very frequently	25	65
Trembling	11	64
Feeling confused or "rattled"	3	53
Feeling weak or faint	4	41
Right after a mission, not being able to remember details of what happened	5	39
Feeling sick to the stomach	5	38
Not being able to concentrate	3	35
Wetting or soiling your pants	1	5

Source: L. F. Shaffer, "Fear and Courage in Aerial Combat," *Journal of Consulting Psychology,* 1947, 11, 137-143. By permission. Based on reports of 1985 flying officers and 2519 enlisted fliers of World War II.

The symptoms will vary according to the situation and the individual. Athletes just before an important contest usually exhibit tense behavior and often report feelings ranging from mild excitement to nausea and intense fear. Other circumstances in life may, of course, evoke similar responses. One of the most important studies of the conscious symptoms of a stressful situation was conducted by Shaffer (1947) with flying men during World War II. In his study, the subjects were asked to indicate the unusual physiological symptoms of which they were aware during a combat flight mission over enemy territory. The results are included in Table 5.

Role of emotion in motor performance and learning

Emotion has long been recognized as an important factor in one's learning and performance of motor skills. Logic, empirical evidence, and research support this concept. The exact nature or extent of its effect, however, has not been determined. This seems to depend heavily upon the nature of the emotion-producing situation. The emotional condition may be one of tension, anxiety, stress, or general excitement regarding a pending situation. Just as the meanings of the terms which are used to describe emotional arousal both differ and overlap in some ways, so does the effect of these different conditions on performance. Therefore, in order for one to clearly discuss the role of these conditions on performance, particular stimuli and responses must be described.

It is clear that emotional excitement has a profound effect on an individual's *performance* in a wide variety of activities, both motor and verbal. For example, there is little question that the level of excitement influences the ability of an individual to lift a heavy load, to throw a baseball for distance or for accuracy, to make a convincing speech, to perform well on a written examination, or to play a piano skillfully. The emotional state is likewise influential in one's ability to *learn* skills of various types. In some situations, high states of emotional excitement seem to help, and in other cases, great excitement seems to prove a detriment. Effects on both performance and learning will be discussed in some detail.

Motor performance

Specific questions are raised by the assumption that one's emotional state affects his performance in motor skills. For example, just how much motivation is needed for maximum performance? Is a condition of emotional excitement equally beneficial for the performance of different types of skills? What are the best techniques for motivating students in different activities? These questions have been investigated by psychologists during the past few years. Some research has been conducted under laboratory conditions, while other investigations have been carried out in regular class or athletic situations.

Different states of emotional excitability seem to have varying effects in different learning and performance situations. Some factors which seem important are (1) the nature of the emotion-inducing stimulant, (2) the type of skill involved, (3) the level of proficiency of the participant, and (4) the personality of the participant. Each must be considered if one is to fully understand the effect of motivation. With each of these conditions, several alternatives are possible. For example, the emotion-inducing stimulant may be a challenge, threat, reward, ridicule, praise, or environmental distraction. The type of skill may vary from a simple to a complex motor response, a fine to a gross movement, or a meaningful to a novel laboratory task. Similarly, studies have shown that the level of skill of the performer is influential in the degree of excitement which may result from a particular set of circumstances. One's personality also plays a major role in his response. For example, empirical evidence indicates that some individuals get unduly rattled under stress while others rise to the occasion. It becomes clear that a blanket generalization cannot be made for all circumstances.

The nature of the stimulant.   Physical educators and coaches have consistently found that individuals seem to try harder if they are competing against another individual or team. The technique of competition has therefore been used as one of the primary means of promoting maximum effort by performers. As early as 1897, Triplett found that the mere presence of other persons caused changes in an individual's performance. Sometimes the performance improved, while on other occasions a decline resulted. He observed that the inconsistency in direction of change seemed to be caused by the personality of the individual.

W. R. Johnson (1949) studied the effect of competition in causing a buildup of anxiety among a group of team sport (football) members and a group of individual sport (wrestling) members. Heart rate, blood pressure, and blood sugar were used as the measures of anxiety. He reported that the wrestlers became more excited immediately before the contest than did football players. The individual challenge seemed to present a greater competitive threat to the participants than did the group challenge. In another study of college football players, Johnson (1950) reported a close relationship between the performers' level of excitement regarding an upcoming game and their performance in the game. Games which were preceded by the highest level of excitement also had the highest level of performance. For the game of football, Johnson theorized that the higher the level of emotional arousal, the better would be the performance.

Several studies have been conducted in which induced noises and other distracting conditions were used to determine their effect on motor performance taking place at the same time. Grimaldi (1958) conducted one such study in which a coordination task was performed under quiet and noisy conditions of various frequency ranges and intensities. There were more errors and less precision when noise was evident. Further, response times were slower and number of errors were greater when noise levels and frequencies were highest. Grimaldi concluded that intermittent noise has a reducing effect on an individual's ability to perform quick and precise movements.

The realization of failure seems to have a detrimental effect on subsequent performance in motor skills. Rasch (1955) investigated this phenomenon with aviation cadets during World War II. After the cadets had taken the final flying test to qualify for their wings, instructors informed each student that he had failed (but accurate scores were kept). After this "failure," students were given subsequent flying tests to determine if their performances would be affected by knowledge of failure. Rasch found (1) subsequent performances were significantly poorer than original test performances; (2) performance was adversely affected for four days after the failure; and (3) flyers who were rated highest in previous performances were more adversely affected than were poorer flyers.

Sullivan (1927) observed a similar phenomenon when he reported that an intellectually superior group of students was hindered more by a realization of failure than was an inferior group. Possibly, this was because the more intelligent group was not as used to failure. Memorization of nonsense syllables was used in Sullivan's study. McClelland and Apicella (1947) found that failure produced less efficient subsequent performance in a card-sorting task. Willingham (1958) also showed a decrease in motor performance following failure.

The type of task. Performance on some tasks seems to be enhanced by a high level of emotional excitement, while proficiency for other tasks is lessened. Matarazzo and Matarazzo (1956) reported that performance on a more complex maze problem is adversely affected by anxiety. A simple maze task, however, was enhanced by a moderate level of anxiety. Taylor and Spence (1952) reported that a high level of anxiety is a detriment to performance in a complex verbal choice-point problem. Wechsler and Hartogs (1945), after research with a mirror-drawing task, concluded that fine motor coordinations and discriminations were adversely affected by anxiety.

Hennis and Ulrich (1958) investigated the effect of psychic stressor on the depth perception, steadiness, blood pressure, and simple eye-hand coordination of freshmen college women. They found that there was an elevation in blood pressure when the stressor was used. There were also changes in depth perception, steadiness, and coordination, but these changes were not consistent in direction. Henry (1961) showed that motivation resulting from electric shock can be effective in speeding simple reaction time. In addition, the resulting speedup was transferable from a simple to a more complicated movement.

L. A. Miller (1960) evaluated the emotional stress of varsity high school track performers immediately before all meets for the months of March and April. The degree of stress was determined by taking pulse and respiratory rates and measuring palm perspiration. The students also completed a checklist to give an indication of their confidence. A significant relationship was found between emotional stress and consistency of competitive performance. Poor competitors (as rated by coaches) showed less emotional stress than did good performers.

Gerdes (1958) had subjects perform tasks involving speed, strength, accuracy, and certain sports skills under several motivation conditions. The speed tasks were the sixty-yard dash and a zigzag run; strength items were pull-ups and push-ups; accuracy items included a volleyball wall volley and basketball passing test; and skill tasks were the baseball throw and basketball wall volley test. Gerdes used such motivating techniques as competition between individuals and groups, encouragement individually and in class situations, scale scores, and individual testing in a class situation. He reported that each of the motivational techniques proved beneficial for performance in most of the activities, but that encouragement and the use of test scores were especially helpful.

The Yerkes-Dodson law, as described by Eysenck (1963), points out the varying effect that a standard amount of drive might have on different tasks. According to this law, complex tasks are performed best when one's drive or motivation is relatively low, but optimum proficiency in simple tasks is attained when drive is high. The relationship between drive and performance is therefore not a simple one. As drive increases, so does performance to a point. Continued increases in drive lead to poorer performance, especially in complex skills. It appears that under a high level of tension, wrong habits are often activated which interfere with both learning and performance. This law was developed by Robert M. Yerkes and John D. Dodson of Harvard University prior to World War I. It has been substantiated both experimentally and observationally since that time.

The level of proficiency. Individuals having different levels of proficiency often react differently to a stressful or motivating condition. In two verbal tests, Gates (1924) found that proficient students performed less well in front of a large audience. Rasch (1955) reported that the most outstanding aviation cadets were more seriously hindered by the realization of failure than were cadets who were not as proficient. Similarly, in a verbal test, Sullivan (1927) found that an intellectually superior group was more adversely affected by failure than was an inferior group.

Not all evidence, however, supports the concept that stress has a more detrimental effect on superior performers. L. A. Miller (1960) reported that track performers who were rated as poor performers by their coaches showed relatively little emotional stress prior to track meets, good performers exhibited a greater degree of emotional stress and also greater consistency of performance. In a simple maze test with young children, Abel (1936) found that the performance of more intelligent subjects was enhanced when a group situation was introduced.

The personality of the individual.   In addition to the individual's level of skill and the type of task, personality plays an important part in determining one's performance in a stressful situation. Highly anxious individuals are more disturbed by stressful conditions and have greater difficulty in novel situations than do less anxious persons. Parsons, Phillips, and Lane (1954) found that stress was detrimental to steadiness. Baker (1961) found that stress inhibited the performance of high anxiety subjects and aided the performance of low anxiety subjects. Breen (1959) showed that there is motor incoordination even among normal subjects under stress. Also, neurotic patients were found to have less general coordination and manual dexterity.

Some people seem more resistive to distraction than do others. Some athletes are more consistent or steady performers while others tend to be "hot" one day and "cold" the next. It can be observed by those who follow major league baseball games that some players are more susceptible than others to slumps and hot streaks. In like manner, there is great variation in the consistency of track and field performers. Characteristically, all people's performances fluctuate from time to time. This variability is evident among both outstanding and poor performers and among anxious and nonanxious individuals. Physiological causes cannot always be found when the individual performs at an unusually high or low level. Personality traits seem more influential in determining one's response to different emotional situations. Although there is little dispute about the influence of personality, very little conclusive evidence has been gathered in this difficult area of investigation.

Motor learning

The direct influence of an emotionally stimulating situation is more obvious in motor performance than in motor learning. Nevertheless, it has been consistently pointed out that the most important condition for learning is motivation on the part of the learner. This widely accepted principle is more important both for motor skills and for verbal concepts, but the exact role of different types and intensities of motivation in the learning of different skills is not entirely clear.

Several factors seem to affect the role of tension or excitement in the learning of motor skills. Most investigators have reported that simple motor tasks are learned more effectively under tension, while the learning of complex tasks is adversely affected by tension. Also, Wechsler and Hartogs (1945) reported that high levels of anxiety hinder the learning and performance of tasks involving fine motor coordination. A third factor is the induced tension's characteristics and relation to the task. Tension from both physical effort and emotional stress tension has been used in studies. Physical tension, which is nearer the performing body part, appears to be most influential.

The existence of tension seems to have varying effects on mental tasks of different degrees of complexity. A moderate amount of tension seems to aid simple mental tasks. Bills (1927), for instance, found that subjects who were squeezing hand dynomometers in both hands were better able to learn nonsense syllables, memorize and add columns of digits, and recite scrambled letters. Zartman and Cason (1934), however, reported that continuous tension (a foot applied to a resisting pedal) did not aid subjects in solving a complete arithmetic problem. Freeman (1938) found uneven effects when he attempted to affix an optimal tension load to different types of mental and motor tasks. He concluded that the more complex tasks would be inhibited by tension.

A number of studies have shown that during the early stages of learning, tension is high, but subsides as greater skill is developed in the task. Stroud (1931), in a maze problem, found that less downward pressure was exhibited by subjects as they developed skill. Greater tension was shown when subjects encountered the more difficult portions of the maze. He also found that physical tension could be induced by suggestion. When subjects were told that they had to produce three perfect trials, greater downward pressure on the stylus was evidenced.

Daniel (1939) and Ghisselli (1936) obtained results which generally agree with those of Stroud. Both found a reduction in tension as learning increased. Daniel reported that high tension was associated with greater speed while lower tension resulted in fewer errors. Stauffacher (1937) found that good learners were hindered by increased tension while poor learners were aided by tension. He theorized that prior to induced tension the poor learners were operating at below maximum level.

Farber and Spence (1953) reported that nonanxious subjects developed proficiency in a stylus-maze task more quickly than did anxious subjects. After arriving at similar findings, Ausubel, Schiff, and Goldman

(1953) concluded that anxious individuals were not able to improvise or adjust to changes in a learning situation. Matarazzo and Matarazzo (1956) reported that subjects learn a simple maze task more easily when a moderate level of anxiety exists rather than a very high or very low level of anxiety. Very anxious or overly tense individuals apparently do less well in most learning situations and perform even more poorly in situations which require progressive discrimination.

In a situation in which airmen were attempting to learn a complex manipulative skill, Fleishman (1958) used verbal encouragement to increase the motivation level. The experimenter made comments which indicated that future assignments would depend upon how well one performed. These comments were made prior to and during the performance. Fleishman reported that performance scores improved significantly when this motivational technique was used. Many other authors have reported that the motivational level which is attained through written or oral praise is beneficial for the learning of both motor and verbal skills.

Generally, the evidence relating to the role of motivation in motor learning and performance suggests that:

1. An above average level of excitement or motivation aids learning and performance in most motor tasks.
2. A high level of excitement is advantageous for performance in gross motor activities involving speed, strength, and endurance, and for the learning of simple motor tasks.
3. A high level of excitement interferes with performances involving fine muscle movements, coordination, steadiness, and concentration, and with the learning of complex motor tasks.

TECHNIQUES IN MOTIVATION

The idea that excitement or tension level has an effect on performance is no longer seriously questioned. For some types of motor performance or learning, a very high level of motivation may be sought by the teacher. Such a situation exists when maximum performance on a pull-up test is sought, or if the coach in football wants his linemen to play at their peak. In another situation, the coach may want the player to develop a relatively low level of motivation. This condition may prove best for the quarterback in football, the novice diver or gymnast in an important meet, or the child who is taking a balance test in a physical education class. In some situations, therefore, the teacher or coach would like to develop a motivation level which is between the two extremes.

In addition to *determining* the most advantageous level of arousal for each type of activity and for children of different personality types, teachers need to give more serious study to the matter of effectively *changing* the tension levels of children. In many situations, students in class or athletes on the field need to be motivated or brought to a higher level of excitability. On other occasions, they need to be demotivated or calmed down for most effective performance.

In regular school classes, motivating techniques are needed very frequently. The arbitrary bell schedule often runs counter to the interests of the child. For example, the student may be interested in a particular problem in history when the bell rings. Then he must immediately be ready for math; another bell and his interest must be in a soccer lead-up game, then in some project in wood shop. Obviously, students may have great difficulty in changing their psychological readiness with the class schedule at school. Sound motivational techniques are therefore needed to quickly capture the student's attention in each class situation.

Numerous motivating techniques have been tried, both in experimental and practical settings. An analysis of the effectiveness of some of these may aid the teacher in determining the most appropriate method to use in several different situations.

Experimental techniques

A number of projects have been conducted in which several motivating techniques were studied at once. In one study, Strong (1963) had sixth-grade boys and girls take physical fitness tests following six different methods of motivation. He reported that best performances took place when subjects were organized as members of a competing team, and then were individually able to choose their desired level of performance. Another effective method was encouraging the children to try to set a record. Individual competition against either (1) a classmate of near equal ability, (2) a classmate of different ability, or (3) all classmates was not as effective. Generally he found that motivated children performed better than unmotivated children. He also reported that these techniques of motivation were more effective with boys than with girls.

Gerdes (1958) compared the techniques of (1) verbal encouragement, (2) team competition, (3) use of previous scores, and (4) retesting on four types of physical tasks which involved speed, strength, accuracy, and sports skills. He pointed out that the motivating techniques did not demand any specially constructed apparatus and therefore were usable in a regular class situation. Gerdes generally concluded that all the techniques resulted in improved performances (especially in strength), but that no method was singularly most effective. He observed that the validity of fitness testing is dependent upon the motivation used.

M. M. Martin (1961) tested the effect of four motivational techniques on performance in a test of reaching skill. Individuals performed either with the group or alone, and some were told their results while others were not. She found that the informed groups did better than the uninformed groups. Also, performing in the presence of classmates, resulted in better achievement than performance alone. J. Nelson (1962) used ten different techniques to get college men to exercise to exhaustion on the elbow-flexion ergograph. The motivating situations varied from verbal encouragement to several competitive situations in which subjects were told that they were being compared with Russian students, or that their performances were being used to set standards for the selection of astronauts. Most of the special techniques resulted in improved performance, with none of the methods proving particularly outstanding.

Occasionally, the practice of *hypnotism* has been used by some researchers in an effort to stimulate the individual to greater effort or to determine his true capacity in such components as strength, endurance, speed, and general muscular control. It has been found that hypnotism can be effectively used to delay fatigue, to enable one to withstand pain, and to control various psychological inhibitions. It has also been reported that hypnotic suggestion can reduce the effective strength of the individual. However, there are inconsistencies among studies in regard to the value of hypnosis for increasing strength. Some researchers have found that inhibitions regarding performing without a warm-up can be effectively controlled by hypnotism. For several reasons, however, hypnosis is not recommended as an appropriate technique to motivate public school children.

Traditional techniques

The techniques most often used to promote greater interest in learning and performance are *reward* and *punishment.* The advisability of selecting either reward or punishment for learning cannot be easily generalized upon because the choice depends upon the circumstances. The personality of the learner is one important consideration. Some individuals respond well to both reward and punishment while others respond better to one method. All experienced teachers have observed children who sulk for long periods after being punished. Quite frequently punishment results in a detrimental effect on subsequent learning and performance. Other factors which influence the effect of these techniques are the age and sex of the individuals, and the manner in which reward or punishment is administered.

Rewards may be (1) symbolic: particularly praise, athletic letters (certificates), school grades, or recognition on all-star teams; (2) material: athletic prizes (watches, blazers, etc.) or money; or (3) psychological: personal knowledge of improvement, a feeling of adequacy, or acceptance. Symbolic and material rewards have often been referred to as "external" motivation while psychological rewards are sometimes called "internal" motivation. Internal motivation is of the highest order and is generally favored by educators.

The most important advantages of rewards seem to be that they tend to create a pleasurable association with the desired act; they engender enthusiasm; and they enhance the learner's ego. Numerous studies with both verbal and motor skills reveal advantages of praise. There are some disadvantages, however, especially if too frequent use is made of praise. The most important disadvantage is the individual's tendency to develop a dependence upon extrinsic rather than intrinsic motivation and, therefore, develop false values (interest in the reward rather than the activity itself). Another disadvantage of external rewards in physical education and intramural activities is that the same few children seem to excel most of the time. It appears that the winners of external rewards are usually the children who need them least for subsequent enthusiasm.

In the use of rewards, Oberteuffer (1956) offers the following guides:

1. The reward should be found within the activity—not separate or unrelated to it.
2. The reward should lead the winner on to further activity in the same line of endeavor.
3. The reward should produce no consequences in the individual winner which are unacceptable socially.
4. Above all, the reward or anticipation thereof should not serve as the principal incentive: the incentive should come from the satisfactions within the activity (p. 178).[1]

Traditionally in schools, reproof or some form of punishment has been used about as frequently as praise and reward. The most important advantage of punishment seems to be that it *is effective* with some children. In motor skills punishment is sometimes associated as a natural result of an activity. As such, the punishment can aid in the elimination of certain undesirable responses. Apparently a degree of discipline is needed by all children, but there are more agreed-upon disadvantages of punishment than advantages. For example, when used often, punishment loses its effect. There are situations in which punishment may reinforce the undesired act by creating fear in the mind of the learner. Very often rapport between the teacher and student is lost. Punishment is often humiliating for some students and reinforces a feeling of inadequacy. This is damaging to the self-concept of the individual. On the

[1] D. Oberteuffer, PHYSICAL EDUCATION, New York: Harper & Row, 1956. By permission.

other hand, some students, especially extroverts, are stimulated more by reproof than by praise. In the use of punishment, however, one drawback is the inability to establish an equal punishment for all students. It is often clear that what is real punishment for one child is only a minor challenge for others.

A popular technique which has been used to stimulate individuals to greater effort has been the *pep talk* immediately before the beginning of athletic contests. The nature of these pregame talks has varied from a tense, stirring, oratorical appeal to the emotions of the participants, to a quiet, logical, and instructional talk. The former type, popularized by Knute Rockne and several other football coaches, has perhaps been the most popular technique for team games in schools and colleges. Recordings of such speeches or events are used for pre-game motivation in a similar manner. Films, with emotional overtones, have been occasionally used before athletic contests and even during wartime to evoke a certain arousal on the part of participants. There can be little doubt that the pep talk and other precontest techniques have often been effective in motivating young people to greater effort.

The use of *music* as a motivating device has recently become popular. However, almost no research has been done to determine the effect of music on one's attitude toward or performance in subsequent activity. The practice of using music in the locker room to generally excite the players for the upcoming contest is increasing. Each year at basketball tournament time there are reports of coaches who use music prior to games and during half-time intermissions. It is logical to assume that certain types of music, with a stirring, rhythmic beat, and with progressively increasing volume and tempo, may result in a measurable increase in excitability on the part of young people.

On other occasions, music is used during the performance of activity for the purpose of stimulating the individual to greater effort. Band music for marching has traditionally been used by armies because of the psychological stimulation as well as for regulating the pace at which the troops walk. "Exercise" records are being used more and more in schools. In addition to the verbal instruction, the music is designed to motivate students to vigorous activity. In the use of such music to accompany exercise, care should be taken to select music which is appropriate for the age level. This author has observed junior high school girls exercising to the accompaniment of rock-and-roll music and elementary school children exercising to the "William Tell Overture" and the "Sabre Dance." These selections seemed to promote maximum effort as well as blend with the interest level of the children. Thus physical educators and coaches, in addition to dance teachers, have begun to use music for the stimulation of positive attitudes as well as for rhythm.

Competition has been one of the most frequently used techniques for motivating young people to perform with greater enthusiasm. Research projects dealing with the role of motivation in physical activity have used several forms of competition. Competition is not only effective, but it is easy to create in almost any school situation. Students may compete against other teams or against other individuals. Team competition may be on the varsity level, the intramural level, or within a particular class. Individual competition may be strictly individual in nature, as in a challenge tournament, or it may involve individuals as team members, as in a gymnastic or track meet. In working with sixth-grade children, Strong (1963) found that competition was more effective in motivating boys than girls. In our culture, boys are apparently more impressed than girls by a competitive situation.

In addition to competing against other persons, one might compete against himself or against various class or school records. Such competitive situations are especially appropriate and easy to establish in physical fitness tests, circuit training or obstacle courses, track and field events, and sports skills tests. A useful and effective method which is employed by many teachers is reminding children of their previous performance on a particular task and encouraging them to surpass that score in subsequent trials. Such competition is particularly dependent upon the student's receiving *knowledge of results* from all his participations. This proves to be a meaningful challenge for most students. Outstanding performers can be encouraged to try to break the class or school record. The total class, as a unit, might compete against established school records. Secondary school boys are often motivated to work harder if a situation is established in which they are competing against Marine Corps scores or scores of children from another country. Competition is most effective when each child has a reasonable chance to win. If one child is either completely outclassed or is an easy winner in a contest, his motivation will be weakened rather than enhanced by the situation.

General motivation or enthusiasm for a class activity may be prompted if the instructor *teaches for success* on the part of the student. There is wisdom in the cliché: "Nothing succeeds like success." It is customary that students will develop greater interest in an activity if their early attempts meet with some degree of achievement. On the other hand, if their first few trials result in total failure, students' interest will rapidly diminish. Therefore, class methods should be varied so that even those with a very low level of skill can, to some extent, reach the objectives of the activity. Modifications can be made in certain drills in order to attain this success. Consider the situation in which the instructor attempts to teach the fast break to a group of novice basketball players. If the drill is organized so that three offensive players are coming down court to be met by three defensive players, it is practically certain that the offensive team will meet with failure. In the early stages of learning basketball, defensive skills are more advanced than are offensive skills.

Therefore, to increase the probability of a successful fast break, the teacher could start with three offensive players against one defensive player. Later, he might use two defensive players, but restrict their movement to about one step. The same general technique might be employed in soccer, since the lack of dribbling and passing skills make it practically impossible to score goals unless certain restrictions are placed on the defensive team. Some technique for assuring a degree of success will certainly add to the interest and general motivation of students.

Sometimes it is desirable for the teacher or coach to demotivate or calm down individuals in certain situations. Demotivation may be necessary both for efficiency of performance and for safety reasons. First, it has been pointed out that a high level of excitement or stress is likely to hinder one's performance in some tasks, especially those involving precision or complexity of fine motor movement. For most efficient performance in such tasks, therefore, efforts should be made to reduce the tension of performers in certain situations. Second, there are certain dangers if individuals with heart ailments, epilepsy, or certain other handicaps get too excited and overexert themselves in vigorous activity. When such individuals show evidence of too great tension, efforts should be made to relieve the tension or to remove them from the situation. Sometimes young people under the stimulation of emotional excitement attempt dangerous activities for which they are not yet ready. In advanced diving, tumbling, or gymnastics, hazardous stunts are often attempted as a result of undue motivation, as is reckless play in such sports as football or soccer.

Ironically, some of the general techniques which are used to motivate performers are also effective in *reducing motivation* or tension. For example, talking with an individual or group in a calm and relaxed manner might have just the opposite effect of a pep talk. Likewise, music which is soft and flowing, rather than loud marching music, might have a calming effect. Hypnotism, progressive relaxation, and deep breathing exercises have also been used to soothe persons who are in a state of high tension.

Since the individual's motivation greatly affects his learning and performance in any mental or physical activity, every effort should be made to develop a most favorable climate. However, many questions remain to be answered, and much research has yet to be done in the complex but vital area of motivation.

LEVEL OF ASPIRATION

A concept which is intimately related to motivation and performance is the topic of level of aspiration. It has long been suspected that a relationship exists between one's goals and his achievement. However, the idea of expectations and their influence on performance was first investigated by Lewin before he left Germany. Frank (1935) reported that the term *"level of aspiration,"* in reference to expectation, was originated by Hoppe. Other authors have reported that Dembo (1931) first coined the phrase. Both Hoppe and Dembo were students of Lewin.

A generally accepted definition of level of aspiration is given by Frank as: "The level of future performance in a familiar task which an individual, knowing his level of past performance in that task, explicitly undertakes to reach" (p. 119). In the general use of this term, primary thought has been devoted to what one *expects* to achieve as opposed to what one would *like* to achieve. In support of this distinction, several researchers, Martire (1956), Clarke and Greene (1963) and Wylie (1961) found no relationship between the level of aspiration and the achievement need of the individual. Other authors, however, have suggested that one's general level of motivation probably has a bearing on his expected achievement. Most authorities agree that *once the level of aspiration is set, it can serve as a strong motivator for the individual to reach it.*

Measurement of level of aspiration poses a problem. Merely asking the subject what he expects to attain in a particular performance does not always provide an accurate score of his expected achievement level. Lewin (1944) suggests that there are three levels for each task: (1) what the person *says* that he expects to attain, (2) what he *really* expects, and (3) what he would *like* to attain. Weiss (1961) had subjects respond to several aspiration questions. On the basis of these, he was able to identify two major categories: the judgmental or expectational dimension, and the motivational or aspirational dimension. Current research seems to indicate that a high or low level of aspiration is not a general personality characteristic which is the same for all tasks. Instead, level of aspiration is specific to a particular task.

If a participant attains or surpasses his level of aspiration for a particular task he could be considered to have succeeded. On the other hand, his inability to reach his predicted level would constitute a failure. The participant's future levels of aspiration are affected somewhat by his previous performances. However, some individuals seem to consistently set levels which are not attained. Others establish levels which are close to their actual performances, while a third group sets levels which are far too low. Children who regularly set unreasonably high levels of aspiration apparently feel a need to put themselves in a high category or promote the feeling that they have tried very hard. Those who select too low levels seemingly need to play it safe and assure themselves of success. It is also possible that they do not wish to try very hard. In general, one's level of aspiration for a task tends to vary up or down with his prior successes or failures. However, subsequent aspiration levels are influenced more by successes than by failures.

Price (1960) had college women take part in a wide variety of motor skills to determine if there was a relationship between level of aspiration and performance. Significant correlations were found between aspiration and achievement. The reason for this relationship was not suggested. Strong (1963) found that one of the most effective ways to motivate children to perform was allowing them to choose their own desired level of performance.

Worell (1959) found that college students who set a reasonable level of aspiration concerning their academic work had greater contact with reality and were generally successful in grade achievement. Students with levels of aspiration far above their previous records were generally unsuccessful or poor students. Walter (1951), in a study of children from the fourth to twelfth grades, found that boys had a higher level of aspiration than girls.

Sears (1940) investigated the level of aspiration of a group of children in grades four, five, and six who had long histories of chronic failure in reading and arithmetic. These children were compared with another group that had histories of consistent success in these subjects. She found that the children with successful backgrounds set their aspirations at a reasonable or realistic level while the failure group set their aspirations with little regard to their previous achievements. Sears inferred that many of the failure group completely ignored reality and were living out of contact with their ability. Apparently these children continuously set higher aspiration levels in an imaginary world where the mere gesture of setting high goals was accepted as achievement instead of real success.

The establishment of aspiration levels seems to be affected by the social setting. Children seem to express aspiration levels which conform to some extent with the group mean. According to Hilgard, Sait, and Margaret (1940), "One with a good score does not wish to brag, and so asserts that it was a matter of good luck and next time the score will be lower. Similarly, one with a low score does not wish to admit that he is a deviate, attributes the low score to bad luck, and expresses an optimistic estimate" (pp. 419–420).

A very important role of the teacher is helping the student to establish realistic goals. In this way, success and failure can be regulated to some extent. Without guidance, some students select tasks or levels of proficiency which are inappropriate for their ability. Such indiscriminant goal setting often leads to frustration or, in some cases, habits of selecting tasks which are not challenging. On the basis of previous performances, students' feelings about their abilities, and other factors, the teacher should suggest appropriate aspiration levels (goals). Individual guidance is especially necessary in physical education activities where performance standards vary so widely. In the same class, one boy may well be encouraged to jump five feet and to run a mile in minutes while another boy should reasonably be expected to jump only four feet and to run a mile in seven and one-half minutes.

Child and Whiting (1949) reviewed the literature and research on level of aspiration and established the following general conclusions which seem to have implications for all phases of education:

1. "Success generally leads to raising of the level of aspiration, and failure to a lowering." Despite the difficulties or luck involved in attaining success, the level of aspiration is raised for subsequent performances. Hope seems to be easily reinforced. This principle is exhibited by children who learn a skill for the first time and make adjustments during the process. All people use previous experiences, among other things, to establish an estimate of their capabilities.

2. "Effect of failure on level of aspiration are more varied than those of success." The unpredictability of failure is similar to the effects of punishment. Perhaps the individual rationalizes about failure so that it is not accepted as a true indication of his skill level. Many golfers, prior to teeing off, assume that they will score better than their previous scores would indicate. The expected level seems to be more related to previous best records or maximum potential rather than to recent average performances. A few failures do not quickly lower the level of aspiration.

3. "The stronger the success, the greater is the probability of a rise in the level of aspiration; the stronger the failure, the greater is the probability of a lowering." Very poor performances tend to "destroy the confidence" of the individual. Since this is not desirable, teachers should avoid placing students in situations where glaring failures are likely to occur. On occasion, however, students need to have their level lowered somewhat so that they can more realistically appraise their ability. For example, a high school pitcher of mediocre ability might aspire to become a major league pitcher. Despite a frank evaluation by his coach, this player may not accept his limitations until he is bombed on several occasions by opposing teams. On the other hand, another performer might have too low an opinion of his ability and, thus, would not aspire to excellence. In such situations the teacher might arrange for some successes in order to raise his level of aspiration to a more reasonable point.

SELECTED READINGS

Cannon, W. B. *Bodily changes in pain, hunger, fear and rage.* (2nd ed.) New York: Appleton-Century-Crofts, 1929.

Cole, L. E., & Bruce, W. F. *Educational psychology.* New York: Harcourt, Brace & World, 1959.

Cratty, B. J., *Movement behavior and motor learning*. Philadelphia: Lea & Febiger, 1964.

Deese, J. *The psychology of learning*. (2nd ed.) New York: McGraw-Hill, 1958.

Hilgard, E. R. *Introduction to psychology*. New York: Harcourt, Brace & World, 1957.

Selve, H. *The stress of life*. New York: McGraw-Hill, 1956.

Ulrich, C. Stress and sport. In W. R. Johnson (Ed.), *Science and medicine of exercise and sports*. New York: Harper & Row, 1960. Pp. 251–269.

Woodworth, R. S., & Schlosberg, H. *Experimental psychology*. (Rev. ed.) New York: Holt, Rinehart and Winston, 1963.

Young, P. T. *Motivation and emotion*. New York: Wiley, 1961.

Part IV

CONDITIONS FOR LEARNING

Introduction

The conditions by which the task is presented to the individual are strategic in the learning process. These instructor-controlled variables affect both the rate and the thoroughness with which the task will be learned. The distribution of practice periods as well as the length and internal make-up of each work session are important conditions which are within the ability of the instructor to control. In addition, the instructor has some role to play in promoting related conceptualization to accompany the physical practice. Such covert rehearsal along with overt practice of the particular skill is a condition which appears to take advantage of the intelligence of human beings for faster learning of skills.

Another condition for learning over which the instructor has control is the organization of the task into units which are most appropriate for acquisition. Learning tasks may be broken into large or small segments and may be related to the whole activity, or each task may be a separate unit in and of itself. Accordingly, this discussion of *conditions for learning* will include the following major areas:

Chapter 8

Practice and rest distribution

Efficiency in teaching and learning is to a great extent dependent upon the intelligent scheduling of work periods. For this reason, the planning of work schedules has always been of concern to teachers and school administrators. Several developments in recent years demand that more serious attention be devoted to the matter of attaining maximum efficiency in programming and in instruction. The "population explosion," resulting in more crowded schools, and the "explosion of knowledge," leading to a more crowded curriculum, highlight these developments. In addition, recent research resulting in a greater understanding of the attention span of children, and more knowledge about the learning process indicates that traditional methods in work scheduling are inadequate. It is imperative that educators synthesize all available information and put it to use for teaching and learning efficiency.

It has long been acknowledged by authorities that individuals do not learn simply because they practice. Thorndike emphasized that exercise must be under favorable conditions in order for effective learning to take place. Still, in today's schools there often seems to be an assumption that learning is simply a factor of time spent in practice or in study, i.e., the more you practice, the more you learn.

Regarding the topic of practice and rest distribution, physical education teachers and athletic coaches have many practical questions about daily, weekly, and yearly schedules of work periods. For example, how long should daily practices be for a high school football team? How can the many skills of field hockey be broken down into short units of practice within a work session for most effective results? In baseball batting practice, is it best to take one round of twelve swings or two rounds of six swings? Should one begin the season with short practices and gradually lengthen them, or with long practices which are later shortened? Should a coach have his team skip days of practice late in the season? Unfortunately, teachers are often guided by nothing more valid than tradition when planning work periods or unit schedules. Athletic coaches seem particularly guilty of arbitrarily scheduling practice sessions with little uniformity in length and structure and with almost no scientific evidence upon which to base their judgments.

Since the publication of Ebbinghaus' memory studies (1885), much discussion and research has taken place concerning the effect of time and practice upon learning. William James (1890) contributed to the interest in this area by suggesting that learning can take place even when we are not practicing. He postulated that people learn to skate during the summer and to swim during the winter.

Much research has been organized and administered to determine the relative effectiveness of massed and spaced practices. *Massed*, or concentrated, schedules are those which have little or no rest (or alternate activity) between the beginning and the completion of practice on the activity. *Spaced*, or distributed, schedules are those in which work periods are spread out or separated by either rest or some activity which is different from the one being practiced.

Research designs

The degree of massing or spacing of work periods is generally expressed in terms relative to alternative schedules. In most experiments, two or more groups are involved, each of which follows a different concentration of practices. A rather typical research design was conducted by Snoddy. In his experiment (1938), he sought to determine the relative effectiveness of three practice schedules on the development of skill in mirror tracing. While looking through a mirror, subjects traced a star-shaped path. Performance score on this task was determined by the length of time required to complete the circuit (from beginning to end) and the accuracy (number of errors) which was exhibited.

All groups completed twenty trials in Snoddy's experiment. One group practiced on a massed schedule in which no rest was allowed between each trial. A second group followed a relatively massed schedule in which a one-minute rest was allowed between each of the twenty trials. The third group practiced on a distributed schedule in which a twenty-four-hour period elapsed between each of the trials. All groups, therefore, had the same amount of practice. Each group was tested at the end of the experimental period to determine which schedule was most effective for the learning of the skill. Snoddy found that the group having the twenty-four-hour period between trials performed significantly better than did either of the other two groups. In addition, the group having a one-minute rest between trials performed better than the group following the massed practice schedule.

Many variations in research designs have been used to solve particular learning problems. Practice schedules most often used are those in which (1) no rest is allowed between practices; (2) a standard rest period is used following each trial; (3) progressively increasing rest periods are administered; and (4) progressively decreasing rests are given. Of course, any number of variations in the relative degree of massing or in the length of practice periods may be arranged. For most studies, the total amount of practice has been held constant for all groups. A second major variable in practice studies is introduced if different amounts of practice time are assigned to the different groups. This is often done to determine if variations in distribution can offset advantages of a greater amount of practice.

STUDIES IN PRACTICE DISTRIBUTION

The important problem is the determination of the optimum *amount* of practice and the most ideal *spacing* of practice periods for maximum learning of different types of skills at different points on the learning curve. Many questions still exist regarding the most efficient means of scheduling practices for different types of learning. Following is a discussion of some (1) research, (2) theories, (3) generalizations, and (4) implications regarding the topic of practice distribution. The research is discussed according to the tasks learned, i.e., verbal materials, laboratory motor skills, and meaningful motor skills.

Verbal materials

The first experimental work dealing with practice schedules and learning was reported by Ebbinghaus (1885). He served as his own subject for extensive research with meaningful poetry as well as nonsense syllables, and he concluded that a given unit of material could be learned in less practice time and retained longer when rest periods are taken between study sessions. This first significant effort to deal with temporal relationships served as a beginning for experimental work in all aspects of learning. Ebbinghaus' work with practice schedules stimulated others to test his findings.

Lyon (1931) had subjects memorize meaningful materials on two practice schedules. One group learned a short section each day while a second group practiced continually until they had learned all the material. The short-section-per-day group retained the material much longer. On the basis of his study, Lyon suggested that: (1) progressively increasing rest periods should be used, and (2) the optimum learning schedule varies with different individuals and different tasks. Hahn and Thorndike (1914) used elementary school children in an arithmetic experiment which lasted for 90 minutes of practice. Most effective work periods varied from 10 to 22½ minutes depending on the grade level. In working with meaningful material, Jost (1897) found that two readings every day for twelve days was far more effective than eight readings a day for three days. English, Welborn, and Killian (1934) showed that fewer readings were required to learn poetry and prose when the readings were distributed.

Pyle (1919) compared results from practice periods of 15, 30, 45, and 60 minutes as subjects took part in a card-distributing experiment. For economy in learning, he found that the 30-minute work period was most effective. He suggested that the 15-minute period was too short for this type of learning, while the 45-minute periods were too long. For the longer periods, very little gain was made after 30 minutes. He presumed this decline in efficiency to be due to fatigue.

The suggestion that fatigue interferes with learning has frequently been made. Pyle's study, however, seemed to indicate that practices which are too short are not desirable, and that, possibly, it takes some time for the person to warm up to the activity. Reed (1924) also varied the length of the practice period from ten minutes to sixty minutes. He found that addition of two-place numbers was learned more quickly in twenty-minute periods than in shorter or longer practice periods. Perkins (1941) used different-sized blocks of nonsense syllables and varying time intervals. She reported that the length of the work period was much more important than the length of the interval. After conducting extensive research with rote learning, Hovland (1940) concluded that distributed practices are most effective because less interference is developed with such practices.

A few researchers have reported some disadvantages in distributed practices under certain circumstances. After experimenting with subjects in learning finger mazes, Cook and Hilgard (1949) concluded that easy skills could best be learned with massed trials, whereas difficult tasks could best be learned with spaced practices. Rubin-Rabson (1940) found no difference in the effectiveness of massed and distributed practices when subjects were memorizing piano music. Eaton (1937) reported that the nature of the interpolated activity between work periods was strategic in determining the value of the interim periods. After working with various types of verbal material, he concluded that the greater the amount of concentration demanded by the interpolated activity, the greater would be the interference with the regular learning material. Franklin and Brozek (1947) suggested that the most advantageous schedule depends upon the individual, the difficulty of the task, and the stage of learning.

Laboratory motor skills

A great deal of research regarding practice distribution has involved novel motor tasks. Experimental psychologists have conducted studies with these skills to establish principles for learning in general. Novel tasks offer distinct experimental control advantages over more meaningful material, whether verbal or motor. These control advantages include equalizing the background for the subjects and reducing the possibility that the task will be practiced at times other than the scheduled practice periods. In addition, since the subjects start from a near-zero level of proficiency, there is a strong likelihood that definite improvement will be shown. The relationship of these tasks to meaningful motor skills is similar to the relationship of nonsense syllables to other verbal tasks.

Foremost among the laboratory motor tasks have been *mirror tracing*, the *pursuit rotor*, and various types of *mazes*. In addition, several coordination and control learning tasks have been developed and used in recent years, especially in learning experiments with Air Force personnel. These have not been standardized and used extensively with civilians or in school situations. Carmichael (1922) explained that some form of mirror drawing was used in Germany as early as 1899; but W. F. Dearborn was the first to develop a learning method with this apparatus in 1905. Koerth (1922) developed the pursuit rotor, a target-tracing apparatus, for the purpose of conducting research in learning. Beginning about 1900, several researchers, working independently, developed many variations of animal mazes, finger mazes, pencil mazes, and total body mazes. These have been used mostly in learning studies.

Snoddy developed a mirror-tracing instrument and used it in several early studies of practice and rest. In one study (1935), he had five groups of university students learn this motor skill, each on a different practice schedule. On the basis of his findings in this study, he suggested that there are two processes in mental growth, and, further, that these processes are directly opposed to each other. These two opposed growth processes were called primary and secondary. Primary growth takes place early and is stable. It is the foundation for secondary growth. Secondary growth comes later and is less stable. The stability of secondary growth is greatly dependent upon the adequacy of primary growth. Snoddy further stated that early growth is enhanced by distributed practices while later growth occurs best when practices are massed. Rest intervals tend to have opposite effects on primary and secondary learning. Snoddy's theory, therefore, advocates spaced practices in the early stages of learning and massed practices later. Lorge (1930) had college students learn mirror tracing as well as verbal tasks involving nonsense syllables, code work, and mirror reading. He found that for each type of task, a twenty-four-hour interval between practice trials was more effective than was a continuous schedule or one with a one-minute rest interval.

Massey (1957) had young women who were training to be teaching nuns learn mirror-tracing according to three different practice schedules. The variables of diet, rest, and daily routine were, to a great extent, controlled. Practice schedules used were daily (Monday through Friday), three times per week, and an *adapted additive* pattern which starts with massed practices and continues with progressively longer rest periods. Each practice period was held constant for all groups. All groups practiced (on their respective schedules) for a five-week period. It was shown that groups with greater massed practices at the beginning exhibited greater initial learning. In later practices, the Monday through Friday group reached a higher level of performance. The higher level of performance for this group, however, was not in proportion to their greater number of practices. The more distributed practices were far more efficient in terms of time spent in practice.

In a study by Oxendine (1965), college students practiced mirror tracing on three different schedules. The length of each succeeding practice period increased progressively for one group. Another group practiced on a schedule in which each succeeding practice became shorter. The third group used constant units of practice throughout the learning period. During the experimental period all groups completed the same amount of practice. At the end of the learning period the group using constant units of practice performed best, followed in order by the increasing practice group and the decreasing practice group. A retention test administered four weeks after the final practice revealed that the groups remained in the same relative positions.

In a study by Harmon and Oxendine (1961), three groups of junior high school boys had different *amounts* of practice while developing mirror-tracing skill. Each group practiced two times a week for five weeks. Only the length of the practice period varied. One group had 2 trials on each practice day, while a second group had 5 trials and a third 8 trials. At the conclusion of the experimental period, therefore, one group had completed 20 trials, another group 50 trials, and the third group 80 trials. The authors reported that during the early stages of the experiment, the groups using relatively long practices showed advantages over the groups using shorter practices; i.e., the 8-trial group performed best, followed by the 5-trial group and the 2-trial group respectively. After the early stages of learning, however, the groups seemed to learn equally fast despite the differences in amount of practice.

The Koerth pursuit rotor was used by Doré and Hilgard (1938) to test Snoddy's claim of two processes in mental growth. College students served as subjects in this experiment which lasted a total of forty-three minutes for each. One group followed a schedule of progressively increasing rest periods, while another group used progressively decreasing rests. The group with early massing and late spacing scored reliably higher than the group on the reverse plan. These results contradict Snoddy's claim that early spacing and late massing is better for the learning of a motor skill. In a different study (1937), Doré and Hilgard found that groups with greater distribution of practices throughout the experiment showed better performances than groups with massed practices.

Humphreys (1936) reported that during the early periods of learning, greater increments took place between practice periods than between trials within the same practice. He found, also, that after a substantial degree of skill had been developed, greater improvement took place during the work period. This appears to support Snoddy's recommendation of early spaced practices followed by later massed practices.

Travis (1936a) had college students develop skill on a modified pursuit rotor called the pursuit oscillator. He varied the rest period between practices and the length of the work period to show advantages for spaced practices. In twelve minutes of continuous practice, performance declined after two or three minutes of work. In another study (1936b) with the same apparatus, he kept the length of the practice periods for all groups constant at five minutes and varied the rest period from five minutes to 120 hours. He found that for a work period of five minutes, a rest period of twenty minutes was better than a shorter or longer period. After a rest period of twenty minutes, performance for the first minute of the work period was superior to the average of the previous work period. He concluded that the rest period proved more important for learning than the last half of the five-minute work period.

Studies by Hilgard and Smith (1942) and Cook and Hilgard (1949) showed advantages of distributed practice when working with the Koerth pursuit rotor. Cook and Hilgard studied 26 college men and women over a three-day examination period. Wherever practices were most widely distributed, there was greatest learning. They found no difference in learning, however, whether the rest periods were increased or decreased. These results conflict with the findings of Snoddy and those of Doré and Hilgard. Ammons (1947) used the same instrument in an elaborate experiment with 34 groups of 14 subjects each. He found the length of the work to be more crucial than the rest period. Work periods of 8 minutes with 5-minute rest periods appeared more effective than any other schedule used.

Kimble˜ has conducted extensive research in recent years with the pursuit rotor to determine optimum spacing of practices. In one study (1949), he reported that learning took place during the first five minutes of practice. After that, all gains occurred during the rest period, and all decrements occurred during practice. Duncan (1951) had college women develop skill with the pursuit rotor. He used four groups in an experiment which lasted twenty minutes for each subject. Each group worked five minutes, had a ten-minute rest; then worked five more minutes. During the five-minute work period, one group practiced continually while the other group worked ten seconds and rested twenty seconds.

The later group, therefore, had only one-third as much practice as the former group. The group that took the twenty-second rest, however, still was superior to the continuous practice group in the prerest and postrest sessions.

Meaningful motor activities and sports skills

Several researchers have used meaningful motor tasks in the search for information regarding the most desirable distribution of practice. The advantage of research with meaningful tasks is that results are more clearly applicable to other gross motor skills offered in the school program. There are certain disadvantages, however, in exercising experimental control. In one study, Harmon and Miller (1950) had four groups of inexperienced college women practice the skill of billiards. One group practiced daily, another group one time a week, the third group three times a week, and the fourth group used an additive pattern (rest periods getting progressively longer). New set shots were added at each practice while one shot was held constant throughout. The additive pattern proved more efficient than either of the other plans. Harmon and Miller concluded that relative massing was desirable during the early stages of learning, but later practices should be more distributed. Lawrence (1949) did a retention check on the same subjects one year later. Based on the 60 per cent of original subjects who took part in his study, Lawrence found that after a twelve-month period, the additive-pattern group retained a significantly higher level of skill than the other groups.

Singer (1965) had college men practice a novel basketball skill according to three practice schedules. In this task, the subjects were required to stand behind the free-throw line and attempt to bounce the ball off the floor and into the basket. All groups had a total of 80 practice shots plus 20 shots on the test. One group practiced the 80 shots consecutively; a second group had a five-minute rest following each 20 shots; and a third group had a twenty-four-hour rest between each of the 20-shot practices. Singer reported that the most distributed practice group (twenty-four hours between 20-shot practices) did best on a test which was administered at the conclusion of practice. However, this group performed poorest at a retention test which was administered one month later.

Wagner (1962) conducted a study to determine the effect of three different lengths of practice periods on the learning of selected fundamental basketball skills. The skills were field goal shooting, speed dribbling, free-throw accuracy shooting, and wall volleying. He reported that the longer-practicing group exhibited early proficiency at a higher level than the shorter-practicing groups. After the initial practices, however, the shorter-practicing groups appeared to learn just as much. More consistent performances were evident among the longer-practicing groups.

Breeding (1958) conducted a study to determine whether women's archery classes held on Monday, Wednesday, and Friday for forty minutes would improve the archery achievement of beginners to a greater or lesser extent than would classes conducted on Tuesday and Thursday for sixty minutes. The participants were 70 freshmen and sophomore women. The final test to measure archery achievement was three rounds shot from a distance of forty yards. The difference between the mean improvement of the two groups was not statistically significant. It was concluded that one method of spacing the archery practices, as set up within the limits of the study, was as effective as the other method in teaching beginners.

In an early study, Lashley (1915) exeprimented with archery target shooting. During the early learning period, he found no distinction in performance whether practices were massed or distributed. During the second half of the experiment, however, better results were obtained when practice periods were spaced. Lashley's results were somewhat different from those of Young (1954), who had students practice archery and badminton on two-day-a-week and four-day-a-week schedules. The four-day-a-week schedule proved more effective for learning archery while the two-day-a-week schedule was more effective for badminton. It should be noted, however, that even a four-day-a-week schedule is relatively spaced.

In other studies, Murphy (1916) found practices on three days a week to be more effective than practices on five days a week when learning to throw the javelin; Webster (1940) reported that shorter, more frequent practice periods were most effective in learning bowling; Pyle (1915) found distributed practice far superior to massed practice when learning the skill of typewriting; and Knapp and Dixon (1950) reported similar results in favor of distributed practices in working with the skill of juggling.

A SYNTHESIS OF RESEARCH ON PRACTICE DISTRIBUTION

Generalizations

1. Distributed practices are generally more efficient for learning and performance than are massed practices.
2. Relatively short practices (in time or in number of repetitions) make for more efficient learning than do longer practices.
3. Progressively decreasing the concentration of practice periods during the learning period seems advantageous.

4. Progressively decreasing the length of practice periods during the learning period appears to make learning more effective.

5. Proficiency which has been gained over a long period of time is retained better than that which is developed within a short period.

6. A high level of motivation enables one to benefit from longer and more concentrated practices than would be possible with a lesser degree of motivation.

7. Individuals or groups who are more competent in a particular activity can effectively practice that activity for longer periods than can persons or groups who are less competent. Similarly, older children are able to practice longer than younger ones.

8. In physical education or sports activities, the number of repetitions or trials (shots, throws, dives, etc.) should be considered as the unit of practice rather than the time spent at the work session.

9. Some group activities can be practiced for a longer period than individual tasks because of the fewer trials that the person may have; i.e., he often has a rest period between his turns in a group activity.

Theories of distributed practice

It is clear that research studies show advantages for some form of distributed practice in most learning situations. Authorities do not agree, however, why this is true. The most prominent explanations have been related to the concept of inhibition associated with massed practices. Other suggestions which have been offered from time to time include fatigue, rehearsal motivation, maturation, and neural "set." The latter explanations have little research support. Certainly some of these factors could play a role in learning and performance, but most studies have been designed to keep their influence to a minimum. Fatigue has been controlled somewhat by keeping the massed schedules relatively short when great effort is required on the part of the participant. To prevent between-practice rehearsal, tasks which are not usually available to the subject have been selected. On other occasions, interpolated activity has been used to prevent the individual from even thinking about the task. Obviously, very little maturation occurs during a typical experimental period of a few hours, days, or weeks.

Lorge (1930) believes that spacing between practices is desirable because ". . . . (1) the neural changes may in some unknown way 'set' or establish themselves more fully when time is allowed them; and (2) the process of learning may be more satisfying and receive better attention when rest periods intervene" (p. 52). Wheeler and Perkins (1932) suggest the most important reasons for the inclusion of rest periods are ". . . (1) to permit a replenishing of the lowered energy supply; (2) to overcome the effect of over-stimulation, which is faulty energy distribution, and (3) to permit maturation with its increased differentiation of energy patterns" (p. 86).

The most widely accepted theory regarding the disadvantages of massed practices relates to the concept of inhibition. The most prominent theory of inhibition is Hull's (1943) reactive inhibition theory, a response theory which implies that once the individual performs a task, he is reluctant to repeat it immediately. Furthermore, the greater the task involved, or the more frequently it is repeated, the greater is the reactive inhibition, Hull has stated. This inhibition subsides naturally with the passage of time so that the person is once again susceptible to maximum response in the activity. According to Hull, reactive inhibition may also cause one to become *conditioned* to not responding or not responding well. Kimble (1949) supported Hull's theory, but he pointed out that an increase in motivation leads the subject to tolerate a greater amount of reactive inhibition. Kimble further indicated that motivation is instrumental in promoting reminiscence.

It seems clear that massed and distributed practices may result in differences in both *performance* and in *learning*. Singer (1965) believes that differences between massed and distributed practices occur in performance rather than learning. His study showed a temporary, but not a permanent, difference between practice schedules. He correctly pointed out that performance has been measured and reported in most investigations. Singer's explanation seems inadequate, however, because if only performance was affected and learning was not, differences between groups would be eliminated with the passage of time. Several studies have included retention tests and are clear in showing permanent as well as temporary differences in learning and performance. Furthermore, any influence which prevents the individual from performing probably will not allow him to learn at maximum efficiency.

Limitations of distributed practices

Short work sessions do not seem to be most advantageous in all situations. Woodworth and Schlosberg (1963) suggest that the advisability of spacing versus massing depends upon (1) the type of skill, and (2) the length of the interval between practices. They present evidence to support the contention that *short lessons* or tasks are best learned in one long practice rather than in several shorter ones. Less forgetting appears to take place if the task can be completed in a short period of time.

Woodworth and Schlosberg also pointed out that widely spaced practices are detrimental to the learning of tasks which demand much exploration to discover the correct response. It is often observed that a brief review or warm-up is valuable in enabling one to get into the swing of the activity. This seems especially important if the activity is very complex. The authors also theorize that massing may aid in the *variability of attack* on a rather unfamiliar problem. If one is taking several trials of a task, there is a tendency to avoid the immediate repetition of an erroneous response. On the other hand, if practices are widely spaced, one is likely to return to a logical but incorrect choice. This is especially true if a fault has been developed in some movement.

PRACTICE DISTRIBUTION IN THE SCHOOL PROGRAM

How can the principles of practice distribution be put to use most effectively in the regular school curriculum? Unfortunately, educators have devoted very little attention to the exploration of implications of the research. Nevertheless, the problem of applying distribution principles derived from the research seems to have implications for (1) the daily conduct of classes, (2) unit planning, and (3) year-to-year schedules. Athletic practices and season schedules should also make use of these principles. Rest intervals may therefore refer to minutes, weeks, months or years.

All teachers must function within the structure of the school day and the school calendar, but even these schedules may be altered to obtain a more effective plan. For example, some school systems now operate on regular six-week to eight-week sessions, followed by a one-week vacation, rather than on the traditional schedule in which vacations are associated only with national holidays. In addition, the length of school days may vary just as the number and length of recesses, or the length of the lunch period, may be altered within the school day. These schedules are based largely on what administrators believe to be the most effective learning regimen for their children.

Nevertheless, for the teacher in the classroom, planning must fall within the time allowed for that class. Therefore "ideal" schedules based on very unusual conditions cannot be used. The 24-hour day, the 7-day week, and the 12-month year are not under the auspices of the teacher. Furthermore, in many cases, physical education classes do not meet every day, but follow schedules such as Tuesdays and Thursdays or Mondays, Wednesdays, and Fridays. Athletic teams, however, usually meet for practice on every school day. Within the school's schedule restrictions, there are still ways in which practices may be arranged effectively. Some of these possibilities will be discussed briefly.

Scheduling during the class period

According to Hull's theory of inhibition, students can be expected to develop inhibitions after performing a given task several times. This means that they will become relatively ineffective (temporarily) in learning that particular task. Students may, however, practice different skills with full effectiveness. Inhibition is, therefore, distinguishable from fatigue which would render the individual incapable of fruitfully practicing anything. Complete rest is not necessary when inhibition occurs, but a frequent change in the task being practiced is useful. All major physical education activities have several subtasks which can be practiced to allow variety in practice without changing to completely different activity.

During a unit of basketball, the instructor may attempt to teach dribbling, lay-up shots (with the right and left hand), jump shots, free throws, pivoting, passing (different types), faking, guarding, fast breaking, and many other fundamentals of individual and team play. Some teachers might take a full period to try to do a thorough job in teaching one or two of these skills. Consequently, a rather long practice (especially in number of repetitions) for the one or two skills will result. On the other hand, the teacher who makes effective use of short, distributed practices would have the students move more rapidly through a greater number of the skills during the class period. This might mean that each player gets only three trials at a particular pivoting maneuver during the early part of the class. However, the teacher might well take the class through more than one round of the skills during a single period. It is probably better that the student practice two rounds of 5 left-handed lay-ups, rather than one round of 10 trials of the same shot. The technique of going through the circuit of skills more than once, or covering a greater number of skills during a class period, seems to be an effective use of short and distributed practices.

The practice session in athletics

The distributed techniques described for class periods can be used equally well by athletic coaches in any sport. The football coach who uses team *A* and team *B* to run alternate plays against the red shirt team is making more effective use of distributed practice than the coach who has team *A* work for ten minutes and team *B* for ten minutes.

In baseball, one skill which needs regular practice for improvement, or even to prevent deterioration, is batting. It is not unusual for a practice session to be arranged so that each player has a total of 15 swings at batting practice pitches. The coach could have each boy come up and take all of his batting practice at one time. However, this does not appear to make the most effective use of the distribution principle. It is likely that the player who takes 15 swings consecutively will not gain as much from his eleventh to fifteenth swing as he did from his first to fifth swing. Only part of the reduction in efficiency will result from fatigue. Therefore, it seems desirable to break up each player's total swings into two rounds of 8 and 7 swings, or three rounds of 5. A coach may also develop a progressively decreasing work schedule with batting rounds of 7, 5, and 3 swings. Such decreasing schedules are often used by professional teams just before a game. Sometimes each of the starting players participate in several one-swing rounds just before the end of the batting session. These techniques seem much more effective for the improvement of skill than the system of taking all the swings at one time.

Even in individual sports which require no waiting, distribution in skill practice can still be realized. For example, after all the skills have been introduced in golf, a person may practice the different strokes by using a different club after every five strokes. Or at the driving range a participant may "play" holes of different distances by first driving, estimating the distance remaining to the imaginary green, and then selecting a club and attempting to hit the ball the proper distance. Holes of various distances would require the selection of different clubs for the second shot on each hole.

Most athletic teams probably practice too long. It is often obvious to the outside observer that late in the practice period the players are not performing any better than they did a half-hour earlier. Fatigue often occurs and learning diminishes. In addition to the cessation of learning, players often lose some enthusiasm for the activity when practices are too long and gruelling. It is understandable that motivation would be lessened when improvement no longer seemed possible. A decline in performance is even more frustrating. Teachers and coaches need to keep in mind that enthusiasm for the activity is vital to both learning and performance. Additional *physical conditioning* is frequently needed even after learning has substantially slowed. A different activity, often more suitable for conditioning, can be selected. The alternate activity, which can be a fun game or drill, will tend to eliminate the negative impressions which often become associated with the original sport when longer and more frustrating practices are used.

Unit and season scheduling

The technique of spacing or distributing units of learning material can be applied to large segments of material which require weeks or months for completion, as well as to smaller units which are completed within one session. Such larger segments include units of verbal material that are taught in the classroom, specific activity units in physical education, or a playing season in a varsity sport.

In physical education, when classes meet only two or three days a week, segments of material are quite naturally presented in a rather distributed manner. The classes are generally separated by at least one day. In most classroom courses, however, lessons are more concentrated, meeting five consecutive days a week. The five-day-a-week schedule is also followed in most varsity sports. Depending on the activity, however, varsity practices are interspersed with one or two games a week.

Providing distribution during the day by frequently changing the task being practiced makes it necessary to introduce the same tasks on several occasions in order to develop adequate skill. For example, in the discussion of daily basketball practice it was mentioned that several fundamental skills should be included each day. During the first few days of practice, it seems desirable to spend a *relatively* long period on each skill as it is introduced. On the following days, after some degree of success has been attained, a shorter period of time will be devoted to the specific skill. Other new skills should be introduced on successive days and handled in a similar manner, with relatively long practices immediately after the skill is introduced. In this manner, several activities will be included within each class period with the possibility of devoting different amounts of time to each. Group activity, whether in a lead-up drill or the total game, can also be conducted in this manner. One way of achieving distribution is to include game play (with other activities) only for a short period during the class time. Another way is to devote the total class time to the game but to introduce sufficient rest periods for the purpose of instruction, whether in fundamentals or in team strategy.

Many athletic coaches have used techniques which seem to be suggested by the research presented earlier in this chapter. One technique is using longer practices in the beginning of the season and gradually shortening work periods as the season progresses. Football coaches often hold two practices a day during the first two or three weeks of the season and then cut down to one practice a day. Another method occasionally used by coaches in all sports is the elimination of practices on certain days during the latter part of the season. In consideration of the small amount learned in some of the late-season practices, this reduction in practices probably should be made more often.

Yearly schedules

If a total of six weeks is to be devoted to volleyball at the junior high school level, should volleyball be scheduled as one 6-week unit for one year, two 3-week units for two years, or three 2-week units for three years? Similar questions exist for the person responsible for organizing health units as well as for teachers in certain other subject areas. The physical education curriculum may be so arranged as to have many of the activities appear in the schedule once every year, every two years, or every three years. Units of material which are to be offered on several occasions should not be spaced too distantly.

If a given amount of time is to be devoted to an activity it seems desirable to include that activity relatively often, even if only for a short session. There is a widespread assumption that a two-week unit every year or a three-week unit every two years would provide only for review, and that advanced learning or depth in the activity could not be attained. Such an assumption is based on the belief that little is retained from year to year, and that the instructor must start each time from the beginning and proceed at about the same rate. This belief appears to be refuted by the study of Purdy and Lockhart (1962) in which 94 per cent of original learning in several gross motor skills was retained by subjects after one year.

When activity units in physical education are reintroduced after a year or two, students should be expected to reach or surpass previous levels of proficiency in one or two class periods. They should then be ready for more advanced work. This is especially true since the students are more mature at each successive grade level. The great problem is that teachers *assume* that students need to continue reviewing for a fairly long period. Very often students are taught in essentially the same manner and at the same pace as they were in earlier grades. This procedure usually results in a considerable waste of time.

In view of the advantages for distributed practices, the high level of retention of skills, and the renewed student enthusiasm that usually greets a change in activity, it appears that a given unit of material such as volleyball may be better learned if spread over two or three years than if offered on only one occasion.

SELECTED READINGS

Cook, B. S., & Hilgard, E. R. Distributed practice in motor learning: progressively increasing and decreasing rests. *J. exp. Psychol.*, 1949, **39**, 169–172.

Doré, L. R., & Hilgard, E. R. Spaced practices and the maturation hypothesis, *J. Psychol.*, 1937, **4**, 245–259.

Doré, L. R., & Hilgard, E. R. Spaced practices as a test of Snoddy's two processes in mental growth. *J. exp. Psychol.*, 1938, **23**, 359–374.

Harmon, J. M., & Miller, A. G. Time patterns in motor learning. *Res. Quart.*, 1950, **21**, 182–187.

Kimble, G. A. Performance and reminiscence in motor learning as a function of the degree of distribution of practice. *J. exp. Psychol.*, 1949, **39**, 500–510.

Knapp, C., & Dixon, R. Learning to juggle: I. a study to determine the effect of two different distributions of practice in learning efficiency. *Res. Quart.*, 1950, **21**, 331–336.

Lorge, I. Influence of regularly interpolated time intervals upon subsequent learning. *Teach. Coll. Contr. Educ.*, 1930, No. 438.

Massey, M. D. The significance of interpolated time intervals on motor learning. *Res. Quart.*, 1959, **30**, 187–201.

Snoddy, G. S. *Evidence for two opposed processes in mental growth.* Lancaster, Penn.: Science Press, 1935.

Travis, R. C. Practice and rest periods in motor learning. *J. Psychol.*, 1936, **3**, 183–187.

Chapter 9

Mental practice

Teachers of physical education and coaches of athletic activities have traditionally viewed practice in terms of the overt or physical performance of the task to be learned. The amount of practice and subsequent learning has generally been assumed to be a function of the period of time the individual participates, or the number of repetitions that are completed. This emphasis on active practice or performance has been consistent with the philosophy of learning by doing. At the same time, relatively little attention has been devoted to the mental, or imaginary, practice which might precede, accompany, or follow the performance. Some recent evidence, however, suggests that physical proficiency might be considerably enhanced by mental rehearsal, by observing others perform, or by just informally thinking about the task.

The term *mental practice* is used to signify the introspective or covert rehearsal that takes place within the individual. Other terms which have occasionally been used in reference to this process are *conceptualization, ideational functioning, introspection,* and *imaginary practice.* Actually, references to mental practice and physical practice are somewhat misleading since they seem to indicate that the individual functions at a purely physical or mental level. The truth is that in the physical performance of a task there is usually some degree of related mental activity, while in mental practice certain neural and muscular responses are evoked. In light of this, the concept of mental practice could perhaps be understood better if it was thought of as sedentary practice.

The emphasis upon overt performance, with a neglect of the associated mental processes, does not take full advantage of man's intellectual abilities. The physical practice technique seems to have been patterned after the conditioning experiments with animals. In these experiments, amount of practice was generally based on the number of repetitions or the length of time spent in practice. Although such a trial-

and-error approach will usually result in learning, it is a rather slow and unpredictable process. Too often learners seem to go through the motions rather mechanically, without much thought or kinesthetic awareness of the essential movement responses.

Despite the traditional emphasis on overt practice, few teachers would doubt that the learner occasionally thinks through the performance *between* the physical work periods. In fact, these mental activities have occasionally been encouraged by teachers. It is not known, at this time, just how much of the practice is "physical" and how much is "mental." Neither is it known how much of the learning results from going through the motions, and how much is from related mental activity. It appears that if the mental and physical practices were effectively combined, the tasks might be learned more rapidly and perhaps with greater understanding.

The role of conceptualization in motor skills has not been widely investigated by general psychologists. Apparently, this is because the concept of applying mental rehearsal to the performance of motor tasks is not characteristic of the type of learning in which they are most interested, i.e., verbal learning. This lack of general application to problems in classroom learning has apparently resulted in the failure to rank mental rehearsal among the major issues in learning.

Why mental practice?

There are several reasons why teachers of physical education should give serious attention to the systematic use of mental practice in addition to traditional overt performance. Perhaps the most important reason is that the learner may develop proficiency in the skill more quickly, more thoroughly, and possibly with greater retention. Research reports have suggested each of these possibilities.

The intelligence of people should be recognized and brought into use when a task is being taught. Too often it has been assumed that motor learning is a rather automatic process. It is reasonable to expect that human beings do some thinking when they go through the motions of a particular activity. Nevertheless, more specific information regarding types of related mental activity can increase the effectiveness of the intellectualizing process.

Another important reason why attention should be devoted to mental practice is that more efficient use might be made of the crowded facilities and limited equipment which prevail in many schools today. Large classes make this problem especially important. If the nature of between-trial learning were more clearly understood, more effective use could be made of these periods. When a facility or a piece of equipment is unavailable, or when one is waiting for his turn, the time might be used to promote learning. Some research has shown that a systematic program of mental practice in conjunction with physical rehearsal might result in as much learning as would spending the full time in physical practice. Alternating groups of students between physical and mental rehearsal, therefore, might allow more students to take advantage of the facility or equipment for physical practice. Alternating physical and mental practice should prove valuable not only in crowded conditions, but even in nearly ideal class conditions.

It is possible that individual differences in mental and motor abilities might be more adequately met when techniques of mental rehearsal are skillfully used. It has been shown that mental rehearsal is an effective practice for individuals of widely differing intelligence levels. In two separate studies, Start (1960, 1962) found that children of low average intelligence could make effective use of mental practice. It is essential, however, that the individual *understand* the skill to be rehearsed. Some variation in technique might therefore be necessary with pupils of very low intelligence.

Getting students into the habit of thinking about or analyzing skills in an intellectual, kinesthetic, and mechanical way, is a desirable result of the use of mental practice. Most people are not used to rehearsing in this manner. Perhaps greater personal discipline is needed to enable the student to make effective use of the time between performances. For each new skill which is learned, the individual will likely gain a greater understanding, which should result in increased retention of the task.

It should be emphasized that mental practice is not proposed as a substitute for, or to the exclusion of, physical performance. Physical practice has numerous advantages which cannot be matched by conceptualization. In addition to helping one learn the skill, overt practice also tends to promote fitness, comradeship among participants, satisfactions from movement, and enjoyment as a result of participating with and against others. Mental practice cannot achieve these goals very effectively. Nevertheless, the full possibilities of conceptualization must be thoroughly explored because of its learning advantages.

Traditional use of mental practice

Mental rehearsal has long been practiced to a limited extent in the learning and performance of motor skills. Undoubtedly, athletes have always gone over in their minds ways by which they might improve their performances in a particular activity. These rehearsals have usually taken one of three forms. In one type, the performer briefly reviews his event or stunt immediately before beginning his performance. This is done in an effort to enable him to exactly duplicate the perfect performance which has been imagined. Such practice is most vividly illustrated by the gymnast, the diver, or the high jumper who hesitates and thinks through his event before beginning.

A second type of mental practice takes place between performances or practice sessions. This mental practice involves both conscious and subconscious imagery. The period between overt practices may last for hours, days, weeks, or months. Benefits from this interim conceptualization have occasionally been revealed when an individual who had experienced little success in an activity, such as rebound tumbling, returns at a later time and exhibits skill which was apparently impossible at an earlier practice. Informal rehearsal of this type is frequently used in all types of motor activity.

The two aforementioned types of rehearsal seem to improve physical proficiency in a particular motor response. A third type of mental practice is frequently used for the purpose of developing game strategy or operational techniques. Performers often make spontaneous reactions in sports which prove successful. These seemingly instinctive responses probably result because the individual has rehearsed numerous alternatives during his idle hours. Conceptualization is often concerned with what could be done in particular athletic situations, or how certain skills might be performed more smoothly, surprisingly, or impressively. This strategy-developing type of mental practice may deal with a technique such as a variation on a routine in gymnastics, or with a new fake which the pass receiver in football plans so that he can evade the defensive back. Thus, conceptualization may involve refinement of old techniques, or it may involve general strategy planning.

These types of mental practice have been observed by teachers and coaches for many years. Often teachers have been pleasantly surprised at the results of mental activity. Yet, the only aid or prompting for this mental activity has been comments such as "Take your time" or "Don't rush." These comments have been assumed to be valuable aids only in getting the performer to relax. More specific guidance is needed to enable the individual to use mental rehearsal for most effective learning and performance. Since most students do not know *how* to mentally rehearse effectively, coaching in the use of techniques should prove valuable.

HISTORICAL DEVELOPMENTS IN THE STUDY OF MENTAL PRACTICE

Despite its use for centuries, mental practice has not been thoroughly investigated or discussed during the past half-century. This is somewhat surprising in view of the fact that learning, in general, has come in for extensive research and theorizing. One reason for the lack of attention to the topic of mental practice has been the obvious difficulty of isolating, observing, and controlling the mental activity related to a particular skill. While it is quite easy to control and measure the number of seconds or minutes a person spends actively practicing a skill, or even the number of trials, the related mental processes cannot be easily detected. The degree of concentration or the intensity of mental activity also cannot be accurately measured.

Another reason why mental practice has not been widely investigated has been the popularity of the concept which stresses that learning is reflected in observable *behavior*. Guthrie and Skinner especially emphasized the need for demonstratable behavior in learning. They were not particularly interested in explaining the functioning in the nervous system. Therefore, learning has generally been viewed as the resulting observable and measureable behavior. Such an outlook has not stimulated interest in the informal mental activity related to the task. Study of this mental activity, however, might result in understandings of the task which would be important in other areas than the specific measurement of learning. The importance of related understandings has generally been minimized.

Gestalt contributions

The concept of mental rehearsal first came into sharp focus with the work of Köhler during the second and third decades of the twentieth century. He devoted considerable attention to the matter of *insight* in relation to gestalt psychology. In his experiments with apes, it became apparent that the animals were figuring out answers to problems without always resorting to overt trial and error. Tolman, another learning theorist, indicated that learning often results from implicit trial-and-error practice. He believed mental rehearsal to be an important element in all types of learning.

It became a basic assumption of the gestalt psychologists that mental activity, or thinking, is important in the learning of any skill. The concept of insight is essentially the belief that the learner actually figures out the answers to problems. Tolman believed that the individual uses his intelligence in problem solving and does not mechanically and automatically make connections. Problem solving is assumed to be a factor in both verbal and motor learning. The emphasis which the gestaltists placed on the learner's intelligence and thought would indicate their assumption of mental practice.

Early studies

Studies of mental practice have generally been organized into the following type of experimental design. First, two or three groups are equated on a new or relatively new skill. One group is then assigned a physical practice schedule which will be followed for a designated period of time. A second group will engage in mental practice by reading a detailed description of the correct execution of the activity, or by imagining themselves performing the task. A third group is sometimes scheduled to follow a combination of physical and mental practice. The allocated practice time each day is usually the same for all groups. Occasionally a control group which does not practice at all is used. The practice schedules usually extend from one to four weeks. At the end of the experimental period, the groups are tested to determine which type of practice schedule promoted the greatest amount of learning for the particular activity.

Wilson (1961) reviewed several studies dating back to 1890 in which mental activity relating to physical performance was suggested. Most of the earliest studies, however, did not clearly isolate and attempt to control mental rehearsal as opposed to overt activity. During the 1930's, Jacobson (1932, 1934) showed in several electrophysiological studies that when subjects imagined their performance of a particular motor response they reacted by subconsciously flexing muscles which were used in the overt performance of the task. In addition to the slight response in the muscle groups used in physical performance, action was also noted in such areas as the eyelids, tongue, and lips. Jacobson also showed that subjects who were skilled in relaxation techniques were unable to visualize movement activities when in a state of relaxation. As a result of his research with progressive relaxation, he concluded that complete relaxation of the body can take place only when the mind is free from activity.

In a somewhat similar study, Shaw (1938) found that weight lifters exhibited muscular action when they imagined themselves lifting weights. He further reported that greater vividness in imagination, or thoughts of lifting heavier weights, resulted in proportionally greater muscular action.

Perhaps the first "mental practice" study was conducted by Sackett (1935). In his experiment, four groups of college women learned a finger-maze skill. One group engaged in overt practice of the task while three groups took part in various amounts of mental rehearsal. One of the mental rehearsal groups was asked to think through the task once at each practice session. A second group was asked to think through the task three times, and a third group had five such practices. A control group was asked not to think about the activity at all. Sackett reported that the physical practice group learned more than any of the mental practice groups. It was found, however, that the symbolic practice did aid subsequent performances and also promoted retention. Sackett reported that the greater the mental rehearsal, the greater the learning. However, he concluded that a small amount of mental practice was relatively more beneficial than a large amount.

Perry (1939) reported that some types of tasks were better learned by mental practice than by physical performance. The relative effectiveness of mental and physical practice seemed to vary according to the type of skill. Rubin-Rabson (1941) reported that mental review reduced the amount of keyboard practice needed in the learning of musical scales. In his experiment, mental review proved especially effective in promoting retention. However, he reported that prolonged periods of mental practice before one had actually taken part in the activity were not of great value. After students had gained some experience in the physical performance of the activity, mental rehearsal was much more effective.

Recent mental practice studies

Recent studies relating to mental practice may be grouped into two categories: (1) those involving novel or unusual tasks, and (2) those in which common skills are used. The novel tasks may be laboratory skills or others which are new to the subjects. The common motor tasks are ones which are relatively familiar to the subjects.

Studies involving novel motor tasks. In W. E. Twinning's (1949) study, 36 college men practiced a ring-tossing task emphasizing accuracy. The subjects, divided into three groups, were tested by throwing 210 rings on the first and twenty-second days. In addition, one group practiced by throwing 70 rings on each day in between the test days. For the same period, a second group was asked mentally to throw the rings for fifteen minutes daily, but to refrain from any simulated movements. A third group did not have any type of practice between the test days. Twinning found that the no-practice group showed no significant improvement when tested on the final test day. The group with the daily ring-tossing practice showed the greatest improvement. The mental practice group showed significant improvement at the final test but not as much as the regular physical practice group. He concluded that both physical and mental practice aid in learning the ring toss.

Egstrom (1964) had six groups of college men learn a novel paddle-ball task. Subjects practiced for ten days, with each group following a different combination of manual drill and conceptualization. He found that the groups which showed the greatest improvement were the group following a regular physical practice schedule for the full period and the group regularly alternating between mental and physical practice. He also reported that a group which followed a mental practice schedule for the first half of the experiment and then changed to physical prac-

tice showed improvement in both phases of the experiment. However, a solid program of conceptualization during the last part of the experiment did not prove beneficial after the first part had been spent in
manual practice. He suggested that a technique of alternating between
physical and mental practice in regular physical education activities
would result in effective learning and would also reduce the pressure on
facilities and equipment in today's programs. He concluded that:

> There appear to be some advantages in the use of a method which alter-
> nates manual and conceptualizing practice during the learning of a gross
> motor skill . . . Perhaps the inclusion of a period of manual practice between
> periods of conceptualizing practice provided reinforcement through additional
> knowledge of results and heightened sensory impressions which resulted in
> more meaningful perceptions and subsequent improved performances.

> . . . There appeared to be cause for considerable skepticism about the
> value of conceptualizing practice which was not accompanied by frequent
> experiences with manual practice (pp. 479–481).[1]

Corbin (1965) had 120 college men practice a novel juggling task
which required them to toss and catch a wand by use of two other
wands which were held in each hand. The wand being manipulated was
not touched by the subjects during the performance. Three groups of
subjects practiced for twenty-one days under conditions of overt practice (30 tries), mental practice (30 imaginary trials), and physical-mental practice (15 overt and 15 imaginary). A fourth group was used as a
control. Corbin found that the schedule of overt practice proved most
effective. In addition, the data offered some support for a schedule which
combined mental-physical practice. It was reported in this study that the
skill level of the subjects was not a factor in determining the most
effective technique of practice; i.e., less skillful subjects benefited from
mental and physical practice in a manner similar to those who were
more proficient. Therefore, he made the recommendation that ". . . the
best method of teaching should be found and used regardless of the
skill level of the S [subject]" (p. 102).

In Corbin's study, mental practice did not appear to be of value
when used as an exclusive practice technique. He suggested that prior
experience was needed before mental practice would prove valuable.
This conclusion is supported by Trussel (1958), who reported that mental rehearsal was ineffective except in combination with physical practice. Her study involved a ball-juggling task which was new to all her
subjects.

---

[1] G. H. Egstrom, "Effects of an Emphasis on Conceptualizing Techniques
During Early Learning of a Motor Skill," *Research Quarterly*, 35, Washington,
D.C.: AAHPER, 1964, pp. 479–481. By permission.

Studies involving common sports skills.   Several studies have involved
meaningful motor tasks, i.e., activities familiar to the subjects. In these
studies there are experimental control disadvantages such as varying
degrees of familiarity with the task or the possibility of unauthorized
practice during the experimental period. However, the ease of applying
such findings to the regular school situation involving gross motor skills
is obvious. Perhaps the earliest study of this type was conducted by Vandell, Davis, and Clugston (1943). These researchers had boys from junior
high school, senior high school, and college practice the skills of basketball free-throw shooting and dart throwing. Three groups which were
equated in motor and mental ability learned the basketball skill. Another
three groups, similarly equated, practiced dart throwing.

All subjects were given proficiency tests in free-throw shooting or
dart throwing on the first and the twentieth days. However, from the
second through the nineteenth days: (1) one group engaged in overt
practice each day; (2) another group had fifteen minutes of mentally
throwing the basketball or darts; and (3) a third group did not take part
in either physical or mental practice. At the test given on the twentieth
day, the physical and the mental practice groups showed significant improvement over the first-day test scores. The amount of improvement was almost identical for these groups. The no-practice group
showed no improvement. Results from the basketball and dart-throwing
skills were very similar. The authors concluded that, under the conditions of the experiment, mental practice was practically as effective as
physical practice for improvement in performance.

Clark (1960) also used the basketball free throw in a mental rehearsal study. High school boys practiced the one-hand foul shot. The
subjects were equated into mental and physical practice groups on the
basis of intelligence, arm strength, and basketball-playing experience. On
the first day, both groups were given instructions followed by 25 practice shots and then 25 shots for score. For each of the next fourteen
school days, the physical practice group practiced 5 warm-up shots and
25 shots for score. For the same period, the mental practice group was
instructed to imagine shooting 5 warm-up shots and 25 shots for score.
The daily mental practice of this group was preceded by their reading
through a work sheet which described the correct execution of the shot.
The work sheet was used to enable the boys to focus their attention
on the task and to concentrate more effectively.

After the fourteen days of practice, Clark administered a retest to
both groups. He found that both the physical practice and the mental
practice groups showed highly significant gains in shooting ability. The

physical practice group showed only a slight advantage over the mental practice group. This advantage was evident primarily with those who were lowest in skill. All mental practice subjects reported a gain in the ability to visualize, or imagine, shooting techniques. Clark also reported that arm strength seemed to make a difference in shooting performance. However, general intelligence (within the range of the subjects in his study) did not appear to be a factor in shooting skill or the ability to benefit from mental practice.

Wilson (1961) investigated the relative effects of mental practice and physical practice in the learning of tennis drives. Her subjects, 75 college women who had recently completed a course in tennis, were divided into a physical practice group, a mental practice group, and a control group. The physical practice group hit tennis balls in the gymnasium daily. The mental practice group engaged in daily imaginary practice in the classroom. This group received coaching cues which were slightly different from day to day. Wilson found that both experimental groups made significant improvement during the practice sessions, while the control group did not improve. The physical practice and the mental practice groups showed approximately the same amount of improvement. In addition, it was reported that highly skilled performers maintained their superiority in each of the groups.

Burns (1953) conducted a study in which girls ranging from junior high school to college age practiced the skill of dart throwing. She found that groups which followed a physical practice schedule or a combination physical-mental practice schedule improved significantly. However, a group engaging only in mental rehearsal did not improve.

J. G. Jones (1963) tested the value of directed versus undirected types of mental practice with 30 college students in the learning of a new gymnastic skill. In the directed rehearsal, subjects received a practice sheet which gave general practice directions as well as a mechanical description of the task. This group's practice was controlled to a great extent by the instructor. The undirected mental practice group had less direction from the instructor and greater freedom in conceptualizing. He found that the undirected mental practice group learned more quickly than the group which was more formally directed by the instructor.

Contrary to some reports, Jones found that combined reading and mental practice could aid in the performance of a new motor skill. He concluded that physical practice is not essential for initial learning of a motor skill. In addition, he found that whether or not the subject sees the skill performed has no effect on the value of subsequent mental practice. General intelligence test scores did not seem to be related to the subject's abilities to use mental rehearsal. Jones theorized that undirected mental rehearsal proved most effective because a better kinesthetic image is achieved if the individual receives the information and is then free to form a pattern on his own.

Start (1960) had a group of 35 boys mentally practice the underhand basketball free throw. Although the boys were familiar with basketball in general, they had not previously practiced the particular task. In addition, the investigator reported that unscheduled practice would be impossible during the period of the experiment. After an initial test to determine the general shooting ability among the boys, nine daily mental practice sessions of five minutes each were given. At the end of the experimental period, a final free-throw test was given. The group showed significant improvement at the final test. According to Start, the effect of the initial test and intelligence were effectively controlled. He believed, therefore, that confidence could be placed in the fact that the improvement resulted essentially from the mental practice.

Start later divided the subjects into two groups to determine if general intelligence was a factor in the amount of gain which resulted from mental practice. He found that the high intelligence group (IQ from 106–117) did not gain more than did the lower intelligence group (IQ from 83–105). The ability to improve motor skill through mental rehearsal, therefore, did not seem to be related to intelligence.

Generalizations regarding mental practice

Certain common findings seem to persist throughout most of the research studies. The following generalizations are supported by the research on mental practice:

1. Mental rehearsal is more valuable in motor learning than is generally assumed. Research has consistently shown that mental practice groups learn and perform at a higher level than do control groups.

2. Mental practice should be used in combination with overt practice, not in place of such practice. There is no evidence which would suggest that exclusive use of mental practice proves superior to exclusive use of physical practice.

3. Some experience or acquaintance with a particular motor task is necessary before mental practice can be fully effective. Most studies have reported that the novice does not profit as much from mental practice as does the individual who has some skill in the particular task. Apparently this is because the inexperienced person is unable to focus his concentration on the appropriate movement responses.

4. Mental practice apparently results in below-threshold muscular responses which usually accompany the overt performance of the par-

ticular task. These responses, however, are so slight as to be negligible for physical-conditioning purposes.

5. Some evidence suggests that mental rehearsal which is rigidly directed by the instructor may prove less effective than rehearsal sessions in which the learner is allowed greater freedom of imagery. After a certain amount of guidance, students apparently need some freedom in organizing their own patterns for conceptualization.

6. Mental practice can be effectively used with students of widely varying intelligence levels. Within the range of abilities usually found in school, intelligence does not seem to be a factor in determining one's ability to profit from mental practice.

Techniques to promote mental practice

Assuming that there are benefits to be derived from the use of mental practice, how can this process be promoted most effectively? How can the track coach get a high jumper to understand the execution of the skill so that he can properly conceptualize the task. For effective use of mental practice, it is essential that the learner understand the task and develop skill in conceptualizing its performance.

If mental practice is to be used at all, it is important that a proper technique be used. When a poor method is used, it is likely to be ineffective, and time may therefore be wasted. More important, if an incorrect movement, or a fault, is practiced mentally, this undesired response will be learned. Some thought should therefore be given to *how* mental practice should be used. A starting point in such an investigation is for teachers to consider some of the techniques which have been used by researchers in the past few years.

No one has yet been able to exactly control or to measure the amount and type of mental activity. As a result, the nature of mental practice is to some extent open to question. Some investigators have gotten subjects' reactions and impressions of mental functioning during periods of practice. Questionnaires or other techniques have been used in an effort to determine how long the subjects could concentrate, what types of suggestions seemed to evoke the most valuable responses, impressions regarding the understanding of the task, and other observations. Such surveys, whether by questionnaire or interview, are limited to the subjective opinions of the learner. Most effective techniques must therefore be determined by analyzing the *results* of different methods used to promote such practice.

Despite the inability to determine scientifically the techniques which stimulate most effective mental activity, a discussion of the different types of programs that have been used should offer some guidance. Two types of mental rehearsal techniques will be discussed: (1) those which have been reported in experimental studies, and (2) the practical techniques which have been observed in informal use.

Experimental techniques

An investigation of the techniques used in experimental studies should provide some useful information on the range of methods which have been used. The effectiveness of the various techniques offers some guidance to the teacher who wishes to promote the use of conceptualization.

In Clark's (1960) study, primary emphasis was placed on getting the student to understand the skill before he began mental practice. Clark believed that comprehension was essential for the skill to be practiced properly. In his basketball free-throw experiment, he set up the following instructional program for those who were to engage in mental practice. First, the student read a printed description of the proper technique. Next, he stepped up to the free-throw line and, as the instructor demonstrated and gave oral instructions, slowly went through the motions of the shot (without the ball). At different sequential positions, the subject was stopped momentarily in an effort to get him to remember all phases of the skill. Clark encouraged the subject to see himself and the instructor in the different bodily positions, and to *feel* the movement with his eyes open and then closed. Next, the subject took twenty-five shots at the conclusion of which any necessary changes were pointed out. The students later reported that they gained greater confidence through this method of mental practice. They also expressed the belief that this technique enabled them to visualize the skills more effectively and to instantly recognize an incorrect response.

Start's (1960) mental practice sessions involved both instructor-led exercises and individual practices. In the first case, the instructor described in detail the proper technique for shooting a free throw. At the same time he asked the boys to picture themselves performing the skill. Next, they were asked to mentally perform the throw without an oral description. This was followed by another short instructor-led practice. Students remained seated for the entire session. At subsequent sessions, the instructor would concentrate on certain specific aspects of the performance. In some practices the students were asked to picture themselves from the time they left the bench in the gymnasium, completely through the execution of the free throw, and until they returned to the bench.

In another study, Start (1964) described the mental practice sessions for a group of young men who were learning a new skill. The study was designed to determine the relationship between kinesthesis and the degree to which one could benefit from mental practice. Start describes in detail the technique used to promote mental rehearsal:

For six days the group met at 1:00 p.m. and were issued with duplicated practice sheets which contained instructions based on a detailed and systematic analysis of the skill of an Olympic gymnast who was also a noted gymnastic teacher. Each movement necessary for the skill was described and consecutively linked until the complete skill had been described from the point of view of the performer.

The instructor worked from a copy of the practice sheets which contained detailed annotations on the procedure to be adopted at each session: i.e., the subjects read through their practice sheets, pausing at indicated points to imagine the sequence of movements about which they had just read; they then closed their eyes and imagined themselves performing the movements as the instructor read them aloud from the practice sheet and allowed set times for the periods of imagination. The subjects next read through the practice sheet as the instructor read out loud again, allowing time for the imagination of the various movements; then they tried to imagine themselves performing the complete movement without cueing either from the instructor or the practice sheet. Next they read through the practice sheet with the instructor once again and finally tried to imagine themselves performing the complete sequence of movements without any form of cueing.

In this way six daily practices, each of five minutes duration, were given (pp. 317–318).[2]

In Wilson's (1961) study, which included the learning of tennis strokes, all subjects came to the mental practice session together, and all left at the same time. During the practice period, they were given coaching cues which varied from day to day. They were asked to review the cues on their own and then mentally practice fourteen forehand and fourteen backhand drives (the same number that the physical practice group was taking). An interesting feature of the study was that the subjects were asked to feel the body going through the stroke, not to picture it, because when a stroke is actually performed, one does not see it. Further, when a poor hit was made, students were asked to analyze it and try to correct it. Eyes could be kept either open or closed during this rehearsal.

In Harby's (1952) study, motion pictures were used in an effort to stimulate the desired mental activity. Harby believed that this technique would have about the same effect as a demonstration, and that it would extend the period of time that the student could effectively engage in mental practice. In his study, however, the films did not prove particularly valuable in helping subjects to learn the underhand free throw.

---

[2] K. B. Start, "Kinesthesis and Mental Practice," *Research Quarterly*, **35**, Washington, D.C.: AAHPER, 1964, pp. 317–318. By permission.

W. E. Twinning (1949) asked subjects of college age to mentally throw rings for fifteen minutes. He reported that they had great difficulty in mentally practicing for this length of time. The college-aged subjects said that they were able to effectively concentrate on this type of activity for only about five minutes. The remainder of the time was usually devoted to trying to figure out new ways of performing the skill or to random mental activity.

Practical techniques

Away from the research laboratories, teachers and coaches often do not take advantage of opportunities to promote mental practice among students. Consequently, skills and habits are not developed in the use of these rehearsal techniques. It can be observed in many activities that performers do not appear to make deliberate efforts to improve through mental practice. For example, the golfer who fails in his first attempt to blast out of the sand trap often rushes into his second or third shot without thoroughly analyzing his first. If the individual would seek to determine the cause of his first failure and then mentally rehearse a perfect performance, his second attempt would often be more successful. When this procedure is not followed, however, a particular fault is often repeated several times. The tendency to rush through performances and repeat mistakes can often be observed among bowlers, young baseball pitchers, high jumpers, and many other performers. The use of mental rehearsal, or review, following the performance may provide feedback which would not otherwise be perceived by the learner.

There are several ways in which the individual might practice mentally for improvement in movement proficiency as well as in game performance. This conceptualization may come in the form of (1) review which immediately precedes, follows, or coincides with the performance; (2) formal or informal rehearsal which takes place between work periods; and (3) decision making which relates to the strategy or other decision-making phases of the activity. The latter may occur *during* the practice or game or *between* these events.

Review techniques. The learner may be encouraged to mentally review the total performance and attempt to sense the kinesthetic and other cues which are associated with the act. Such a rehearsal should be used to enable the individual to exactly duplicate the perfect performance which has just been imagined. This brief pre-performance review is often used by individuals in such diverse activities as gymnastics, bowling, diving, the high jump, and the pole vault. Although such a rehearsal may be used in most motor activities, it seems most easily applied in individual activities of short duration. During this short rehearsal, the performer focuses his attention on the task at hand and thinks his way through it. This is done so that during the actual performance which follows, the sequence of movements will be most vivid in his mind. Frequently, it can be noticed that the individual who is upset following a failure will proceed with the performance without such a rehearsal.

On some occasions the learner may attempt to analyze a previous performance and concentrate on avoiding a particular fault, or error, which may have been committed. For example, the diver may realize that in his previous dive he opened out of his tucked position too soon, or that his knees were not drawn into his body tightly enough. During the ensuing mental rehearsal period, this individual can review his total performance and make a special effort to avoid duplicating his specifically erroneous responses. The high jumper might realize that his trailing leg was held at the wrong angle. In like manner, the basketball player who has missed the first of two free throws can concentrate on making the necessary adjustment on the second one. Not all review must be based on the need to make adjustments, however. Quite often the learner may attempt to duplicate a previous performance which was apparently perfect.

One famous golf professional *replays* each poorly hit shot; i.e., he takes a second swing at an imaginary ball from the same position. He apparently analyzes the first shot, determines his error, and attempts to correct it, or play it the way it should have been played. This seems to be an effective way of preventing the remembrance of an incorrect swing. The technique used by this golfer is an effort to reorient himself to the proper swing to insure that it will be remembered. Perhaps a similar procedure after a perfect performance would also be desirable as a means of reinforcing the correct response. The technique of mental rehearsal and simulated movement which is used by this golfer seems to be an excellent procedure which teachers should advocate.

Some individuals verbally remind themselves to perform correctly *during* the performance of the activity. For example, the golfer may tell himself to take a slow backswing, to keep his eyes on the ball, or to keep his head down during the backswing. The skier sometimes tells himself to shift his weight or to execute other bodily maneuvers while descending the hill. The bowler sometimes reminds himself of the correct technique during his approach. Other performers such as the baseball pitcher, the discus thrower, or the free-throw shooter orally remind themselves to focus their attention on the most important aspects of the performance. Such methods are actually the result of the instructors' frequent and forceful emphasis of particular points and the performers' belief that they will forget these points unless they remind themselves. Of course, it is not essential that one talk to himself while performing. However, this practice is indicative of accompanying mental activity which is advantageous to learning and performance.

Teachers can aid the performance of their students by encouraging them to slow down, relax, and review the skill before beginning. This technique should be encouraged in athletic coaching and with students in a regular class. Instructors can be very helpful by developing habits of preperformance rehearsal among learners.

Between-practice mental rehearsal. Conceptualization between daily practice periods has rarely been emphasized by teachers when they attempted to develop motor skill among students. However, there is research evidence to support the belief that a planned program of mental rehearsal might effectively supplement physical practice. Occasionally an individual who has experienced little success in rebound tumbling or in shooting a jump shot will return to the activity at a later time and exhibit skill which was seemingly impossible at an earlier practice. The learner often says, "I think I've figured out how to do it," or "I know what I've been doing wrong." The phenomenon of reminiscence (improvement between practice periods) may result from this type of informal practice. Perseveration, or the persistence of imagery after the cessation of practice, is frequently offered as the reason for this improvement. Mental deliberation may be a conscious or a subconscious act. Nevertheless, a planned program, and one in which some specific guidance is offered, seems more likely to result in useful conceptualization than will an informal or unstructured program.

Research seems to suggest homework assignments in which students would conceptualize the tasks which are being overtly practiced in school. In addition to techniques such as mentally performing the task a given number of times or reading a detailed description, the learner may gain a clearer concept of the correct performance by observing outstanding participants in action or by watching a demonstration film. Simulated practice may also be advocated in which the learner stands before a mirror and executes the movement response, whether it is swinging a baseball bat, or stepping through a dance routine. When he observes himself exhibiting the skill by watching the mirror or possibly by an instant film replay and develops a kinesthetic awareness of the action, the learner's improvement will be apparent during the next practice session.

Situational decision-making. The type of mental activity most frequently stressed by athletic coaches has to do with game strategy or rapid decision-making during a contest. It is assumed that more intelligent behavior will result if the performer engages in concentrated rehearsal of the various eventualities which might occur in the game. This type of conceptualization might take place during the contest, by replaying the game after its completion, or by planning ahead for the next contest. It is not uncommon for a baseball coach to tell a player, "Assume that every ball will be hit to you and plan ahead so that you'll know what to do with it." This planning ahead is probably the reason some players seem to have intuition in certain game situations. Performers who repeatedly make such correct decisions are assumed to have good athletic "sense." It is likely that such individuals simply plan ahead for various possibilities.

Teachers and coaches should devote greater attention to the matter of getting students to make valuable use of the time which is available during a team activity. There are many ways in which an individual can spend his idle moments. For example, between pitches the shortstop in baseball might (1) mentally prepare himself for any situation which might occur on the next pitch, (2) think about unrelated activities, or (3) simply rest. Coaches should encourage all performers to plan what they will do if certain situations arise during the next play. Assuming that there is a man on first base, what will the shortstop do if a ground ball is hit hard to his left or slowly straight at him? If he has considered all the likely possibilities, he will be able to react more intelligently than if he has been idling away his time. Coaches who encourage this type of mental rehearsal or situational planning will find that their players make fewer mental errors.

The individual may surprise an opponent more often if he plans ahead. This planning should be based on his previous actions and his opponent's responses, as well as the strength and weaknesses of both. With such planning, the end in football might figure out ways in which he can run a pass pattern which will be unexpected by his opponent. The pitcher in baseball, the wrestler, the fencer, and the quarterback should think through the available possibilities rather than routinely do what seems to come naturally. Without considerable reasoning, the individual will usually do the natural and the obvious thing. Teachers should emphasize the habit of thinking ahead. Spot-checks and drills can be conducted for this purpose.

Mental rehearsal, or review, should be used at the beginning of a class or practice period more often than it is currently used. Mental review of recently learned skills can save time by reducing the usual amount of routine physical practice. In addition to general class orientation, each particular task should be mentally rehearsed prior to the beginning of performance. After this technique has been developed into a habit, time need not be taken from general class activity for such individual conceptualization. The teacher can be very effective in promoting both general class and individual mental rehearsal sessions.

In mental practice, as in other aspects of learning, a high level of motivation is essential for optimal benefits. There is a strong tendency for individuals to think often about things in which they are interested and to ignore things in which they are uninterested. It, therefore, is advantageous for teachers to keep interest in the task to be learned at a high level. In addition, they have a responsibility for teaching learners how to conceptualize effectively and to develop the learner's understanding of the importance of mental practice. Because of the relative newness of this topic, many questions regarding mental rehearsal remain to be answered. Research will continue in this area in coming years. Meanwhile, teachers should take advantage of the intelligence of their students by having them use their heads while learning motor skills.

SELECTED READINGS

Clark, L. V. The effect of mental practice on the development of a certain motor skill. *Res. Quart.*, 1960, **31**, 560–569.

Egstrom, G. H. Effects of an emphasis on conceptualizing techniques during early learning of a gross motor skill. *Res. Quart.*, 1964, **35**, 472–481.

Jacobson, E. Electrical measurement of neuromuscular states during mental activities. II. imagination and recollection of various muscular acts. *Amer. J. Physiol.*, 1934, **94**, 22–34.

Richardson, A. Mental practice: a review and discussion, part I. *Res. Quart.*, 1967, **38**, 95–107.

Sackett, R. S. The relationship between amount of symbolic rehearsal and retention of a maze habit. *J. genet. Psychol.*, 1935, **13**, 113–130.

Start, K. B. The relationship between intelligence and the effect of mental practice on the performance of a motor skill. *Res. Quart.*, 1960, **31**, 644–649.

Start, K. B. Kinesthesis and mental practice. *Res. Quart.*. 1964, **35**, 316–320.

Twinning, W. E. Mental practice and physical practice in learning a motor skill. *Res. Quart.*, 1949, **20**, 432–435.

Vandell, R. A., Davis, R. A., & Clugston, H. A. The function of mental practice and the acquisition of motor skills. *J. gen. Psychol.*, 1943, **29**, 243–350.

Chapter 10

Programming units for instruction

In order to achieve maximum efficiency in the teaching situation, it is essential that consideration be given to the manner in which bodies of material are presented to the learner. An analysis of this topic requires both a study of the manner in which the learning units are organized, or programmed, and the size and form of the units. In this chapter the organization of learning material into a context of self-teachable units will be viewed with reference to the relatively recent development of *programmed* instruction. The selection of units of this material will be discussed in terms of *whole* and *part* concepts.

PROGRAMMED INSTRUCTION IN PHYSICAL EDUCATION

Programmed instruction is essentially a method of organizing learning material into progression steps so that it can be easily acquired by the individual. A *program* is generally arranged so that the learner can make progress without the constant aid of the instructor. This auto-instruction has generally taken the form of teaching machines or programmed textbooks. Although the principles upon which such practices are founded have been established for many years, the widespread use of programmed methods is only now coming into existence. Today, almost all subject areas, from the primary grades to the college level, are making some use of programmed techniques.

There are numerous advantages in the use of programmed materials in the school. With these materials the individual is able to learn by himself and at his own rate. Individual differences, therefore, do not prove to be a major problem since fast learners are not held back by slower children who, in turn, are not lost by the pace established by other class members. When instruction is programmed, teachers are freed from routine tasks to deal with particular students or problems which need special attention. Since programs are arranged to reward each correct response, a higher level of motivation may be developed than exists in the traditional teaching situation. In addition, well-developed programs tend to compensate for teacher inadequacies.

There are also several problems or disadvantages related to the use of programmed instruction. One of the most serious complaints is that while programs are good for promoting minute step-by-step learning, they are ineffective in developing general or whole concepts. Another oft-stated complaint is that students' attitudes or values cannot be developed by use of programmed techniques. Several authors have expressed the belief that programmed learning does not require serious thought or creativity on the part of the learner. They hold that the programmer does all the thinking while the learner merely becomes conditioned to respond in a particular way. Other problems often associated with learning programs are that after a time students sometimes lose interest; one can cheat in most programs by looking ahead; extensive use of programs tend to make the school program impersonal; and programs are expensive to develop and maintain. These problems related to programmed learning are especially apparent when the instructor removes himself from the teaching situation and depends too greatly upon the program. However, most of these problems can be minimized when the program is kept in proper perspective and is only one technique used by the teacher.

Problems in programming physical education

Despite the widespread use of teaching machines and programmed texts during recent years, only limited use of these techniques has been made in physical education. The reason for this difference appears to be the nature of the learning material. Verbal tasks are apparently more easily programmed than are motor skills. While most courses have been primarily concerned with the acquisition of verbal concepts, physical education has placed major emphasis on the development of physical skills and secondary emphasis on related knowledges. Of course, the verbal skills associated with physical education, as well as health and safety education, are as appropriate for programming as are other primarily verbal courses. A recent series of health and safety programmed texts by the Behavioral Research Laboratories (1966) as well as Penman's (1964) text on college physical education give evidence of this.

While the knowledge areas of physical education are easily adaptable to programming, efforts to program movement tasks have not been very successful. Effective programming is dependent upon the individual's reception of immediate and accurate feedback regarding appropriate and inappropriate responses. This type of information is difficult to arrange for all the graduated steps in learning skills. This difficulty in providing feedback is probably why general concepts are also not effectively taught by programmed techniques. In complex tasks especially, conscious awareness of body position is not very vivid for the person who is performing a skill for the first time. Some simple motor tasks, however, offer more definite knowledge of results.

An example of a program which involves some motor activity is the set of instructions that one attempts to follow in assembling a piece of equipment or machinery which has been purchased. Detailed instructions for each step, along with checkpoints and illustrations, are usually provided. When parts lock into place or line up so that bolts fit properly or resemble the sequence of illustrations the individual knows that the verbal instructions have been followed accurately. When mistakes are made in these assembly tasks, the person can revert back to an earlier step to check his progress. Unfortunately, the progression steps in such programs are often too great for the unskilled individual.

Despite certain inherent problems, the programming of physical skills has been accomplished, or appears to be feasible, in each of the following situations: (1) the learning of new motor skills and the improvement of old ones, (2) the notation, or writing, of dance movements and sequences, (3) the development of regular conditioning programs, and (4) the arrangement of remedial activities. The status and prospects of each of these situations will be discussed.

Programming the learning of a new motor skill

Very limited programming has been accomplished in the teaching of regular physical education skills. The possibilities of autoinstruction in these activities have not been fully explored. Consequently, the extent to which motor tasks can be taught by the programmed technique is not yet known. It seems obvious that this method of instruction is more applicable to certain types of tasks than to others. Where a particular sequence of separate responses can be isolated and described, programming is rather easily accomplished. The equipment assembly task referred to earlier is an example of this. It appears that the sequence of events in archery, i.e., nock, stance, draw, aim, may also be broken down into rather definite steps for programming. The sensorimotor skill of typewriting has essentially been programmed for quite a long time. Typing textbooks simply list a series of progressively more advanced drills which the learner is to perform. Success or failure can be easily observed in typing.

The programming of a complex motor task which involves the movement of the body in space appears more difficult. The high jump, fancy dive, golf swing, or basketball jump shot seems to defy a step-by-step analysis for particular feedback. It may be, however, that some progress in the beginning stages of learning can be made by the autoinstruction method. The following hypothetical program for teaching the high jump is offered for illustrative purposes.

A program for the straddle roll as a high-jumping technique.[1]

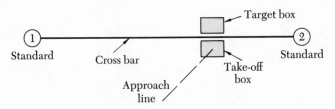

Figure 7. Physical layout.

Instructions	*Desired responses*
Step 1. Take two quick steps along the approach line, beginning with the right foot.[2] Start from a short distance so that with normal running steps the left foot lands in the take-off box. Execute five times.	The left foot lands in the take-off box on the second step.
Step 2. Take the two running steps and with a continuous motion, kick the right foot up to shoulder height. Execute five times.	The left foot lands in the take-off box; the right foot reaches shoulder level.
Step 3. Complete steps 1 and 2 and during the kick, *lift off* the ground using the left foot to push. Land on the left foot in the take-off box. Execute five times.	The same responses as in previous steps, plus lift-off from and return to the take-off box on the left foot.
Step 4. Complete the previous steps, but also thrust arms upward at the lift-off for added height. Execute five times.	Greater height should be attained by using arms.
Step 5. Complete the previous steps, but during the lift-off simultaneously *roll the body* to the left (facing downward and toward standard 1) and land	Same checkpoints as in previous steps, and the right foot should land in target box.

[1] This program was suggested by Albert Paolone in a graduate class taught by the author.

[2] This description is written for the person who favors the approach from the left side. For individuals who prefer the other side, a right-left substitution must be made throughout the program.

on the right foot in the target area (no cross bar is used). Use the hands to break the fall. Execute ten times.

Step 6. Put the crossbar up to waist height. Perform all the steps as before. Execute ten times.

The right foot is the first over the bar and is the first thing to touch the ground in the target area.

Step 7. Use a four-step approach. Start two steps farther away from the bar (along the approach line) and complete all phases as in step 6. Execute ten times.

Adjust the starting distances so that the left foot naturally lands in take-off box.

This program for teaching the high jump would be valuable only in the beginning stages of the skill. However, a large group might reach a minimum standard of proficiency with such a technique. More refined techniques at the advanced level would require individual instruction from the teacher.

Programming the dance

One type of motor-skill programming that has been used rather extensively is dance notation. This does not deal with the *learning* of a dance movement but with the arrangement of previously learned techniques. However, since the particular dance is a new activity, its acquisition does involve learning. Dance notation is the process of using symbols to record on paper the elements of bodily motion, time, and space. From the symbolic description, these elements can be reinterpreted into movement. Dance movements, from the most simple to the most complex, can be recorded and subsequently interpreted by any person who knows the method of notation. In this way, written dance is comparable to written music. However, dance notation appears more complex because it involves variations in magnitude of movement for different body parts simultaneously.

According to Hutchinson (1954), attempts to devise a system of dance notation have been made for at least five centuries. There is evidence of elementary forms of notation dating back to the ancient Greeks. Somewhat more sophisticated forms of dance notation have been attempted from the fifteenth century. During the early part of the twentieth century several dance choreographers devoted some effort to this topic. The first well-developed system of dance notation was devised by Rudolf Laban during the period from 1925 to 1950. Because of his pioneering work and the general acceptance of his system, *Labanotation* is today widely accepted as the foremost system of dance notation.

While most early systems of dance notation made use of a horizontal staff similar to the one used for music, Laban introduced the vertical staff. This innovation, along with variations in the length of the symbol on the staff, provided for greater description than was possible in previous systems. Hutchinson states that, "Since Labanotation records in vividly legible form all possible movements of the body in space and time (and in a dimension heretofore unattempted—dynamics), it overcomes the obstacles which had impeded the progress of all earlier systems" (p. 4). This system is effective in describing (1) the parts of the body that move, (2) the use of space, (3) timing, (4) the dynamics or strength of the movement, and (5) the pattern or flow in the movement.

The staff is the basic structure within which the meaningful symbols must be placed. In Labanotation, three vertical lines are used for the staff. However, placement of symbols within and beyond these lines provides particular information regarding the part of the body to be used. In the following illustration (from Hutchinson, p. 2), dotted lines are added to the Laban staff for descriptive purposes.

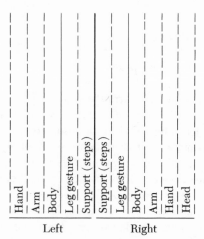

Left   Right

Figure 8. THE LABAN STAFF.

Source: Copyright 1954 by The Dance Notation Bureau, Inc. "Laban Staff," Copyright 1954 by Rudolf Laban. Reprinted with the permission of the Publisher, Theatre Arts Books, New York.

Directional symbols are placed within the staff to indicate the type of movement for particular body parts. The eight principal directions are as follows:

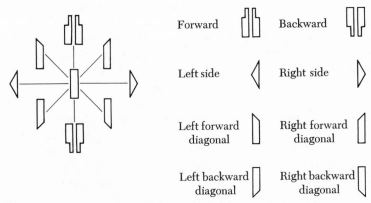

Figure 9. THE EIGHT MAIN DIRECTIONS.

After the part of the body has been determined (by placement of the symbol in the staff), and the direction of movement (by the shape of the symbol), further information is provided regarding the level of movement (by shading or markings within the symbols) and timing (by the length of the directional symbol). Many other notations are made for refinement and standardization of all aspects of Labanotation.

Numerous programs, or dances, have been written and may be purchased for class use. Effective use of this system assumes a knowledge of the movement and an ability to read the dance. Although movement notation has been used with dance, principally classical and modern ballet, this system is applicable to any area in which bodily movement needs to be recorded.

Programming conditioning exercises

Not all programs are developed for the purpose of promoting *learning* in an activity. In physical education, some of the most useful plans are those designed to develop or maintain fitness. Once such a program has been established, the regular attention of the instructor is no longer required. Individually prescribed programs for physical development have traditionally been used in weight training. In recent years, *circuit training* and the Royal Canadian Air Force conditioning programs have proven popular. To take part in such planned activities, the individual must first learn how to perform each of the skills. The instructor must usually devote some time to teaching these items when they are used in the school setting. Thereafter, a particular schedule of exercises is prescribed. In the initial stages of the program, there is a progressive increase in the work load. This increase may be regulated by (1) the number of repetitions which must be completed, (2) the amount of weight or resistance used, (3) the speed with which the work must be performed, or (4) the length of time that the individual must continue working.

An example of a circuit-training program is that developed by Morgan and Adamson (1957) to improve the strength and endurance of college-aged men. Activities are designed for the development of (1) arms and shoulders, (2) back, (3) abdomen, (4) legs, and (5) overall body. Specific exercises are devised and arranged in the program for the development of each of these body parts. For example, arm and shoulder exercises include gripping, hanging, climbing, pulling, pressing, and lifting. Other exercises are distributed throughout the program to develop each of the different body parts.

In Morgan and Adamson's program for circuit training, from six to twelve exercises are taught to the individual. After he becomes proficient in the performance of these conditioning tasks, he is assigned a particular work program which is based on his exhibited fitness level. The daily work load involves the completion of three rounds, or circuits, of the series of exercises. Generally, the time required for completion is from fifteen to twenty minutes. Adjustments in the program (progressively more difficult work loads) are made by increasing the number of repetitions which must be completed or the amount of resistance used. The variables in the program are, therefore, speed and resistance. Reinforcement is provided when certain speed standards are achieved.

In summary, the circuit-training program is initially established on the basis of the individual's fitness level. It is so arranged that the person is able to immediately detect any capacity changes on the basis of his performance. Self-evident adjustments are made in the work load because of observed improvement.

In 1962, the Royal Canadian Air Force established two planned programs of exercises, *The VBX Plan for Physical Fitness* for men and *The XBX Plan for Physical Fitness* for women. These programs include basic exercises which are designed to develop and maintain fitness. They chart the level at which the individual should start (based on age), how fast he should increase the work load, and how far he should progress to attain a desirable level of fitness. This work program, which requires no equipment, is designed for about twelve minutes of work each day. Graduated scales are included to provide particular guidance regarding progressive changes in the program. The automated character of these programs makes them very similar to the programmed instructional materials in other subject areas.

In addition to their use for conditioning purposes, programs could be established for particular units of practice in a regular physical education activity. Such plans could be devised to promote learning or to improve one's proficiency in a particular task. The high school basketball player might be programmed to practice certain skills during the drill phase of each workout. For example, a particular player could be required to take twenty-five free-throw attempts, shoot ten jump shots from each side of the basket, complete two trials of ten rebound-taps of the backboard, and dribble through a particular obstacle course for speed. Such a program designed for the individual or group would insure a minimum amount of daily practice of skills which need to be emphasized.

The programs which have been discussed for conditioning or for skill learning incorporate within them the means for measurement. The individual immediately observes, and can therefore record, any improvement or decline. This raises a question about the possibility of programming other testing programs. For items in which the instructor is not required for the administration of the test, there appears to be no important reason why most motor performance tests in school cannot be established on the basis of an individual-testing or dual-testing procedure. Such a program could promote more testing and therefore more inherent reinforcement than traditional teacher-administered tests which are usually infrequent.

Programming remedial exercises

The type of physical education activity which has, traditionally, most closely resembled programmed learning is the exercises associated with remedial programs. The operation of some of the complex apparatus has been very similar to the operation of some teaching machines. Such remedial equipment is often used for exercise purposes and for measurement. Apparatus designed for the alleviation of problems associated with the feet, posture, or with limited flexibility is often arranged so that the individual must move the apparatus through a given distance as the body parts are exercised in a particular manner. In this way, the subject can observe progressive changes in his performance as his specific ailment or condition improves.

The student with a flexibility problem may be on a program which requires him to perform a given amount of stretching exercises every day. Whether or not these exercises are done with apparatus, it is important that the student be able to determine small changes in status. For example, he should be shown if he can stretch two inches further than he could on a previous occasion. This type of regular reinforcement is strategic in such a program. In like manner, dynamometers can be used to show slight changes in strength for various body parts.

The program of exercises should be prescribed by the remedial physical education instructor in conjunction with a medical specialist. Such a work program is developed in view of the person's particular limitation. The subject follows the prescribed schedule in much the same manner as the conditioning program described earlier. An integral part of the remedial program should be the regular testing of one's status. It is preferable that this evaluation be a daily procedure and that it be a self-testing routine. It is even more ideal from a programming standpoint if the exercise itself is an exhibition of status, as is the use of a strength dynamometer or a flexion device which must be extended through observable angles or landmarks as the individual exercises. In simpler exercises one can easily notice the number of push-ups or sit-ups or the time required for the completion of a certain conditioning stunt.

WHOLE AND PART PRESENTATION

During recent years considerable attention has been devoted to the study of techniques by which materials may be organized for presentation to the learner. Much of this investigation has centered on the topic of whole versus part learning. Answers have been sought to such questions as the following: Is it more economical to memorize a poem by studying it as a whole or part by part? Can a folk dance be learned easier if it is presented as a total unit or if it is broken into parts? In teaching the game of soccer to a group for the first time, should skills in dribbling, passing, and kicking for goal be developed first, or should one begin with a game situation?

The term *whole learning* has been used in reference to situations in which the total block of material is seen or studied at once. An example of this in verbal learning is the study of a poem as a unit (reading it from start to finish) until it can be recited in its entirety. In *part learning*, initial attention is devoted to only a portion of the material. In memorizing a poem by this method, a line, a sentence, or verse is studied until it is thoroughly learned before the next segment is studied. After all the parts have been learned, the individual connects them so that the total poem can be recited. In addition to these very different techniques, several variations or combinations of the two methods are used, for example, whole-part and progressive-part techniques. In such plans, whole and part techniques are used alternately in an effort to take advantage of the special values of each.

In motor activities, part learning refers to the plan in which practice is devoted to a particular phase of the task until it is learned quite well before other parts of the overall task are introduced. For example, if one were to learn the tennis serve by the part method, he would first practice tossing the ball into the air until this could be done properly. Next, he would practice shifting his body weight, then various aspects of the swing. When all the separate parts of the service had been learned, he would practice the serve as a unitary response. On the other hand, if the whole learning approach were used with this task, the learner would be made aware of the total act of serving by demonstration, explanation, film, or some other method. Then he would begin to practice the total act of serving.

In team games, such as basketball or soccer, the part method emphasizes the early development of proficiency in the separate fundamentals, such as dribbling, passing, and shooting. When the whole method is used, early attention is devoted to acquainting the learner with the total activity or at least with combinations of several parts. It is important to note that the whole method does not simply throw groups of children into an activity without instruction and guidance. Rather, the whole method organizes the material so that the learners are able to view the total activity from the beginning.

The concept of part learning has been most closely related to stimulus-response theories of learning. Within this framework, students have been encouraged to learn one thing at a time and to learn it well. Educational methods have been based traditionally on proceeding from the simple to the complex. Although the part principle has considerable merit, its extreme use has been challenged by cognitive psychologists. These theorists insist that learning is not additive in nature, i.e., knowledge about any given activity or task is not simply knowledge of the sum of the individual parts. Interpretations of gestalt psychology from its earliest days have led to the belief that learners should become acquainted with the broadest possible view at the earliest moment. Recent gestaltists have urged that unitary wholes be developed first and that parts or skills be refined later. According to this view, stress should be placed on the learner's perception of the interrelations of the parts of the material to be learned. Current evidence, however, does not suggest that one method should be used exclusively. Rather, each method seems to have merit in different situations.

Factors influencing the method to be used

There are several factors which determine whether the whole or part method should be used. Under certain conditions, the whole approach may prove most effective, while in other situations the part method seems best. On occasion, they may be equally effective. Some learners, especially those who are highly motivated, seem to learn well in all situations.

One of the most important factors in determining the most effective method is the *learner* himself. More mature learners are able to comprehend larger units of material than can less mature individuals. Likewise, more intelligent learners can understand larger wholes or relationships among more complex parts. Such individuals are more likely to become bored with continuous repetition of small segments of the task. At the same time, slow learners are likely to become bewildered and frustrated with the complexity of some large blocks of material. In their case, smaller units would be advisable. Of course, some activities or bodies of material are so large or so complex that they must be broken down for even the most advanced learners.

The nature of the *material* or task to be learned is also influential in determining the appropriate technique. Most important considerations are the difficulty and length of the material, and whether or not there is a relationship among the parts which gives meaning to the whole. In some situations there is no particular advantage in attempting to learn all the parts at once. Certain movement skills in sports activities are not very closely related to other aspects of the sport. For example, batting in baseball does not form any logical whole with sliding into second base. Therefore, regularly practicing these skills in close relation does not seem particularly beneficial. On the other hand, movements which follow each other in a logical sequence probably have a relationship to each other. The whole method is therefore advocated for the learning of such sequential activities.

The *instructor* is also important in determining the best method to be used in particular situations. Some teachers seem to be more skillful with one technique or the other. Either method, to be very effective, must be mastered by the instructor. Other considerations in determining the best method to use are (1) the manner in which *practice periods* are distributed, (2) the particular *variation* of the part or whole method used, and (3) the method to be used for *measuring* the amount of material which is learned.

Research involving whole and part presentation

Studies which have been organized to determine the relative merits of whole and part teaching techniques have generally been designed in the following manner: (1) one group is designated to practice the total task, or some major part thereof, from the beginning; (2) a second group practices a particular part of the overall task and does not go on to the next part until the first part is well learned; and (3) a third group is sometimes included to practice some combination of the whole and part techniques. At the conclusion of the training period, the groups are compared to determine which technique proved more effective.

Most of the early research in whole and part learning dealt with the memorization of verbal material or the learning of various novel types of physical tasks. In recent years, however, a significant number of studies have involved more common motor activities. Knapp and Dixon (1952) compared the whole method with the part method for developing skill in juggling. Paired groups of college students were used. The group following the whole method learned juggling more rapidly. Cross (1937) used whole methods, minor games, and whole-part methods in teaching basketball to ninth-grade boys. He found advantages for each method, depending on the complexity of the skills to be learned. The simpler skills were learned best by the whole method, while the more complex ones were acquired more quickly with the whole-part method. McGuigan and MacCaslin (1935) found that army trainees learned rifle marksmanship better by means of the whole method. The whole method was superior to the part method for both slow and sustained firing.

Theunissen (1955) compared the whole method to the part method in teaching golf. After ten weeks of instruction according to these methods, the paired groups played eighteen holes of golf. Instruction was continued for six more weeks after which another round of golf was played. The group on the part method proved superior in the first test, but those following the whole method did best on the second test. The whole method also proved best for indoor golf instruction. O'Donnell (1956) showed that college women learned tennis better by the whole method than by either the part or progressive-part methods. It was noted that in final playing ability (as measured by the Dyer test), the whole-method group was significantly better. In specific tests of forehand, backhand, and serving ability, however, the whole-method group was not significantly better. Thomas (1923) found that junior high school boys developed skill in ordinary sports activities when they were placed in a competitive situation faster than when attention was concentrated on the movement patterns of the activities. This seems to support the whole activity concept rather than specific skill practice. Lambert (1951) found that interference resulted when a two-handed manipulatory skill was taught separately with each hand.

Although the bulk of experimental evidence shows some advantage for the whole method, the results have not been unanimous. Niemeyer (1958) taught 336 students to swim, to play volleyball, and to play badminton by whole and part methods. He found that persons who were taught by the whole method learned to swim sooner, faster, farther, and with better form than those who were taught by the part method. In learning to swim by the whole method, arm and leg action, as well as breathing, was developed simultaneously while, in the part method these skills were introduced separately. In volleyball, greater improvement was shown by the group which followed the part method, i.e., individual skills (serving, setting up, spiking) were developed before being put together in a game. In badminton, neither method proved superior. On the basis of his study, Niemeyer suggested that (1) the part method is best for the learning of team sports; (2) the whole method is best for individual activities; and (3) dual sports are learned equally well by either method. Although this may be an oversimplification, it does point out that different methods prove best in different situations.

Naylor and Briggs (1961) investigated the effects of task complexity and organization on the efficiency of whole and part methods. They reported that when tasks were unorganized, part practice was most efficient. However, under conditions of higher organization, the whole method proved most efficient.

In a study of a gymnastic stunt on the horizontal bar, Shay (1934) found that a progressive-part method resulted in greater speed of learning than did the whole method. Peckstein (1917), Reed (1924), and McGeoch (1931) have also reported good results with the progressive-part method for the learning of various types of verbal material. In this technique, the individual first learns one part of the task, then a second part and, at this point, practices both parts together. This procedure is followed until all parts are learned and practiced as a total unit.

ORGANIZING MATERIALS FOR TEACHING

It is important to point out that teachers need not adhere completely to the whole method or to the part method. A good teaching program might well combine both of these concepts to a greater or lesser degree. Recent research seems to indicate, however, that the whole method should be used to a greater extent than it has been in the past. The size of the whole should be given serious study by those who are planning teaching units. The amount of material which can be comprehended will depend largely upon the intelligence of the learners. Research seems to indicate that less intelligent learners should be given smaller wholes than brighter pupils. Some may learn a whole dance routine, while others would need it broken into several "wholes."

In discussing the whole and part concepts in the teaching of tennis, Ragsdale (1950) states that:

It is probably well to begin with a concept of the game as a whole and some preliminary trial in it as a whole. Very soon, however, special practice on part-activities must be begun. As each part is moderately learned, it should be applied in further trial of the game as a whole. This alternation of part and whole practice carries all parts along approximately together and keeps them constantly adapted to the requirements of the total activity. This procedure also assures that no important part is underlearned, that practice is constantly motivated by reference to the whole game, that transition between part-activities is learned as the parts are learned, and that meaning and relationship are preserved and developed at all stages of skill (p. 85).[3]

Whole learning

In whole learning, the separate parts and the integration of these parts into a meaningful unit is established at once. When the part-learning technique is used, extra effort is needed to connect the parts together after they have been learned. A situation in which the individual has learned the parts but not the whole can sometimes be noted in classes where sports skills are tested. The author has had students who scored high on tests of individual sports skills, but in subsequent class tournaments in the activity did not rank at the same relatively high position. Some boys are excellent shooters in basketball, but when harassed by opposing players they cannot make routine shots. Dance teachers likewise report that some students are skillful in the various techniques or positions of a particular dance but are mediocre in overall dance performance.

The introduction of a new activity by the whole method is much more complex than just starting with a game. Putting children in an unfamiliar team game would, in fact, not often result in any clear understanding of the total game. The concept of the whole method implies that the learner gains an *understanding* of the whole and the relationship of the parts to the whole. An experienced teacher of soccer knows that to put children immediately into a game without some preparation would result in mass chaos. Little understanding of the real game would take place. For many activities, therefore, alternative measures must be taken. The teacher might discuss the basic purposes and rules of the game along with chalkboard illustrations of positions and movements. He might show a film in which soccer is played as a game, or he could even take students to see a soccer game. These techniques would all give the student a general acquaintance with the game and an idea of the necessary skills. The student might then be taken onto the field and walked through some game situations. At this time, emphasis would be placed on position responsibilities, and team strategy. Later, the students might move to activities such as full speed games, practicing skills, and lead-up games. This whole-part approach is, therefore, very different from merely rolling out the ball.

In a discussion of the gestalt approach in the teaching of tumbling, Dahlern (1960) encouraged the grouping of tumbling activities into families of similar stunts. According to him, the student should not view each stunt as an isolated entity but should be made to see that rolls, cartwheels, and turns are all activities involving rotation of the body. This big family of activities can be further broken into subfamilies depend-

[3] By permission of the National Society for the Study of Education.

ing upon the type of movement involved. Stands and balances can be grouped because of similar general principles. Using combined tumbling stunts also gives the student a larger perspective of total body movement. Dahlern emphasizes that individual stunts are easier to understand and learn if one sees them as part of a larger whole.

Teaching wholes in sports skills. From a practical standpoint, a division of the whole may be necessitated when the total material is too long or complex. Just as a poem or play may be broken into stanzas or acts a complex motor activity may be broken into several wholes. Any individual who is familiar with sports can think of situations where several skills together make a logical sequence. For example, consider the end in football who is practicing pass catching. The customary procedure is to have the player take his set position, start on the snap of the ball, run to a given spot, fake, accelerate his movement, catch the ball, and sprint for about ten more yards. This sequence involves a number of parts which obviously go together. Practicing the parts separately would not enable the player to run the pass pattern smoothly. Learning to fake well is not of much value unless the individual can move quickly away from the unsteady defender. Learning to catch the ball well and quickly moving into a full gait (with ball properly cradled in arms) involves more than being able to catch the ball and being a fast runner. The total pass pattern, therefore, is a logical whole. There are many other sports situations in which sequential skills should be practiced together. The baseball player practicing the drag bunt should follow each bunt by taking a few quick steps toward first base. Knowing how to bunt the ball and being able to run fast will not necessarily make one a good drag bunter. The two skills must be put together for the fast getaway that is needed in a game. In like manner, the most effective infield practice for the shortstop involves fielding the ground ball *and* throwing to first or to second base. This makes for a more effective play than does fielding grounders at one time and throwing to the base at another time.

Conversely, one can think of other situations in sports where it is meaningless to try to tie things together into a whole. Sometimes this is done rather artificially with little apparent advantage. The football coach, for example, might have the receivers break from the huddle, go to the line of scrimmage, wait for the signal, and start the play pattern. When the players get set to wait for the signal, the first "whole" has been terminated. The next meaningful sequence starts with the signal. The pass receiver who practices extensive broken-field running after the catch seemingly has no whole-method advantage over the one who stops after a few steps. Broken-field running can be practiced in isolation from pass catching. In trying to determine the advantage of whole or part techniques, therefore, one must determine whether any "connecting" advantage is gained by putting them together.

Novice wrestlers often learn one move at a time, and unfortunately continue to use moves in isolation. The sit-out, turn-in, switch, wrist roll, and take-down might be learned quite well as separate skills. However, unless the instructor devotes some time to aiding the wrestler in putting these skills into a rapid and smooth sequence, they may be of little value in a wrestling match. Practices should be conducted so that several series of moves can be put together for greater effectiveness. Also, boxers who have a good repertoire of punches will be much more effective if "combinations" are developed. The dancer who learns a particular movement or position without understanding how to smoothly get to the next position or movement will exhibit a disjointed style. In a wide range of activities, from fencing and wrestling to all varieties of dance, greater fluidity and effectiveness are promoted by encouraging learners to practice several skills in sequence.

In addition to possible learning advantages, the whole-game approach, or a modification, might offer motivational advantages. It is obvious that learning to dribble in soccer will interest the learner little unless he can see some relationship between dribbling skill and success in the total game. Learning to trap the ball without understanding the use of trapping in the game is next to useless. Young children, especially, are interested in early gratification of their efforts. This gratification is most often supplied in an activity which has variety and climax in itself. Modified or lead-up games offer excellent variations from the total game situation.

Part and whole-part learning

There are definite limitations in the use of the whole concept in teaching which make strict adherence to this technique inadvisable in several situations. Sometimes the learner cannot effectively comprehend large units of material or the complexity of an activity. In such situations, the learning material can be organized in parts which are adjusted to the capacity of the individual. Sometimes motivation can best be promoted by the part method because of the more immediate improvement which the learner is often able to observe. For example, students who are exposed only to the whole method for the learning of a complex dance may leave an early learning session with the idea that they really do not know any part of the dance. Such an experience usually leads to a lack of interest on the part of the learner. On the other hand, if some attention is devoted to a particular part of the dance, that phase may be mastered with the result being greater satisfaction.

Part learning is also essential on occasion to enable the learner to improve particular responses. When the whole technique is used exclusively, improper responses, or faults, are likely to be practiced repeatedly. If not isolated for special attention in the early stages, these faults will be well learned and thus more difficult to eliminate at a later time. Coaches who have been especially interested in correct form and technique have traditionally devoted a great deal of attention to the practice of parts.

Combination techniques in which learners are exposed to both whole and part learning, perhaps on an alternating basis, have been used with considerable success. Variations of this method have been described as whole-part, part-whole-part, and progressive-part. The whole-part method has been used in situations in which the students are first introduced to, and begin work on, the total activity and later revert back to practice on particular parts. It is assumed that when learners understand the place of the separate skills in the overall activity, practice of the skills will be more meaningful. The whole-part approach is used quite often in teaching beginning swimming. The individual must be taught the overall act of swimming before refinement of arm strokes, kick, breathing, and other parts can effectively take place.

The part-whole-part technique, as generally used, is similar to the whole-part technique except that alternation back and forth occurs more regularly. In using the part-whole-part, teachers or coaches have learners practice the fundamental skills, participate in the overall activity, and then return to practice of the skills. This technique often has advantages over the exclusive practice of specific skills in terms of meaningfulness and motivation. Similarly, the part-whole-part technique is often better than exclusive game play because more specific attention can be directed toward the improvement of weak skills.

The progressive-part method refers to the gradual accumulation and combination of the separate parts of the activity. If this technique was used in basketball, the students would first learn passing and then a second skill such as dribbling. The two skills would then be combined in an activity requiring the use of both. Now a third skill (such as shooting a lay-up) would be practiced separately. Then the skills would be combined in an activity such as a weave which results in a lay-up shot. Similarly, the remaining skills would be learned, one at a time, and connected to previously learned skills.

A traditional and effective way of combining several parts into a whole has been the use of *lead-up* games in sports. In these activities, several fundamental skills are combined to form an interesting game. There are several advantages in the use of lead-up games. Such activities are usually more interesting to the participant than practice of the separate skills. With the enthusiasm which is engendered in this competitive situation, it is reasonable to expect that greater learning of skills will result. In addition, several of the skills are related or tied together in these activities much as they are in the regular game. Students are able to see the importance of the separate skills toward success in the total activity.

Numerous examples of developmental lead-up games are presented in a recent book by Blake and Volpe (1964).

Selecting the best technique

Whether or not the whole or part method should be used with a particular activity depends on many factors. Numerous studies have shown that material which is meaningful is learned more readily than material which is not meaningful. It has been suggested that practicing the total or complex task is preferable when a reasonable degree of success is possible. If the total concept is within the grasp of the learner, the part method, which requires learning the parts *and* putting them together, probably wastes some time. However, if meaning in the overall activity is not apparent, a key part or a simplified whole is desirable. Neither the whole nor the part method is invariably better than the other. The desirable method depends upon the complexity, length, organization, age, intelligence, and motivation of the learner.

The whole method seems best when the amount of learning does not exceed what the learner can comprehend. This method is also better when learners are older, brighter, more highly motivated, and have a background in the task The whole technique is also favored in late stages of the learning process and when practices are distributed. When the opposite conditions exist, then part methods seem best. A combination of the two methods is sometimes most successful. It seems desirable, therefore, that all teachers be able to make effective use of each technique and a combination of the two. An essential of good teaching seems to be flexibility, which is also important in the use of whole and part organization of learning tasks.

SELECTED READINGS

Cratty, B. J. *Movement behavior and motor learning.* Philadelphia: Lea & Febiger, 1964.

Deterline, W. A. *An introduction to programmed instruction.* Englewood Cliffs, N. J.: Prentice-Hall, 1962.

Hutchinson, A. *Labanotation.* New York: New Directions, 1954.

Margulies, S., & Eigen, L. D. (Eds.) *Applied programmed instruction.* New York: Wiley, 1962.

Morgan, R. E., & Adamson, G. T. *Circuit training.* London: G. Bell, 1957.

Niemeyer, R. K. Part versus whole methods and massed versus distributed practice in learning of selected large muscle activities. Unpublished doctoral dissertation, Univer. of Southern California, 1958.

Penman, K. A. *Physical education for college students.* St. Louis: Mosby, 1964.

Royal Canadian Air Force. *VBX Plan for physical fitness.* Ottawa: Roger Duhamel, F.R.S.C., Queen's Printer and Controller of Stationery, 1962.

Royal Canadian Air Force. *XBX Plan for physical fitness.* Ottawa: Roger Duhamel, F.R.S.C., Queen's Printer and Controller of Stationery, 1962.

Theunissen, W. V. Part teaching and whole teaching of beginning group-golf classes for male college students. Unpublished doctoral dissertation, Indiana Univer., 1955.

Woodworth, R. S., & Schlosberg, H. *Experimental Psychology.* (Rev. ed.) New York: Holt, Rinehart and Winston, 1963.

Part V

Individual differences in learning and performance

Introduction

When children report to school at the beginning of the year, there are differences which are immediately apparent to the teacher. Many other differences, perhaps more important, are not so easily detected. These individual differences (both obvious and subtle) are influential in the child's learning and performance in all areas of the school curriculum. Of course, certain types of differences are more strategic in some subject areas than in others. In order for the teacher to be most effective in promoting the development of the child, he must understand (1) the nature of the differences and (2) the effect of these differences on the learning and performance of the child in different activities.

In the area of motor skills, children seem to vary a great deal in their capacity to benefit from practice and in their ability to attain outstanding proficiency in skills. It has been noticed that different children seem to excel in different physical activities. Physical educators have long been interested in determining the particular elements which contribute to differences in motor capacities. Also of interest has been the question of whether these components are inherited or whether they can be developed through practice. Most often investigated have been the following *individual differences in learning and performance*, which will be discussed in this section.

Chapter 11

General and intellectual differences

When one observes a group of young children playing a run-and-tag game, or skipping, or even bouncing a ball, it becomes apparent in a short time that some of the children are more skillful than others. When a new activity is introduced, a few of the children will almost immediately get the idea and exhibit a reasonably high level of proficiency. Other children will work hard at the activity but with little success. Still others will have no interest in the game and will pay little attention to instructions. In performance in motor activities, therefore, it soon becomes clear that physical, mental, and personality factors are important. Individuals differ in each of these areas in ways which are important for the learning and performance of motor skills.

Despite the problems which may be presented to the teacher, individual differences prove a distinct asset in our culture. Vocational and avocational pursuits in our society require the full range of motor and verbal skills. Great variety in interests and backgrounds also proves valuable. Even in sports, different types of strength are required for the many athletic activities (and positions in each) which are available in the modern school program. Then too, differences among individuals, and the resulting variety in attitudes and activities, add interest and strength to both small and large groups.

Nevertheless, in the school setting, the teacher is faced with an important problem when attempting to meet the needs of the different class members. His success will depend upon an understanding of the important differences among his pupils and his resourcefulness in reacting to these differences. Even the neophyte teacher can usually pick out gross differences among children, but he may have little skill in making program adjustments to meet these differences. However, the effectiveness of the teacher in dealing with pupils' differences will determine how well students reach the direct and related objectives of his programs.

The problem of differences cannot be solved completely by homogeneous grouping, which reduces only the range of the trait that is used as a basis for grouping. Other physical, mental, and social traits may vary widely for such a grouped class. For example, if general motor ability were used as a means for grouping in physical education, special sports skills as well as interests in the activities might still cover the total range of the school population. Therefore, the practice of ability grouping, despite certain pedagogical advantages, does not lessen the need for the teacher's attention to differences within his group.

Among the most highly skilled as well as the most poorly skilled groups, differences become readily apparent. Among high school varsity basketball players, for example, some shoot the ball more accurately, pass with greater speed and accuracy, and generally perform better than their teammates. Some boys and girls seem to be natural players in certain activities, while others, with great effort and perseverance, manage to perform only adequately. Even on professional athletic teams, some players consistently perform at a high level and become the stars in the league, while others barely make the squad. When observing baseball players, one can see that certain outfielders get the jump on the ball and run a true course to the point where the ball is to be fielded. Others, sometimes with greater running speed, get off to a slower start and often misjudge the flight of the ball.

Teachers have often wondered why some children are much better than others in the performance of certain skills. One might hypothesize that the more proficient children have had more experience in the particular activity. Even with a new activity, however, some children learn more rapidly and perform at a higher level than do others. It seems that some people have a greater innate capacity for learning and performing in certain skills. Upon close observation, it can be detected that the better performers are not always the biggest children or the smallest. Physical size and body build do not always give a reliable clue to the reason for differences in abilities to learn and perform motor skills. Physical educators have shown some concern in recent years for determining the physiological and psychological components which contribute to differences in motor skills. In addition, they have been interested in establishing whether or not these traits are inherited, to what extent they can be developed, and how they can be measured most effectively.

The scope of differences

The Declaration of Independence states that "all men are created equal." It is obvious, however, that this equality is a legal rather than a biological concept. It was clear even before the document was written that not all men were the same height, weight, or had the same shoe size. Experimenters today, with more sophisticated measuring instruments, have discovered countless traits in which human beings differ. Probably the most widely used instruments in American schools during the past decades have been those designed to determine the students' intelligence or special mental abilities. Today, physical educators, as well as specialists in other subject areas, are becoming more interested in determining the basic traits which enable an individual to attain outstanding success in their particular specialty.

Garry (1963) has categorized individual differences into the following areas, each of which might affect school performance to a greater or lesser degree:

1. Physical differences include age, height, weight, sex, vision, hearing, motor ability, and handicaps.
2. Social differences include socioeconomic status, religious and ethnic background, family relationships, and peer group relationships.
3. Personality differences include character traits, motivational needs, interests, attitudes, and affective reactions.
4. Capacity differences refer to general intelligence and a wide variety of special aptitudes.
5. Achievement differences refer to previous accomplishments in school and out-of-school activities.

Within any class there are variations among students in each of these components. Teachers in different subject areas are, of course, interested in the traits which are most influential in their particular field. Physical differences, therefore, are of greatest importance to the physical educator. However, the influence of physical and other differences overlaps in several areas. Certainly social and personality components help to determine the child's interest and work habits in certain motor activities. On the other hand, it is obvious that physical components such as vision, hearing, and general state of health can affect the child's achievement in reading. Similarly, general intelligence is a component which seems to influence the individual's performance in a wide range of activities.

General motor ability

In Garry's list of physical differences, motor ability has received the greatest attention from physical educators. In recent years, this term has been used to describe one's proficiency in a wide variety of rather basic skills and general fitness activities. Clarke (1959), Fleishman (1964), and several other authors have outlined and described the components of motor ability. Clarke's list includes elements which have traditionally been assumed to be important in the performance of gross motor skills. This list, which has attained considerable acceptance among physical educators, includes the following:

Muscular strength. The maximum force which can be exerted in a single muscular exertion.

Muscular endurance. The ability to continue muscular exertions of a submaximal magnitude.

Cardiovascular endurance. The ability to continue moderate contractions of large muscle groups for a relatively long period of time and required adjustments in the cardiorespiratory system.

Speed. The rapidity with which successive movements of the same kind can be made.

Agility. Speed in changing body position or direction.

Balance. Ease in maintaining or controlling body position.

Muscular power. The release of maximal muscular force in the shortest period of time.

Eye-hand coordination. The ability to make precise movements of the hands when vision is used.

Eye-foot coordination. The ability to make precise movements of the feet when vision is used.

Fleishman identified the following list of *psychomotor ability components* which he believed to be somewhat independent of physical proficiency or fitness factors. These motor abilities were established after extensive factor analysis studies:

Control precision. Fine movement dexterity with the hands or feet.

Multilimb coordination. Simultaneous control of the movements of a number of limbs.

Response orientation. The ability to make rapid and correct movements to different stimuli.

Reaction time. The speed with which the individual is able to respond to a stimulus.

Speed of arm movement. The rapidity with which the person can make a gross discrete movement where accuracy is not required.

Rate control. The ability to make anticipatory adjustments to objects which change speed and direction.

Manual dexterity. Speed of skilled arm-hand movements of relatively large objects.

Finger dexterity. The ability to manipulate small objects which primarily involves use of the fingers.

Arm-hand steadiness. The ability to make finely controlled positioning movements.

Wrist-finger speed. The ability to make rapid movements of the wrist and fingers, such as in tapping.

Aiming. The ability to make rapid controlled movements requiring the touching of targets placed in an irregular order.

In addition to differences of age, size, and the generally accepted motor ability components just listed, additional distinctions among children appear to cause variations in their achievement in physical activities. The most important of these differences seem to occur in (1) general intelligence, (2) kinesthesis, (3) visual abilities, (4) reaction and movement time, (5) lateral dominance, and (6) anthropometry. These components are somewhat related to both learning and performance in a wide range of motor skills. Because of this relationship and because of the differences among individuals, each will be discussed in the following chapters.

INTELLECTUAL DIFFERENCES

The role of general intelligence in motor learning and performance has intrigued the physical educator for many years. Certain questions relative to this topic have been investigated and are still being explored. For example, is an intelligent person likely to learn a rather simple motor task, such as shuffleboard, more quickly than a person with less intelligence? Does the same rule apply for a more complex skill, such as an intricate rhythmical drill? Does the learning of a motor skill require the use of one's intellect? Does general intelligence include motor aptitude, or is there a special kind of motor intelligence?

An investigation of these questions first requires an analysis of the topic of general intelligence. Is intelligence inherited, or is it developed? Several years ago this was a popular question for debate, research, and general discussion. The nature-nurture controversy has never been completely resolved because of the difficulty of isolating and controlling all the important variables. However, extreme "hereditarians" and "environmentalists" are decreasing in number. Most psychologists today agree that both heredity and environment interact to influence the development of one's intelligence.

In a similar fashion, the question of inheriting motor ability has been debated. A number of factors have contributed to the traditional belief that motor abilities are inherited. One factor has been the occurrence of occasional father and son participants in professional sports or participation of several brothers from the same family. Another contributing factor is the obvious role of heredity in body size and physique, which certainly plays a part in sports performance. However, motor learning, as well as proficiency in movement activities, is quite separate from size and shape. The nature-nurture argument in motor ability, like that of IQ, has been supported more by opinion and observation than by scientific evidence.

What is intelligence?

Intelligence has been pragmatically defined as that which intelligence tests measure, or the ability to do well on an intelligence test. Although these explanations apparently contain a degree of truth, they do little to clarify the issue. It is extremely difficult to get a consensus among authorities on a clear definition of intelligence. In view of this, Spearman (1923) stated that ". . . this word in its present day usage *does not possess any definite meaning* . . . neither its utterers nor its hearers appear to have behind it any clear idea whatever" (p. 20). In recent years, however, intelligence has variously been described as (1) the ability to adjust to a new situation, (2) the ability to do abstract thinking, (3) that which distinguishes man from lower animals, (4) the ability to learn rapidly, and (5) the ability to solve problems. A synthesis of the many definitions would include most of these qualities.

Wechsler (1944) offers the following definition which has attained a reasonable degree of acceptance: "Intelligence is the aggregate or global capacity of the individual to act purposefully, to think rationally and to deal effectively with his environment" (p. 3). He points out that intelligence is made up of differential elements or abilities and their *combination*. According to Wechsler, therefore, intelligence is more than the sum of one's special abilities.

Ideas about intelligence have changed considerably during the past century. A great deal of generality has traditionally been assumed to exist among the various abilities of the individual. Stern (1914) advocated this concept of intelligence in his general factor theory, which implied that if a person has outstanding intelligence or ability in one activity or trait, he will also have outstanding intelligence in all other areas of human ability. All specific abilities (referred to as *s*) accrue from the general factor (referred to as *G*). A person is, therefore, equally intelligent in all areas. According to Stern's theory, the more intelligent person learns mathematics, mechanics, music, or spelling better than the person of lesser ability. Apparently uneven abilities or skills are assumed to result from one's environment or one's greater interest and experience in some areas.

Spearman (1927) explained intelligence as a general factor plus specific abilities. He described two integers: a general factor *g* common to all tasks, and a specific factor *s* peculiar to a particular task. No two people have identical combinations of *g* or *s*. The specific factors or abilities were listed as verbal, numerical, mechanical, attention, imagination, and mental speed. Unlike Stern's theory of a large G with perfect intercorrelations among special abilities, Spearman described a small g with the suggestion of a *tendency* towards a correlation among abilities. The individual who was above average in numerical ability was assumed to have above-average ability in mechanics, mental speed, and all other capacities.

Thorndike and Hagen (1927) described intelligence as an accumulation of specific abilities (S). According to his theory an individual's general intelligence was derived by adding all the S factors, i.e., $S_1 + S_2 + \ldots S_n$. He discussed intelligences rather than intelligence and indicated that there is a special intelligence for each task. He assumed no g factor, and the S abilities were viewed as unrelated. The fact that a person is intelligent in one area is no indication that he will be above average in another field. For example, the skilled mechanic may exhibit a very low level of skill when thrust into a group leadership role. The politician may experience similar failure when presented with a mechanical problem.

Thurstone (1938) believed general intelligence to be made up of seven "primary mental abilities." His theory is similar to the one proposed by Thorndike. Thurstone, however, assumed some correlation to exist among certain of the abilities. The primary abilities were listed as (1) numbers, (2) word fluency, (3) verbal meaning, (4) memory, (5) reasoning, or ability to solve problems, (6) space, and (7) perceptual speed. The last two abilities listed seem especially important in the learning and performance of motor skills. Although the question of intelligence is not yet settled, the most popular ideas on this topic do not appear to differ greatly from Thurstone's theory.

The relationship of intelligence to physical proficiency

It has often been assumed that intelligence is important in enabling one to learn motor skills. Aptitude in motor activities may be one of the many "intelligences," or special abilities, which every person has. The ability of some persons to more quickly determine the relationship between a particular physical response and desired result may be considered an example of motor intelligence. Anyone who observes a group of elementary school children can see that some can more easily coordinate all parts of their bodies for certain types of activities. Those with greater aptitude in motor coordination can more quickly learn to perform in activities which depend heavily upon that aptitude. Is general intelligence also a factor in this motor aptitude?

Several authors have suggested a relationship between intelligence and the ability to improve with practice in motor skills. Among them,

R. A. Davis (1935) claims a relationship between intelligence and the learning of *complex* skills but no relationship with easy tasks. He states that:

Skills of the simple types require a limited amount of mental coordination and direction and therefore bear little relation to intelligence. The simpler skills are primarily dependent upon reflexes and instincts where intelligence and training are not essential. In the complex skills intellectual control and training are necessary. Complex skills, therefore, become an index to intelligence (pp. 138–139).[1]

Vince (1953) also emphasizes the relationship between intellectual and motor activity in the following statement:

At the same time it has been shown that this intellectual activity cannot be considered in separation from the motor activity: in that the subject's idea of the pattern is to some extent determined by it, and in that the development of the intellectual activity may depend very largely on the character of the motor response . . . (p. 85).

Several studies dealing with the topic of intelligence and motor performance have been conducted in recent years. However, the variability in design and conduct of research has often confused the issue. For example, some studies have related *physical fitness* to academic achievement. Such studies are based on the assumption that good health and fitness enable one to more nearly reach his potential capabilities in various intellectual activities. Typical of such studies was a recent analysis of the dropouts from U.S. military academies. A disproportionate percentage of the failures was especially low on physical fitness components. Also, Nason (1965) recently stated that, "children with high motor proficiency make higher grades in reading and writing than children with poor coordination" (p. 36). Though lending support to the relationship between fitness and school achievement, these statements do not provide a strong clue to the role of intelligence in the ability to learn a new skill.

Several studies have been designed to analyze the effect of athletic *participation* on academic achievement. In such studies, the school grades of athletes and nonathletes have been compared. Comparisons have also been made among participants during the sports season and during the off-season. Participants in a single sport have been compared with participants in several sports, and varsity players with intramural players. Such studies have generally led to the conclusion that those who participate in athletic activities represent the full range of ability and achievement levels found in the school. But, these studies have added little to an understanding of intelligence and motor learning ability.

It seems reasonable to assume that intelligence would have little to

[1] From PSYCHOLOGY OF LEARNING by R. A. Davis. Copyright 1935 by McGraw-Hill Book Company. Used by permission of McGraw-Hill Book Company.

do with one's ability to perform a simple muscular response involving power, speed, or endurance. For example, items such as pull-ups, a softball throw for distance, and a running speed test appear not to be affected by intelligence. However, when several types of movements are combined into a rather complex activity involving coordination, reaction to different stimuli, and use of general strategy a relationship seems more plausible.

Several studies have been conducted in recent years which considered rather directly whether high intelligence (as determined by performances on a general intelligence test) aids one in the learning of new skills. Some studies have also dealt with the relationship between intelligence and speed of improvement in relatively familiar skills. A positive relationship was reported in some studies, while no significant relationship was shown in other studies.

Research favoring a positive relationship

Harmon and Oxendine (1961) investigated the relationship between the intelligence of junior high school boys and their ability to develop skill in mirror tracing. Scores on the Pintner Intermediate Test (Form A) were obtained for 135 boys. These scores were then correlated with the subjects' initial performance in mirror tracing as well as performance at various points throughout a five-week learning period. The authors reported low positive correlations between general intelligence scores and mirror-tracing performance. There was a tendency for subjects with higher intelligence to exhibit better initial proficiency and to perform better at all phases of the learning process than did subjects with lower intelligence scores. The correlations were too low, however, to be a predictive value.

Kulcinski (1945) had fifth-grade and sixth-grade boys and girls learn eleven easy and eleven hard stunt exercises. He reported a definite relationship between various degrees of intelligence and the learning of the exercises. Children in the high IQ group exhibited slightly superior motor performance in the new skills than did children in the normal intelligence group. The normal group exhibited a greater degree of superiority than the subnormal group. Ellis (1938) investigated the learning ability and performance of groups of normal and defective children. He found that normal children learned more quickly, had better overall performance and better retention than did defective children. There was also less inhibitory potential among normal children.

In an early study, Burt and Moore (1912) reported a correlation coefficient of .60 between general intelligence scores and mirror-tracing scores. Elementary school children in England were used as subjects. Others who have studied the relationship between general intelligence and mirror tracing were Schott (1923), Calfee (1913), and Snoddy (1926). All reported low positive correlations. Subjects in these experiments ranged in age from elementary school to college age.

Garfiel (1923) compared intelligence scores to general motor ability. Although he found a low positive correlation, he concluded that motor ability represents a group of abilities different from mental ability. Thompson (1952) found only a slight relationship between motor ability and general intelligence. Ray (1940) compared mental and physical abilities with scholastic achievement among high school boys. He reported that physical ability was a more reliable predictor of academic standing then was one's intelligence quotient. Brace (1946) tested the ability of feeble-minded girls to learn gross motor skills. The mean IQ of the girls was 53. He found a slight relationship between intelligence and the ability to learn sports skills.

Fitzhugh and Fitzhugh (1965) reported a significant relationship between certain small motor movements and general intelligence in a group of brain-damaged patients. Children were organized into intelligence levels from below 60 to above 90. Each group was given tests in finger-tapping speed, tactile finger recognition, and fingertip number writing. They reported that intelligence, within the range of the group, was positively related to each of the skills.

Studies not showing a relationship

Not all research has shown a relationship between general intelligence and motor learning. Clinton (1930) gave intelligence tests to a group of elementary, high school, and college students. Each of the subjects then took a five-minute mirror-drawing test. The score on the test was simply the amount which could be traced during this initial period. Mirror-tracing performances of pupils with the highest and lowest intelligence were then compared. There was no significant difference between these scores. This led Clinton to conclude that "There is no positive relation between mirror-drawing ability and general intelligence" (p. 228).

Start (1962) tested 180 grammar school boys in Australia to determine if there was any relationship between game performance, intelligence, and "streaming" (selection for a tract, or particular course of study, in secondary school). Game performance, which was used as an indication of motor ability, was determined by whether or not the boy was selected for either rugby union or association football. Streaming was based upon the boy's performance on the annual scholastic examinations. The intelligence scores used were those obtained in the Secondary School Selection Examination which was taken prior to the boy's entering grammar school. Start reported an insignificant correlation between game performance and intelligence quotient. The difference in game performance between the group with IQs from 121–141 and boys in the 106–120 range was insignificant.

In addition, Start found no significant difference in the proportion of school players in each stream. This would indicate a lack of relationship between school achievement and sports performance. He also reported a low positive correlation (.19) between intelligence quotient and performance on the annual scholastic examinations. Although this was reported as significant at the 1 per cent level of confidence, it is admittedly low. A high score on an intelligence test, therefore, did not give strong assurance of success in a grammar school.

Start indicated that the selection of the sample may have been an important factor in showing no relationship between intelligence and athletic performance. The measured intelligence quotients of the subjects ranged from 106 to 141. He suggested the need for determining whether similar results would be found if a lower intelligence group is used. One should therefore conclude from this study that *for boys in the 106 to 141 intelligence range* there is no relationship between general intelligence and motor skill as measured by selection on a rugby or football team.

Ryan (1962a) tested the speed with which 80 male college students learned a novel balancing skill. He then correlated each subject's score with academic capacity, academic achievement, athletic ability, and relative achievement (academic achievement related to ability). The only significant correlation was between motor learning and relative achievement. He suggested that the *motive to succeed* was a more general characteristic than either intelligence or motor ability.

Westerdarp (1923) showed a negative correlation between mental ability and the physical traits of agility and coordination. Hertzberg (1929) compared motor ability tests with the intelligence scores of kindergarten children. He found no relationship at this age level. DiGiovanna (1937) found no relationship between general intelligence scores and (1) athletic ability or (2) motor ability of college men. G. B. Johnson (1942) showed that there was no relationship between the performance of college freshmen on the Thurstone Psychological Examination and the Johnson Physical Skills Test.

Intelligence and motor learning

Evidence concerning the relationship of general intelligence to motor learning is not consistent and, therefore, not entirely conclusive. Several studies report a low positive correlation, while others show no significant relationship. Almost no studies report a negative correlation between intelligence and the ability to learn skills. It seems reasonable to assume that, within the IQ ranges in most regular school situations, there is no more than a slight relationship between intelligence and the ability to learn the types of tasks reported in the literature. It should also be noted that correlations between general intelligence scores and school grades are also low, usually between .40 and .60. However, when feeble-minded or very low IQ subjects are used, a more substantial positive relationship is found between intelligence and motor-learning ability. This suggests the existence of a point below which intelligence becomes important in learning.

From the available evidence, it must be assumed that motor intelligence and general intelligence (as measured by tests today) are different components. Does this mean that the ability to learn skills is not related to intelligence or that this learning is not an intellectual process? This question has not been answered in the research. Immediately open to question is the validity of current IQ tests for determining overall general intelligence.

One might well question which of the following is the more accurate indication of general intelligence: (1) the ability to remember the definition of a word or to analyze the sequence of a series of numbers, or (2) the ability to learn to drive an automobile or to coordinate one's body in a skilled gymnastics movement. Word definitions and number analysis are rather arbitrarily described as intelligence measures, while the last two items are not. Therefore, if intelligence is defined as "the ability to do well on an intelligence test," then this factor is no more than slightly related to the learning of most skills. If on the other hand, intelligence is the "capacity of the individual to act purposefully" (Wechsler) or to adapt to new situations, perhaps motor-learning proficiency is as accurate an indication of intelligence as is the learning of a mathematical skill.

It can be concluded that the ability to learn motor skills, i.e., to relate specific body responses to results and to use coaching suggestions and cues, is *different* from the ability to solve certain mathematical problems or to do some types of verbal reasoning. Which of these is most closely related to general "intelligence" is still an unanswered question.

Motor intelligence

The term which has traditionally been used to indicate a person's aptitude for learning new physical skills is *motor educability*. This concept differs from general motor ability, which refers to capacity to perform a variety of tasks at any given time. Motor intelligence, as used in this discussion, includes both of these ideas and is related to motor skills in much the same way as general intelligence is related to verbal tasks.

However, less progress has been made in defining and measuring motor intelligence than has been made in the area of general intelligence.

Several factors have complicated efforts to measure motor intelligence. In addition to the problem of previous experience (which is also troublesome in general intelligence measurement), the matter of maturation and many physical traits such as vision, reaction time, strength, and kinesthesis play a vital role in one's ability to perform motor tasks. Also, they affect his ability to show improvement with practice over a short period of time. Theoretically, motor intelligence should be reflected in the ability to learn different tasks, i.e., to show improvement between the initial trial and some subsequent performance. Such a procedure, however, has proven difficult to administer with proper controls. Most motor intelligence measures, therefore, have been based on the individual's ability to exhibit initial skill in an activity which is new to him.

Motor educability

Tests for the determination of motor educability seemed to offer great promise during the 1920's and 1930's. However, they have not proven especially valuable in predicting one's ability to benefit from practice in a wide variety of motor skills. Neither have they been particularly useful in predicting initial performance in a variety of different activities. They continue in popular use, however, mostly as a means of grouping children for participation. Some of the most popular motor educability tests will be reviewed briefly.

Brace (1927) published perhaps the first test designed to measure motor ability. This test, along with subsequent variations, has been the most popular test of motor educability. His battery of tests was made up of twenty self-testing stunts. All items on the initial test were on a pass or fail basis, and no consideration was given to age or size. McCloy (1937) revised the original Brace test and included separate units for boys and girls at the elementary, junior, and senior high school levels. This twenty-one item Iowa-Brace test (including ten items from the original Brace test) has probably been the most widely used motor-educability test. Gire and Espenschade (1942) reported that the Brace test related highly to the ability of high school girls to learn and perform basketball, volleyball, and baseball skills. Later Brace (1946) reported that the "stunt" or rhythm-type skills, requiring manipulation of the total body, involve different abilities from those required for "sport-type" skills.

G. B. Johnson (1932) developed a test designed to group children for performance. This ten-item test included variations of jumps, hops, forward and backward rolls, and turns. In a study of the Johnson test, Carpenter (1935) identified the components of strength, control, locomotive strength of arms, and the ability to solve new motor skill coordination in the test. Gire and Espenschade (1942) reported a reliability coefficient of .61 for the test. Metheny (1938) found that scores in four selected items of the Johnson test correlated .997 with the overall test score. These items were validated by comparison with the subject's ability to learn tumbling stunts. For boys and girls, she determined that the strategic items were the ability to do forward and backward rolls with precision and to jump and turn. On this basis she developed a simplified Johnson-Metheny test.

McCloy (1934) developed a test which was designed to determine the innate motor capacity of the individual. Items in this test were the Sargent jump, squat thrusts, and pull-ups, plus the Iowa-Brace classification of size and maturity. Later McCloy (1940) listed the following prerequisites for motor learning: muscular strength, dynamic energy, the ability to change direction, flexibility, understanding the technique involved, and the absence of inhibiting factors.

A. R. Adams (1954) contended that neither the original Brace test nor the Iowa revision could be classified as a test of sport-type motor educability. After experimenting with forty-nine test-items, he determined that the tests which correlated highest with his motor educability criterion were (1) the basketball wall volley test, (2) throwing and catching a ball from a supine position, and (3) a basketball shooting contest. These test results had a multiple correlation of .79 with four sport-type learning tests. Fleishman (1964) found the following traits to be important in the performance of general motor skills: reaction time, tapping, manual dexterity, finger dexterity, steadiness, aiming, and motor kinesthesis. He also suggested a possible relationship between the general traits of psychomotor coordination, ambidexterity, and psychomotor precision.

Generally, the literature regarding motor educability testing indicates that: (1) the three most popular tests have been the original Brace test, the Iowa-Brace test, and the Johnson test; (2) two general types of motor educability have been described as sport-type and stunt-type; (3) despite some weaknesses, the Johnson test is probably the most valid test of stunt-type motor educability; and (4) no available test is a very reliable index of sports-skill educability.

Generality and specificity in motor learning

A question intimately involved with the matter of motor educability is whether a person can learn different types of motor skills with approximately the same degree of ease. Traditionally, it has been assumed that the person who could develop skill unusually fast in one task would be able to acquire skill in another motor activity more quickly than most persons. This traditional idea is consistent with Stern and Spearman's views of intelligence.

The concept of generality in performance seemed to be supported in a study by Robichaux (1960) in which 75 college women were classified into high, average, and low skill groups on the basis of general sports ability. The women then practiced five new gross motor skills different from any previously learned. A definite relationship was shown between performance in the previously learned skills and performance in the new tasks; i.e., the high ability group did best in the new skills, followed in order by the average and the low groups. In a somewhat similar study, Vernon (1951) reported a relationship between performance in fine and gross motor skills.

Soares (1958) studied the relationship of certain physical abilities to motor learning. The physical abilities measured were agility, balance, reaction time, speed, and fine motor-coordination. Subjects learned the skills of bongo board balancing, double ball toss, cut step, and double arm extension. She found significant correlations between the following measures: (1) speed with agility, (2) reaction time with agility, (3) right-hand accuracy with left-hand accuracy, (4) Scott motor-ability test with speed, (5) Scott motor-ability test with reaction time, (6) kinesthetic awareness of the right arm with kinesthetic awareness of the left arm, (7) balance with agility, (8) speed with reaction time, and (9) kinesthetic awareness of the left arm with balance. Generally, it was concluded that a high degree of intercorrelation existed among the motor-ability items tested.

The most recent researchers in this area have cast doubt on the validity of generality in the learning or the performance of skills. Bachman (1961) used two balancing tests to investigate this question. Male and female subjects from ages six to twenty-six practiced a ladder climb and balancing board task. The investigator compared beginning and final scores in both activities. No significant correlations were found for any of the age groups. He concluded that motor learning (on the items tested) was task specific.

Even prior to Brace's original work with motor-educability tests, Perrin (1921) attempted to identify fundamental motor components which would serve as a basis for general motor performance. He administered three complex motor tests and fourteen simple motor tests to college students. The complex tests included the Bogardus test, card sorting, and a coordination test involving both hands. The simple tests included reaction time, tapping, steadiness, and tracing. He found little correlation among these tests and concluded that motor ability is specific to the particular task and therefore, is not a general trait.

Seashore (1942) stated that, "No overall or general positive dependence or interrelatedness of fine motor abilities and gross motor abilities has been found" (p. 273). He concluded that there was little justification for such terms as *general motor ability* or *general muscular coordination.* Seashore, Buxton, and McCollum (1940), however, later identified certain fine motor traits as having general applicability. These included speed of simple reaction, steadiness or precision, hand speed in oscillatory movements, and skill in manipulatory spatial relations.

Henry (1958) reviewed research regarding the specificity as compared with commonality of motor-learning ability. He indicated that numerous test batteries will, by necessity, give some appearance of general motor ability, even if there is none. However, he concluded that ability to learn and perform in motor activities is extremely task specific. He stated that, ". . . individual differences in ability to profit by practice are specific to that skill and definitely do not predict the ability to improve by practice in some other skill" (p. 126). Other studies generally supporting this concept have been conducted by Cumbee, Meyer, and Paterson (1957) who worked with coordination, and Muscio (1922) who worked with tapping, reaction time, and steadiness.

Tyler (1956) indicated that motor characteristics of individuals are more specific than are mental characteristics. According to him, there is no *g* factor among motor skills. Excellence in one activity is no basis for predicting how an individual will perform in another. For predictive purposes, therefore, specific tests have to be given for each activity. He did suggest, however, that separate motor abilities are not as narrow and specific as was thought by early investigators.

SELECTED READINGS

Anastasi, A. *Psychological testing.* (2nd ed.) New York: Macmillian, 1961.

Brace, D. K. *Measuring motor ability.* New York: Barnes, 1927.

Buros, O. K. (Ed.) *The sixth mental measurement yearbook.* Highland Park, N. J.: Gryphon Press, 1965.

Clarke, H. H. *Application of measurement to health and physical education.* (4th ed.) Englewood Cliffs, N. J.: Prentice-Hall, 1967.

Fleishman, E. A. The perception of body position in the absence of visual cues. *J. exp. Psychol.,* 1953, 46, 261–270.

Garry, R. *Psychology of learning.* Washington: Cen. appl. Res. Educ., 1963.

Guilford, J. B. A system of psychomotor abilities. *Amer. J. Psychol.,* 1958, 71, 164–174.

Jenkins, J. J., & Peterson, D. G. *Studies in individual differences: the search for intelligence.* New York: Appleton-Century-Crofts, 1961.

Thurstone, L. L. Primary mental abilities. *Univer. of Chicago psychometr. Monogr.*, 1938, No. 1.

Tyler, L. E. *The psychology of human differences.* New York: Appleton-Century-Crofts, 1956.

Chapter 12

Visual and kinesthetic perception

The senses offer the means by which man learns from his environment. The sense organs, therefore, contribute greatly to the manner in which people respond. The senses which seem most strategic for motor learning and performance are those which relate to perception, from both external and internal stimuli, and particularly vision and kinesthesis. Even though other senses may prove important in certain physical performance situations, general applicability is not extensive. This chapter will therefore be devoted entirely to perception resulting from visual and kinesthetic cues. As with general intelligence, individuals differ in their capacities of kinesthesis and vision. In fact, abilities in these traits are distributed over a normal curve.

The relationship of vision and kinesthesis to the acquisition and performance of skills becomes clear when investigated closely. For example, vision is clearly a capacity which is both distributed over a wide range among different individuals and is strategic in motor performance. There are several types of visual abilities, each of which falls into a normal distribution curve much the same as do general intelligence scores. This is contrary to the often held concept that one's vision is either 20–20 or poor. The important role of vision in overall school performance makes an investigation important for all teachers. Physical education teachers, especially, should be familiar with (1) the different types of visual abilities, (2) the range of these abilities among different persons, (3) how each can be measured, and (4) their role in motor learning and performance.

VISUAL PERCEPTION

There are many kinds of school achievement in which visual perception plays a vital role. Teachers in several subject areas have only recently begun to gain a full realization of the important effect that the various visual capacities may have. One school activity which is very strongly influenced is that of motor-skill acquisition and performance. Recent research is beginning to answer some long-standing questions regarding the relationship of vision to athletic performance. For example, must one have exceptional vision to be an outstanding athlete? In what particular activities is good vision most beneficial? Can an individual develop or improve his depth perception or peripheral vision? In what activities can the visually handicapped person participate most effectively? Can visual tests be used as a screening device to determine one's potential for performing at a high level in certain activities.

In areas other than physical education, individual differences in vision also result in variations in performance. It seems likely that the person who learns to read with great speed has special visual abilities which may be measurable. Such abilities may be special inherited capacities or acquired skills. For efficiency and for safety in driver education or industrial arts, it is important that the individual's visual abilities be appraised. In addition, the student's ability in painting or other artistic work may be influenced by special perceptual abilities. Teachers in the arts, as well as those in physical education, have a particular interest in visual differences.

Some learning theorists have expressed great interest in visual perception. The gestalt psychologists especially emphasized that perception is intimately involved with learning. The manner in which one observes his environment is considered strategic to his learning. Despite their attention to perception, the gestaltists placed little emphasis on individual differences in vision and the role of these differences in learning. Neither did they identify or discuss the different types of visual abilities.

Unfortunately, thorough and scientific investigations of vision and its relationship to the learning and performance of motor skills have not been undertaken on a large scale. Perhaps this lack of attention has resulted from an assumption that differences in vision within the normal range are not important in performance. Although it has been accepted that a weakness in vision proves a handicap in activities in which seeing is important, little attention has been devoted to the possibility that outstanding vision might prove to be an asset. Some of the special visual abilities which have been identified in relation to motor performance will be discussed briefly.

Depth perception

Depth perception refers to the ability to distinguish the distance of objects or to make judgments about relative distances. This capacity, also called distance perception, adds the third dimension to height and width. Binocular vision (simultaneous vision with both eyes) is the primary basis for depth perception. The two eyes focus on an object from slightly different angles. These overlapping fields of view help to provide depth in one's perception. Monocular vision (seeing with one eye) tends to flatten things in the distance. In illustrating this concept, Bannister and Blackburn (1931) reported that rugby players had greater distances between their eyes than did nonplayers. The authors assumed that the players' greater interpupillary distance provided them with outstanding depth perception and, therefore, contributed to their playing ability. However, more recent research has not substantiated a relationship between interpupillary distance and depth perception.

In addition to binocular vision, the individual is aided in making judgments about the distance of objects by certain visual cues. The distinctiveness of the object, its relative size, its relative motion (in some cases), and its shadows may also aid one in making accurate judgments. Objects of a known size which are closer, beside, or farther away help the individual in estimating an object's size and distance. For example, when driving, the distance of an oncoming automobile can be guessed fairly accurately by observing its relationship to the highway and other objects in the visual field. At night, judgments are often based on the observed distance between, and the intensity of, the headlights. However, these guides may prove inadequate for passing, since a smaller-sized automobile with a shorter distance between the headlights would appear farther away.

In motor activities, there are many opportunities for making judgments about the distance of people or objects. For example, the passer in football needs to determine with considerable accuracy the distance of his receivers and his opponents. Similarly, the receiver must be able at all times to make an accurate judgment about the distance of the thrown ball. The golfer on the fairway must make an accurate estimate of the distance of the pin so that he can determine which club to select and how hard to swing. The high jumper, pole vaulter, or broad jumper in track needs to make an accurate estimation of the distance to the take-off point, or he will be required to make a last-second adjustment in stride. A misjudged fly ball in baseball results from a poor estimation of the distance and speed of the ball. The batter with poor depth perception is most susceptible to a change-up pitch. In most motor activities, and especially in ball games, the ability to distinguish distances is strategic to efficient performance.

Depth perception is generally assumed to be an inherited physiological trait which cannot be appreciably improved by practice. However, the ability to identify distances in terms of absolute measures can apparently be improved to some extent. Gibson and Bergman (1954) conducted an experiment in which individuals observed targets at distances ranging from 39 to 435 yards. During a pretest period, the subjects made eighteen different judgments and were told the correct distance after each. They had five practice trials of eighteen judgments each and a posttest. The percentage of error decreased considerably during the pretest trials but changed very little during the remaining practice and posttrials. Therefore, a short training period for judging distances seems to be implied for activities such as golf or field archery. The armed services often use similar techniques to train personnel for shooting in combat.

Olsen (1956), using the Howard-Dolman apparatus,[1] found that male college varsity athletes had better depth perception than did male students who participated in the intramural program. The intramural group in turn had significantly better depth perception than did a group of male students who had never participated in athletic activities on formal teams. Olsen assumed that depth perception was a necessary component for outstanding performance in the varsity team sports used in his study. He concluded that college athletes were able to perform at a higher level because of their greater inherent depth perception and that the trait was not being developed as a result of participation.

Montebello (1953) found a keener depth perception among baseball players than among nonplayers. However, there was no significant correlation between depth cues and batting averages among the players. Graybiel, Jokl, and Trapp (1955) reported that differences in depth perception were found between Olympic performers and nonperformers. He also found differences among performers in different sports activities. D. M. Miller (1960) showed depth perception to be one of the important distinctions between outstanding performers and low-skilled performers in a variety of sports activities. Krieger (1962) found that figure-ground perception (as measured by the Gottshaldt Embedded-Figures Test) was significantly related to spatial adjustment in tennis. He reported that college men and women with high figure-ground perception were better able to orient the racquet for successful ball contact. The relationship was greater for the more advanced performers.

In a study by Dickson (1953), however, no relationship was found between depth perception and basketball-shooting ability. He administered five tests of depth perception to three groups of college men. The groups were skilled, semi-skilled, and unskilled players. He found that the five measures of depth perception used did not identify those who performed well in the shooting tests.

---

[1] The apparatus was devised by Howard in 1919 to serve as a screening test for determining those aviation cadets who might not have keen depth perception. The test requires the subject to line up two black rods from a distance of twenty feet. The rods are mounted on parallel tracts and are maneuvered by tugging on the twenty-foot-long cords.

Peripheral vision

Peripheral vision is often called "field of vision" and refers to the ability of an individual to see to the side while looking straight ahead. This looking out of the corners of the eyes can be done without moving the head or the eyes. An individual who has very limited peripheral vision is said to have "tunnel vision." Peripheral vision is determined by the placement of rods and cones in the eyes. While looking straight ahead, most individuals are able to see about a 90° angle to each side, or a total field of vision of 180°. Among a group of normal individuals differences in peripheral vision range from approximately 155° to 205°. From a central point, it seems that most people see farther to the right than to the left. Peripheral vision cannot be appreciably improved by practice. One might, however, become more alert and possibly make greater use of his innate field of vision.

Peripheral vision has been measured with several types of apparatus. In using most apparatus, the head and eyes are held stationary while the subject is required to respond to stimuli which are presented on each side. In Olsen's (1956) experiment, the McClure perimeter was used. With this apparatus, the subject presses his face against a darkened periscope-type viewer which has movable arms on each side. As the arms swing farther to each side, the subject responds to miniature lights which flash in either or both arms. Some driver education programs have used a cruder method in which the subject's face is pressed against the apparatus while pegs are moved farther to each side until the subject indicates they are out of his visual range.

In his study to determine the relationship between certain physical capacities and proficiency in sports, Olsen (1956) found that varsity athletes in college had a wider range of vision than did those who did not take part in varsity sports. Also, intramural participants had greater peripheral vision than did college men who had no history of organized athletic competition. Olsen surmised that greater inherited peripheral vision aids one to perform at a higher level than persons with more limited vision. McCain (1950) reported slight visual differences between high school athletes and nonathletes. Stroup (1957) found that basketball players had above-average peripheral vision.

Graybiel et al. (1955) reviewed some research relative to peripheral vision which was conducted at the 1952 Olympic Games. A test project was set up in which athletes performed in various activities under conditions of normal vision, limited peripheral vision, central vision, and no vision (blindfolded). In javelin throwing, movements became clumsy, and the distances of the throws were significantly shorter when peripheral vision was excluded. The javelin also could no longer be thrown in a direction at right angles to the base line. The throwers with imposed limited peripheral vision reported that they were unable to see the tip of the javelin at the moment of maximal thrust of the arm, and this fact was believed to be responsible for the disorganization of the normal performance patterns. Throwing performances were poorest when vision was totally eliminated.

Discus performances were very poor when peripheral vision was excluded and best with unimpeded vision. Total elimination of vision proved at times to be less of a handicap than did interference with peripheral vision. Similar results were found with hammer throwers. In a 400-meter track race, no appreciable decline in efficiency was found with the elimination of peripheral vision.

With slalom skiers, the elimination of peripheral vision resulted in marked deterioration in performance. The athletes found it difficult to follow the course, and their judgments of distance were extremely poor. Figure skaters experienced a serious loss of symmetry, precision, and timing of movements when peripheral vision was excluded; on elimination of central vision, less difficulty was encountered than resulted from the exclusion of peripheral sight. Gymnasts experienced similar problems.

The importance of peripheral vision in sports activities is clear when one considers the many situations in which this lateral vision is essential. The middle man on a fast break in basketball needs to be able to see to each side without turning his head. The defensive football player with limited peripheral vision is likely to be hit from the "blind" side most often. In soccer, field hockey, and all other team sports, it is advantageous for the individual to be able to observe both teammates and opponents over a wide range. However, it seems that for certain other activities, such as track, tennis, golf, or bowling, the ability to see well to the side is not particularly important.

Individuals who have an especially limited visual field, either to the right or left, may be wisely placed in certain positions on the team so that their weakness will not play a major part in their performance. For example, the soccer forward with a weakness in vision to the right side may be positioned at right wing because in this position most of the action would be to his left side. Such a practice, however, is dependent upon accurate measurement of peripheral vision.

In activities other than sports, good lateral vision is often important for performance and for safety. The automobile driver who is entering an intersection or who is driving in the center lane of heavy traffic will have a safety advantage if he can see at wide angles to each side. It is also to the pedestrian's advantage to be able to see cars approaching from either side. In many work situations with moving machinery or vehicles, one's safety is enhanced if he has good vision to both sides.

Speed of vision

The speed with which individuals are able to observe objects may be discussed in terms of two types of capacities: (1) span of apprehension, and (2) pursuit movements. Span of apprehension refers to the individual's ability to observe several objects in a short period of time and retain a knowledge of what has been seen. This component may be measured by use of a tachistoscope which flashes several numbers, words, or images on to a screen for a short period of time. The subject then identifies what has been presented. Pursuit speed is the ability of the individual to visually follow an object or image which is moving at particular velocities. This component is often measured by use of high speed eye-movement cameras. As with other visual traits, people differ in speed of vision.

In Olsen's (1956) study, span of apprehension was measured by means of a tachistoscope which flashed black dots on to a white screen for one-fifth of a second. The number of dots varied from four to thirteen. After each exposure subjects were asked to write down the number of dots which appeared. If twelve dots were flashed, the individual did not have time to count to twelve by the one-two-three technique. Rather, he had to try to get an impression within one-fifth of a second and retain the image long enough to count during the brief period after the flash had passed. Subjects differed greatly in the ability to see and distinguish objects quickly. Olsen reported that almost all persons could accurately distinguish four or five dots within one-fifth of a second, but very few could consistently count twelve or thirteen accurately.

How is span of apprehension important in motor activities? Very often the player in a team game situation will look up and see the total field within his view. A quick analysis of the position of his opponents and teammates in relation to his goal can be of great importance. A momentary delay in seeing the set-up, if it results in a delay in decision and action, can allow compensatory actions on the part of opponents. The person with a limited span of apprehension will often make his move just a little too late. The halfback in football who breaks through the line of scrimmage must size up the situation and make a quick decision. There are many other situations in sports where a multiplicity of visual stimuli must be observed and analyzed in a minimum of time. Olsen reported a relationship between scores on his test and proficiency in team sports among college men. Perhaps this same speed of vision in spanning is what enables some children to span a greater number of words and therefore read faster than other children.

When one observes a moving object, the retinal image becomes blurred unless the eyes keep pace with the object. If the eye follows the moving object in a smooth sweep, vision of the object remains vivid. When this occurs, stationary objects within the field of vision become blurred. Individuals develop some skill in tracking objects as a result of learning what kind of movement to expect and by practicing. New visual activities involving movement, especially when the movement is caused by an external force, result in difficulties in focusing. After all, as the fixed object starts to move, the image is displaced from the center of vision. The individual must then make corrective movements in order to catch up to the target. The pursuit movement may be too fast or too slow until experience with the particular task has been gained. Individuals, however, differ in their ability to develop skill in tracking objects moving very fast. Some persons are able to develop a smooth pursuit movement while others must rely upon jerky (jump-pause, jump-pause) action. Hubbard and Seng (1954) and Mott (1954) have reported a relationship between pursuit speed and proficiency in motor skills.

General acuity

General visual acuity is a form of brightness discrimination which contributes to one's ability to see his way around, to read, or to take part in routine daily activities. This type of vision may be adequately measured by the Snellen eye-chart which contains rows of printed letters or symbols of decreasing size. The importance of visual acuity in most motor activities is clear. Just as a person on the street needs to see people in order to keep from walking into them, the player on the athletic field needs to see his opponents clearly so that he may avoid or intercept them and to see his teammates so that he may work with them.

Visual acuity among different individuals seems to be spread over a range which approximates a normal distribution with the typical person having 20–20 vision. This means that the individual with such vision can see at a distance of 20 feet what the average person can see at 20 feet. Almost all people fall within the 20–10 to 20–40 visual range. The child with 20–10 vision has excellent visual acuity in that he can see at 20 feet things that the average child can see only at 10 feet. Such outstanding visual acuity would appear to give the child an advantage in activities requiring keen vision at some distance. On the other hand, the child with 20–40 vision can only see at 20 feet what the average child can see at a distance of 40 feet. This unusually poor vision would prove a disadvantage in most activities requiring good vision.

When visual acuity has been weak enough to handicap an athlete's performance, glasses or contact lenses have been used with satisfactory results to improve the visual acuity of the performer. Performers in all sports activities are using glasses or lenses more than ever before. Traditionally, players have hestitated to wear glasses because of the fear of serious injury or the possible stigma attached to wearing them. It is not unusual today to find two or three players on a major league baseball team wearing glasses. If eye glasses can aid in overcoming visual acuity handicaps, they should be worn.

Other visual characteristics

Several other visual abilities seem to have a limited relationship to general motor performance. These include eye dominance, color vision, night blindness, and glare recovery. *Eye dominance* refers to the fact that one eye is stronger in acuity or is preferred for certain sightings over the other eye. It has generally been established that the right eye is dominant in most children. Special training does not appear to affect eye dominance. *Color vision* refers to the ability to make discriminations on the basis of wave length as well as intensity of light. *Night blindness* is a term used to indicate the unusual difficulty which some persons experience in becoming acclimated to relative darkness. *Glare recovery* refers to the ability of an individual to recover normal vision after being exposed to bright lights. The last three characteristics are especially important for the safe operation of an automobile.

Apparently the individual's total visual capacity is more important than particularly strong vision in any one of the components discussed. The gestalt, or combination of visual abilities, seemingly offsets a weakness which may exist in one area. This strength from the combined visual abilities appears to be present in certain outstanding athletes who are especially poor in one or more of the individual vision traits.

While most ball games and many other activities make great use of vision, many motor activities do not place such a high premium on visual perception. Vision is apparently of minor importance in swimming and in some types of dancing. Some outstanding swimmers and dancers have very poor vision. Some dances, however, do emphasize space perception and require the individual to coordinate his movements with those of his partner.

KINESTHESIS

Kinesthesis has often been referred to as the muscle sense or the motor sense. In addition, it has popularly been called the sixth sense because it was the first recognized addition to the original five senses. Although physiologists demonstrated the existence of the kinesthetic sense approximately a century ago, it is still relatively unknown to persons outside the scientific fields. Until very recently, a surprisingly small amount of study had been devoted to kinesthesis even in the scientific area. This neglect probably results from a number of factors including (1) problems and differences of opinion in defining kinesthesis, (2) difficulties in measuring it, and (3) problems related to isolating and studying kinesthesis without the interference of other senses.

Definitions

The kinesthetic sense is generally considered to be the "feel" or awareness of body position and body movement. However, more thorough and specific definitions offered by authorities may help to clarify and outline the scope of this capacity.

Scott (1955) defined kinesthesis as ". . . the sense which enables us to determine the position of segments of the body, their rate, extent, and direction of movement, the position of the entire body, and the characteristics of total body motion" (p. 325). According to Magruder (1963) kinesthesis is (1) the ability to recognize muscular contractions of a known amount, (2) the ability to balance, (3) the ability to assume and identify body position, and (4) the ability to orient the body in space. Phillips and Summers (1954) referred to kinesthetic perception as "the conscious awareness of the individual of the position of the parts of the body during voluntary movement" (p. 456).

After looking at these and other definitions, it can be noted that there is considerable agreement regarding the general meaning of kinesthesis. Four factors seem to be quite common in the many statements: (1) positioning of body segments, (2) precision of movement, (3) balance, and (4) space orientation. These concepts offer a basis for developing tests to measure kinesthesis. When tests have been developed, however, a great deal of specificity has been noted in kinesthesis. This in turn has required more specific listings of what abilities are to be measured.

Basis for kinesthesis

Most sense organs depend upon stimulation from outside the body. For example, the eyes, nose, ears, skin, and taste receptors receive external impulses. The kinesthetic sense, however, is dependent upon internal stimulation. Nerve endings, called spindles or proprioceptors, are located in the muscles, tendons, and ligaments, and apparently aid in the coordinated movement of the body. Labyrinthine receptors located in the inner ear are strategic for body balance. Both coordination and balance are important elements of kinesthesis.

Authorities do not entirely agree regarding the physiological basis for the kinesthetic sense. Traditionally, it has been assumed that the proprioceptors in the muscles are stimulated by contraction or stretching of the muscle cells. Tendon and ligament proprioceptors are stimulated by the stretching or movement which results from muscular contractions. The constant flow of stimuli from these receptors enables the individual to sense the position of the body part without the benefit of vision. In addition, he is able to make smooth coordinated movements and antigravity adjustments without even being conscious of sensations from receptors.

This explanation of kinesthesis is supported by Cooper and Glassow (1963) who identify the sense receptors as muscle spindles, Golgi tendon organs, and Pacini corpuscles. They state that each of these is stimulated by changes in tension, and nerve impulses initiated in them are conducted to the cerebral cortex where they serve as the basis for kinesthetic sensation and perception. The 1965 edition of *Neuro-Functional Anatomy* lists four types of proprioceptors as endings; the first three are related to the sense of position and movement, while free nerve endings (and Pacini corpuscles) are sensitive to deep pressure.

There is some difference of opinion, however, regarding the exact source of kinesthetic information. Rose and Mountcastle (1959) express doubt that stretch receptors in muscles provide information regarding movement or position. They state that ". . . it appears that classical proprioceptors may not contribute at all to the arousal of 'proprioceptive' sensations" (p. 388). Gardner (1963) also expresses the belief that muscle spindles do not play an important role in kinesthetic reception. Rather, she states the Ruffini endings and Pacini corpuscles are primarily responsible for kinesthesis. Thus, the precise source for the reception and transmission of kinesthetic information during movement has not been determined to the satisfaction of all those who have worked in this area.

Equilibrium, or balance, is very closely related to the overall kinesthetic sense. Just as the individual is aware of general position changes, he is also aware of head movement and position. Labyrinthine receptors located in the inner ear are activated by changes in head position or movements of the head in connection with movements of the body as a whole. The ability to assume good posture or to maintain an upright position when external force is exerted against the body is evidence of the usefulness of these receptors. Since effective motor performance is dependent not only upon coordinated body movement but upon balance control of the body, the equilibrium receptors are assumed to be part of the mechanism for kinesthesis.

Measurement of kinesthesis

Research in the area of kinesthesis has generally fallen into two categories: (1) studies dealing with the selection of tests and the measurement of kinesthesis, and (2) studies dealing with the relationship between kinesthesis and motor performance or learning. Even research in the second category has been forced to deal with the matter of measurement. The concept of kinesthesis is relatively easy to define, but is is very difficult to measure effectively. As a result, there is more consistency among the definitions than among the tests which have been developed. Although many evaluative tools have been used for measuring kinesthesis, most do not possess established validity.

Authorities who are most familiar with this topic have concluded that *the kinesthetic sense is not a general capacity.* Rather, it is composed of specific elements. For example, Scott (1955) suggested the following specific abilities as those which determine the kinesthetic sense: (1) muscular contractions of a known amount, (2) balance ability, (3) ability to assume and identify body positions, (4) precise use of the hands, and (5) orientation of the body in space. Others have developed different lists of specific abilities. Therefore, in order to measure kinesthesis, a number of different capacities must be measured. This requires not one but several tests. In attempting to measure the many elements involved in kinesthesis, various researchers have administered batteries of tests involving fifteen to twenty-five items. Very low correlations have usually been shown among the different tests. This lack of relationship has substantiated the belief that no single ability or single test item is sufficient to cover the total kinesthetic sense.

Analysis of the different measures of kinesthesis reveals that most test batteries are designed to measure the following capacities: (1) dynamic and static arm functioning, (2) thigh and leg functioning, (3) balance, and (4) vertical and horizontal arm movements. It is assumed that visual or tactile senses should not be used in these measures. No single test is adequate for measuring all these kinesthetic traits.

A second major problem encountered in testing for kinesthesis is similar to the difficulty in measuring other traits ranging from intelligence to motor ability. It is virtually impossible to select test items which are equally novel for all subjects. Research has shown that performance on most tests used in the measurement of kinesthesis can be improved with practice. Therefore, a basic question arises regarding the results of kinesthetic testing: Did the individual perform well because of a high degree of sensory capacity, or did his outstanding performance result from his previous experience in the test activity or an activity similar to it? Although there is little research on the subject, one is led to suspect that, like intelligence, kinesthetic performance is affected by both heredity and environment.

Typical tests of kinesthesis require the subject to perform the following types of activities:

1. Duplicate or assume a given space, position, or angle with the arms and legs.

2. Exhibit accuracy in arm movements on a horizontal and on a vertical plane.
3. Exert a given amount of force against some measurable resistance.
4. Jump a given distance or height.
5. Walk a certain pathway in a particular manner.
6. Throw an object for accuracy in direction or distance.
7. Touch or point at a particular target.

Phillips and Summers (1954) described one technique for measuring body alignment or position. In their study, subjects were blindfolded and asked to assume a certain standing position. A floodlight was placed in front of the subject which caused his shadow to be cast on a board which was marked off in degrees. The subject's score was determined by the number of degrees of variation from the desired position. A similar technique is used when the individual stands against a board which is marked off in degrees at fingertip distance from the body. Here the subject assumes different arm positions, and measurements are taken in variations from the desired position.

In summary, efforts to develop a test of kinesthesis have resulted in the conclusion that there are several specific elements which require a *battery* of tests for adequate measurement. Although several of these elements have been identified by different researchers, no agreement exists regarding the best means for measuring each of them. Since kinesthesis is assumed to be dependent upon the proprioceptors and labyrinthine receptors, it is generally concluded that tests for kinesthesis should not make use of one's vision. Finally, several of the tests used for kinesthesis have shown a high level of reliability, but validity has not yet been established.

Relationship of kinesthesis to motor performance

Several researchers have reported a high positive relationship between performance on kinesthetic tests and general tests of motor ability. In addition, it has been shown that outstanding athletes score higher on kinesthetic tests than do nonathletes. Conclusions from such studies, however, are limited by the unproven validity of the tests.

Phillips and Summers (1954) reported a relationship between motor-learning ability in bowling and kinesthesis. They classified 115 college women as fast and slow learners on the basis of improvement in bowling scores shown in twenty-four class periods. Then a kinesthetic test involving positional measures was administered to all subjects. The authors reported that kinesthesis was more highly related to early learning than to the later learning stages of bowling. In this study, the authors also reported a difference in kinesthetic perception between the preferred and nonpreferred arm. It was suggested that habitual use of the arm might result in this perceptual difference. In another study involving bowling, Greenlee (1958) found a relationship between dynamic balance and bowling, but not between measures of kinesthesis, strength, and static balance with bowling.

Mumby (1953) developed a test which required subjects to maintain constant pressure on a moving object. He then administered this test to twenty-one students in wrestling classes and reported that the better wrestlers scored higher. He concluded that wrestling ability is related to one's sensitivity to pressure and his ability to react accurately to it. Phillips (1939) administered several kinesthetic measures to sixty-three college men in a golf class. He reported a relationship between certain kinesthetic measures and putting ability, but little or no relationship with driving performance.

Clapper (1957) administered tests of kinesthesis to high school girls who were grouped into low, medium, and high socioeconomic levels. The tests involved target pointing, arm raising, finger spreading, and ball balancing. She reported a low correlation between motor-learning ability and the accumulative scores of the test battery. When test items were analyzed individually, insignificant findings were reported. She also reported that performance in the test items used in the study could be improved somewhat with practice. Wiebe (1954) reported that varsity athletes performed at a higher level than did nonathletes on twenty-one tests of kinesthetic ability. Taylor (1952) found that boys who were successful in making the varsity basketball team scored higher on a kinesthetic test than did unsuccessful candidates. Gross and Thompson (1957) reported that individuals who have better dynamic balance can swim faster and have better overall swimming ability than do individuals with poorer balance. The Bass test of dynamic balance was used to establish one's balance score.

Young (1945) investigated the relationship between kinesthesis and selected movements used in gymnastics and sports. A group of 37 college women took movement tests involving arm and leg movements, throwing, kicking, hitting, grip, and balance. Although some question was expressed regarding the validity of the kinesthetic test items used, the author concluded that there is a positive relationship between kinesthesis and some typical movements used in gymnastics and sports. In another experiment involving college women, Roloff (1953) administered the Scott motor ability test and eight tests for kinesthesis to 200 students in physical education classes which reflected different levels of ability. A positive relationship was shown between these two test batteries. Roloff concluded that there was merit in the kinesthetic tests used, and further, she developed a regression equation for a battery of the test items involving arm raising, weight shifting, arm circling, and the stick balance.

Norrie (1952) had instructors divide students in physical education classes into good and poor groups according to physical ability. A battery of kinesthetic tests was then administered to each group, and it was found that a positive relationship existed between performance in these tests and motor ability as evaluated by the instructors. Witte (1962), however, reported no relationship between positional measures of kinesthesis and the ball-rolling ability of boys and girls in the first and second grades. Also, there were no differences between boys and girls in these measures of kinesthesis.

Development of kinesthesis

The possibility of improving the kinesthetic sense has been of considerable interest to physical educators. However, the probability of improving a basic sensory capacity through practice seems remote. There is no convincing evidence that kinesthesis can in fact be improved. What *can* be improved is a particular position or movement response. Generally, the more one practices a certain response the more skillful he will become in that movement or similar movements. For example, Widdop (1963) showed that ballet training improved the ability of college students in limb positioning and limb position awareness. There is little doubt that such an activity might enable one to perform better on certain types of kinesthetic tests. Nevertheless, it appears that the Widdop study, as well as several similar ones, shows only that certain types of movements and positions can be learned.

Despite the assumption that no basic capacity of kinesthesis can be developed through a program of exercises, there appear to be distinct advantages for participating in a wide range of motor activities. Greater body control, balance, and movement skill should result from this widespread activity. The more movement responses and positions that the individual practices, the more likely he will develop some skill for movement behavior which will be required in the future. Therefore, the person who takes part in a variety of dance, gymnastic, and sports skills will probably be able to exhibit a higher score on any future measure of kinesthesis which involves bodily movement. Such a general development of movement skills gives the appearance of kinesthetic development. Actually, it only represents the development of skills which will be duplicated or transferred to similar skills in the future.

Use of kinesthesis in teaching

Persons with a keen kinesthetic sense apparently remember correct motor movements easily because of vivid position sensations received from the proprioceptors. For example, such an individual when learning to type develops an early awareness of what it feels like to touch each of the keys. Once this sensation has been established he can thereafter depress the correct key with the proper finger without looking. The finger will not often come down between keys or strike two keys at once. The same kinesthetic knowledge may be put to use by the piano player or by the automobile driver who is able to step on the brake pedal or the accelerator without looking.

In sports activities the ease and skill with which the individual is able to initially assume certain positions or execute particular movements is evidence of his level of kinesthesis. The individual with a high level of kinesthesis will therefore be able to easily repeat the proper starting position for track or football, or the baseball batting stance, once it has been done correctly the first time. In addition, he will be able to duplicate or execute a movement more consistently. The ability to regularly execute a cartwheel, fancy dive, or a baseball swing properly is evidence of good kinesthesis. In order to perform in this manner the individual must clearly sense the movement involved.

To perform effectively and consistently in motor skills, the learner must be guided by his own sensory clues. On the spot instruction by the teacher can be helpful, but in the final analysis the performer must know if he is performing correctly. He must develop a feel for the correct way to swing, to throw, or to jump. In most situations, instruction is necessary in order to effect the initial performance in gymnastics, dance or some other activity. Following this, the person must remember the sensations of the movement in order to duplicate it at a subsequent time.

The instructor can be helpful in enhancing the performer's kinesthetic awareness of the movement necessary for a particular response. In addition to the natural and obvious sensations which the learner receives without guidance, the teacher should help him in conceptualizing the movements for more conscious awareness of the sensations. This greater receptivity to the sensations from proprioceptors should aid the learner in reviewing the performance and mentally rehearsing for future performances.

Some aids are occasionally used by the teacher to promote proper mechanics in movement and student awareness of these responses. The traditional body mechanics technique of having students balance a book on the head while walking up and down stairs, sitting and standing, or walking around the room is one method. Techniques in sports include the use of the weighted golf clubs, baseball bat, or tennis racket (with press) to help the learner develop a proper follow-through. Such a weighted bat or club will *force* the individual to follow-through and perhaps experience this response for the first time. Once the correct movement is being performed, the instructor can be very helpful in alerting the performer to its sensations.

Selected Readings

Gagné, R. M., & Fleishman, E. A. *Psychology and human performance.* New York: Holt, Rinehart and Winston, 1959.

Graybiel, A., Jokl, E., & Trapp, C. Russian studies of vision in relation to physical activity and sports. *Res. Quart.,* 1955, **26**, 480–485.

Hochberg, J. *Perception.* Englewood Cliffs, N J.: Prentice-Hall, 1964.

Mueller, C. G. *Sensory psychology.* Englewood Cliffs, N.J.: Prentce-Hall, 1965.

Olsen, E. A. Relationship between psychological capacities and success in college athletics. *Res. Quart.,* 1956, **27**, 79–89.

Phillips, M., & Summers, D. Relation of kinesthetic perception of motor learning, *Res. Quart.,* 1954, **25**, 456–469.

Scott, G. M. Measurement of kinesthesis. *Res. Quart.,* 1955, **26**, 324–341.

Woodworth, R. S., & Schlosberg, H. *Experimental psychology.* (Rev. ed.) New York: Holt, Rinehart and Winston, 1963.

Chapter 13

Structural and dominance differences

One of the most obvious differences that one notices when he observes a group of boys and girls is the variation among their sizes and shapes. These differences are considerable from the time the children first enter school. Once the children start to participate in physical activities, whether they are writing, throwing, kicking, or swinging clubs, handedness and footedness become immediately apparent. For any age level, anthropometrical or structural differences are normally distributed over a wide scale. Such an even distribution does not exist in dominance since most children favor right-sidedness. However, among children who exhibit a right or a left dominance, there appear to be strengths or degrees of this dominance.

Differences in both structure and lateral dominance characteristics are related to learning and performance in motor skills in two important ways. First, these differences have an effect on how successfully, as well as the manner in which, the individual performs in various activities. In most school activities size differences have limited importance for performance, but this does not hold true in physical skills. Generally, the big child with a good physique will excel the child who is small or has a frail body structure. Although body structure alone cannot be used as a means for determining performance potential, it is one important factor. Differences in handedness or footedness affect the manner, and possibly the level, of performance. Adjustments on the part of the teacher and the child must be made in the case of left-handed children.

The second way in which structural and dominance differences are related to motor activity is influential in the development of these characteristics. Children who engage in vigorous activity from an early age will have a somewhat different structural development from children who are more restricted or limited in their activity. Similarly, the nature of one's early activity plays a role in the development of handedness or footedness. Physical educators have an excellent opportunity to observe, and possibly affect, both of these characteristics.

ANTHROPOMETRY

The term *anthropometry* refers to the investigation of variations in body structures. This topic has been of particular interest to physical educators because of the effect of body structure on performance, and the effect of physical activity on body structure. Certain other persons, including psychologists and medical doctors, have also shown an interest in this area because of the possible relationship between body type and personality, physical health, and mental health.

It is a truism in any sport that "A good big man can beat a good little man." The same principle holds for children in physical activities. In addition to greater maturity, the larger, well-developed children will have distinct performance advantages in general motor performance. Among older children and adults, specific performance advantages for particular types of body dimensions are not so clearly understood. Some authorities, though, have described particular physiques as best suited for various sports activities. They encourage greater investigation of this topic so that children and adults may be more intelligently guided in the selection of appropriate activities. Sills (1950) suggests that children be grouped, and therefore graded, in physical education according to their body type.

Today there are two general methods used to describe the physique of the individual. First, there is the classification of the total body into one of several categories. Traditionally, such descriptions as heavy, medium, and slender were used for classification. This is slightly subjective procedure, although the techniques are now reasonably well standardized. Second, the body may be described in relation to specific body proportions. For example, the length of the forearm, upper arm, lower legs, the trunk, or the total body may be measured and compared with the width of the hips and shoulders, the width and depth of the chest, the girth of the neck, upper arm, or waist. Such measurements and comparisons may be used as means for describing body structure. Each of these measurements, and many more, may be studied in relation to some other factor such as performance in some physical activity.

Historical background

It has long been recognized that no two human beings are exactly alike in physical characteristics. Man's interest in body variations and in ways of classifying them dates back more than two thousand years at least to the Athenian Greeks. Perhaps the people most influential in pioneering the area of anthropometry in relation to physical education have been Edward Hitchcock, in the latter half of the nineteenth century; Ernest Kretschmer, in the 1920's; and William Sheldon, in the 1940's.

Hitchcock (1893) at Amherst College began the first systematic work in anthropometric measurement in the United States. Measurements were taken on each student soon after he entered Amherst and again near the end of each school year. These measurements included ". . . eight items of age, weight, height, chest girth, arm girth, forearm girth, lung capacity and pulse. . . ." (p. 5). Each student was shown how he compared with others in these measurements, and how his own measurements had changed since previous measurement periods.

Kretschmer (1925) divided body types into the following classifications: (1) *asthenic*: characterized by a lack of thickness and width in all parts of the body and generally a low level of strength; (2) *athletic*: a vigorous body build with strong skeletal and muscular developments, and (3) *pyknic*: compact development of the body cavities and a great deal of fat distribution around the trunk. After working with mental patients for several years Kretschmer concluded that physique was related to temperament.

Today, the most widely used system for describing body types is the plan developed by Sheldon (1954). This system, which is similar to that of Kretschmer, uses the following terminology for describing three body types: (1) endomorphy: relative predominance of soft, round tissue throughout the body with short, heavy arms and legs, and a large midsection; (2) mesomorphy: relative predominance of muscle, bone, and connective tissue throughout body; a heavy, rectangular body outline; and (3) ectomorphy: relative predominance of linearity and fragility; a frail, thin body.

Body type and general motor performance

R. N. Walker (1952) reported that important relationships exist between the motor behavior and body types of two-, three-, and four-year-old children. Using Sheldon's terminology, he described mesomorphic children as having good gross coordination and being energetic. Thin ectomorphs, however, exhibited poor gross coordination with a lesser degree of energy and drive for active participation. Cunningham (1927) found that among nursery school children, body build was more important in the performance of gross motor tasks than was instruction or verbal ability. In a study of first-grade boys and girls, Bauer (1956) reported that boys of medium build tended to be stronger than boys of linear or lateral physique. For girls of this age, however, physique did not seem to be related to measures of strength.

Bookwalter (1952) investigated the relationship of body size to physical performance among 1,977 elementary school boys. Each boy's Wetzel Grid rating was compared with his performance on the Indiana Physical Fitness Test. Bookwalter reported that (1) boys of average size and thin physique perform better than boys of average size who have a medium physique; (2) very obese boys were the poorest performers of any group studied; (3) maximum size and shape do not produce maximum physical performance; (4) very large boys who are thin perform equally well with those who are average weight; and (5) large and fat boys vary more in physical performance than do normal or thin boys.

Cozens (1929) administered several tests of athletic performance to college men who were grouped according to weight. The tests included measures for strength, speed, jumping, throwing, kicking, diving, and agility. The author found distinct relationships between stature and athletic performance. Specifically, he reported that (1) both tall men and those of medium height were superior to short men; (2) heavier men were superior to slender ones; and (3) men of medium weight were superior to those who were slender.

Morris (1960) compared women athletes to unselected college women in body strength, anthropometric measurements, and somatotype. Comparisons were also made among athletes who competed in different sports. Significant anatomical differences between performers in particular sports were found in limb lengths, hip widths, and the ratio of shoulders to hips. The athletic group was more mesomorphic and less ectomorphic than were the unselected women. The athletes were generally rated as mesomorphic-endomorphs, whereas divers, gymnasts, and track women were particularly high in mesomorphy, and participants in hockey, basketball, swimming, softball, and golf were relatively high in endomorphy. Morris reported that total strength was not as important in athletic performance as was the ratio between strength and weight. Perbix (1954) found that women physical education majors in college exhibit high mesomorphic traits. She also reported a significant relationship between mesomorphy and knee push-ups but no relationship between body type and flexibility.

Hawthorne (1952) investigated the relationship between the somatotype ratings of college men and their performance on selected motor ability tests. The tests included strength, speed, jumping, throwing, and coordination items. The ectomorphic-mesomorphic group did best on these tests, while the mesomorphic-ectomorphic did poorest. In general motor ability, those high in ectomorphy were best and the mesomorphs were highest in strength items. Sills and Everett (1953) related performance in physical fitness items to the somototype of the participants. The authors reported that the mesomorphs did best, with the ectomorphs and endomorphs following in that order. Willgoose and Rogers (1949) reported that strength increases with mesomorphy, and that the fitness level of extreme mesomorphs is very high.

Physical size, with age, serves as the basis for two widely used methods of grouping children for physical activity. The McCloy *classification index,* long used as a means for class grouping and equating teams for athletic competition, includes the components of height, weight, and age. A different index is used for the elementary school, the high school, and the college levels. In the elementary school, only age and weight are used, thus indicating that height is not a major determinant for performance at this age level. The index for the college level includes only height and weight, but the high school index includes all three characteristics. The *Neilson and Cozens classification index* is very similar to that of McCloy except that it is limited to the elementary and high school levels. Both of these indices emphasize the role of height and weight in athletic performance.

Anthropometry and special skills

There is little doubt that mesomorphic individuals generally exhibit greater physical achievement than either ectomorphic or endomorhpic persons. However, a more refined analysis of limb lengths, hip and shoulder widths, and the relationships of various body parts is needed for a thorough knowledge of the physical characteristics for most efficient performance. It is clear at this time that the individual who is structurally most efficient for one activity may not be for others. In this regard, several investigators have described body types which are ideally suited to performance in particular activities.

Cureton (1941) reported that people with relatively long legs make good jumpers, runners, vaulters, and hurdlers. Individuals so structured, however, are weak in the performance of heavy and sustained work. However, short heavy-set people make good heavy laborers. He reported that performers in running and jumping events were high in ectomorphy, but weight men had a tendency toward endomorphy. All outstanding American athletes were high in mesomorphy. In a later study of champion athletes, Cureton (1951) reported that swimmers were heavier than track men, who are typically slight in skeletal framework. Track men also have long forelegs in relation to thighs and long overall legs compared to trunk length. Conversely, he found that wrestlers, gymnasts, weight lifters, and divers had longer and larger trunks in relation to limb length. The body density of the athletes was considerably greater than that of a sampling of normal men of comparable age.

After studying track and field competition at the Olympic games in Rome, Tanner (1946) arrived at several conclusions similar to those of Cureton. Tanner reported a gradient of decreasing mesomorphy and increasing ectomorphy as runners move from sprints to longer races. Sprinters were found to be muscular and relatively short (especially in the legs) when compared to middle-distance runners. Generally, he found that runners tend to be slim. High jumpers were tall men, with the shortest competitor being over six feet. Pole vaulters were found to have outstanding arm and shoulder development. Throwers were tall and heavy, with long arms in relation to their legs. Discus throwers, on the average, were the largest of all athletes. Weight lifters had short arms and legs in relation to trunk length.

Cobb (1936) also studied the relationship between body build and performance in special track events. He concluded that the large, heavily muscled athletes put the shot and throw the hammer the farthest. The leading high hurdlers were found to be tall, while the outstanding distance men were found to be medium to slender. DiGiovanna (1943) showed marked differences between the structural and functional measurements of various athletic groups and of a nonathletic group. Tests of strength and power, as well as body structural items, were administered to 836 college men. In addition to showing a general relationship between body structure and athletic success, he further reported that the sports of baseball, basketball, football, gymnastics, tennis, and track and field work seem to have their own unique patterns for success.

Racial differences

It has been observed that there are disproportionate percentages of persons from different racial groups in certain sports activities. For example, during the past half-century, boxing has had, during different periods, an abundance of Americans whose heritage was Irish, Italian, Negro, and Latin American. During recent years, Negroes have excelled in short-distance running events and jumping, but not in middle- and long-distance running events. They have also been outstanding in baseball and basketball, but not in swimming, golf, or tennis. For years, the Australians did especially well in swimming, and recently a team of five Japanese took the first four places in the Boston Marathon.

These occurrences have given rise to the question of why some groups seem to perform especially well in certain activities. Among the reasons offered has been the suggestion of anthropometric advantages of certain racial groups for some activities. Some related physiological differences have also been offered as a reason.

Aside from a few obvious situations, such as the height and weight disadvantage that oriental performers might have in basketball or American football, are there physical differences among racial groups which are important in athletic performance? Unfortunately, there has been much more speculation than research on this question. Wyndham, Strydom, Morrison, Peter, Williams, Bredell, and Joffe (1963) found that there was no difference among various ethnic groups in oxygen intake when the physical condition of the subjects was similar. This is contrary to alleged reports that Negroes are incapable of performing well in distance or endurance events because of limitations in lung physiology.

In an early study, Metheny (1939) reported numerous differences in anthropometric measurements between Negro and white students at the college level. She theorized that these differences offered the Negro advantages in athletic activities. She pointed out especially that the structure of the lower leg and ankle may offer some advantage in jumping events. However, no effort was made in her study to determine if there was a relationship between the observed structure and performance level. Despite the fact that Metheny's study has been quoted often since its publication, very little effort has been made to duplicate its findings. Neither has research demonstrated the relationship between the anthropometric characteristics described and outstanding athletic performance. In a comparison of Negro and white college women, however, Steggerda and Petty (1940) reported that all linear measurements of appendages were larger for the Negro group. The arm span of the Negro women was reported as 105 per cent of the standing height, whereas for the white group the relationship was 99 per cent.

Tanner (1964) described Negro athletes at the Olympic games as having longer arms and legs than white athletes competing in the same event. Also, Negro athletes had more muscle in the arms and thighs, but slenderer calves and hips. In a performance study, Hutinger (1959) found that Negro children in the elementary school ran faster in a thirty-five-yard dash than did white children at the same grade level. He suggested that the difference may have been due to a faster reflex time, although this was not tested in Hutinger's study. Age, size, and environmental differences wer not controlled or suggested as factors in the speed differences. Herzstein (1961) found that at the college level, Negro men had higher scores on the Sargent vertical jump test than did white men.

A word of caution must be offered regarding the tendency to categorize all athletes according to particular body dimensions. It has consistently been found that persons with widely differing somatotypes excel in each sport. Also, many who have an ideal body type for some activities fail to win over others who are apparently less well endowed. One must conclude, therefore, that there are many factors which go into making an outstanding performer. Body structure is only one of these components.

LATERAL DOMINANCE

Lateral dominance refers to the habitual use, in unilateral motor tasks, of one hand, foot, or eye in preference to the opposite member. In bilateral tasks, dominance is exhibited by the member which performs the more complex maneuvers or provides the greatest power. Other terms used in reference to the concept of lateral dominance are *laterality, preference, sidedness, dominance,* and in a more limited context, *handedness.*

In addition to common motor tasks, people exhibit sidedness in smiling, chewing, winking, sleeping positions, handling eating utensils, and many small manual skills. Lateral dominance and body asymmetry, with resulting habits, are characteristic to some extent of lower animals. The most easily observed aspect of lateral dominance in man is handedness. This trait also affects more movements and habits than the other dominance characteristics. As a result, most of the attention in the area of dominance centers on handedness.

Handedness has been a phenomenon of considerable social interest for centuries and in all cultures. Since the beginning of recorded history, man has been concerned with the occurrence and significance of left-handedness. Sinister moral and mental implications have been associated with this trait. Recent scientific interest has also been devoted to this topic and particularly to questions such as: Is handedness inherited, or is it developed as a result of environmental conditions? Can handedness be changed without resulting in stuttering or other emotional problems? Are there particular advantages or disadvantages in performing motor skills either right-handed or left-handed? Is it advisable to change handedness, and if so, how can this be done most effectively?

Several terms have been developed to describe the conditions which exist in lateral dominance. The predominant use of the right hand for unilateral skills is referred to as *dextrality.* When the left hand is used for such tasks this is called *sinistrality. Ambidexterity* refers to a condition in which the two hands exhibit approximately equal skill and are used to perform similar tasks. Perfect ambidexterity, however, is rarely found. Hildreth (1950) has inferred that most ambidextrous people are naturally left-handed but have acquired a great deal of skill with the right hand.

Homolaterality refers to the situation in which the hand, eye, and foot on the same side are dominant. *Contralaterality* is used to denote mixed dominance in which the individual has some dominance characteristic on each side, such as being right-handed and left-eyed. The term *ambisinistrality* has been used recently in reference to a condition in which neither hand has been developed to an adequate level of efficiency and, therefore, no dominance is present. This is contrasted with ambidexterity in which a relatively high level of skill has been developed in both hands.

The incidence of dominance

Percentages of lateral dominance of one type or another seem to vary with the particular culture. In the United States, it is estimated that approximately 5 per cent of the population is left-handed. However, the range in research reports often varies from about 3 to 12 per cent. It has been reported that in Russia and in China the percentage of left-handers is far less than in the United States. Anthropologists indicate that in some cultures, past and present, the proportion of left-handers to right-handers more closely approached a 50–50 ratio. According to Hildreth (1949a), incidence of left-handedness has run as high as 33 per cent in prehistoric times.

It has been theorized by one psychologist that about 25 per cent of the population are naturally right-handed, 25 per cent are naturally left-handed, and 50 per cent have no innate dominance. According to this theory, all those who are naturally right-handed remain so; all those with no dominance become right-handed; and most of the naturally left-handed persons develop a right-handed dominance.

Right-handedness has apparently prevailed in all cultures as far as man can trace. Tools, relics, and drawings, however, indicate that left-handedness was more prevalent among primitive men than among people today. The strong shift to right-handedness probably originated in religious ceremonies and was reinforced by the design of military weapons and methods. Superstitions which associated left-handedness with evil spirits resulted in great pressure for the development of right-handedness in all children. Dextrality then became a social code and a cultural law. Prejudice and superstition regarding sinistrality still exists in some cultures.

Incidence of lateral dominance seems to be related to the age and sex of the individual as well as to the culture in which he lives. Left-handedness is more common among boys and men than among girls and women. In a study of 13,438 elementary school children, Blair (1945) reported that 6.4 per cent of the children used the left hand for writing. Of this sinistral subgroup, 62 per cent were boys and 38 per cent were girls. Brain (1945) found that left-handedness was twice as common among males as females. Apparently boys are less concerned with conformity in laterality, or possibly they participate in more activities in which the left hand is developed. In addition to dominance preference, boys exhibit less strength difference between the hands than do girls. In one study, it was shown that among boys the strength difference between the right and left hand was 6 to 7 per cent, while among girls the difference was 10 to 12 per cent.

Children exhibit a greater degree of ambidexterity than do older persons. For example, more five-year-old children will show a right-handed dominance than will three-year-olds. In fact, during the first few years of life, there is a fluctuation in hand preference. The tendency toward right-handedness increases during the first few years of school. Thereafter, any significant change in handedness is rare. College students appear to have the lowest incidence of left-handedness of any group reported.

Simply reporting the number of people who are right-handed or left-handed does not present a complete picture of hand dominance. There appears to be *levels* or *degrees* of handedness which vary among people and among tasks. Rife (1951) has indicated that 5 to 8 per cent of the population are totally left-handed while 30 per cent are inclined to be left-handed in certain activities. The particular method used to identify or measure handedness makes a difference in the percentage reported. Some persons write with one hand but throw a ball with the other one. Some may swing a tennis racket with the right hand but swing a baseball bat from the left-handed side of the plate. In addition, some people have approximately equal strength in each hand while others have a great difference between the two. For these reasons, labeling a person as "right-handed" or "left-handed," or simply reporting the percentage of people who fall into each category, does not completely illustrate the status of handedness.

Dominance of the feet and eyes do not follow the extremely one-sided pattern which is prevalent in handedness. That is, a much higher percentage of people are left-footed or ambidextrous with the feet than are left-handed. This may be due to the fact that since foot dominance is less obvious, less pressure is exerted upon people to make dominant use of one foot. The situation often results in a condition of contralaterality. It is estimated that from 65 to 85 per cent of all right-handed people are also right-eyed, but probably a smaller percentage have foot dominance on the same side as hand dominance. In a study by L. M. Jenkins (1930), for example, it was reported that at age five, 3.3 per cent of the subjects exhibited both left-hand and left-foot dominance, whereas 7.7 per cent were left-handed and right-footed.

People are able to make a pretty accurate judgment of their hand dominance, but an accurate identification of foot dominance is more difficult. Even the selection of hand dominance can be troublesome, however, as reported by Fox (1963), who found that a sizable percentage of people preferred the use of the right hand even though tests indicated that the left hand was stronger and more skilled. Most people assume that the right foot will be greatly dominant, but left-handed people will select the left foot. In many activities, the individual performs in a manner which seems most natural without being aware of which leg is being used in a dominant manner. Personal judgments about eye dominance or leg dominance are often inaccurate. Visual tests, however, can easily be established for acuity, peripheral vision, or other capacities.

Measurement of lateral dominance

A series of tests must be administered before a clear determination can be made of the type or degree of handedness. Fuzak (1961) indicated that lateral dominance can be expressed only in terms of the traits measured. To be most accurate, therefore, one must indicate the skill or activity in which the person exhibits a preference. Since people exhibit different hand preferences for different activities, no single test can be adequate for measuring dominance.

One technique, which has been used in some studies, is to solicit information from the subject by means of a *questionnaire* or *interview*. Rather than seeking the subject's general estimation of his dominance, it is more accurate to ask specific questions about his habitual performance of certain routine tasks. For example, which hand does he use in cutting with scissors, writing, throwing a ball, or using a tennis racket? Also, in what manner does he swing a baseball bat, chop wood, or rake leaves? Which foot is used to kick a football, as a takeoff for a high jump or broad jump; and which leg is used for the hurdle step in diving? Such questions can give a fairly accurate picture of the individual's preferred or habitual use of hands and legs.

A second technique for determining functional handedness, footedness, or eyedness, is to have the individual actually *perform* tasks as the investigator observes. Such a procedure is often used with preschool children as they draw a picture, throw a ball, use a hammer, cut a form with scissors, screw nuts on a bolt, sight objects, or jump over an obstacle. This will provide information regarding functional dominance in cases where it cannot be given by the individual verbally.

Dominance may also be tested by administering a *series of tests* and comparing the strengths and weaknesses of different body parts in each. Tests of speed, strength, fine and gross dexterity, and skill level may be administered to both hands or both feet. Comparisons between the right and left can be made to determine not only the dominant member, but the amount of difference in each type of movement. Provins (1956) tested each hand of subjects for speed of tapping and for sensitivity to applied pressure against a steel bar. The same measures were administered to the big toe on each foot. In addition, an aiming test (dart throwing) was taken with each hand. Significant differences were found in tapping speed in favor of the preferred hand and in accuracy for the preferred hand. No differences were noted for the sensitivity test.

A comparison of the capacities of each hand and foot offers the most helpful means of classifying handedness and footedness. Manuometer tests can be administered to determine the strength of each hand. The ball throw for distance and for accuracy can provide a valuable comparison of the power and skill associated with each. Different dexterity and skill tests may be used for other types of comparison. Tests for leg strength, kicking for distance and accuracy, and jumping distance off each foot can provide similar comparisons. Only when such a battery of tests is used, can a thorough analysis be made of the individual's dominance.

Theories of dominance development

There are two major beliefs regarding the development of lateral dominance. One of these is that dominance is *inherited*. This theory holds that lateral dominance is caused by a dominant hemisphere of the brain which controls the opposite side of the body. Nevertheless, it is assumed that the opposite hand or foot can be trained to perform the chores generally performed with the naturally dominant hand or foot. The inheritance theory of dominance was perhaps more popular several decades ago than it is today. Beeley (1918), Rife, (1951), Brain (1945), and Tuttle and Travis (1935) offer empirical evidence to support this point of view. Rife, for example, pointed out that where one parent is left-handed, one out of six children is left-handed; where neither parent is left-handed, one child out of sixteen is left-handed.

The second major theory is that lateral dominance is strictly *developmental* in nature. According to this belief, all normal children can develop either a right or a left dominance with appropriate training from birth. This is, of course, opposite to the hereditary theory. In one investigation, Peterson (1934) was not able to demonstrate a hereditary factor in seven generations of rats. He concluded that if dominance is hereditary it does not follow a Mendelian recessive schedule. Hildreth (1949a) offers perhaps the most extensive case in support of the developmental nature of dominance and against the heredity theory with the following observations: left-handedness decreases sharply from infancy to adulthood; young children show an inconsistency in handedness; more boys than girls are left-handed (social influence); the percentage of left-handedness has increased due to modern techniques and freedom to the left-hander; mental defectives or untrainables have a higher ratio of left-handers than do the normal population; the skills most definitely right-handed are those which are specifically taught (such as writing, throwing, and eating); and skills which have previously been performed with the right hand can be learned with the left if the need arises.

Gesell and Ames (1947) conducted a study of eight children for several years as handedness was being developed. Moving pictures were taken periodically of each child engaging in varied motor activities. These movies were analyzed for the determination of handedness at the different age levels. The authors found that the development of lateral dominance does not take a straight course but fluctuates periodically. A typical case for a future right-handed person was described as follows:

16 to 20 weeks—exhibition of contact laterality, with the left hand slightly more active.

24 weeks—bilaterality.
28 weeks—unilaterality, with the right hand most often.
32 weeks—bilaterality.
36 weeks—bilaterality, with the left hand predominating.
40 to 52 weeks—four-week observations during this period revealed fluctuations between the right and left hand.
52 to 56 weeks—dominance of right hand.
80 weeks—interchangeable use of both hands.
2 years—clear use of right hand.
2½ to 3¼ years—some shift to bilaterality.
4 to 8 years—right hand generally predominant, with occasional shifts to bilaterality.

Other authors claim that hand dominance is developed as early as the fourth month. Sinclair and Smith (1957) indicated that dominance is firmly established by the eleventh or twelfth month. They point out that handedness develops from the general to the specific and from bilateral handedness to one-handed dominance. According to these authors, the dominant hand is used to learn early skills and assumes control in activities in which both hands are used. The recessive hand is used for support in two-handed activities and later may develop skill in tasks which have been previously learned with the dominant hand.

Characteristics of left-handed persons

It has often been asserted that stuttering or other speech defects are associated with left-handedness, and with children to whom attempts have been made to change handedness. Durost (1934) reported that sinistrality is linked with reading difficulties, stuttering and stammering, and a lack of physical coordination. He expressed the view that these difficulties resulted from both neural confusion and environmental pressures. It has also been reported that confusion resulting in opposite hand movements such as typing the letter *d* instead of *k*, or *i* instead of *e* is more prevalent among left-handed persons.

Several researchers have reported a disproportionate number of mentally retarded and defective persons to be left-handed. In one study of institutions for the feebleminded and psychopaths, K. L. Martin (1952) found from 16 to 30 per cent of the patients to be left-handed. Other studies have also reported three or four time as many left-handers in such institutions as are found in the general population.

Authors who have reported a connection between left-handedness and school failure or other difficulties have not usually suggested a cause-and-effect relationship. Rather, it has generally been theorized that the frustrations and pressures encountered by the left-hander in a right-handed culture have been considerable. Lack of success, lack of appropriate facilities or equipment, and efforts to subdue the preferred hand in favor of the unpreferred hand may result in *some* children developing emotional or motor development problems. Apparently, these problems do not adversely affect all, or even the majority, of left-handed children.

Traditionally, the left-handed person has been forced to modify or adjust to many situations in and out of school. For example, when the right-handed teacher explains or demonstrates the proper technique for throwing, batting, jumping, or kicking, the sinistral person is required to interpret or adapt this technique to the opposite side for his own purposes. Further, left-handed persons are required to use right-handed desks, tools, baseball gloves, bowling balls, and, in some cases, omit an activity entirely. In short, the left-hander is a member of a minority group. Some persons respond healthily to such stimulation, while others do not.

Some attention, recently, has been devoted to the need for developing a dominant side. It has been reported that individuals with no clear dominance and with little motor skill exhibit more severe problems than do persons with either a right or left dominance. Doman (1960) and Delacato (1963) reported that when a clear dominance is established in retarded children, significant motor and intellectual development will result.

Changing handedness

There are special problems which a left-handed person, growing up in our society, will naturally encounter. Some of these were alluded to in the previous section. For this reason, it has often been considered fortunate if a child naturally grew up to be right-handed. Furthermore, some parents and teachers have thought it desirable to change any children who seemed to be developing left-handedness. In some quarters, this desire to reverse handedness assumed a degree of urgency. Most often these attempts centered around the task of handwriting during the early school years.

Efforts to switch the handedness of children resulted in many problems (real and imaginary) of speech and general school progress. A fear of changing handedness, therefore, developed. Recent research, however, has cast serious doubt on the belief that attempts to change handedness will necessarily result in emotional or other problems. In fact, most authorities today do not feel that this procedure causes stuttering or is emotionally upsetting. However, particular attention should be devoted to the manner in which the change is attempted. One of the most extensive studies dealing with the reversal of writing-handedness was conducted by Blau (1946) in Elizabeth, New Jersey. In this study, an effort was made to reverse 250 students during the first years of school. Within a four-year period, all but 66 of the children were regularly writing with the right hand. No cases of defective speech or emotional problems were reported. It may be assumed that since 66 children were *not* reversed, undue pressure was not exerted upon them. While some children are quite susceptible to reversal training, others are very resistive. Blau's study points out that training to a degree sufficient for reversing most children may be conducted without emotional problems.

When attempting to change handedness among children, patience and understanding are needed to avoid emotional repercussions. It is also best that the reversal be attempted early, preferably before the ages of seven or eight, although some children can be changed years later. When developing the unpreferred hand, simple gross movements should be initiated. After some skill has been developed, finer and more complex tasks can be introduced. For example, in developing handwriting skill, large figures written on the chalkboard may serve as an appropriate preliminary activity for paper and pencil writing.

It is important that parents and educators keep in mind that children do not *have* to become right-handers. Before attempting to reverse the left-handers, some thought should be devoted to whether or not it is worth the effort. Accommodations are more readily available, and the culture is more tolerant of left-handers than ever before. In some situations, including certain sports activities, they appear to have an advantage. As a result of these developments, researchers indicate that the number of left-handed persons in this country is growing.

Lateral dominance and motor performance

In athletics it has often been suspected that left-handed performers had a slight advantage over right-handers when competing in a face-to-face situation. This was based on the assumption that the left-handed person is more used to such a confrontation than is the right-hander. For example, in combative activities, such as boxing, wrestling, fencing, and judo, the strengths and typical moves of the right-handed participant may be quite familiar to his left-handed opponent, whereas the reverse is not true. In football, the quarterback who rolls out to his left and throws with the left hand may cause some adjustment problems for the charging defensive lineman. In baseball, the left-handed pitcher may have a slight advantage because his delivery is not as common. However, in sports not requiring interacting competition, such as swimming, track and field, bowling, and gymnastics, handedness would seem to make little difference.

Research relating lateral dominance to motor proficiency has been slight. Several related studies, however, are reported in the literature. Sinclair and Smith (1957) investigated the relationship of hand, eye, and foot dominance to proficiency in swimming the crawl and side strokes. Subjects were freshmen and sophomore college women. The investigators reported that swimmers who breathe to the right side while doing the crawl stroke generally swim the side stroke on the left side. Similarly those who breathed to the left side in the crawl stroke did the side stroke on the right side. Dominance of the hand, eye, or foot was not established as important for side selection in swimming or breathing. Rather, the authors concluded that teaching methods and social customs were more important factors in determining sidedness in swimming.

Fox (1957) administered a response test to determine hand dominance of women students in a bowling class. Twenty subjects were selected who exhibited a left-handed dominance, but who preferred bowling with the right hand. In the experiment, sixteen of these subjects were taught to bowl with the preferred hand while four were taught to bowl left-handed. The two groups of students were equated in general motor ability. After equal sessions of practice, the right-handed bowlers performed better. In this particular study, therefore, the *preferred* hand proved more effective in bowling than did the *dominant* hand (as determined by Fox). Though the sample was very limited, the author theorized that the total body coordination and previous experience were perhaps as important in performance as was hand and arm dominance. It was suggested that hand preference rather than hand dominance be used as the basis for arm choice in bowling.

In another study, Fox (1963) investigated the dominance indices of girls with high and low motor ability. No difference was found between these ability groups in dominance indices. Mixed dominance was prevalent among both groups. From this study, she concluded that lateral dominance was not related to motor performance.

Way (1958) administered tests in archery, bowling, badminton, and tennis to 410 college women to determine the relationship between these activities and certain measures of lateral dominance. Hand, eye, and foot dominance were established for each of the subjects. Certain laterality measures seemed particularly important in activities stressing accuracy of direction toward a fixed target, such as archery and bowling. The author concluded that women with mixed dominance are superior in motor ability to those with homolateral preferences.

Teaching for ambidexterity

In many athletic activities, it is desirable for the instructor to teach for ambidexterity in the performance of the particular task because of the need for the performer to be able to use both hands or both feet skillfully. For example, in basketball the good player must be able to dribble or to shoot lay-up shots with both the right and left hand. If he does not have this ability with each hand, the defensive team will have a decided advantage by concentrating their attention against only one side. In soccer, the player who can kick with only one foot is limited in his effectiveness. In football, the ability to block or tackle on either side is advantageous. Many other examples can be brought to mind in which ambidextrous skill is essential for effective participation. In some activities, however, bilateral dexterity is not of particular value. In handwriting, playing tennis, pitching baseball, or shooting archery there is little advantage to having a high level of skill with the nondominant hand.

When developing skill in the nondominant or less skillful hand it is desirable to emphasize large and simple movements in the beginning. After some skill has been developed in basic, or fundamental, elements, practice can then begin with finer and more complex movements. This technique has been used where handwriting has been developed in the unpreferred hand for the reversal of handedness. Large, smoothly curved figures have usually been presented in the early sessions. The development of skill in the nondominant hand is therefore similar to the recommended practices for original learning.

When introducing soccer to a group for the first time, should skill in dribbling and passing be developed first with one foot or should practice take place with both feet concurrently? The advisability of simultaneous versus separate practices has not been clearly determined for gross motor skills. The possibilities for positive bilateral transfer as well as negative transfer (interference) must be considered in each situation. The majority of evidence suggests, however, that practice with both hands or both feet should proceed simultaneously. Lambert (1951) conducted a study in which male college students learned a novel two-handed psychomotor task. In this experiment, some subjects practiced the skill first with the dominant hand, while others practiced initially with the nondominant hand. The author concluded that for learning the two-handed task, it made little difference which hand was trained first. When subjects switched from the use of a single hand to the use of two hands, poorer performance resulted. Lambert recommended, therefore, that attention be devoted to training both hands concurrently.

SELECTED READINGS

Blau, A. The master hand. *Amer. orthopsychiatr. Ass. Res. Monogr.*, 1946, No. 5.

Cureton, T. K. *Physical fitness of champion athletes.* Urbana, Ill.: Univer. of Illinois Press, 1951.

Delacato, C. H. *The treatment and prevention of reading problems.* Springfield, Ill.: Charles C Thomas, 1959.

Garrity, H. M. Relationship of somatotype of college women to physical fitness performance. *Res. Quart.,* 1966, **37,** 340–352.

Gesell, A., & Ames, L. B. The development of handedness. *J. genet. Psychol.,* 1947, **70,** 155–175.

Hildreth, G. The development and training of hand dominance: I. characteristics of handedness. *J. genet. Psychol.,* 1949, **75,** 197–220.

Jones, H. E. *Motor performance and growth.* Berkeley, Calif.: Univer. of California Press, 1949.

Metheny, E. Studies of the Johnson test of motor educability. *Res. quart.,* 1939, **9,** 105–114.

Provins, K. A. Handedness and skill. *Quart. J. exp. Psychol.,* 1956, **8,** 79–95.

Sheldon, W. H. *Atlas of men.* New York: Harper & Row, 1954.

Sills, F. D. Anthropometry in relation to physical performance. In W. R. Johnson (Ed.), *Science and medicine of exercise and sports.* New York: Harper & Row, 1960.

Tanner, J. M. *The physique of the Olympic athlete.* London: G. Allen, 1964.

Chapter 14

Reaction and movement speed

An important behavioral characteristic in which individuals differ greatly is speed of reaction. This component seems strategic in distinguishing between outstanding, average, and poor performers in many motor skills. Athletic coaches have traditionally assumed that the best athletes are those with the fastest reaction time. For this reason, they have shown considerable interest in the speed of reaction and in determining the performers who can move most rapidly. Experimental psychologists have also exhibited a great deal of interest because reaction speed is one of the important response variables among people and because it is conveniently available for rather objective measurement.

Reaction time versus movement time

Several meanings are often attached to the term "reaction time." Some people use it in reference to such traits as the ability to get quick starts, i.e., to take the first few steps most rapidly, or to have quick movements. Others have a more limited concept of the term. For the measurement of reaction time, some physical educators and psychologists have restricted the subject's response to small, finger movements. Occasionally, large motor responses have been used. To clarify the issue, reaction time and movement time will be discussed as components of speed of reaction.

Reaction time is the period from the stimulus to the beginning of the overt response. It is not what the term might seem to imply, i.e., the time occupied by the execution of the response. Rather, reaction time is the time required to get the overt response started, or the stimulus-to-response interval. Following the stimulus, there is a latent period while the impulse is transmitted from the sense organ to the central nervous system and then back to the muscles. The muscles must then contract to begin movement. Although all of these actions take some time, the most time is probably taken in the motor areas of the brain. This is especially true if any decision making is required. According to Woodworth and Schlosberg (1963), reaction time ". . . includes sense-organ time, brain time, nerve time, and muscle time" (p. 8). In experimental situations the measurement of reaction time has involved some simple response such as releasing or depressing a button or telegraph key. Since even these small responses require some movement through a distance, they are not "pure" measures of reaction time, but they have been acceptable as reasonably accurate.

In addition to reaction time, movement time has been of special interest to athletic coaches and physical educators. Experimental psychologists, on the contrary, have not investigated or discussed this component widely. *Movement time* refers to the period from the beginning of the overt response to the completion of a specified movement. In the measurement of movement time, a rather large movement is usually employed. The total movement response, therefore, encompasses both reaction and movement times; reaction time being the stimulus-response interval, and movement time being the period required for the response itself. The term "reaction time" has occasionally been used erroneously to include both of these concepts, even when the movement phase was quite long.

The concept of movement time has been developed because of the interest of physical educators in how quickly an individual can do something which might be important in a motor activity. Athletic coaches have been interested in determining which players can perform certain acts most rapidly. For example, in a bully situation in field hockey, can the person move fast enough to gain control of the ball? The same question would apply in a drop-ball situation in soccer. In other situations, does the player have quick hands so that he can catch a fast moving ball or one that suddenly appears from a short distance? The individual with fast movement time exhibits this capacity in numerous sports situations. Speed of movement is, therefore, quite different from the speed of the neural impulses in reaction-time testing.

It has traditionally been assumed that there is a rather high relationship between reaction time and movement time. That is, the individual with a fast reaction time was believed to be able to move more quickly or to run faster than a person with a slower reaction time. This particular question has been investigated quite thoroughly during the past few years. As a result of this research, considerable doubt has been cast on the traditional assumption. According to Guilford (1958) and Henry (1952), the natures of reaction time and movement time are quite different.

Guilford (1958) classified *impulsion* (the rate of starting movements from a stationary position) and muscular strength as general factors which are primarily dependent upon heredity. *Speed* (the rate of movement after it is initiated), static precision, dynamic precision, coordination, and flexibility are listed as traits which seem to be dependent upon experience. According to Guilford, therefore, simple reaction time (impulsion) is inherited, while the movement phase of reaction time (speed) is developed. This would suggest little, if any, relationship between the components of reaction and movement time.

Henry (1961b) stated ". . . muscular force causes the speed of a limb movement, whereas reaction latency reflects the time required for a pre-movement operation of a central nervous system program-switching mechanism" (p. 65). Movement time, on the other hand, is caused by muscular force. On the basis of these concepts and his research, he suggests a zero correlation between the two traits. This is contrary to the widespread beliefs of some coaches and physical educators.

Hodgkins (1962) found that reaction time and movement time were unrelated for subjects ranging in age from six to eighty-four. In several studies, Henry (1952, 1960a, 1960b, 1960c) found no relationship between reaction time and speed of movement. Slater-Hammel (1952) and L. E. Smith (1961) have also reported insignificant correlations between these two components. However, Kerr (1966), Pierson and Rasch (1959), and Hipple (1954) have reported statistically significant correlations between measurements of reaction time and movement time. They theorize that reaction time is an aid to one's movement speed. It appears, however, that the majority of research generally supports no relationship.

Another question which has been investigated during recent years is the *generality of reaction time,* i.e., do people who have fast reaction with the right hand also have fast reaction with the left hand, the feet, or other parts of the body? Evidence regarding this topic is rather inconsistent. Seashore and Seashore (1941) reported a high correlation among the reaction time of hands, feet, and even biting movements. In their study, the speed of the hands did not differ greatly from each other, nor did the speed of the feet. These correlations demonstrated a high degree of individual consistency. However, they did show that foot movement was slower than hand movement. Rangazas (1957) also reported hand movement to be faster than foot movement. After an extensive study with children between the ages of seven and thirteen, McArthur (1957) differed with Seashore and Seashore's assumption of generality in bodily movement speed. He found no relationship among the movement speed of various parts of the body, or among different types of movement. McArthur concluded that: "No satisfactory conclusions regarding the general response patterns of subjects can be drawn from a series of testings based on one neuromuscular response such as the tapping of a finger, the flexion of a hand or the extension of a foot" (p. 128).

Simple and choice reaction time

In the literature and in discussions of speed of reaction, a distinction is made between simple reaction time and choice reaction time. In *simple reaction time* testing, the individual may be asked to make a simple response, such as depressing or releasing an electric key or switch when a light goes on. Under these conditions, one type of stimulus is given, and one response is solicited. When the stimulus of light is used in such an experiment, reaction time will generally be in the vicinity of .20 to .25 seconds. If a buzzer or another sound stimulus is used, the time will be slightly less. These times are relatively fast because there are no alternatives which the subject must consider. He knows in advance what stimulus to expect and what response he should make.

In *choice reaction time*, there are alternatives for the subject to consider. Other terms used in reference to this type of response are *discriminative* or *disjunctive* reaction. It might be that a red light requires the depression of key 1, while a green light requires the depression of key 2. In such an experiment of choice reaction, the stimuli are alternated in an irregular order. The subject, therefore, must observe the stimulus and make a choice of which response is appropriate. Needless to say, the time for choice reaction is slower than that for simple reaction. The choices might vary from two to five or ten. It has been found that the greater the number of choices, the slower is the reaction.

Researchers are interested in both simple and choice reaction time. In sports, there are numerous occasions when the player must make a decision on the most appropriate response. For example, the batter must make a decision whether or not the ball will be a strike before starting his swing. The defensive halfback must decide whether he has a chance for an interception on a pass, or whether he should stay back and play the receiver. On other occasions, a simple movement response is called for. The defensive guard in football, for example, looks for a single stimulus (movement of the ball by the center) as a key to his making a single, predetermined response (charging into the opposing player).

In nonathletic situations, similar reactions must be made. Most often, reactions in the adult world require a choice. The automobile driver, upon entering an emergency situation, must decide the most appropriate response. He may slam on the brakes, speed up, blow the horn, or steer the car to the right or to the left. In such a situation, it is of little value for the response to be fast if it is the wrong response. Certain workday situations require that the worker "grade" products before they are processed. This necessitates a selection of several choices and the corresponding responses. In other occupations, however, simple reactions are often the rule. In routine machine work, especially, the worker expects one type of stimulus and is prepared to make one type of response. In such a situation involving rapid response, a fast, simple reaction time is most advantageous.

There is no doubt that there are *individual differences* in reaction time. All researchers report differences among individuals, whether the testing is on simple reaction, choice reaction, or movement time. Within individuals, however, there are a number of factors which contribute to speed of reaction.

Factors affecting reaction time

The reaction time of an individual depends upon several variables. These variables may be classified as (1) external: principally dealing with the stimulus; or (2) internal: having to do with the state of the individual. Several of these conditions can be controlled by the experimenter. A thorough knowledge of them is therefore essential if the tester is to get optimum reaction speeds, or if he is to get accurate measures which can be compared. In addition, some knowledge of the influential conditions is essential if the reader is to make valid judgments about particular research reports. The most important variables affecting reaction time will be discussed briefly. The first two of these, of course, are external, having to do with the stimuli used, while the remainder deal with the individual's condition.

Stimulation of the sense organs. In pioneer work on reaction time at Columbia University, Cattell (1947) found that which sense organ is stimulated makes a difference in the speed of reaction. He established the following order of senses for speed from fastest to slowest: hearing, seeing, pain, taste, smell, and touch. This order has generally been corroborated by other researchers. Rangazas (1957) also showed that reaction to sound was faster than reaction to vision. However, it has been shown that touch may elicit as fast a response as sound, especially when the more sensitive spots, and those closest to the brain are used. In testing, the senses of sight, hearing, and touch are relatively easy to isolate and stimulate separately. However, the senses of taste and smell, as well as the temperature receptors, are extremely difficult to stimulate suddenly without affecting the touch receptors. Mowbray (1960) found that choice reaction is improved when more than one sense is stimulated simultaneously. From various studies, it seems evident that the individual who reacts quickly to one stimulus also reacts quickly to others.

Intensity of the stimulus. Cattell reported that the intensity or strength of the stimulus makes a difference in the speed of reaction. Research by

Rangazas substantiated this conclusion. A very loud noise is likely to result in a faster response than noise at a lower intensity. The sharp sponse than would the oral command, "Go." When color is used as a sound of a starter's gun in track should therefore elicit a quicker re-stimulus, a brilliant or vivid color will result in a faster reaction than the softer shades. The general physical setting of visual stimuli also affects one's response. Similar findings regarding the effect of more intense stimuli seem to prevail for the other senses. Woodworth and Schlosberg (1963) after reviewing the research, suggest that each increase in intensity of stimulus results in a faster reaction time. The decrements become smaller and smaller with each subsequent increase in stimulus. The correlation between reaction time and intensity is a curving rather than a straight line. It seems, therefore, that above a certain point, additional increases in intensity of stimulus would not prove beneficial.

Height of readiness. Researchers have long been interested in the period of greatest attention, or the time at which the subject is likely to exhibit the fastest reaction. This is an important factor in the speed of reaction. Investigators have consistently found that the peak of attention does not last indefinitely. If the foreperiod is too short, the subject will not have time to get sufficiently ready; but if it is too long, the readiness will gradually fade away. Cattell (1947) suggested the period between two and four seconds following the stimulus as the moment for maximum response. Other recent researchers have generally established the period of highest concentration as from one to three seconds following the stimulus.

General muscular tension is natural during the foreperiod. This tension is especially evident in the muscle to be used in the expected response. R. C. Davis (1940) attached electrodes to the skin over the muscles to study muscular tension during expectant periods. He concluded that muscular tension begins about .20 to .40 seconds after the "ready" signal and tends to increase until the moment of reaction. He also found that the reaction was quickened with greater tension.

Knowledge about the moment of greatest readiness has significance for physical education teachers and athletic coaches. Starters in a sprint race in track are interested in the length of delay between set and the gun. If the length of the foreperiod is regular, tension will be greatest at the point of expected stimulus, and the reaction quicker. Starting signals in football, from the time the team is down in position until the snap of the ball, should be arranged to fall within the period of maximum concentration. Of course, efforts may also be made to avoid the opposing team's maximum readiness period. Either a long count or a quick snap of the ball may prove effective. The pitcher in baseball, after coming to a set position with a man on base, often tries to avoid a regular one-second delay, either by waiting a shorter or a longer period, in order to evade the period of highest attention for either the batter or the runner.

Practice as a factor. The effect of practice on the speed of reaction has been investigated by a number of individuals. These investigations have been aimed at determining whether reaction time, as usually measured, is inherited or developed. Simple reaction time is so routine that one would expect a person to reach his maximum after a very few trials, i.e., once he gets the idea. However, Woodworth and Schlosberg (1963) report that the average person continues to improve for several days or for several hundred trials, though change after the first fifty or one hundred trials is slight. About a 10 per cent improvement is shown after the first day of practice. Blank (1934) showed very small diminishing values for practice after the first day. McArthur (1957) administered five trials of a reaction time test to boys and girls. He found the fourth and fifth trials were faster than the first. For the five trials, there seemed to be gradual improvement. Hodgkins (1962), however, reported that reaction time was not significantly improved from the first through the tenth trial. Tweit, Gallnick, and Hearn (1963) found that total body movement time can be improved. This was "movement time" as previously defined, and they concluded that athletes may develop this type of reaction.

Age. During the developmental years, reaction time improves rapidly. As the peak period is approached during the late teens and early twenties, there is a leveling off of speed of reaction. After the adult level has been reached, there is very little change up to the age of sixty. The lengthening of reaction time begins to occur rapidly when the individual approaches feebleness. Miles (1929) showed that maximum speed of reaction was reached at about twenty-five, and practically no change was evident up to age sixty. Hodgkins (1962) reported that peak reaction time was reached at age nineteen, and noted a greater drop-off than Miles by age sixty. In her study, movement speed and reaction time developed and deteriorated in almost identical patterns, even though there was no relationship between the two components.

Sex. Hodgkins (1962) and Rangazas (1957) showed that males are faster than females in both reaction and movement time. Also, peak performance is maintained longer among males in movement time. Females, however, retained a relatively high level longer in reaction time. McArthur (1957) found boys to be faster than girls in movement time, and boys were also less variable.

Drugs and alcohol.   The effect of drugs on one's reaction time has long been a matter of interest to researchers. Cattell (1947) found that alcohol slows reaction time to the extent that it is evident in the blood system. The detrimental effect of alcohol and several drugs on reaction time has been shown by a number of recent investigators. Straub (1938) reported that reaction time is lengthened by 10 per cent when the alcoholic content in the blood reaches .35 and by 24 per cent when the 1.4 level of alcohol in the blood is reached. This problem has been especially important in traffic safety research. Most drugs, when taken in normal doses, do not have an appreciable influence on reaction time. When large doses are absorbed, most drugs slow one's reaction and speed of movement. However, certain drugs have recently been found to improve reaction time slightly. Nevertheless, use of these drugs for the purpose of improving speed has been strongly discouraged. Since the possibility of harmful or habit-forming effects has not been determined, such drugs have no place in school athletic programs at this time.

Reaction time and athletic performance

Westerlund and Tuttle (1931) reported a high relationship between reaction time and running speed in the seventy-five-yard dash. Several subsequent studies, however, have failed to show a relationship between reaction time and running speed or similar activities. On the other hand, correlations have been reported quite frequently between general athletic performance and various measures of speed of movement. Most studies designed to determine the relationship between reaction time and performance have compared individuals of different ability or experience in athletics.

Keller (1940) reported a relationship between movement time and athletic ability among male subjects. He found that athletes performed better in "quickness of movement" than nonathletes at both the high school and college levels. He also found that team-sport athletes (baseball, football, track) were quicker than individual-sport athletes (wrestlers, gymnasts, swimmers). Olsen (1956) found that varsity athletes in college exhibited faster reaction times than did intramural participants who, in turn, showed greater speed than nonathletes. In another study of male athletes, Wilkinson (1958) reported that athletes had a faster reaction time than nonathletes. Further, he found that wrestlers and baseball players exhibited greater speed than did several other groups of athletes. In a study by Cureton (1951), champion athletes in different sports activities were shown to have different reaction speeds. Pierson (1959) reported significant differences between male fencers and nonfencers in movement speed.

In a study of women athletes and nonathletes, Younger (1959) found the athletes to be significantly faster than the nonathletes. Also, among the athletic group, performers in different sports differed in speed of movement, but not in reaction time. Swimmers tended to be the slowest movers, but, among the others (field hockey, fencing, and tennis performers), no difference was found in movement speed. In an earlier study, Beise and Peaseley (1937) also found that skilled women had faster reaction times than did unskilled women.

SELECTED READINGS

Cattell, J. McK. The influence of the intensity of the stimulus on the length of the reaction time. *Brain,* reprinted 1947, **9**, 512–515.

Guilford, J. B. A system of psychomotor abilities. *Amer. J. Psychol.,* 1958, **71**, 164–174.

Henry, F. M. Factoral structure of speed and static strength in a lateral arm movement. *Res. Quart.,* 1960, **31**, 440–447

Hodgkins, J. Reaction time and speed of movement in males and females of various ages. *Res. Quart.,* 1963, **34**, 335–343.

Olsen, E. A. Relationship between psychological capacities and success in college athletics. *Res. Quart.,* 1956, **27**, 79–89.

Slater-Hammel, A. T. Reaction time and speed of movement. *Percept. mot. Skills, Res. Exch.,* 1952, **4**, 109–113.

Woodworth, R. S., & Schlosberg, H. *Experimental psychology.* (Rev. ed.) New York: Holt, Rinehart and Winston, 1963.

References

Abel, T. A comparison of tactual, kinesthetic, and visual perception of extent among adults, children and subnormals. *Amer. J. Psychol.*, 1936, **48**, 269–296.

Adams, A. R. A test construction study of sport-type motor educability for college men. Unpublished doctoral dissertation, Louisiana State Univer., 1954.

Adams, J. A. *An evaluation of test items measuring motor abilities.* Lackland AFB, Texas: Air Force Personnel and Train. Res. Cen., Res. Report 56-55, 1955.

American Association for Health, Physical Education, and Recreation. *AAHPER Youth Fitness Test Manual.* Washington, D. C.: Author, 1965. (a)

American Association for Health, Physical Education, and Recreation. *This is physical education.* Washington, D. C.: Author, 1965. (b)

Ammons, H., & Irion, A. L. A note on the Ballard reminiscence phenomenon. *J. exp. Psychol.*, 1954, **48**, 184-186.

Ammons, R. B. Rotary pursuit performance with continuous practice before and after a single rest. *J. exp. Psychol.*, 1947, **37**, 393–411.

Ammons, R. B. Le movement. In G. H. Seward & J. P. Seward (Eds.), *Current psychological issues.* New York: Holt, Rinehart and Winston, 1958.

Ammons, R. B., & Willig, L. Acquisition of motor skill: effects of repeated periods of massed practice. *J. exp. Psychol.*, 1956, **51**, 118–126.

Anastasi, A. *Psychological testing* (2nd ed.) New York: Macmillan, 1961.

Anderson, G. L., & Gates, A. T. The general nature of learning. *Yearb. nat. Soc. Stud. Educ.*, 1950, **49**, 12–35.

Arnold, M. B. Physiological differences of emotional states. *Psychol. Rev.*, 1945, **52**, 35–48.

Asmussen, E., & Heebell-Nielsen, K. A dimensional analysis of physical performance and growth in boys. *J. appl. Psychol.*, 1955, **7**, 593–603.

Astrand, P. O. *Experimental studies of working capacity in relation to sex and age.* Copenhagen: Munksgoard, 1952.

Ausubel, D. P. *The psychology of meaningful verbal learning.* New York: Grune & Stratton, 1963.

Ausubel, D. P., Schiff, H. M., & Goldman, M. Qualitative characteristics in the learning process associated with anxiety. *J. abnorm. soc. Psychol.*, 1953, **48**, 537.

Bachman, J. C. Specificity vs. generality in learning and performing two large muscle tasks. *Res. Quart.*, 1961, **32**, 3–11.

Bagley, W. C. *The education process.* London: Macmillan, 1905.

Baker, K. E., & Wylie, R. C. Transfer of verbal training to a motor task. *J. exp. Psychol.,* 1950, **40,** 632–638.

Baker, K. E., Wylie, R. C. & Gagné, R. M. Transfer of training to a motor skill as a function of variation in rate of response. *J. exp. Psychol.,* 1950, **40,** 721–732.

Baker, K. E., Wylie R. C., & Gagné, R. M. The effects of an interfering task on the learning of a complex motor skill. *J. exp. Psychol.,* 1951, **41,** 1–9.

Baker, R. F. The effects of anxiety and stress on gross motor performance. Unpublished doctoral dissertation, Univer. of California, Los Angeles, 1961.

Baller, W. R., & Charles, D. C. *The psychology of human growth and development.* New York: Holt, Rinehart and Winston, 1961.

Bannister, H., & Blackburn, J. H. An eye factor affecting proficiency at ball games. *Brit. J. Psychol.,* 1931, **21,** 382–384.

Barch, A. M. The effect of difficulty of task on provocation facilitation. *J. exp. Psychol.,* 1953, **46,** 37–43.

Bauer, T. A. Body build as a factor related to variations in strength and tissue components of first grade children. Unpublished doctoral dissertation, Univer. of Wisconsin, 1956.

Bauer, W. W., & Hein, F. V. *Exercise and health.* Chicago: A.M.A., 1958.

Bayley, N. Some comparisons between growth in motor and in mental abilities in young children. *Psychol. Bull.,* 1934, **31,** 608.

Bayley N. The development of motor abilities during the first two years. *Soc. Res. in Child Develpm. Monogr.,* 1936, No. 1.

Bayley, N. Some psychological correlates of somatic androgeny. *Child Develpm.,* 1951, **22,** 47–60.

Bayley, N., & Espenschade, A. Motor development from birth to maturity. *Rev. educ. Res.,* 1941, **11,** 562–572.

Beeley, H. An experimental study in left handedness. *Univer. of Chicago Suppl. Educ. Monogr.,* 1918, No. 8.

Behavioral Research Laboratories. *American health and safety series.* Palo Alto, Calif.: Author, 1966.

Beise, D., & Peaseley, V. The relation of reaction time, speed, and agility of big muscle groups to certain sport skills. *Res. Quart.,* 1937, **8,** 133–142.

Bell, H. M. Retention of pursuit rotor skill after one year. *J. exp. Psychol.,* 1950, **40,** 648–649.

Belmont, L., & Birch, H. G. Lateral dominance and right-left awareness in normal children. *Child Develpm.,* 1963, **34,** 257–270.

Bennett, C. L. The relative contributions of modern dance, folk dance, basketball, and swimming to selected and general motor abilities of college women. Unpublished doctoral dissertation, Indiana Univer., 1956.

Bernard, H. W. *Psychology of learning and teaching.* (2nd ed.) New York: McGraw-Hill, 1965.

Bigge, M. L., & Hunt, M. P. *Psychological foundations of education.* New York: Harper & Row, 1962.

Bills, A. The influence of muscular tension on the efficiency of mental work. *Amer. J. Psychol.,* 1927, **38,** 227–251.

Bilodeau, E. A. (Ed.) *Acquisition of skill.* New York: Academic Press, 1966.

Birney, R. C., & Teevan, R. C. (Eds.) *Reinforcement; an enduring problem in psychology.* Princeton, N. J.: Van Nostrand, 1961.

Blake, O. W., & Volpe, A. M. *Lead-up games to team sports.* Englewood Cliffs, N. J.: Prentice-Hall, 1964.

Blank, G. Brauchbarkeit Optischer Reaktionsmessungen. *Indust. Pstechnik,* 1934, **11,** 140–150.

Blau, A. The master hand. *Amer. orthopsychiatr. Ass. Res. Monogr.,* 1946, No. 5.

Bloom, V. S. *Taxonomy of educational objectives.* New York: McKay, 1956.

Bontz, J. Some problems in physical education in the elementary school. *J. Hlth, phys. Educ., Recreat.,* 1948, **19,** 406–407, 440–441.

Bookwalter, K. The relationship of body size and shape to physical performance. *Res. Quart.* 1952, **23,** 271–279.

Bortner, D. M. Pupil motivation and its relationship to the activity and social drives. In W. C. Morse & G. M. Wingo (Eds.), *Readings in educational psychology.* Chicago: Scott, Foresman, 1962.

Brace, D. K. *Measuring motor ability, a scale of motor ability tests.* New York: Barnes, 1927.

Brace, D. K. Studies in motor learning of gross motor skill. *Res. Quart.,* 1946, **17,** 242–254.

Brain, R. Speech and handedness. *Lancet,* 1945, **249,** 837–841.

Bray, C. C. Transfer of learning. *J. exp. Psychol.,* 1928, **11,** 443–467.

Breeding, B. A. A study of the relative effectiveness of two methods of spacing archery practice. Unpublished master's thesis, Univer. of Colorado, 1958.

Breen, J. L. Anxiety factors related to some physical fitness variables. Unpublished doctoral dissertation, Univer. of Illinois, 1959.

Bruner, J. S. *The process of education.* Cambridge, Mass.: Harvard, 1963.

Bryant, W. L. On the development of voluntary motor ability. *Amer. J. Psychol.,* 1892, **5,** 123–204.

Burack, B., & Moss, D. Effect of knowing the principle basic to solution of a problem. *J. educ. Res.,* 1956, **50,** 203–208.

Burns, P. L. The effect of physical practice, mental practice and mental-physical practice on the development of a motor skill. Unpublished master's thesis, Pennsylvania State Univer., 1953.

Buros, O. K. (Ed.) *The sixth mental measurements yearbook.* Highland Park, N. J.: Gryphon Press, 1965.

Burt, C., & Moore, R. C. Mental differences between the sexes. *J. exp. Psychol.,* 1922, **6,** 355–361.

Burtt, H. E. An experimental study of early childhood memory: final report. *J. genet. Psychol.,* 1941, **58,** 435–439.

Cain, L. F., & Willey, R. deV. The effect of spaced learning on the curve of retention. *J. exp. Psychol.,* 1939, **25,** 309–214.

Calfee, M. College freshmen and four general intelligence tests. *J. educ. Pedag.,* 1913, **24,** 227.

Calvin, S. An analysis of the effect of progressive heavy resistance exercise on the motor coordination of a group of high school boys ages fourteen to eighteen. Unpublished doctoral dissertation, Univer. of Maryland, College Park, 1958.

Cannon, W. B. *Bodily changes in pain, hunger, fear and rage.* (2nd ed.) New York: Appleton-Century-Crofts, 1929.

Carmichael, L. The history of mirror drawing as a laboratory method. *Pedag. Seminary & J. genet. Psychol.,* 1922, **34**, 90–91.

Carpenter, A. Strength, power, and femininity as factors influencing the athletic performance of college women. *Res. Quart.,* 1935, **9**, 120–127.

Carroll, H. A. *Genius in the making.* New York: McGraw-Hill, 1940.

Cattell, J. McK. The influence of the intensity of the stimulus on the length of the reaction time. *Brain,* reprinted 1947, **9**, 512–515.

Child, I. L., & Whiting, J. W. Determinants of level of aspiration: evidence from everyday life. *J. abnorm. soc. Psychol.,* 1949, **44**, 303–314.

Clapper, D. J. Measurement of selected kinesthetic responses at the junior and senior high school levels. Unpublished doctoral dissertation, State Univer. of Iowa, 1957.

Clark, L. V. The effect of mental practice on the development of a certain motor skill. *Res. Quart.,* 1960, **31**, 560–569.

Clarke, H. H. *Application of measurement to health and physical education.* (4th ed.) Englewood Cliffs, N. J.: Prentice-Hall, 1967.

Clarke, H. H., & Greene, W. H. Relationships between personal-social measures applied to 10-year-old boys. *Res. Quart.,* 1963, **34**, 288–298.

Clinton, R. J. Nature of mirror drawing ability: norms on mirror drawing for white children by age and sex. *J. educ. Psychol.,* 1930, **21**, 221–228.

Cobb, W. M. Race and runners. *J. Hlth, phys. Educ., Recreat.,* 1936, **7**, 1–9.

Coladarci, A. P. (Ed.) *Educational psychology.* New York: Holt, Rinehart and Winston, 1955.

Cole, L. E., & Bruce, W. F. *Educational psychology.* New York: Harcourt, Brace & World, 1959.

Colville, F. M. The learning of motor skills as influenced by knowledge of mechanical principles. *J. educ. Psychol.,* 1957, **48**, 321–327.

Cook, B. S., & Hilgard, E. R. Distributed practice in motor learning: progressively increasing and decreasing rests. *J. exp. Psychol.,* 1949, **39**, 169–172.

Cook, T. W. Massed and distributed practice in the learning of rats. *Psychol. Rev.,* 1934, **41**, 330–355. (a)

Cook, T. W. Studies in cross education: kinesthetic learning of an irregular pattern. *J. exp. Psychol.,* 1934, **17**, 749–762. (b)

Cooper, J., & Glassow, R. *Kinesiology.* St. Louis: Mosby, 1963.

Corbin, C. The effects of mental practice on the development of a unique motor skill. NCPEAM Proc., 1966.

Cozens, F. W. The measurement of general athletic ability in college men. *Univer. of Oregon phys. Educ. Ser.,* 1929, **1**, No. 3.

Crampton, C. W. Physiological age—a fundamental principle. *Child Develpm.,* 1944, **15**, 1–52.

Cratty, B. J. Comparison of learning a fine motor task with learning a similar gross motor task, using kinesthetic cues. *Res. Quart.,* 1962, **33**, 212–221.

Cratty, B. J. *Movement behavior and motor learning.* Philadelphia: Lea & Febiger, 1964.

Cronbach, L. J. Book review. *J. educ. Psychol.*, 1954, **45**, 314–317.

Cronbach, L. J. *Educational psychology* (2nd ed.) New York: Harcourt, Brace & World, 1963.

Cross, T. A comparison of the whole method, the minor game method, and the whole-part method of teaching basketball to 9th grade boys, *Res. Quart.*, 1937, **84**, 49–54.

Cumbee, F. Z., Meyer, M., & Paterson, G. Factoral analysis of motor co-ordination variables for third and fourth grade girls. *Res. Quart.*, 1957, **28**, 100–108.

Cunningham, B. V. An experiment in measuring gross motor development of infants and young children. *J. educ. Psychol.*, 1927, **18**, 458–464.

Cureton, T. K. Body build as a framework of reference for interpreting physical fitness and athletic performance. Suppl. to *Res. Quart.*, 1941, **7**, 301–330.

Cureton, T. K. *Physical fitness of champion athletes.* Urbana, Ill.: Univer. of Illinois Press, 1951.

Cureton, T. K. Improving the physical fitness of youth. *Monogr. soc. Res. in Child Develpm.*, 1964, **29**, No. 4 (Serial no. 95).

Dahlern, G. G. Gestalt approach to tumbling. *J. Hlth, phys. Educ., Recreat.*, 1960, **31**, (No. 1), 38.

Daniel, R. S. The distribution of muscular action potentials during maze learning. *J. exp. Psychol.*, 1939, **24**, 621–629.

Dashiell, J. F. A survey and synthesis of learning theories. *Psychol. Bull.*, 1935, **32**, 261–275.

Davis, E. C., & Lawther, J. D. *Successful teaching in physical education.* (2nd ed.) Englewood Cliffs, N. J.: Prentice-Hall, 1948.

Davis, R. A. *Psychology of learning.* New York: McGraw-Hill, 1935.

Davis, R. C. Set and muscular tension. *Indiana Univer. Sci. Ser.*, 1940, No. 10.

Day, R. H. Relative task difficulty and transfer of training in skilled perform-ance. *Psychol. Bull.*, 1956, **53**, 160–168.

Deese, J. *The psychology of learning.* (2nd ed.) New York: McGraw-Hill, 1958.

Delacato, C. H. *The treatment and prevention of reading problems.* Spring-field, Ill.: Charles C Thomas, 1959.

Delacato, C. H. *The diagnosis and treatment of speech and reading problems.* Springfield, Ill.: Charles C Thomas, 1963.

Dembo, T. Der Arger als dynamishers. *Psychol. Forsch.*, 1931, **15**, 1–144.

Dennis, W., & Dennis, M. G. The effect of cradling practices upon the onset of walking in Hopi children. *J. genet. Psychol.*, 1940, **56**, 77–86.

Deterline, W. A. *An introduction to programmed instruction.* Englewood Cliffs, N. J.: Prentice-Hall, 1962.

Dickson, J. F. The relationship of depth perception to goal shooting in basket-ball. Unpublished doctoral dissertation, State Univer. of Iowa, 1953.

DiGiovanna, V. G. A comparison of the intelligence and athletic ability of college men. *Res. Quart.*, 1937, **8**, 96–106.

DiGiovanna, V. G. The relation of selected structural and functional measures to success in college athletics. *Res. Quart.*, 1943, **14**, 199–216.

Doman, G. *Treatment procedures utilizing principles of neurological organi-*

zation. Philadelphia: Inst. for Achievement of Human Potential, 1964.

Doman G., et al. Children with severe brain injuries. *J.A.M.A.*, 1960, **174**, 257–262.

Doré, L. R., & Hilgard, E. R. Spaced practices and the maturation hypothesis. *J. Psychol.*, 1937, **4,** 245–259.

Doré, L. R., & Hilgard, E. R. Spaced practices as a test of Snoddy's two processes in mental growth. *J. exp. Psychol.*, 1938, **23**, 359–374.

Douglass, H. R., & Kittleson, K. L. An experimental evaluation of a modified Morrison procedure in teaching American history. *J. exp. Educ.*, 1935, **4**, 20–25.

Duffy, E. The psychological significance of the concept of arousal or "activation." *Psychol. Rev.*, 1957, **64**, 265–275.

Duncan, C. P. The effect of unequal amounts of practice on motor learning before and after rest. *J. exp. Psychol.*, 1951, **42**, 257–264.

Durost, W. N. The development of a battery of objective group tests of manual laterality with the results of their application to 1300 children. *Genet. Psychol. Monogr.*, 1934, **16** (4), 229–335.

Eason, R. G. Relation between effort, tension level, skill and performance efficiency in a perceptual-motor task. *Percept. mot. Skills*, 1963, **16**, 297–318.

Eason, R. G., & White, C. T. Relationship between muscular tension and performance during rotary pursuit. *Percept. mot. Skills,* 1960, **10,**199–210.

Eason, R. G. & White, C. T. Muscular tension, effort and tracking difficulty: studies of parameters which affect tension level and performance efficiency. *Percept. mot. Skills,* 1961, **12**, 331–373.

Eaton, M. L. The conditioned reflex technique applied to a less specialized type of learning. *J. exp. Educ.*, 1937, **6**, 68–83.

Ebbinghaus, H. *Uber das Gedachtnis: Untersuchungen Zur Experimentellen Psychologie.* Leipzig: Dunker and Humblet, 1885.

Ebbinghaus, H. *Grundzüge der Psychologie.* (3rd ed.) Vol. I. Leipzig: Veit, 1911.

Edwards, A. L. The retention of affective experiences—a criticism and restatement of the problem. *Psychol. Rev.*, 1942, **49**, 43–53.

Egstrom, G. H. Effects of an emphasis on conceptualizing techniques during early learning of a gross motor skill. *Res. Quart.*, 1964, **35**, 472–481.

Eichorn, D. H., & Jones, H. E. Maturation and behavior. In G. H. Seward & J. P. Seward (Eds.), *Current psychological issues.* New York: Holt, Rinehart and Winston, 1958. Pp. 211–248.

Ellis, W. D. *A source book of gestalt psychology.* New York: Harcourt, Brace & World, 1938.

English, H. B., Welborn, E. L., & Killian, D. C. Studies in substance learning and retention. *J. genet. Psychol.*, 1934, **16**, 233–260.

Espenschade, A. Motor development. *Rev. educ. Res.*, 1947, **17**, 354–361.

Espenschade, A. Kinesthetic awareness in motor learning. *Percept. mot. Skills,* 1958, **8**, 142.

Eysenck, H. J. The measurement of motivation. *Sci. Amer.*, 1963, **208** (May), 130–140.

Farber, L. E., & Spence, K. W. Complex learning and conditioning as a function of anxiety. *J. exp. Psychol.*, 1953, **45**, 120–125.

Fitzhugh, K. B., & Fitzhugh, L. C. Effects of early and later onset of cerebral dysfunction upon psychological test performance. *Percept. mot. Skills,* 1965, **20,** 1099–1100.

Fleishman, E. A. A relationship between incentive motivation and ability level in psychomotor performance. *J. exp. Psychol.,* 1958, **56,** 78–81.

Fleishman, E. A. *The structure and measurement of physical fitness.* Englewood Clifts, N. J.: Prentice-Hall, 1964.

Fleishman, E. A. The perception of body position in the absence of visual cues. *J. exp. Psychol.,* 1953, **46,** 261–270.

Fleishman, E. A., & Parker, J. Factors in the retention and relearning of perceptual-motor skill. *J. exp. Psychol.,* 1962, **64,** 215–226.

Fort, M. A study of the emotions of high school football players. Unpublished doctoral dissertation, Boston Univer., 1959.

Fox, G. The relation of dominance to motor ability. Paper read at AAHPER nat. Convent., Minneapolis, Minn., April, 1963.

Fox, M. G. Lateral dominance in the teaching of bowling. *Res. Quart.,* 1957, **28,** 327–331.

Frank, J. D. Individual differences in certain aspects of the level of aspiration. *Amer. J. Psychol.,* 1935, **47,** 119.

Franklin, J. C., & Brozek, J. M. Relation between the distribution of practice and learning efficiency in psychomotor performance. *J. exp. Psychol.,* 1947, **37,** 16–24.

Freeman, G. L. The optimal muscular tension for various performances. *Amer. J. Psychol.,* 1938, **51,** 146–150.

Frostig, M., & Horne, D. *The Frostig program for the development of visual perception.* Chicago: Follett, 1964.

Fuzak, J. A. Physical maturation and fine motor coordination. In T. L. Harris & W. E. Schwahn (Eds.), *Selected readings on the learning process.* New York: Oxford, 1961. Pp. 365–379.

Gage, N. L. *Metatechnique in educational research.* Urbana, Ill.: Univer. of Illinois Bur. educ. Res., 1961.

Gagné, R. M. Training devices and stimulators: some research issues. *Amer. Psychologist,* 1954, **9,** 95–107.

Gagné, R. M. *The conditions of learning.* New York: Holt, Rinehart and Winston, 1959.

Gagné, R. M., & Fleishman, E. A. *Psychology and human performance.* New York: Holt, Rinehart and Winston, 1959.

Gagné, R. M., & Foster, H. Transfer of training from practice on components in a motor skill. *J. exp. Psychol.,* 1949, **39,** 47–68.

Gardner, E. *Fundamentals of neurology.* Philadelphia: Saunders, 1963.

Garfiel, E. The measurement of motor ability. *Arch. Psychol.,* 1923, **9,** 1–47.

Garrity, H. M. Relationship of somatotype of college women to physical fitness performance. *Res. Quart.,* 1966, **37,** 340–352.

Garry, R. *Psychology of learning.* Washington: Cen. appl. Res. Educ., 1963.

Gates, G. The effect of an audience upon performance. *J. abnorm. soc. Psychol.,* 1924, **18,** 333–341.

Gerdes, G. R. The effects of various motivational techniques upon performance in selected physical tests. Unpublished doctoral dissertation, Indiana Univer., 1958.

Gesell, A., & Ames, L. B. The development of handedness. *J. genet. Psychol.*, 1947, **70**, 155–175.

Gesell, A., & Thompson, H. Learning and growth in identical infant twins. *Genet. Psychol. Monogr.*, 1929, **6**, 1–124.

Getman, G. N., & Kane, E. R. *The physiology of readiness.* Minneapolis: P.A.S.S., Inc., 1964.

Ghisselli, E. Changes in neuro-muscular tension accompanying the performance of a learning problem involving constant choice time. *J. exp. Psychol.*, 1936, **19**, 91–98.

Gibson, E. J., & Bergman, R. The effect of training on absolute estimation of distances over the ground. *J. exp. Psychol.*, 1954, **48**, 137–149.

Gire, E., & Espenschade, A. The relationship between measure or motor educability and the learning of specific motor skills. *Res. Quart.*, 1942, **13**, 43–56.

Graybiel, A., Jokl, E., & Trapp, C. Russian studies of vision in relation to physical activity and sports. *Res. Quart.*, 1955, **26**, 212–223.

Greenlee, G. A. The relationship of selected measures of strength, balance and kinesthesis to bowling performance. Unpublished doctoral dissertation, State Univer. of Iowa, 1958.

Greulich, W. W., & Pyle, S. I. *Radiographic atlas of skeletal development of the hand and wrists.* Stanford, Calif.: Stanford, 1959.

Grimaldi, J. V. Sensori-motor performance under varying noise conditions. *Ergonomics*, 1958, **2**, 34–43.

Grose, R. F., & Birney, R. C. *Transfer of learning.* Princeton, N. J.: Van Nostrand, 1963.

Gross, E. A., & Thompson, H. L. Relationship of dynamic balance to speed and to ability in swimming. *Res. Quart.*, 1957, **28**, 342–346.

Guilford, J. B. A system of psychomotor abilities. *Amer. J. Psychol.*, 1958, **71**, 164–174.

Guthrie, E. R. *The psychology of learning.* (Rev. ed.) New York: Harper & Row, 1952.

Gutteridge, M. V. A study of motor achievements of young children. *Arch. Psychol.*, 1939, **34**, No. 244, 1–178.

Hahn, H. H., & Thorndike, E. L. Some results of practice in addition under school conditions. *J. educ. Psychol.*, 1914, **5**, 65–84.

Hale, C. J. What research says about athletics for pre-high school age children. *J. Hlth, phys. Educ., Recreat.*, 1959, **30**, 19–21.

Halverson, L. E. A comparison of three methods of teaching motor skills. Unpublished master's thesis, Univer. of Wisconsin, 1949.

Hamblen, A. A. An investigation to determine the extent to which the effect of the study of Latin upon a knowledge of English derivatives can be measured by conscious adaptation of content and methods to the attainment of this objective. Unpublished doctoral dissertation, Univer. of Pennsylvania, 1925.

Hammerton, M. Retention of learning in a difficult tracking task. *J. exp. Psychol.*, 1963, **66**, 108–110.

Harby, S. F. *Comparison of mental practice-physical practice in the learning of physical skills.* Human Engineering Report. S.D.C. 269–27 to Spec. Device Cen. Office of Naval Res. Prepared at Pennsylvania State Coll., 1952.

Harlow, H. F. The formation of learning sets. *Psychol. Rev.,* 1949, **56,** 51–56.

Harmon, J. M., & Johnson, W. R. The emotional reactions of college athletes. *Res. Quart.,* 1952, **23,** 391–397.

Harmon, J. M., & Miller, A. G. Time patterns in motor learning. *Res. Quart.,* 1950, **21,** 182–187.

Harmon, J. M., & Oxendine, J. B. Effect of different lengths of practice periods on the learning of a motor skill. *Res. Quart.,* 1961, **32,** 34–41.

Harris, T. L., & Schwahn, W. E. (Eds.) *Selected readings on the learning process.* New York: Oxford, 1961.

Harrison, V. F. A review of the neuromuscular bases for motor learning. *Res. Quart.,* 1962, **33,** 59–69.

Havighurst, R. J. *Developmental tasks and education.* New York: McKay, 1950.

Havighurst, R. J. Educational imperatives in a changing culture. Speech at Schoolmen's Week, Univer. of Pennsylvania, March, 1966.

Hawthorne, J. J. Somatotype and its relationship to selected motor performance of college men. Unpublished doctoral dissertation, Univer. of Texas, 1952.

Hebb, D. O. *The organization of behavior: a neuropsychological theory.* New York: Wiley, 1949.

Hebb, D. O. *A textbook of psychology.* Philadelphia: Saunders, 1958.

Hellebrant, F. A. *Education.* December 1961.

Hellebrant, F. A., & Waterland, J. C. Indirect learning. The influence of unimanual exercise on related groups of the same and opposite side. *Amer. J. phys. Med.,* 1962, **41,** 44–55.

Hendrickson, G., & Schroeder, W. H. Transfer of training in learning to hit a submerged target. *J. educ. Psychol.,* 1941, **32,** 205–213.

Hennis, G. M., & Ulrich, C. Study of psychic stress in freshmen college women. *Res. Quart.,* 1958, **29,** 172–179.

Henry, F. M. Increase in speed of movement by motivation and by transfer of motivated improvement. *Res. Quart.,* 1951, **22,** 219–228.

Henry, F. M. Independence of reaction and movement times and equivalents of sensory motivators of faster response. *Res. Quart.,* 1952, **23,** 45–53.

Henry, F. M. Specificity vs. generality in learning motor skills. *Annu. Proc. Coll. phys. Educ. Ass.,* 1958, **61,** 126–128.

Henry, F. M. Factoral structure of speed and static strength in a lateral arm movement. *Res. Quart.,* 1960, **31,** 440–447. (a)

Henry, F. M. Increased response latency for complicated movements and a "memory drum" theory of neuromotor reaction. *Res. Quart.,* 1960, **31,** 448–457. (b)

Henry, F. M. Influence of motor and sensory sets on reaction latency and speed of discrete movements. *Res. Quart.,* 1960, **31,** 459–468. (c)

Henry, F. M. Stimulus complexity, movement complexity, age, and sex in relation to reaction latency and speed in limb movements. *Res. Quart.*, 1961, **32**, 353–366. (a)

Henry, F. M. Reaction time-movement time correlations. *Percept. mot. Skills*, 1961, **12**, 63–67. (b)

Hertzberg, O. E. Relationship of motor ability to the intelligence of kindergarten children. *J. exp. Psychol.*, 1929, **20**, 507–519.

Herzstein, J. N. A comparison of the jumping of American Negro male college students with American white male college students as measured by the Sargent vertical jump test. Unpublished master's thesis, Univer. of Maryland, College Park, 1961.

Hicks, J. A. The acquisition of motor skill in young children—an experimental study of the effects of practice in throwing at a moving target. *Univer. Iowa Stud. in Child Welf. J.*, 1931, **4**, No. 5.

Hildreth, G. The development and training of hand dominance: I. characteristics of handedness." *J. genet. Psychol.*, 1949, **75**, 197–220. (a)

Hildreth, G. The development and training of hand dominance: II. developmental tendencies in handedness. *J. genet. Psychol.*, 1949, **75**, 221–254. (b)

Hildreth, G. The development and training of hand dominance: IV. developmental problems associated with handedness. *J. genet. Psychol.*, 1950, **76**, 39–100.

Hilgard, E. R. *Theories of learning*. New York: Appleton-Century-Crofts, 1948.

Hilgard, E. R. *Theories of learning*. (2nd ed.) New York: Appleton-Century-Crofts, 1956.

Hilgard, E. R. *Introduction to psychology*. New York: Harcourt, Brace & World, 1957.

Hilgard, E. R. Learning theory and its application. In W. Schramm (Ed.), *New teaching aids for the American classrooms*. Stanford, Calif.: Stanford Univer. Inst. communicat. Res., 1960.

Hilgard E. R., Sait, E. M., & Margaret, G. A. Level of aspiration as affected by relative standing in an experimental social group. *J. exp. Psychol.*, 1940, **27**, 411–421.

Hilgard E. R., & Smith, M. B. Distributed practice in motor learning: score changes within and between daily sessions. *J. exp. Psychol.*, 1942, **30**, 136–146.

Hilgard, J. R. Learning and maturation in preschool children. *J. genet. Psychol.*, 1932, **41**, 31–56.

Hilgard, J. R. The effect of early and delayed practice on memory and motor performances studied by the method of co-twin control. *Genet. Psychol. Monogr.*, 1933, **14**, 493–566.

Hill, W. F. *Learning: a survey of psychological interpretations*. San Francisco: Chandler Publishing Co., 1963.

Hipple, J. E. Racial differences in the influence of motivation on muscular tension, reaction time, and speed of movement. *Res. Quart.*, 1954, **25**, 297–306.

Hitchcock, E. *An anthropometric manual*. Amherst, Mass.: Press of Carpenter and Morehouse, 1893.

Hochberg, J. *Perception*. Englewood Cliffs, N. J.: Prentice-Hall, 1964.

Hodgkins, J. Influence of age on the speed of reaction and movement in females. *J. Geront.*, 1962, **17**, 385–389.

Hodgkins, J. Reaction time and speed of movement in males and females of various ages. *Res. Quart.*, 1963, **34**, 335–343.

Hovland, G. C. Experimental studies in rote-learning theory: VII. distribution of practice with varying lengths of list. *J. exp. Psychol.*, 1940, **27**, 271–284.

Howell, M. L. Influence of emotional tension on speed of reaction and movement. *Res. Quart.*, 1953, **24**, 22–32.

Hubbard, A. W. Learning and conditioning. *Coll. phys. Educ. Ass. Annu. Proc.*, 1956, **59**, 234–235.

Hubbard, A. W., & Seng, C. N. Visual movements of batters. *Res. Quart.*, 1954, **25**, 42–51.

Hubel D. H. The visual cortex of the brain. *Sci. Amer.*, 1963, **209** (Nov.), 54–62.

Hull, C. L. *Principles of behavior.* New York: Appleton-Century-Crofts, 1943.

Humphreys, L. G. The factor of time in pursuit rotor learning. *J. Psychol.*, 1936, **3**, 429–436.

Humphreys, L. G. Transfer of training in general education. *J. gen. Educ.*, 1951, **5**, 210–216.

Hutchinson, A. *Labanotation.* New York: New Directions, 1954.

Hutinger, P. W. Differences in speed between American Negro and white children in performance of the 35-yard dash. *Res. Quart.*, 1959, **30**, 366–368.

Irving, R. N. Comparison of maturity, structural, and muscular strength measures for five somatotype categories of boys through fifteen years of age. Unpublished doctoral dissertation, Univer. of Oregon, 1959.

Irwin, L. W. A study of the relationship of dominance to performance of physical education activities. *Res. Quart.*, 1938, 9, 98–119.

Jacobson, E. Electrical measurement of neuromuscular states during mental activities. II. imagination and recollection of various muscular acts. *Amer. J. Physiol.*, 1934, **94** (July-Sept.), 22–34.

Jacobson, E. Electrophysiology of mental activities. *Amer. J. Psychol.*, 1932, **44**, 677–694.

James, W. *Principles of psychology.* New York: Henry Holt, 1890.

James, W. *The principles of psychology.* New York: Holt, Rinehart, and Winston, 1918.

Jenkins, J. G., & Dallenbach, K. M. Oblivescence during sleep and waking. *Amer. J. Psychol.*, 1924, **35**, 605–612.

Jenkins, J. J., & Paterson, D. G. *Studies in individual differences: the search for intelligence.* New York: Appleton-Century-Crofts, 1961.

Jenkins, L. M. Comparative study of motor achievements of children five, six, and seven years of age. *Teach. Coll. Contr. Educ.*, 1930, No. 414.

Johnson, G. B. Physical skill tests for sectioning classes into homogeneous units. *Res. Quart.*, 1932, **3**, 128–136.

Johnson, G. B. A study of the relationship that exists between skill as measured and general intelligence of college students. *Res. Quart.*, 1942, **13**, 57–59.

Johnson, G. B., Jr. Motor learning. In W. R. Johnson (Ed.) *Science and medicine of exercise and sports.* New York: Harper & Row, 1960, Pp. 600–619.

Johnson, W. R. A study of emotion revealed in two types of athletic contests. *Res. Quart.,* 1949, **20,** 72–80.

Johnson, W. R. (Ed.) *Science and medicine of exercise and sports.* New York: Harper & Row, 1960.

Jokl, E. R. *Medical, sociological and cultural anthropology of sport and physical education.* Springfield, Ill.: Charles C Thomas, 1964.

Jones, E. I., & Bilodeau, E. A. Differential transfer of training between motor tasks of different difficulty. *U.S.A.F. Human Res. Cen. Res. Bull.,* 1952, No. 52–35.

Jones, H. E. *Motor performance and growth.* Berkeley, Calif.: Univer. of California Press, 1949.

Jones, J. G. Motor learning without demonstration of physical rehearsal, under two conditions of mental practice. Unpublished master's thesis, Univer. of Oregon, 1963.

Jost, A. Assoziationsfestigkeit in ihrer Ablangigkeit von Verteilong der Wiederholungen, *Z. Psychol.,* 1897, **14,** 436–472.

Judd, C. H. The relation of special training to special intelligence. *Educ. Rev.* 1908, **36,** 28–42.

Kappers, C. V. A. Further contributions on neurobiotaxis. IX. *J. comp. Neurol.,* 1917, **27,** 261–298.

Keller, F. S. *Learning: reinforcement theory.* New York: Random House, 1954.

Keller, L. P. The relation of quickness of bodily movement to success in athletics. Unpublished doctoral dissertation, New York Univer., 1940.

Kephart, N. C. Perceptual-motor aspects of learning disability. *Except. Child.* 1964, **31,** 201–207.

Kerr, B. A. Relationship between speed of reaction and movement in a knee extension movement. *Res. Quart.,* 1966, **37,** 55–60.

Kimble, G. A. Performance and reminiscence in motor learning as a function of the degree of distribution of practice. *J. exp. Psychol.,* 1949, **39,** 500–510.

Kimble, G. A. Evidence for the role of motivation in determining the amount of reminiscence in pursuit rotor learning. *J. exp. Psychol.,* 1950, **40,** 248.

Kimble, G. A. *Principles of general psychology.* New York: Ronald, 1956.

Kimble, G. A., & Garmezy, N. *Principles of general psychology.* (2nd ed.) New York: Ronald, 1963.

Kingsley, H. L. *The nature and conditions of learning.* Englewood Cliffs, N. J.: Prentice-Hall, 1946.

Kingsley, H. L., cited in R. C. Birney & R. C. Teevan (Eds.), *Reinforcement.* Princeton, N. J.: Van Nostrand, 1961.

Kingsley, H. L., & Garry, R. *The nature and conditions of learning* (2nd ed.) Englewood Cliffs, N. J.: Prentice-Hall, 1957.

Knapp, C., & Dixon, R. Learning to juggle: I. a study to determine the effect of two different distributions of practice in learning efficiency. *Res. Quart.,* 1950, **21,** 331–336.

Knapp, C., & Dixon, R. Learning to juggle: II. a study of whole and part methods. *Res. Quart.,* 1952, **23,** 389–401.

Koerth, W. A pursuit apparatus: eye-hand coordination. *Psychol. Monogr.,* 1922, **31,** 288–292.

Koffka, K. *The growth of the mind.* (2nd ed.) New York: Harcourt, Brace & World, 1929.

Koffka, K. Review of Tolman's "Purposive behavior in animals and men." *Psychol. Bull.,* 1933, **30**, 440–451.

Köhler, W. *The mentality of apes.*, Trans. E. Winter. New York: Harcourt, Brace & World, 1925.

Köhler, W. *Dynamics in psychology.* New York: Liveright, 1940.

Köhler, W. *Gestalt psychology.* New York: Liveright, 1947.

Kretschmer E. *Physique and character.* New York: Harcourt, Brace & World, 1925. Cited by P. V. Karpovich, *Physiology of muscular activity.* Philadelphia: Saunders, 1961. P. 292.

Krieger, J. C. The influence of figure ground perception on spatial adjustment in tennis. Unpublished master's thesis, Univer. of California, Los Angeles, 1962.

Krueger, W. C. F. The effect of overlearning on retention. *J. exp. Psychol.,* 1929, **12**, 71–78.

Krueger, W. C. F. Further studies in overlearning. *J. exp. Psychol.,* 1930, **13**, 152–163.

Kulcinski, L. E. The relation of intelligence to the learning of fundamental muscular skills. *Res. Quart.,* 1945, **16**, 226–276.

Kusinitz, I., & Keeney, C. E. Effects of progressive weight training on health and physical fitness of adolescent boys. *Res. Quart.,* 1958, **29**, 294–301.

Lambert, P. Practice effect of non-dominant vs. dominant musculature in acquiring two-handed skill. *Res. Quart.,* 1951, **22**, 50–57.

LaPlace, J. P. Personality and its relationship to success in professional baseball. *Res. Quart.,* 1954, **25**, 313–319.

Lashley, K. S. The requisition of skill in archery. *Papers Dep. marine Biol. Carnegie Instn of Washington,* 1915, **7**, 105–128.

Lawrence, D. P. A reliability check of two interpolated time patterns in motor learning. Unpublished master's thesis, Boston Univer., 1949.

Lawther, J. D. Learning motor skills and knowledge. In C. E. Skinner (Ed.), *Educational psychology.* (4th ed.) Englewood Cliffs, N. J.: Prentice-Hall, 1959. Pp. 499–525.

Lawther, J. D. Directing motor skill learning. Symposium on motor learning. *Quest,* 1960 (May), 68–76.

Leavitt, H. J., & Schlosberg, H. The retention of verbal and of motor skills. *J. exp. Psychol.,* 1944, **34**, 404–417.

Leuba, C. J. *Man: a general psychology.* New York: Holt, Rinehart and Winston, 1961.

Lewin, K. *Principles of topological psychology.* Trans. F. Heider & G. M. Heider. New York: McGraw-Hill, 1936.

Lewin, K. *Field theory in social science.* New York: Harper & Row, 1951.

Lewin, K., Dembo, T., Festinger, L., & Sears P. S. Level of aspiration. In J. McV. Hunt (Ed.), *Handbook of personal and behavioral disorders.* New York: Ronald, 1944. Pp. 333–378.

Lincoln, R. S., & Smith, K. U. Transfer of learning in tracking performance at different target speeds. *J. appl. Psychol.,* 1951, **35**, 358–362.

Lindeburg, F. A. A study of the degree of transfer between quickening exercises and other coordinated movements. *Res. Quart.*, 1949, **20**, 180–195.

Lindeburg, F. A., & Hewitt, J. E. Effect of an oversized basketball on shooting ability and ball handling. *Res. Quart.*, 1965, **36**, 164–167.

Lloyd, R. P., & McIntyre, A. K. Dorsal column conduction of group 1 muscle afferent impulses and their relay through Clarkes column. *J. Neurophysiol.*, 1950, **13**, 209–218.

Lordahl, D. S., & Archer, E. J. Transfer effects on a rotary pursuit task as a function of first task difficulty. *J. exp. Psychol.*, 1958, **56**, 421–426.

Lorge, I. Influence of regularly interpolated time intervals upon subsequent learning. *Teach. Coll. Contr. Educ.*, 1930, No. 438.

Lyon, D. O. The relation of length of material to time taken for learning and the optimum distribution of time, part III. *J. educ. Psychol.*, 1931, **14**, 400–413.

McArthur, W. D. Speed of various neuro-muscular responses in children ages seven to thirteen. Unpublished doctoral dissertation, Oregon State Coll., 1957.

McCain, S. R. A comparison of the motion perception fields of athletes and non-athletes. Unpublished master's thesis, Univer. of Alabama, 1950.

McClelland, D. C., & Apicella, F. S. Reminiscence following experimentally induced failure. *J. exp. Psychol.*, 1947, **37**, 159–169.

McCloy C. H. *The measurement of athletic power.* New York: Barnes, 1932.

McCloy, C. H. The measurement of general motor capacity and general motor ability, Suppl. to *Res. Quart.*, 1934, **5**, 128.

McCloy, C. H. A preliminary study of factors in motor educability. *Res. Quart.*, 1940, **11**, 28–39.

McConnell, T. R. The psychology of learning. *Yearb. nat. Soc. Stud. Educ.*, 1942, **41**, Part II.

McCraw, L. W. A factor analysis of motor learning. *Res. Quart.*, 1949, **20**, 316–335.

McCraw, L. W. Comparison of physical growth and development of athletes and nonathletes at the junior high school level. Report to Res. Sect., AAHPER Convention, Chicago, April 1956.

McGeoch, G. O. The intelligence quotient as a factor in the whole-part problem. *J. exp. Psychol.*, 1931, **14**, 333–358.

McGeoch, J. A., & Irion, A. L. *The psychology of human learning.* (2nd ed.) New York: McKay, 1952.

McGeoch, J. A., & Whitely, P. L. The recall of observed material. *J. educ. Psychol.*, 1926, **17**, 419–425.

McGraw, M. B. *Neuromuscular maturation of the human infant.* New York: Columbia, 1943.

McGraw, M. B. Maturation of behavior. In L. Carmichael (Ed.), *Manual of child psychology.* New York: Wiley, 1946.

McGuigan, F. J., & MacCaslin, E. F. Whole and part methods in learning a perceptual motor skill. *Amer. J. Psychol.*, 1935, **68**, 658–661.

Magruder, M. A. An analytical study of the testing for kinesthesis. Unpublished doctoral dissertation, Univer. of Oregon, 1963.

Malmo, R. B. Activation: a neuropsychological dimension. *Psychol. Rev.*, 1959, **66**, 367–386.

Mandler, G., & Kuhlman, C. K. Proactive and retroactive effects of over-learning. *J. exp. Psychol.*, 1961, **61**, 76–81.

Margulies, S., & Eigen, L. D. (Eds.) *Applied programmed instruction.* New York: Wiley, 1962.

Martin, K. L. Handedness: a review of the literature on the history, development and research of laterality preference. *J. educ. Res.*, 1952, **45**, 527–533.

Martin, M. M. A study to determine the effects of motivational techniques on performance of the jump and reach test of college women. Unpublished master's thesis, Univer. of Wisconsin, 1961.

Martin, R. B. The effect of pelvic tilt on vertical jumping ability. Unpublished master's thesis, Univer. of California, Los Angeles, 1961.

Martire, J. G. Relationship between the self concept and differences in the strength and generality of achievement motivation. *J. Pers.*, 1956, **24**, 364–375.

Maslow, A. H. A preface to motivation theory. *Psychosom. Med. Monogr.*, 1943, **5**, 370–396.

Massey, M. D. A study of the significance of interpolated time intervals on motor learning. Unpublished doctoral dissertation, Boston Univer., 1957.

Massey, M. D. The significance of interploated time intervals on motor learning. *Res. Quart.*, 1959, **30**, 189–201.

Matarazzo, R. G., & Matarazzo, J. D. Anxiety level and pursuit meter performance. *J. consult. Psychol.*, 1956, **20**, 70.

Mead, M. *Growing up in New Guinea.* New York: New American Library, 1958.

Mednick, S. A. *Learning.* Englewood Cliffs, N. J.: Prentice-Hall, 1964.

Melton, A. W. The science of learning and the technology of education methods. *Harvard educ. Rev.*, 1959, **29**, 96–106.

Metheny, E. Some differences in bodily proportions between American Negro and white male college students as related to athletic performance. *Res. Quart.*, 1939, **10**, 41–53.

Miles, W. L. Ocular dominance demonstrated by unconscious sighting. *J. exp. Psychol.*, 1929, **12**, 113–126.

Miller, A. G. The effect of various interpolated time patterns on motor learning. Unpublished doctoral dissertation, Boston Univer., 1948.

Miller, D. M. The relationships between some visual-perceptual factors and the degree of success realized by sports performers. Unpublished doctoral dissertation, Univer. of Southern California, 1960.

Miller, L. A. The effects of emotional stress on high school track and field performance. Unpublished master's thesis, Univer. of California, Los Angeles, 1960.

Minami, H., & Dallenbach, K. M. The effect of activity upon learning and retention in the cockroach. *Amer. J, Psychol.*, 1946, **59**, 1–58.

Mirenva, A. N. Psychomotor education and the general development of pre-school children: experiments with turn controls. *J. genet. Psychol.*, 1935, **46**, 433–454.

Montebello, R. A. The role of stereoscopic vision in some aspects of basketball playing ability. Unpublished master's thesis, Ohio State Univer., 1960.

Morgan, R. E., & Adamson, G. T. *Circuit training.* London: G. Bell, 1957.

Morris, P. C. A comparative study of physical measures of women athletes and unselected college women. Unpublished doctoral dissertation, Temple Univer., 1960.

Morse, W. C., & Wingo, G. M. (Eds.) Readings in educational psychology. Chicago: Scott, Foresman, 1962.

Mott, J. A. Eye movements during initial learning of motor skills. Unpublished doctoral dissertation, Univer. of Southern California, 1954.

Mowbray, G. H., & Rhodes, M. V. On the reduction of choice reaction time with practice. Quart. J. exp. Psychol., 1959, 11, 16–23.

Mueller, C. G. Sensory psychology. Englewood Cliffs, N. J.: Prentice-Hall, 1965.

Müller, G. E., and Pilzecker, A. Experimentelle Beiträge Zur Lehre vom Gedachtnis. Z. Psychol., 1900, 1, 312, 322, 447.

Mumby, H. H. Kinesthetic acuity and balance related to wrestling ability. Res. Quart., 1953, 24, 327.

Munn, N. L. Bilateral transfer of learning. J. exp. Psychol., 1932, 15, 343–353.

Murphy, H. H. Distribution of practice periods in learning. J. exp. Psychol., 1916, 7, 150–162.

Murray, E. J. Motivation and emotion. Englewood Cliffs, N. J.: Prentice-Hall, 1964.

Murray, H. A. Explorations in personality. New York: Oxford, 1938.

Muscio, B. Motor capacity with special reference to vocational guidance. Brit. J. Psychol., 1922, 13, 157–184.

Mussen, P., Conger, J., & Kagan, J. Child development and personality. (2nd ed.) New York: Harper & Row, 1963.

Nason, L. J. Physical coordination helps improve grades. Nason on education, 1965.

National Association for Physical Education of College Women & National College Physical Education Association for Men. A symposium on motor learning. Quest, 1966 (May), No. 6.

Naylor, J. C., & Briggs, G. E. Long-term retention of learned skills, and review of the literature. Lab. of aviation Psychol., Ohio State Univer. & Ohio State Univer. Res. Found., 1961.

Neilson, N. P., & Cozens, F. W. Achievement scales in physical education activities for boys and girls in elementary and junior high schools. New York: Barnes, 1934.

Nelson, D. O. Effect of swimming on the learning of selected gross motor skills. Res. Quart., 1957, 28, 374–378. (a)

Nelson, D. O. Studies of transfer of learning in gross motor skills. Res. Quart., 1957, 28, 364–373. (b)

Nelson, J. Analysis of the effects of applying various motivational situations to college men subjected to a stressful physical performance. Unpublished doctoral dissertation, Univer. of Oregon, 1962.

Newman, E. B. Forgetting of meaningful material during sleep and waking. Amer. J. Psychol., 1939, 52, 65–71.

Niemeyer, R. K. Part versus whole methods and massed versus distributed practice in learning of selected large muscle activities. Unpublished doctoral dissertation, Univer. of Southern California, 1958.

Nissen, H. W. Analysis of a complex conditional reaction in chimpanzees. *J. comp. physiolog. Psychol.*, 1951, **44**, 9–16.

Nissen, H. W., Chow, K. L., & Semmes, J. Effects of restricted opportunities for tactual, kinesthetic, and manipulative experience on the behavior of a chimpanzee. *Amer. J. Psychol.*, 1951, **64**, 485–507.

Norrie, M. L. The relationship between measures of kinesthesia and motor performance. Unpublished master's thesis, Univer. of California, Berkeley, 1952.

Oberteuffer, D. *Physical education.* New York: Harper & Row, 1956.

O'Donnell, D. J. The relative effectiveness of three methods of teaching beginning tennis to college women. Unpublished doctoral dissertation, Indiana Univer., 1956.

Olsen, E. A. Relationship between psychological capacities and success in college athletics. *Res. Quart.*, 1956, **27**, 79–89.

Olson, A. L. Characteristics of fifteen year old boys classified as outstanding athletes, scientists, fine artists, leaders, scholars, or as poor students or delinquents. Unpublished doctoral dissertation, Univer. of Oregon, 1961.

Oxendine, J. B. A study of the significance of varying lengths of practice periods on the growth of a motor skill. Unpublished doctoral dissertation, Boston Univer., 1959.

Oxendine, J. B. Effect of progressively changing practice schedules on learning of a motor skill. *Res. Quart.*, 1965, **36**, 307–315.

Oxendine, J. B., Generality and specificity in the learning of fine and gross motor skills. *Res. Quart.*, 1967, **38**, 86–94.

Parsons, O. A., Phillips, L., & Lane, J. E. Performance on the same psychomotor task under different stressful conditions. *J. Psychol.*, 1954, **38**, 457–466.

Pavlov, I. P. *Conditioned reflexes.* Trans. E. V. Anrep. New York: Oxford, 1927.

Peckstein, L. A. Whole vs. part methods in motor learning: a comparative study. *Psychol. Monogr.*, 1917, **23**, 2.

Penman, K. A. *Physical education for college students.* St. Louis: Mosby, 1964.

Perbix, J. Relationship between somatotype and motor fitness in women. *Res. Quart.*, 1954, **25**, 84–90.

Perkins, W. L. Distributed practice with nonsense syllables. *Brit. J. Psychol.*, 1914, **7**, 253–261.

Perrin, F. A. C. An experimental study of motor ability. *J. exp. Psychol.*, 1921, **4**, 25–57.

Perry, H. M. The relative efficiency of actual and imaginary practice in five selected tasks. *Arch. Psychol.*, 1939, **34**, 5–75.

Peterson, G. Mechanisms of handedness in the rat. *Comp. phys. Monogram,* 1934, **5**, 27–34.

Phillips, B. E. The relationship between certain phases of kinesthesis and performance during the early stages of acquiring two perceptuo-motor skills. Unpublished doctoral dissertation, Pennsylvania State Coll., 1939.

Phillips, M., & Summers, D. Relation of kinesthetic perception of motor learning. *Res. Quart.*, 1954, **25**, 456–469.

Piaget, J. *The origins of intelligence in children.* New York: International Universities Press, Inc., 1952.

Piaget, J. Psychology of intelligence and education. *Pennsylvania Sch. J.,* 1966, 114, 7–318.

Pierson, W. R. A comparison of fencers and nonfencers by certain psychomotor, space perception, and anthropometric measures. Unpublished master's thesis, Michigan State Univer., 1953.

Pierson, W. R. The relationship of movement time to reaction time from childhood to senility. *Res. Quart.,* 1959, 30, 227–231.

Pierson, W. R., & Rasch, P. J. Determination of representative score for simple reaction and movement time. *Percept. mot. Skills,* 1959, 9, 107–110.

Pierson, W. R., & Rasch, P. J. Generality of a speed factor in simple reaction and movement time. *Percept. mot. Skills,* 1960, 11, 23–28.

Pond, F. L. Influence of the study of Latin on word knowledge. *Sch. Rev.,* 1938, 46, 611–618.

Price, N. The relationship between the level of aspiration and performance in selected motor tasks. Unpublished master's thesis, Women's Coll., Univer. of North Carolina, 1960.

Provins, K. A. Handedness and skill. *Quart. J. exp. Psychol.,* 1956, 8, 79–95.

Provins, K. A. The effects of training and handedness on the performance of two simple motor tasks. *Quart J. exp. Psychol.,* 1958, 10, 29–39.

Purdy, B. J., & Lockhart, A. Retention and relearning of gross motor skills after long periods of no practice. *Res. Quart.,* 1962, 33, 65–72.

Pyle, W. H. Concentrated versus distributed practices. *J. educ. Psychol.,* 1915, 5, 247–258.

Pyle, W. H. Transfer and interference on card distributing. *J. educ. Psychol.,* 1915, 9, 107–110.

Radler, D., & Kephart, N. C. *Success through play.* New York: Harper & Row, 1960.

Radosavijevich, P. R. Das Behalten und Vergessen bei Kindern und Erwachsenen Nach experimentellen Untersuchungen. *Päd. Monogr.,* No. 1. Cited by R. S. Woodworth & H. Schlosberg, *Experimental psychology* (Rev. ed.) New York: Holt, Rinehart and Winston, 1963. P. 892.

Ragsdale, C. E. How children learn motor types of activity. *Yearb. nat. Soc. Stud. Educ.,* 1950, 49, 69–91.

Rains, D. D. Growth of athletes and non-athletes in selected secondary schools as assessed by the grid technique. Unpublished doctoral dissertation, Indiana Univer., 1951.

Rangazas, E. P. A comparative analysis of selected college athletes and non-athletes on several hand-foot reaction-time measures. Unpublished doctoral dissertation, Indiana Univer., 1957.

Rarick, L. Growth and development theory and practice: implications for physical education. *Mich. osteopath. J.,* 1965, 30, (Oct.), 21–24.

Rarick, L., & McKee, R. A study of twenty third-grade children exhibiting extreme levels of achievement on tests of motor proficiency. *Res. Quart.,* 1949, 20, 142–152.

Rarick, L., & Thompson, J. J. Roentgenographic measures of leg muscle size and ankle extensor strength of seven-year-old children. *Res. Quart.*, 1956, 27, 321–332.

Rasch, A. G. Improving personnel selection through research. *Civil Serv. Assembly Personnel Rep.*, 1955, No. 552.

Rasch, P. J., & Burke, R. K. *Kinesiology and applied anatomy.* Philadelphia: Lea & Febiger, 1963.

Ray, H. C. Interrelationships of physical and mental abilities and achievements of high school boys. *Res. Quart.*, 1940, 11, 129–141.

Reed, H. B. Part and whole methods of learning. *J. exp. Psychol.*, 1924, 15, 107–115.

Reed, H. B. Distributed practice in addition. *J. educ. Psychol.*, 1924, 15, 592–595.

Rejall, A. E. Studies on long term retention. Cited by J. A. McGeoch, *The psychology of human learning.* New York: McKay, 1946. P. 328.

Richardson, A. Mental practice: a review and a discussion, part I. *Res. Quart.*, 1967, 38, 95–107.

Richter, C. P. Total self regulatory functions in animals and human beings. *Harvey Lecture Ser.*, 1942, 38, 63–103.

Ries, S. C. Dominance, discrimination and accuracy in fencing. Unpublished master's thesis, Univer. of California, Los Angeles, 1962.

Rife, D. C. Heredity and handedness. *Sci. Mon.*, 1951, 73, 317–325.

Robichaux, W. A. Relationship between demonstrated skill in performing sports activities and learning new gross motor skills. Unpublished doctoral dissertation, Univer. of Southern California, 1960.

Robinson, E. S. Some factors determining the degree of retroactive inhibition. *Psychol. Monogr.*, 1920, 28, No. 128.

Robinson, E. S. The "similarity" factor in retroaction. *Amer. J. Psychol.*, 1927, 39, 297–312.

Roloff, L. Z. Kinesthesis in relation to the learning of selected motor skills. *Res. Quart.*, 1953, 24, 210–217.

Rose, J. E., & Mountcastle, V. B. Touch and kinesthesis. In J. Field (Ed.), *Handbook of Physiology.* Vol. 1. Baltimore: Williams & Wilkins, 1959.

Royal Canadian Air Force. *VBX Plan for physical fitness.* Ottawa: Roger Duhamel, F.R.S.C., Queen's Printer and Controller of Stationery, 1962.

Royal Canadian Air Force. *XBX Plan for physical fitness.* Ottawa: Roger Duhamel, F.R.S.C., Queen's Printer and Controller of Stationery, 1962.

Rubin-Rabson, G. Studies in the psychology of memorizing piano music: II. A comparison of massed and distributed practice. *J. educ. Psychol.*, 1940, 31, 270–284.

Rubin-Rabson, G. Studies in the psychology of memorizing piano music: VI. a comparison of two forms of mental rehearsal and keyboard overlearning. *J. educ. Psychol.*, 1941, 32, 593–602.

Ruch, F. L. *Psychology and life.* (6th ed.) Chicago: Scott, Foresman, 1963.

Ryan, E. D. Effects of stress on motor performance and learning. *Res. Quart.*, 1962, 33, 111–119. (a)

Ryan, E. D. Relationship between motor performance and arousal. *Res. Quart.*, 1962, 33, 279–287. (b)

Ryan, E. D. Retention of stabilimeter and pursuit rotor skills. *Res. Quart.*, 1962, **33**, 593–598. (c)

Sackett, R. S. The relationship between amount of symbolic rehearsal and retention of a maze habit. *J. genet. Psychol.*, 1935, **13**, 113–130.

Sapora, A. V., & Mitchell, E. A. *The theory of play and recreation.* New York: Ronald, 1961.

Schott, E. L. The development of learning capacity. Unpublished master's thesis, Univer. of Missouri, 1923.

Scott, G. M. Measurement of kinesthesis. *Res. Quart.*, 1955, **26**, 324–341.

Scripture, E. W. Recent investigations at the Yale laboratory. *Psychol. Rev.*, 1899, **6**, 165.

Sears, P. S. Levels of aspiration in academically successful and unsuccessful children. *J. abnorm. soc. Psychol.*, 1940, **35**, 498–536.

Seashore, H. G. Some relationships of fine and gross motor abilities. *Res. Quart.*, 1942, **13**, 259–274.

Seashore, P. H., Buxton, C. E., & McCollum, J. Multiple factorial analysis of fine motor skills. *Amer. J. Psychol.*, 1940, **53**, 251–259.

Seashore, S. H., & Seashore, R. H. Individual differences in simple auditory reaction times of hands, feet and jaws. *J. exp. Psychol.*, 1941, **29**, 342–345.

Seils, L. G. The relationship between measures of physical growth and gross motor performance of primary grade school children. *Res. Quart.*, 1951, **22**, 244–260.

Selye, H. *The stress of life.* New York: McGraw-Hill, 1956.

Shaffer, L. F. Fear and courage in aerial combat. *J. consult. Psychol.*, 1947, **11**, 137–143.

Shaw, W. A. The distribution of muscular action potentials during imaging. *Psychol. Rec.*, 1938, **2**, 195.

Shay, C. The progressive-part vs. the whole method of motor skills. *Res. Quart.*, 1934, **5**, 62–67.

Sheldon, W. H. *Atlas of men.* New York: Harper & Row, 1954.

Shilling, M. An experimental investigation of the effects of a decrease in the delay of reinforcement upon instrumental response performance. Unpublished master's thesis, Univer. of Iowa, 1951.

Shirley, M. M. *The first two years.* Minneapolis: University of Minnesota Press, 1933.

Sills, F. D. A factor analysis of somatotypes and of their relationships to achievement in motor skills. *Res. Quart.*, 1950, **21**, 246.

Sills, F. D. Anthropometry in relation to physical performance. In W. R. Johnson (Ed.), *Science and medicine of exercise and sports.* New York: Harper & Row, 1960.

Sills, F. D., & Everett, P. The relationship of extreme somatotypes to performance in motor and strength tests. *Res. Quart.*, 1953, **24**, 223–228.

Simon, J. R., Shaw, M. E., & Gilchrist, J. C. Some effects of prearranged performance scores upon the level of aspiration. *J. exp. Psychol.*, 1954, **47**, 10–12.

Sinclair, C. B., & Smith, I. M. Laterality in swimming and its relationship to dominance of hand, eye, foot. *Res. Quart.*, 1957, **28**, 395–402.

Singer, R. N. Massed and distributed practice effects on the acquisition and retention of a novel basketball skill. *Res. Quart.*, 1965, **36**, 68–77.

Skinner, B. F. *The behavior of organisms: an experimental analysis.* New York: Appleton-Century-Crofts, 1938.

Skinner, B. F. *Science and human behavior.* New York: Macmillan, 1953.

Skinner, B. F. Reinforcement today. *Amer. Psychologist*, 1958, **13**, 94–99.

Skinner, C. E. *Educational psychology.* (4th ed.) Englewood Cliffs, N. J.: Prentice-Hall, 1959.

Skubic, E. Emotional responses of boys to little league and middle league competitive baseball. *Res. Quart.*, 1955, **26**, 342.

Slater-Hammel, A. T. Reaction time and speed of movement. *Percept. mot. Skills, Res. Exch.*, 1952, **4**, 109–113.

Slater-Hammel, A. T., and Stumpner, R. L. Choice batting reaction time. *Res. Quart.*, 1951, **22**, 377–380.

Smith, K. R. Intermittent loud noise and mental performance. *Science*, 1951, **114**, 132–133.

Smith, K. U. Cybernetic foundations of physical behavioral science. *Quest*, 1967 (May), No. 8, 26–82.

Smith, L. E. Reaction time and movement time in four large muscle movements. *Res. Quart.*, 1961, **32**, 88–92.

Smith, L. E., & Lewis, F. D. Handedness and its influence upon static neuromuscular control. *Res. Quart.*, 1963, **34**, 206–212.

Snoddy, G. S. Learning and stability. *J. appl. Psychol.*, 1926, **10**, 1–36.

Snoddy, G. S. *Evidence for two opposed processes in mental growth.* Lancaster, Penn.: Science Press, 1935.

Snoddy, G. S. Reply to Doré and Hilgard. *J. exp. Psychol.*, 1938, **23**, 375–383.

Soares, P. L. A study of the relationship between selected elements of coordination and the rate of learning complex motor skills. Unpublished master's thesis, Women's Coll., Univer. of North Carolina, 1958.

Sparks, J. L. Relative effects of various verbal incentives on learning and retention of a gross motor skill. Unpublished master's thesis, Pennsylvania State Univer., 1963.

Spearman, C. E. *The nature of 'intelligence' and the principles of cognition.* New York: Macmillan, 1923.

Spence, K. W. *Behavior theory and conditioning.* New Haven, Conn.: Yale, 1956.

Spence, K. W. The relation of learning theory to the technology of education. *Harvard educ. Rev.*, 1959, **29**, 84–95.

Start, K. B. The relationship between intelligence and the effect of mental practice on the performance of a motor skill. *Res. Quart.*, 1960, **31**, 644–649.

Start, K. B. The influence of subjectively assessed games ability on gain in motor performance after mental practice. *J. genet. Psychol.*, 1962, **67**, 169–173.

Start, K. B. Kinesthesis and mental practice. *Res. Quart.*, 1964, **35**, 316–320.

Start, K. B., & Richardson, A. Mental practice and imagery. *Brit. J. educ. Psychol.*, 1964, **34**, 85–90.

Stauffacher, J. C. The effects of induced muscular tension upon various phases of the learning process. *J. exp. Psychol.*, 1937, **21**, 26–46.

Steggerda, M., & Petty, C. An anthropometric study of Negro and white college women. *Res. Quart.*, 1940, **11**, 110–118.

Stell, W. L. The effects of mental practice in the acquisition of a motor skill. *J. phys. Educ.*, 1952, **44**, 101.

Stern, W. *The psychological methods of testing intelligence.* Trans. G. M. Whipple. Baltimore: Warwick and York, Inc., 1914.

Stevens, M. L. Measurement in kinesthesis of college women. Unpublished doctoral dissertation, Indiana Univer., 1951.

Straub, W. Psychische Alkoholwirkung and Blutalkoholgehalt, *Z. Arbeitsps,* 1938, **11**, 127–130. Cited by R. S. Woodworth and H. Schlosberg, *Experimental psychology.* (Rev. ed.) New York: Holt, Rinehart and Winston, 1963, P. 38.

Strong, C. H. Motivation related to performance of physical fitness test. *Res. Quart.*, 1963, **34**, 497–507.

Stroud, J. B. Apparatus for measuring muscular tension. *J. exp. Psychol.*, 1931, **14**, 184–185.

Stroup, F. Relationship between measurement of the field of motion perception and basketball ability in college men. *Res. Quart.*, 1957, **28**, 72–76.

Sullivan, E. B. Attitudes in relation to learning. *Psychol. Monogr.*, 1927, **36**, (1), 1–12.

Swift, E. J. Studies in the psychology and physiology of learning. *Amer. J. Psychol.*, 1903, **14**, 201–251.

Swift, E. J. Memory of a complex skillful act. *Amer. J. Psychol.*, 1905, **16**, 131–133.

Symonds, P. M. Human drives. *J. educ. Psychol.*, 1934, **25**, 694.

Tanner, J. M. *Growth and development.* Springfield, Ill.: Charles C Thomas, 1955.

Tanner, J. M. *The physique of the Olympic athlete.* London: G. Allen, 1964.

Taylor, J. A., & Spence, K. W. The relationship of anxiety level to performance in serial learning. *J. exp. Psychol.*, 1952, **44**, 61–64.

Theunissen, W. V. Part teaching and whole teaching of beginning group-golf classes for male college students. Unpublished doctoral dissertation, Indiana Univer., 1955.

Thomas, W. I. *The unadjusted girl.* Boston: Little, Brown, 1923.

Thompson, M. E. A study of reliabilities of selected gross muscular coordination test items. *Human Resources Res. Cen. Res. Bull.*, 1952, 52–59.

Thorndike, E. L. *Animal intelligence, experimental studies.* New York: Macmillan, 1911.

Thorndike, E. L. *Educational psychology.* Vol. 2. *The psychology of learning.* New York: Teachers College, 1913.

Thorndike, E. L. Mental discipline in high school studies. *J. educ. Psychol.*, 1924, **15**, 1–22, 83–98.

Thorndike, E. L. *Human learning.* New York: Appleton-Century-Crofts, 1931.

Thorndike, E. L. *Selected writings from a connectionist's psychology.* New York: Appleton-Century-Crofts, 1949.

Thorndike, E. L., & Hagen, E. *The measurement of intelligence.* New York: Teachers College, 1927.

Thorndike, E. L., & Woodworth, R. S. The influence of improvement in one mental function upon the efficiency of other functions. *Psychol. Rev.,* 1901, 8, 247–261, 384–395, 553–564.

Thurstone, L. L. Primary mental abilities. *Univer. of Chicago psychometr. Monogr.,* 1938, No. 1.

Titchener, E. B. Relearning after forty-six years. *Amer. J. Psychol.,* 1923, 34, 468–469.

Tolman, E. C. Theories of learning. In F. A. Moss (Ed.), *Comparative psychology.* Englewood Cliffs, N. J.: Prentice-Hall, 1934.

Tolman, E. C. The determiners of behavior at a choice point. *Psychol. Rev.,* 1938, 45, 1–41.

Tolman, E. C. There is more than one kind of learning. *Psychol. Rev.,* 1949, 56, 144–155.

Towne, B. M. An individual curve of learning: a study in typewriting. *J. exp. Psychol.,* 1922, 5, 79–92.

Travers, R. M. W. *Essentials of learning.* New York: Macmillan, 1963.

Travis, R. C. Practice and rest periods in motor learning. *J. Psychol.,* 1936, 3, 183–187. (a)

Travis, R. C. The effect of the length of the rest period in motor learning. *J. Psychol.,* 1936, 3, 189–194. (b)

Triplett, N. The dynamogenic factors in pace-making and competition. *Amer. J. Psychol.,* 1897–1898, 9, 507–533.

Trow, W. C. *Educational psychology.* Boston: Houghton Mifflin, 1950.

Trussel, E. M. Mental practice as a factor in learning a complex motor skill. Unpublished doctoral dissertation, Univer. of California, Berkeley, 1958.

Tsai, C. A comparative study of retention curves for motor habits. *Comp. psychol. Monogr.,* 1924, 2, No. 2.

Tuttle, W. W., & Travis, L. E. The relation of precedence of movement in homologous structures to handedness. Supp. to *Res. Quart.,* 1935, 6, 3–14.

Tweit, A. H., Gallnick, P. D., & Hearn, G. R. Effect of training program on total body reaction time of individuals of low fitness. *Res. Quart.,* 1963, 34, 508–513.

Twinning, P. W. The relative importance of intervening activity and lapse of time in the production of forgetting. *J. exp. Psychol.,* 1940, 26, 483–501.

Twinning, W. E. Mental practice and physical practice in learning a motor skill. *Res. Quart.,* 1949, 20, 432–435.

Tyler, L. E. *The psychology of human differences.* New York: Appleton-Century-Crofts, 1956.

Ulrich, C. Stress and sport. In W. R. Johnson (Ed.), *Science and medicine of exercise and sports.* New York: Harper and Row, 1960.

Underwood, B. J. The effect of successive interpolations on retroactive and proactive inhibition. *Psychol. Monogr.,* 1945, 59, No. 273.

Underwood, B. J. Speed of learning and amount retained: A consideration of methodology. *Psychol. Bull.,* 1954, 51, 276–282.

Upshaw, J. S. The relationship of somatotype to motor performance. Unpublished master's thesis, Springfield Coll., 1960.

Vandell, R. A., Davis, R. A., & Clugston, H. A. The function of mental practice and the acquisition of motor skills. *J. gen. Psychol.*, 1943, **29**, 243–350.

Van Dusen, F., & Schlosberg, H. Further study of the retention of verbal and motor skills. *J. exp. Psychol.*, 1948, **38**, 526–534.

Van Ormer, E. B. Retention after intervals of sleep and waking. *Arch. Psychol. N. Y.*, 1932, **21**, No. 137.

Vernon, P. E. *The structure of human abilities.* New York: Wiley, 1951.

Vince, M. A. The part played by intellectual processes in a sensori-motor performance. *Quart. J. exp. Psychol.*, 1953, **5**, 75–86.

Wagner, C. G. The effect of different lengths of practice on the learning of certain basketball skills among junior high school boys. Unpublished master's thesis, Temple Univer., 1962.

Walker, L. C., DeSoto, C. B., & Shelly, M. W. Rest and warm-up in bilateral transfer on a pursuit rotor task. *J. exp. Psychol.*, 1957, **53**, 394–398.

Walker, R. N. Body build and behavior in young children, body build and nursery school teacher's ratings. *Monogr. Soc. Res. Child Developm.*, 1952, **3**, 27, 84.

Walter, L. M. The relation of sex, age, and school achievement to levels of aspiration. *J. educ. Psychol.*, 1951, **42**, 285–292.

Waterland, J. C. The effect of mental practice combined with kinesthetic perception when the practice precedes each overt performance of a motor skill. Unpublished master's thesis, Univer. of Wisconsin, 1956.

Watson, G. What psychology can we feel sure about? In W. C. Morse & G. M. Wingo (Eds.), *Readings in educational psychology.* Chicago: Scott, Foresman, 1962.

Way, E. E. Relationship of lateral dominance to scores of motor ability and selected skill tests. *Res. Quart.*, 1958, **29**, 360–369.

Webster, R. W. Psychological and pedagogical factors involved in motor skill performance as exemplified in bowling. *Res. Quart.*, 1940, **11**, 42–52.

Wechsler, D. *Measurement of adult intelligence.* (3rd ed.) Baltimore: Williams & Wilkins, 1944.

Wechsler, D., & Hartogs, R. The clinical measurement of anxiety. *Psychiatr. Quart.*, 1945, **19**, 618–635.

Weig, E. L. Bilateral transfer in the motor learning of young children and adults. *Child Develpm.*, 1932, **3**, 247–368.

Weiss, R. F. Aspiration and expectations: a dimensional analysis. *J. soc. Psychol.*, 1961, **53**, 249.

Wells, K. F. *Kinesiology.* Philadelphia: Saunders, 1960.

Westerdarp, D. Mental capacity and its relation to physical efficiency. *Amer. phys. Educ. Rev.*, 1923, **28**, 216–219.

Westerlund, J. H., & Tuttle, W. W. Relationship between running events in track and reaction time. *Res. Quart.*, 1931, **2**, 95–100.

Wetzel, N. C. *Grid for evaluating physical fitness.* Cleveland, Ohio: N.E.A. Service, 1940.

Wheeler, R. H. & Perkins, F. T. *Principles of mental development.* New York: Crowell, 1932.

Wickstrom, R. L. Comparative study of methodologies for teaching gymnastics and tumbling stunts. *Res. Quart.*, 1958, **29**, 109.

Widdop, J. Unpublished manuscript, Dep. of phys. Educ., McDonald Coll., McGill Univer., 1963.

Wiebe, V. R. A factor analysis of tests of kinesthesis. Unpublished doctoral dissertation, State Univer. of Iowa, 1950.

Wiebe, V. R. A study of tests of kinesthesis. *Res. Quart.*, 1954, **25**, 222–230.

Wiener, N. *Cybernetics.* (2nd ed.) New York: Wiley, 1961.

Wilkinson, J. J. A study of reaction-time measures to a kinesthetic and a visual stimulus for selected groups of athletes and non-athletes. Unpublished doctoral dissertation, Indiana Univer., 1958.

Willgoose, C. E., & Rogers, M. L. Relationship of somatotype to physical fitness. *J. educ. Res.*, 1949, **42**, 704.

Williams, J. R., & Scott, R. B. Growth and development of Negro infants: IV. motor development and its relation to child-rearing practices in two groups of Negro infants. *Child Develpm.*, 1953, **24**, 103–121.

Willingham, W. W. Performance decrement following failure. *Percept. mot. Skills*, 1958, **8**, 197–202.

Wilson, M. E. The relative effect of mental practice and physical practice in learning the tennis forehand and backhand drives. Unpublished doctoral dissertation, State Univer. of Iowa, 1961.

Witte, F. Relation of kinesthetic perception to a selected motor skill for elementary school children. *Res. Quart.*, 1962, **33**, 476–484.

Wolfe, J. B. Effectiveness of token-rewards for chimpanzees. *Comp. psychol. Monogr.*, 1936, **60**, 1–72.

Woodrow, H. The effect of type of training upon transference. *J. educ. Psychol.*, 1927, **18**, 159–172.

Woodruff, A. D. *The psychology of teaching.* New York: McKay, 1948.

Woodward, P. An experimental study of transfer of training in motor learning. *J. appl. Psychol.*, 1943, **27**, 12–32.

Woodworth, R. S. The accuracy of voluntary movement. *Psychol. Monogr.*, 1899, No. 13.

Woodworth, R. S., & Schlosberg, H. *Experimental psychology.* (Rev. ed.) New York: Holt, Rinehart and Winston, 1963.

Worcester, D. A. Retention after long periods. *J. educ. Psychol.*, 1923, **14**, 113–114.

Worell, L. Levels of aspiration and academic success. *J. educ. Psychol.*, 1959, **50**, 47–50.

Wylie, R. C. *The self concept.* Lincoln, Nebr.: University of Nebraska Press, 1961.

Wyndham, C. H., Strydom, N. B., Morrison, J. F., Peter, J., Williams, C. G., Bredell, G. A. R., & Joffe, A. Differences between ethnic groups in physical working capacity. *J. appl. Physiol.*, 1963, **18**, 361–366.

Young, O. C. A study of kinesthesis in relation to selected movements. *Res. Quart.*, 1945, **16**, 277–287.

Young, O. G. The rate of learning in relation to spacing of practice periods in archery and badminton. *Res. Quart.*, 1954, **25**, 231–243.

Young, P. T. *Motivation and emotion.* New York: Wiley, 1961.

Younger, L. A comparison of reaction and movement times of women athletes and nonathletes. *Res. Quart.,* 1959, **30,** 349–355.

Zartman, E. N., & Cason, H. The influence of an increase in muscular tension on mental efficiency. *J. exp. Psychol.,* 1934, **17,** 671–679.

Zigrossi, N. A. An analysis of the relationship between visual performance and the batting and slugging average of college baseball players. Unpublished master's thesis, Univer. of Maryland, College Park, 1961.

Name index

Subject index